The Sum of Our Parts

In the series

ASIAN AMERICAN HISTORY AND CULTURE,
edited by Sucheng Chan, David Palumbo-Liu, and Michael Omi

The Sum of Our Parts

Mixed-Heritage Asian Americans

EDITED BY

Teresa Williams-León
and Cynthia L. Nakashima

FOREWORD BY

Michael Omi

TEMPLE UNIVERSITY PRESS

PHILADELPHIA

For our families

and

in memory of Jan R. Weisman

Temple University Press, Philadelphia 19122
Copyright © 2001 by Temple University
All rights reserved
Published 2001
Printed in the United States of America

♾ The paper used in this publication meets the requirements of the American
National Standard for Information Sciences—Permanence of Paper for
Printed Library Materials, ANSI Z39.48-1984

Library of Congress Cataloging-in-Publication Data

The sum of our parts : mixed-heritage Asian Americans / edited by Teresa
Williams-León and Cynthia L. Nakashima ; foreword by Michael Omi.
        p. cm.—(Asian American history and culture)
    Includes bibliographical references.
        ISBN 1-56639-846-0 (cloth : alk. paper) — ISBN 1-56639-847-9 (pbk. : alk. paper)
        1. Asian Americans—Race identity.   2. Racially mixed people—United States—
Race identity.   3. Asian Americans—Social conditions.   4. Racially mixed
people—United States—Social conditions.   5. United States—Race relations.
    I. Williams-León, Teresa, 1963–   II. Nakashima, Cynthia L., 1966–   III. Series.

E184.O6.S86 2001
305.895073—dc21

                                                                    00-055214

Contents

Section IV: Asian-Descent Multiraciality in Global Perspective 183

Foreword

Michael Omi

What is fascinating about the topic of multiraciality is the manner in which it renders suspect and throws into question deeply held notions of race, racial classification, and racial identity. To consider an individual or group as "mixed race" presupposes the existence of clear, discernible, and discrete "races." But the concept of race as a biological category has been roundly discredited in the sciences,[1] and we are left struggling over the social construction of multiraciality and its cultural and political meaning.

Consider, for example, the quandary of Tiger Woods's identity. Why isn't this superb golfer touted as the first Asian American to achieve a Grand Slam by winning the masters, the U.S. open, and the British Open golf tournaments? While popularly regarded as a "black" golfer, Woods himself has written that he is "Asian" on forms requesting racial and ethnic data. "Actually," Woods has stated, "I am 90 percent Oriental, more Thai than anything" (*AsianWeek,* 1997).[2] On a 1997 Oprah Winfrey show, Woods complicated his identity further by declaring himself "Cablinasian"—an amalgamation of Caucasian, Black, Indian, and Asian. Yet the rigid "one-drop" hypodescent rule that has historically buttressed the color line in the United States renders Woods "black" within a dominant framework that narrowly recognizes and privileges the categories of black and white.

The repeal of antimiscegenation laws, the marked lessening of social distance between racial groups, and dramatic rates of interracial marriage between specific groups have contributed to the demographic growth of the multiracial population. While the number of people of "mixed racial descent" is unclear and contingent on self-definition, the 1990 U.S. Census counted two million children (under the age of eighteen) whose parents were of different races (Marriott, 1996). In 1990, there were 39 percent more Japanese/white births in the United States than monoracial Japanese American births (U.S. Bureau of the Census, 1992).

The increased visibility of "mixed-race" or "multiracial" individuals has led to an expanding discussion and literature on multiracial identity and consciousness, and its

meaning for a racially stratified society. But much of this discussion has not deeply inter-
rogated the racial meanings that pervade distinctive combinations of multiracial identity. For example, one's experience of being white and Asian in most university settings
is significantly different from being black and Asian in the same situations. An important task for any scholarly and/or activist multiracial agenda is to deconstruct multiraciality and examine the meanings that correspond to specific types of racial categories
and identities.

This volume, *The Sum of Our Parts: Mixed-Heritage Asian Americans,* makes several important interventions with respect to the broader literature on multiraciality.
First, it disrupts the prevailing black/white paradigm of racial discourse by focusing on
Asian American mixed-race identity. The essays gathered here offer an important departure from the emphasis on the dominant racial categories of black and white to expand
our notion of multiracial identity. This text does not essentialize the category of "Asian
American" nor treat it as a uniform and monolithic group identity. Several of the essays
are attentive to the specific experiences of different Asian (pan)ethnicities such as Pacific
Islanders, Southeast Asians, and Filipinos. In addition, the volume does not exclusively
focus on white-Asian multiracials, but explores "minority-minority" positions and
identities. Whiteness is decentered in this examination, and the notion that different
groups of color serve as dynamic referents for each other is affirmed.

A second important dimension of this volume is its emphasis on how concepts of ethnicity, gender, sexuality, and nation articulate and interpenetrate to shape specific forms
of multiracial identity, consciousness, and community. While much has been abstractly
theorized about "intersectionality," little has been said about how interlocking modes
of domination/subordination manifest themselves in everyday experience. Many of the
essays here, by contrast, emphasize the importance of different axes of stratification and
difference to the social construction of the multiracial Asian American subject.

Previous volumes on mixed-race identity have been largely framed by the disciplines
of social and counseling psychology. By contrast, a clear majority of the essays here are
sociological studies. Many are attentive to the "linguistic turn" in the social sciences,
and incorporate postmodern and cultural studies perspectives. What is emphasized in
these accounts are the discursive practices that individuals and groups employ in fash-
ioning identities, in "making" culture, and in advancing political claims.

Lastly, this volume expands the interrogation of multiracial Asian identity by going
beyond the borders of the United States. Several essays illustrate how multiracial consciousness and classification unfold in different national settings, and what social meanings these identities have for specific social formations. While not explicitly comparative
in nature, these explorations allow us to think comparatively, to reflect on the specificity of U.S. patterns, and to discern their global implications.

In many ways, this volume is long overdue. As the editors point out, multiracial Asian
American identity is nothing new. From the initial arrival and settlement of Asian immigrants on these shores, multiraciality has been a reality. From the Punjabi-Mexican families in California to the Chinese-Irish ones in New York, mixed-race Asian American
identities have proliferated. Beginning with World World II, U.S. military conflicts in

Asia have created an influx of Asian "war brides" in their immediate wake. Since the mid-1960s, specific Asian American ethnic groups (including Japanese, Chinese, and Filipinos) have displayed high rates of interracial marriage. The current interest in multiraciality among Asian Americans, therefore, has long and deep roots; such histories are thus not marginal to a broader Asian American historical narrative, but rather central to it.

This said, what do we make of the increased racial hybridity of the Asian American subject? From the vantage point of the assimilationist paradigm (Gordon, 1964), increasing intermarrriage between minority and majority groups is read as an important indicator of a narrowing of social distance, a reduction in group prejudice and discrimination, and a lessening of group boundaries. But increasing intermarriage could also be reflective of inequalities rooted in the complex articulation of racial and sexual hierarchies (Shinagawa & Pang, 1996). What this suggests is that any examination of Asian American multiraciality needs to be attentive to the issue of *power*—in its various manifestations—as deployed in different levels and sites of social life. This includes acknowledging and assessing the power to identify oneself, the power to define and establish categories, the power to promote cultural representation, and the power to advance political claims effectively.

Such power struggles do not simply occur across the color line, but also erupt within a community of color to reveal often invisible fault lines. The intense and bitter debate between Asian American civil rights groups and multiracial Asian Americans over a proposed multiracial category for Census 2000 is illustrative of this point. Since the 1980s, multiracial advocacy groups have challenged the notion of mutually exclusive racial categories and the policy of a "single-race" checkoff, employed by the Census. In the 1990s, both the Association of MultiEthnic Americans (AMEA) and Project RACE (Reclassify All Children Equally) actively lobbied for multiracial recognition.[3] But this was met with resistance from Asian American/Pacific Islander organizations that feared such a policy would reduce the Asian/Pacific Islander count and erode civil rights protections. The National Coalition for an Accurate Count of Asians and Pacific Islanders (NAPALC) stated that "adding a multiracial category would undermine the effectiveness of civil rights enforcement agencies because of the inconsistent counts and the uncertainties it introduces in being able to analyze trends" (Hearings on Federal Measures, 1997: 418).

In 1997, the U.S. Office of Management and Budget decided to allow people to mark one or more of the designated racial categories when identifying themselves in the Census and for other government programs. Debate has now shifted to issues of how to tabulate multiracial responses for different data sets and policy purposes. At issue here is not only Census enumeration, but its impact on federal voting rights and civil rights.

Multiracial advocacy organizations applauded the Department of Justice decision in August 1999 to adopt a "full distribution approach" for redistricting purposes. Under this system, people would be placed in a racial category that corresponds to the exact combination of races they list, and they would not be reassigned to monoracial categories. In all, the various combinations would yield sixty-three officially recognized racial categories.

The debate over the multiracial category is a revealing example of how competing groups make claims to the state for racial recognition, or non-recognition, and the policy implications that flow from these claims. The proposal to add a multiracial category to the Census drew attention to the inherent fluidity and slipperiness of our concepts of race—a move that had ironic political consequences. Former House Speaker Newt Gingrich (1997), for example, used the issue of multiraciality to illustrate the indeterminacy of all racial categories and to advocate vigorously for their abolition in government data collection. The mixed-race issue, it would seem, is susceptible to being politically defined in a number of competing and contradictory ways. How will it be read in the immediate future?

"Race Is Over"—or so declared Stanley Crouch in the title of an essay he wrote for the *New York Times Magazine* in 1996, speculating on what the next 100 years may bring. In an article accompanied by portraits of twenty racially mixed children from five to fourteen years of age (whose specific race/ethnic lineages were noted below their pictures), Crouch stated that in the future, race will cease to be the basis of identity and "special-interest power." Such a belief in race mixing as the most effective antidote to race consciousness and racism has been a long-standing liberal dream. Senator Jay Bulworth, Warren Beatty's character in the film *Bulworth,* comes to realize that the only way to end racism is for the races to disappear through intermarriage. If we as a people cannot be color-blind, then we need to get rid of the colors. He raps, "All we need is a voluntary, free-spirited, open-ended program of procreative racial deconstruction."

But it's not that simple. Drawing on contemporary intermarriage patterns, Michael Lind (1998) suggests that both multiculturalists and nativists have misread trends, with multiculturalists celebrating increased racial hybridity and nativists bemoaning the eclipse of the white population. Lind argues that intermarriage trends actually suggest that a new, disturbing dichotomy between blacks and nonblacks is emerging. In the twenty-first century, he envisions "a white-Asian-Hispanic melting-pot majority—a hard-to-differentiate group of beige Americans—offset by a minority consisting of blacks who have been left out of the melting pot once again" (p. 39). Such a dire racial landscape presents a number of troubling political questions regarding the formation of group interests, social stratification, and the distribution of resources.

Multiracial consciousness cannot elide the question of racialized power—who wields it and how it is deployed. The rigidity of the "one-drop rule" of race, long-standing eugenic fears of racial pollution, and the persistence (until the 1967 Supreme Court decision in *Loving v. Virginia*) of antimiscegenation laws demonstrate how the color line historically has been policed in the United States. In this context, multiracial identities were contained, disregarded, or denied. The emerging multiracial consciousness is grappling with this historical legacy, the contemporary persistence of white supremacy, and the ways that race intersects with class, gender, and sexuality. Multiraciality disrupts our fixed notions about race and opens up a new set of possibilities with respect to dialogue and engagement across, and beyond, the color line. But it does not mean, as Crouch claims, that "race is over." Far from it.

Notes

1. This is not to say that biologistic arguments regarding race are completely dead. As a recent example, see Rushton, 1995.

2. Hybridity abounds in his family. His father, Earl, is half-black, one-quarter Native American, and one-quarter Chinese. His mother, Klutida, is half-Thai, one-quarter Chinese, and one-quarter Dutch.

3. There were, however, sharp differences between AMEA and Project RACE with respect to political consciousness and the intent of multiracial categorization. AMEA supported the multiple checkoff option that was eventually adopted by the U.S. Office of Management and Budget.

Acknowledgments

We would like to thank the following people and institutions for the many contributions to our conceptualizations that made this anthology possible: Janet Francendese, Margaret Weinstein, Michael Omi, Sucheng Chan, Gary Okihiro, David Lopez, Don T. Nakanishi, Walter Allen, G. Reginald Daniel, Ronald Takaki, Evelyn Nakano Glenn, Melvin Oliver, Que Dang, Jeff Yoshimi, Glenn Omatsu, Gregory Trianosky y Velasco, Nancy Brown, Kenyon Chan, David Lopez, George Uba, Gordon Nakagawa, James Sobredo, Enrique de la Cruz, Shirley Hune, Velina Hasu Houston, Steven Masami Ropp, Rika Houston, Russell Leong, Jorge Garcia, Evelyn Rodriguez, Kathy Shamey, Leslie Kawaguchi, CSUN College of Humanities, CSUN Asian American Studies Department, and Hapa Issues Forum.

We are very grateful to each of the authors in this anthology—for without them this volume would not have been possible. We pay special tribute to Jan R. Weisman, whose contributions to the field of multiracial studies have been enormous; we miss her. And, finally, we are most fortunate for having the unwavering love and support of our families, which enable us to do our work and find great meaning in it. We express our heartfelt thanks to Tracy James and Nobue S. Williams and Art and Wendy Nakashima, our parents; our brothers, Tracy Jay Williams and Dan Nakashima; and our own families, Fabian León, Pebbles Williams-León, Shawn Conway, Madeline Nakashima-Conway, and Charlotte Nakashima-Conway.

Introduction

Reconfiguring Race, Rearticulating Ethnicity

Teresa Williams-León
Cynthia L. Nakashima

> *Anybody who's mixed knows they're of the black race. It's all right*
> *for some reason to say Japanese and black or Japanese and Italian or*
> *Chinese and Swedish. But the minute you say black and white. . . .*
>
> —MARIAH CAREY

According to the popular vocalist Mariah Carey (quoted in the November 1998 issue of *Vibe*), the "one-drop rule" of racial categorization defines Black-White biracial people as "Black," whereas multiracial/multiethnic peoples of Asian descent are considered more "socially acceptable" and are therefore "permitted" the luxury of being identified as "racially mixed." Perhaps one way of understanding Carey's point is to note that Black-White issues loom so large in discussions of race that little about Asian-descent multiracial/multiethnic peoples is ever even addressed except as a social marker that confirms the primacy of the Black-White dichotomy.

As we enter the twenty-first century, questions of "race" that have plagued American society since its inception remain unanswered. This was vividly illustrated when, during the 2000 presidential campaign, Republican candidate George W. Bush was characterized as being racist and anti-Catholic for his failure to condemn Bob Jones University's prohibition of interracial dating among students and its public anti-Catholic stance. However, the media attention prompted university officials to rescind its long-held ban on interracial dating, contingent upon written parental approval. During the same campaign, in Orange County, California, Bush's Republican opponent John McCain was criticized by Asian American protestors for having referred to the Vietnamese as "gooks." Thus as "race" increasingly informs and affects the realities of American life in more complex and multifaceted ways, the phenomenon of multiracial and multiethnic Asian Americans complicates Asian America's relationship to the larger society and demonstrates that issues of "race" go beyond the dynamics of Black-White relations.

As part of the "millennium buzz," Ellis Cose (2000: 42) has speculated that

> the color line is fraying all around us. The American future certainly will not be circumscribed by one long line with whites on one side and the "darker" races on the other; there will be many lines, and many camps, and few will be totally segregated. Disparities will remain. But with the rudest reminders of racism washed away, it will be a lot easier to tell ourselves that we finally have overcome.

The qualitatively varied experiences of multiethnic/multiracial people simultaneously contest and reify the very structure of U.S. race relations, confirming that "race" is a sociopolitical construct, not a biologically based, scientific reality. Hence the layers of social meanings that accompany racial matters—whether during interpersonal interactions or within and across institutional arrangements—seem only to become more entangled as multiethnic/multiracial people enter the racial equation in the United States. Just as W.E.B. DuBois (1994) so insightfully predicted that the dilemma of the "color line" would dominate the twentieth century, the same issue will persist in the twenty-first century as it twists, turns, and morphs into multidimensional shapes.

Multiracial Chic

Multiracial characters, as products of vastly different and sharply contradictory worlds—whether real or fantasy, whether heroes or villains—have played symbolic roles in contouring social boundaries, drawing lines of demarcation, and differentiating "us" from "others." From Tabitha in *Bewitched* to Mr. Spock in *Star Trek,* from Johnny Mnemonic to Voldemort in the *Harry Potter* series, from Mariah Carey to Tiger Woods, "mixed beings" have been and continue to be an iconographic source of enigma and intrigue within American popular culture.

In the 1990s multiracial Asian Americans too have found themselves as part of the American social fabric in highly conspicuous and recognizable ways. On college campuses, for example, multiracial student organizations have been formed from coast to coast. In 1999 Diana Alvarado published an article on what faculty and campus leaders need to know about multiracial students, and highlighted the concerns of several Asian-descent multiracial students. Courses on multiracial identity are now part of the curriculum on several campuses (Alvarado, 1999; Gaskins, 1999; Williams et al., 1996), and academic works on this subject proliferate (Houston & Williams, 1997; Root, 1992a, 1996; Ropp et al, 1995; Zack, 1993, 1995).

Popular magazines like *Mavin, Metisse Magazine, Interracial Voice, Interrace,* and *New People* have been founded to represent and promote multiracial identities and lifestyles. Major Asian American magazines and newspapers like *A., Yolk, AsianWeek, Hokubei Mainichi,* and *Pacific Citizen* have come to cover multiracial and "Hapa" feature stories on a regular basis, and popular writings on multiracial identity have hit the book stores in record numbers (Arboleda, 1998; Gaskins, 1999; Hara & Keller, 1999; Nash, 1999; O'Hearn, 1998). More than any other arena, popular culture has enjoyed the contributions of Asian-descent multiracials. In the early 1990s, the quintessential American hero, Superman, was portrayed by a Japanese–European American actor, Dean Cain, in the television series *Lois and Clark*. The nation wakes up every morning to Ann Curry, a Japanese–European American newswoman on NBC's top-rated *Today Show,* affectionately referred to as "America's first family." Tiger Woods, a self-proclaimed "Cablinasian," has been heralded as America's "golden boy" of golf after winning the Master's tournament in 1996. Brooke Lee, a Korean–Native Hawaiian–European American, was crowned Miss U.S.A. in 1997. A Filipino–European American multiracial man, Andrew Cunanan, an alleged "spree killer," found himself on the FBI's most wanted list, taking America on a nationwide manhunt for several weeks in the summer of 1997. And the Chinese–Hawaiian–European American star Keanu Reeves has become the first multiracial Asian man to command $20 million per film.

Journalists describe "multiracial chic" (Gaskins, 1999), writers declare 2000 the official "year of the mulatto" (Senna, 1998), and academics put forth the significance of a multiracial "critical mass" (Root, 1992a, 1996). With all of the buzzing spin on the prevalence of Asian-descent multiracial peoples in everyday American life, their demographic justification need not be made. However, we are left with the question of the social, cultural, political, and theoretical implications of their presence on the discourse encompassing Asian American identity and multiracial identity as a whole.

The Impact of Multiraciality on Asian America

The dramatic increase in intermarriage among many Asian American groups in the last three decades of the twentieth century has contributed to the instrumentalist formation and reformation of family and identity dynamics within and across Asian America (Fong, 1998; Fong & Shinagawa, 2000). As debates around the shifting significance of race continue to mount on college campuses, in the media, and across dinner tables, the impact of Asian-descent multiracial people is beginning to take hold of the public imagination.

While Asian American history has been periodized as "pre-1965" and "post-1965" migration/immigration, it is perhaps more useful to characterize Asian American history as having three periods: (1) pre–World War II, a period of antimiscegenation laws as well as interracial cohabitation, marriage, and families; (2) World War II to 1967; and (3) post-1965 immigration and the post-1967 biracial baby boom. Furthermore, U.S. government and military involvement in Asia throughout the twentieth century has produced a continuous flow of multiracial Asian American births, which comprises the largest portion of the multiracial Asian American population.

The removal of legal barriers and ideological shifts around racial constructions and locations have provided the context for growth in legal interracial marriages and multiracial families in the post–civil rights era. Indeed, for Asian Americans, social integration and open-door immigration policies have contributed to an increase in intermarriage that Joel Crohn (1995) has termed a "quiet revolution." It has also led to the exponential growth of the multiracial population, or what Maria P. P. Root (1992a) has called "the biracial baby boom."

While the dramatic increase in interracial marriages and multiracial offspring is most definitely affecting all racial and ethnic communities, it is perhaps most keenly felt in Asian American communities. The U.S. Census statistics and social scientific studies for the 1990s indicate that Asian Americans are among the highest to outmarry (Fong & Yung, 1995–96; Root, 1997a; Shinagawa & Pang, 1996; Sung, 1990). On May 16, 1997, the *New York Times* reported that of the 1.5 million interracial marriages counted by the Census, 31 percent had an Asian spouse, 22 percent had a Native American or Native Alaskan spouse, and 14 percent had an African American spouse. Considering the fact that Asian Americans make up only 3 percent of the U.S. population, these statistics show their strong presence in the population of interracially married Americans. Likewise, mixed-race Asians are vastly overrepresented among multiracial young people in the United States. For example of 1,037,420 children from interracial households identified by the 1990 U.S. Census, nearly one-half (466,590) were in families where one parent is marked as "Asian" and the other parent as "White."

Asian America has become an important sociopolitical site of racial reconfiguration and ethnic rearticulation. For example, in a third-grade classroom at a Japanese American summer school in the San Francisco Bay area, ten of the fifteen students are multiracial and multiethnic. The hair colors of these eight-year-olds range from blondy brown to black, and the eye colors from deep brown to blue. Their first, last, and middle names reflect their Japanese, Chinese, Filipino, European, and African American heritages. In this small group of children, we see the concepts of race, ethnicity, culture, and community challenged and redefined. In 1995 F. James Davis asked, "Who is Black?" In the new millennium, it is equally compelling to ask, "Who is Asian American?"

Reassessing Assimilation

Because many Asian American communities have outmarriage rates of 30–60 percent, a significant portion of the multiracial population in the United States is of Asian descent. In the Japanese American community alone, according to 1990 Census data, there were nearly 40 percent more Asian-White babies than monoracial babies with two Japanese-descent parents. The U.S. Bureau of the Census has conservatively estimated that within the next twenty-five years, "among Asian Americans, the percentage able to claim some other ancestry in addition to Asian is expected to reach 35%" (*USA Today*, September 7, 1999, p. 1). In some Asian American communities, this projection has already been surpassed. Moreover, if and when we include in these statistics of Asian-descent multiracials here in the U.S. (despite the relatively small percentage of Asian Americans—3 percent—in the overall population), those who are Asian–African American, Asian-Latino, Asian–Native American, etc., the Asian-descent multiracial numbers will expand further. Hence, examining multiraciality *in relationship to* Asian America is long overdue.

Do these demographic trends among Asian Americans suggest processes of structural assimilation? In the social sciences, questions about their linear incorporation and assimilation have dominated the discussions around intermarriage and biracial children (Kitano et al., 1984; Tinker, 1973). Underlying the issue is the binary conceptualization of what it means to be an American: one is either American or not. For Asian Americans, this dilemma has resulted in a near-perpetual foreign status in which social and legal exclusion marked their "American" experience, regardless of citizenship or generation. However, intermarriage with the dominant group, according to assimilationist views, was treated as an important indicator of structural incorporation into mainstream American society (Gordon, 1964). Thus, from this paradigmatic vantage point, multiracial/multiethnic Asian Americans, especially those with European ancestry, have been seen as fulfilling the assimilation promise of becoming a *real* (deracialized) American.

The theoretical and ideological primacy of assimilation continues to influence the articulation of ethnic (and racial) group incorporation, thereby implying that mixed-race Asian Americans are symbols of Asian American assimilation. However, those who have examined European American ethnicity (Alba, 1990; Gans, 1979; Waters, 1991; Yancey et al., 1976, 1985; Yinger, 1981) *and* Asian American ethnicity (Espiritu, 1992; Fugita & O'Brien, 1991) argue that irreversible, straight-line assimilation and dissipation of ethnicity have not been the sole reality (if any part of the reality) of these monoracially identified parent groups of multiracial Asian–European Americans. In addition, the increasingly popular "Whiteness studies" (Allen, 1993; McIntosh, 1992; Nakayama & Martin, 1999) and examinations of peoples of color (including Asian Americans) as "racialized" populations purport that the maintenance and reemergence of ethnicity transgress assimilation in important ways. Moreover, the impact of race in the face of assimilation's prevalence appears to heighten (rather than disappear) among monoracially identified groups (Omi & Winant, 1994; Sanjek, 1996) and among Asian-descent multiracial and multiethnic peoples, as the chapters in this volume illuminate. Thus, the notion of multiracial Asian Americans as an indicator of assimilation and racial erasure is reassessed here.

Multiracial Asian Americans Reconfiguring Race and Rearticulating Ethnicity

The essays in this anthology expound and elaborate on the processes of racial reconfiguration and ethnic rearticulation by the various Asian-descent multiracial populations across historical time periods and geographical locations. Each chapter focuses on the different aspects of the historical constructions, ethnocultural affirmations, sociopolitical negotiations, and formations of identities by these groups.

Previous writings on multiracial identity have had to argue that the subject was worthy of authentic examination (Root, 1992a, 1996; Zack, 1995; Houston & Williams, 1997; Gaskins, 1999; Hara & Keller, 1999). Questions of "Who am I?" and "What are you?" have been the primary emphases of multiracial and multiethnic identity. They tended to explore the personal and psychological identity issues of acceptability versus rejection. Much of the research also focused on the racialized identities of multiracial and multiethnic adolescents, often in contextual and processual vacuums. While these subjects and their foci have been undoubtedly important and groundbreaking, providing a literary base and exploratory foundation for the study of multiracial and multiethnic identities in general, the maturation of the topic and the proliferation of social scientific research have allowed for a more specific, in-depth, and multidimensional examination of Asian-descent multiracial/multiethnic peoples.

This collection focuses on Asian-descent multiracial individuals, their identity formations, and their social locations within Asian America and across their multiply racialized communities in relationship to the White-majority society, issues that have often been ignored or underrepresented in the public discourse on multiraciality and race relations. It also examines the social processes by which multiracial/multiethnic people with Asian ancestry construct, negotiate, and sustain identity. To understand the complexity of multiracial identity this anthology demonstrates that the whole can indeed be greater than the sum of its parts. (See Hall and Turner, Chapter 7.) Furthermore, its major contribution to the growing literature in the field is that it moves beyond the Black-White discourse to explore multiraciality within Asian and Asian American contexts.

This ensemble of social scientifc articles illuminates: 1) the complexity of this subject matter beyond personal identity issues discussed, analyzed and addressed by the vast collection of chapters; 2) multiraciality as social processes and structural arrangements; 3) the processes of multiraciality and its relationship to Asian American and Asian realities in the U.S. and abroad, and; 4) the applicability and implications of racialization and ethnic articulations for other groups through specific examinations of Asian-descent multiracial realities and identities.

Social scientific discourses have come to contest innate and primordial notions of identity by instead emphasizing the sociopolitical formations, shaped by context, condition, and agency, by which levels of identity take hold, an approach that is taken in this volume as we attempt to trace the construction and reformation of Asian American identities across multiracial/multiethnic borderlands, time periods, and cultures. The book is divided into four sections. The essays in Section I, Multiraciality and Asian America: Bridging the Hybrid Past to the Multiracial Present, identify multiracial/multiethnic sociohistorical themes in Asian America and provide sociohistorical contexts from which to problematize them. The chapters in Section II, Navigating Sociocultural Terrains of Family and Identity, examine how multiracial/multiethnic identity is informed by race, culture, gender, family relations, and generational differences and negotiated within and across various social boundaries. The writings in Section III, Remapping Political Landscapes and Communities, highlight some of the most important political issues and social organizations in which race, class, gender, and sexuality collide and interpenetrate, accentuating the social construction of multiracial/multiethnic identities among those of Asian ancestry and demonstrating that the notion of identity extends beyond the personal realm. And finally, the collection of essays in Section IV, Asian-Descent Multiraciality in Global Perspective, offers a comparative perspective on Asian multiracial/multiethnic communities and realities outside of the United States. Taken together, these chapters delve into the complexity, diversity, and multiplicity of multiracial/multiethnic Asian American identities and illustrate that Asian American communities are now, more than ever, critical social, cultural, and political sites wherein processes of racial reconfiguration and ethnic rearticulation are being undertaken in great part by mixed-race people.

Notes on Terminology

Names and terms are important to the self-determination and self-definition of any individual or group. For multiracial/multiethnic individuals who live within, between, and across cultural and racial borderlands (Root, 1996), how and what they name themselves (as well as how and what they are named) are of critical significance. The essays in this anthology examine how Asian American interracial families and Asian-descent multiracial individuals challenge, reinforce, reify, and/or expand boundaries of race and ethnicity among the groups in which they claim ancestry. Thus Asian Americans, as well as European Americans, African Americans and Chicano/Latino Americans are figured in the discussions that follow. A key aspect of this book is that it refuses the racist utility of racial categorization while recognizing the social realities of race and affirming the significance of ethnicity in the lives of multiracial/multiethnic Asian Americans. Each author employs different terms and labels to illuminate the sociopolitical realities of Asian-descent multiracial/multiethnic populations in their various historical, social, and geographic contexts. The attentive reader will also notice that certain spellings, accents, and styles of capitalization and hyphenation vary from one chapter to another in this volume. Given the diversity represented here, the editors did not attempt to impose consistency.

"Race" and "ethnicity" are the core concepts that weave together the subjects of this anthology. Both are defined and treated as social constructs by each author. Whereas race is discussed in reference to the sociopolitical meaning of shared genetics and gene frequencies, ethnicity is employed to recognize cultural formations, shared history, geneological affiliations, and a perceived sense of peoplehood that may or may not exist among groups. Some authors (for example, Michael C. Thornton, Harold Gates, and Stephen Murphy-Shigematsu) emphasize the concept of ethnicity over race when discussing Asians of mixed heritage, whereas others (for example, Cynthia Nakashima, Maria P. P. Root, Rebecca Chiyoko King, and Kieu Linh Caroline Valverde) mostly employ the concept of race in their analysis.

The terms "monoracial" and "monoethnic" are utilized to distinguish those who are socially identified as "unmixed," whereas the terms "multiracial" and "biracial," and "multiethnic" and "biethnic," are employed to describe those who are of mixed racial and/or ethnic ancestries. Thus, ultimately, these labels are attempts at expressing personal and social identities—how one sees oneself in relationship to others—within particular social contexts and racialized realities. When one debates who is an "Asian American," "African American," "Chicano/Latino," "mixed," "multiracial," and "multiethnic," one is not really talking about biological race, for a person's identity encompasses and criss-crosses multiple social boundaries—race, phenotype, ethnicity, culture, language, age, nativity, class, gender, sexuality, temperment, occupation, family structure, and so on. Along with phenotypical and genotypical characteristics—but not conclusively—one's racial and ethnic identity is shaped by one's lived experiences, social arrangements, historical consciousness, generational continuity, and shared sense of peoplehood with "like others."

The terms "multiracial Asian American" and "Asian-descent multiracials" are interchangeably used. Sometimes "biracial Asians," "biethnic Asian Americans," "Asian Americans of mixed heritage," "Interracial Asian Americans," "Amerasians," "Eurasians," "Afroasians," "Hapas," and "mestizos" are also employed. Some terms are geographically, experientially, and historically specific, while others are used more generally and broadly across regions, time periods, and ethnic/national experiences. And, as the difference in terms suggests, mixed-race peoples of Asian descent can have histories, social locations, and therefore identifications that differ from those of others with Asian ancestry as well as from those of their multiracial counterparts who are not of Asian heritage.

While we, as co-editors, do not make any distinctions between our use of the terms "multiracial Asian American" and "Asian-descent multiracials," it is noteworthy to indicate some of the differences in identity implications each can imply. For example, one who employs "multiracial Asian American" and "multiracial Asian" (and variations such as "interracial Korean American," and "biracial Chinese American") to describe himself or herself is locating his or her multiracial identity within an Asian American or Asian context. By contrast, someone who utilizes "mestizo Filipino American" arguably references the mixed-race Filipino experience to Spanish colonialism and situates it within an ethnic-specific Asian (i.e., Filipino) American identity. However, a person who uses the term "Asian-descent multiracial" is likely to be centering his or her identity within his or her multiraciality, while acknowledging his or her Asian ancestry as a descriptive.

As we have seen with other groups, labels and terms are transformed through experience, political movements, and time. But for now, we hope that by putting forth common referents by which we can communicate and convey the social processes and organization of peoples who possess a multitude of social experiences, we will assist readers in framing our discussion on multiracial/multiethnic peoples of Asian descent.

Section I

Multiraciality and Asian America: Bridging the Hybrid Past to the Multiracial Present

As we consider the rapid increase in interracial marriages and multiracial births in the United States since the late 1960s, it is easy to forget that there has never been a time when intergroup contact has not resulted in some version of a ethnic/tribal/national hybrid. Our historical amnesia allows us to forget this nation's "race-mixing" past with its complex tradition of hypodescent, one-drop rules, and "passing." Today, most of those who would be categorized as "Latino" or "African American" could also be considered "racially mixed"—usually from many generations back. The same can be said for many Americans who are typically identified as "European American," "Native American," "Pacific Islander," or "Asian American."

In the first section of this book, we will look across time at multiraciality in Asian America and at the many complex relationships that exist between our hybrid past and our multiracial present.

Chapters 1 and 2, by Paul Spickard and Yen Le Espiritu, respectively, take somewhat different approaches to the history of multiraciality in Asian America. In his examination "Who Is an Asian?," Spickard explores the historical relationship between mixed-race people and several of the Asian American communities, including the panethnic Asian American community. Spickard argues that in most of these communities a "monoracialist impulse" had dominated, placing multiracial people and families low on the hierarchies of belonging and acceptance.

Espiritu also offers a telling of Asian American history that acknowledges the existence of interracial couples and mixed-race people. But while Spickard emphasizes the ways in which multiracials have been marginalized in Asian America, Espiritu argues that multiraciality has always been and continues to be central to who and what are Asian Americans. She makes the point that by recognizing the racial/ethnic blending in our past and present, we open up the "critical space to explore the strategic importance of cross-group affiliation."

Chapters 3 and 4, by Cynthia L. Nakashima and John Chock Rosa, respectively, examine mainstream American discourses on Asian American/Pacific Islander multiraciality. Nakashima considers how, historically and contemporarily, treatments of mixed race reflect cultural anxieties regarding race and ethnicity. By looking at three time periods over the past 150 years, she discusses how a highly racialized society such as the United States can utilize multiraciality as a symbolic tool for exploring issues that are hypersensitive and hyperpoliticized.

Rosa exposes an American fascination with Hawai'i's racial, ethnic, and cultural mixing that began in the 1920s and 1930s, and that served as a precursor to current romanticized images of Hawai'i as a racial paradise and its mixed-race people as a safely assimilated "future face of America."

CHAPTER I

Who Is an Asian?
Who Is a Pacific Islander?
Monoracialism, Multiracial People,
and Asian American Communities

Paul Spickard

This essay explores historically the social contours of multiraciality among people we today call collectively "Asian Americans." It further examines the relationship between multiracial Asian Americans and the monoracialist impulses of the various Asian American communities at various points in time. Beginning with the period before there was an Asian America (i.e., before the late 1960s), it then discusses the effects of new immigration and the Asian American movement on constructions of monoraciality and multiraciality among people of Asian American ancestry.

Before Asian America (1850–1960)

"Asian American" was not a term that meant anything before the late 1960s. There was rather a series of separate Asian immigrant communities—Korean, Chinese, Japanese, Filipino, and so forth. European-derived Americans tended to call them all "Orientals," but that was not an internally generated identity, nor did it organize the lives of individuals or communities in any meaningful way, except for bringing them common discrimination from Whites. Among multiracial people of Asian descent, there was a disconnected series of monoracialist discourses in the several separate communities. Most (but not all) of those communities neither accepted intermarried couples nor acknowledged multiracial people.

Chinese Americans

The experiences of multiracial people of Chinese descent in this period must be divided in two, for the situation on the U.S. mainland was very different from that in Hawai'i.

The U.S. Mainland   Before the 1960s, there was only a small Chinese population of American birth on the U.S. mainland, where Chinese men formed a mainly bachelor society. Many had wives and children back in China; others hoped to have such families one day. Only a small number of merchants brought wives over before World War II, and very, very few Chinese women came on their own. Because of the predominance of this trans-Pacific family pattern and the antimiscegenation laws of most western states, there were few interracial marriages by Chinese Americans in this period, and consequently very few racially mixed people. As noted elsewhere in this volume, some Chinese men found ways to circumvent the laws and marry non-Chinese women, and others formed less formal interracial relationships. Some of those begat children, although how many we do not know, partly because of the relentlessly monoracialist ways that both Chinese Americans and Whites have interpreted Chinese American history.

Those few mixed-race Chinese Americans who did exist generally were strangers to Chinese communities. That was even true for Edith Maude Eaton, now revered as the pioneer Chinese American writer Sui Sin Far. Eaton was the daughter of a Chinese mother and a British father who lived her adult life in Canada and the United States. She wrote sympathetic portrayals of Chinese Americans a century ago, but she had no personal place in Chinese America (Spickard & Mengel, 1997; Far, 1996).

The Chinese American family began to change in the aftermath of World War II, as several thousand Chinese American men who had served in the armed forces brought over their wives and children who had stayed behind in China (Zhao, n.d.). But although a family society would now develop in the United States, it was still a monoracial community very hostile to intermarriage, partly as a response to White oppression, but also as an expression of Chinese chauvinism. Most Chinese Americans were hostile even to marriage between different varieties of Chinese (Spickard, 1989). In addition, almost no Chinese war brides were brought back by non-Chinese servicemen. As a result, through the 1960s, Chinese American identity on the mainland was monoracial; there were few multiracial people, and there was no place for them in Chinese America.

Hawai'i.   The situation was very different in Hawai'i, where almost the entire Chinese community was racially mixed (Takaki, 1983; Glick, 1980: 132–33; Char, 1975: 238–239; Linnekin, 1985: 28–34).[1] The first couple of generations of Chinese working on the plantations experienced substantial social mixing with Native Hawaiians and to a lesser extent with other ethnic groups. Many Chinese men who worked in Hawai'i married Hawaiian women even if they already had wives back home. As a result nearly everyone Chinese in Hawai'i whose ancestry goes back to the plantations has some

Hawaiian forebears, and nearly everyone Hawaiian has some Chinese ancestry. Chinese churches have members who are phenotypically Hawaiian and bear Hawaiian names. The Kamehameha Schools, a private institution for Hawaiians only, admits students with names like Chan and Ing who are phenotypically Chinese. To be sure, there was some mixing between Chinese and other island groups—Japanese, Filipinos, Koreans, and some Haoles (Whites). But Chinese Hawaiians in this period had negative images of Koreans and Filipinos, and resentments against Japanese born of generations of conflict between their ancestral nations. Thus the predominant mixed-race group in Hawai'i in the generations before the creation of an Asian American identity was the Chinese-Hawaiians.[2]

This Chinese-Hawaiian nexus is the foundation of Local identity. It is expressed in the mixture of cuisines that is Local Food.[3] If one goes to Zippy's or Rainbow Drive-In, one can eat poi and kalua pig alongside Chinese dim sum delights (charsiu bow and siumai renamed manapua and pork hash), Japanese noodles, and Spam—the ultimate expression of island self-identity and culinary mixedness. Local identity also expresses itself in Pidgin, the polyglot language based on Hawaiian grammar that does the most to distinguish islanders from outsiders. It is this multiracial, multicultural mixing and blending to form a third cultural space that Kathleen Tyau, herself a Hawaiian-Chinese, describes so vividly in her award-winning novel, *A Little Too Much Is Enough* (1996).[4] This third-space culture comes from several generations of racial and cultural mixing on a footing of relative equality, which means that among the Chinese in Hawai'i there was widespread acknowledgment of racial mixedness and acceptance of mixed-race people into their community from a very early era.

Japanese Americans

Before the 1960s the situation for multiracial Americans of some Japanese ancestry was more like that for multiracial Chinese Americans on the mainland: there were not very many of them, and they were not welcome in the Japanese community. There were more married Japanese Americans than Chinese Americans, for the anti-immigrant movement did not succeed in banning Japanese women who came to join their husbands until after 1924. But, as with Chinese Americans on the mainland, intermarriage remained relatively infrequent—less than 5 percent in the immigrant generation (Spickard, 1989)—for much the same reasons as with the Chinese—antimiscegenation laws prohibited marriages with Whites, and Japanese Americans had strong prejudices against most other groups found in the West, including Chinese, Filipinos, and other Asians. Because of those prejudices, the Japanese American outmarriage rate in Hawai'i was even lower than on the mainland, despite Hawai'i's ideology of racial mixing. The prejudices were strong. For example, in the World War II concentration camps in the United States, Japanese American women who had been partners with Filipino men before the war were ostracized. They had to live and eat separately from other inmates, were talked about by other Japanese American women, and were sexualized by Japanese American men as fair game (Spickard, 1986).

The idea of intermarriage carried enough stigma that those multiracial people who did exist were not welcome in Japanese American families and communities. In 1940 the Japanese American Children's Home of Los Angeles was more than half-full with mixed-race children who had been abandoned by their parents (Spickard, 1986). Others roamed the streets and had to raise themselves. Very few found a place within Japanese America. As Japanese-Caucasian Kathleen Tamagawa (1932:1) described herself: "The trouble with me is my ancestry. I really should not have been born." She spent her youth trying to find a place in Japan or Japanese America before finally reconciling herself to a middle-class White identity with few Japanese connections.

As with Chinese Americans on the mainland, the keepers of the community's memory ignored intermarried Japanese Americans and multiracial people. The one study of Japanese American intermarriage before the 1960s (Ishikawa, 1938) looked only at Japanese Americans on the East Coast and was published in a journal so obscure that its findings have almost entirely escaped notice by historians of Japanese America. The important thing to note is that, like the Chinese community on the U.S. mainland and unlike the Chinese in Hawai'i, Japanese Americans in both places constituted themselves as a monoracial group and cast out the few people of mixed descent.

South Asian Americans

In its initial family structure, the much smaller South Asian population in the United States was a bit like the Chinese American community. Made up mainly of men who worked in California agriculture, the South Asians formed a bachelor society, although quite a few had wives and families back in the Punjab. But this was not so relentlessly a monoracial community. One group of a few hundred Punjabi men settled down in the Imperial Valley of California and married immigrant women from Mexico (Leonard, 1992). They and their mixed-race children formed almost the only Indian community in the United States in the years before there was an Asian America. They identified strongly with the Punjab, but there was little Indian content to their lives. The families spoke English and Spanish, and most were Catholic, although they did tend to eat a mixture of Mexican and South Asian dishes. Identificationally, the mixed people grew up with the label "Hindu," but as with the Hawaiian Chinese, this meant mixed—Punjabi–Mexican American.

After 1946 the immigration ban on South Asians was ended, and small but significant numbers of new arrivals came from India. This meant that there was a new generation of unmixed South Asians, including some wives of the original Punjabi men. These new migrants tended not to recognize the mixed Punjabi–Mexican Americans as South Asians. Thus early on among South Asian Americans there was a fairly high level of interracial mixing, an acknowledgment of multiraciality, and a place in the Asian Indian community for mixed-race people. With new immigration in the postwar era, however, a new monoracial discourse was asserted, and mixed people tended not to be acknowledged any longer.

Filipino Americans

The situation for mixed-race people of Filipino descent was strikingly different. In the era before a common Asian American identity was formed, Filipino communities were full of mixed couples and multiracial children. The main Filipino migration came somewhat later than for the other groups, beginning after 1920. Like the South Asians and Chinese, this was a bachelor society made up largely of farmworkers, both in Hawai'i and on the West Coast. But unlike those groups on the mainland, there was lots of intermarriage, mainly with Whites, although Filipino-White couples had to go to the same extremes as others to circumvent the antimiscegenation laws. Enough did, and had children, so that at some point nearly all second- or third-generation Filipino Americans were racially mixed (Posadas, 1989; Lasker, 1931: 92–95, 196–97; Vallangca, 1977: 36–37, 50–53; Espiritu, 1995: 53–63, 74, 127, 193–203). One of the subjects that has not been explored, but which is surely worthy of study, is the close relationships between Filipinos and Mexican Americans in agricultural districts from the Imperial Valley to Yakima. Surely more intermarriages and mixed people came from that interaction than from the South Asian–Mexican American nexus. There were also mixed families of Filipinos and Native Americans in the Pacific Northwest and Alaska. For Filipino Americans, unlike most other Asian groups, there has long been broad acceptance of intermarriage and inclusion of multiracial people.

In summary, we may conclude three things: (1) there were more interracial marriages and multiracial people among Asian Americans than has generally been recognized, but the total numbers were still relatively small; (2) in three situations—among South Asians, Filipinos, and Chinese in Hawai'i—group identity in this period depended on the fact of mixedness; (3) two groups—Japanese Americans and Chinese Americans on the U.S. mainland—kept multiracial people on the margins or denied them group membership altogether, as those communities pursued monoracial identities.

Other Asian American Diversities and Mixednesses

The complexity presented by racially mixed people was not the only kind of multiplicity experienced by Asian Americans before the coming together of a common Asian American identity. There were in fact several other ways in which Asian Americans constituted a mixed multitude. First, there were the several nations of ancestral origin—China, India, Korea, and so forth. There also were regional differences within each of the groups. For Japanese Americans, the sharpest split was between Okinawan and Naichi Japanese (they still form almost separate communities in Hawai'i), but there were also immigrant-generation splits between people from different prefectures. The division was equally strong in the Chinese community between city Cantonese, Toisanese, Hakka, and Hong Kong Chinese, as well as between all of these groups, which were from greater Canton, and others who came from Taiwan, Fujian, Shanghai, and other parts of China. Among Filipinos, the differences among Ilocanos, Tagalog-speakers, Cebuanos, and others played a similarly divisive role.

In addition, there were significant class divisions among Asian Americans—between merchants and workers in the Chinese community; between Japanese and Punjabi farm owners and managers and their Filipino field laborers; and so forth.

What is striking about this heterogeneity in the pre–Asian American period is the small amount of social and marital mixing among the various groups. Early on, some Filipinos and Punjabis did mix with and marry Whites and Mexicans, and their multiracial children were integrated into the Filipino and Indian communities; and some Chinese did marry Hawaiians. But beyond that there was not a lot of mixing across any of these lines, even across those subethnic lines within various national-origin groups. Although there was more mixing than the keepers of the Japanese American and Chinese American communities' monoracialist histories have recognized, there just were not many marriages between Chinese and Japanese, between Filipinos and Koreans, and so forth.

Outsiders' Views

White Americans did not see all this very clearly. They had a monoracialist discourse for Asian Americans that did not perceive the divisions within Asian America and that failed to recognize the place of multiracial Asian Americans.[5] Their perception of all Asians as a monolith amounted to lumping together the unlumpable. Non-Asian Americans' gathering of Asians together conceptually went so far as to include Pacific Islanders; regularly, in movies, travel advertisements, and television commercials, Asians were put in the places of Hawaiians and other Polynesians, and no one seems to have noticed (Spickard, 1989).

One mechanism by which Whites lumped Asians (and Pacific Islanders) together was the Census. When Asians first emerged out of the "other" category, they were all classified as "Orientals," and later as "Asians and Pacific Islanders" (U.S. Bureau of the Census, 1963). But the White perception of commonality among Asians was more broadly cultural than just the bureaucratic labeling device that was the Census, for pulp fiction and B movies throughout the twentieth century have assumed an Asian cultural homogeneity extending from Hawai'i to Pakistan and beyond, and a sameness to people whose ancestors came from those places.

The idea of the "Orient" goes very deep in European intellectual history, dating long before the creation of Europe. Herodotus, writing in the fifth century B.C., depicted the Persian invaders of Greece as a faceless, unfeeling mass (Herodotus, 1954). From that day on, European-derived perceptions have grouped together everyone from anywhere east of the Bosporus. Edward Said (1978) has written about this as "Orientalism," although the Arab-and-Turk-focused British Orientalism he describes has a rather different content than the East-Asia-focused Orientalism that operates among White Americans.

The point is that White Americans constructed a monoracialist discourse to describe Asian Americans, and did not differentiate among the various sorts of Asian Americans, including multiracial people of Asian ancestry. As far as Whites were concerned, such people were consigned to the Asian group, even though before 1965 the largest Asian groups would not have them. This left multiracial Asian Americans with no place to be.

Pulling Apart: Monoracial Immigration Since 1965

Two countervailing forces have been at work on Asian American unity and the place of multiracial people in the last third of the twentieth century and into the twenty-first. One has been the immigration of unprecedentedly large numbers of Asian Americans as a result of the 1965 Immigration Act and various forces set in motion by the Vietnam War. The other has been the coming together of Asians of many sorts into a panethnic coalition with something like a shared identity. Both of these, however, have been mainly monoracialist discourses that have not explicitly determined what they intend to do with multiracial people of Asian ancestry.

Lots of new immigrants have come to the United States from Asia since about 1970: from China nearly three-quarters of a million; from South Asia more than four hundred thousand; from Korea more than six hundred thousand; from Vietnam more than half a million; and from the Philippines over eight hundred thousand (Ong et al., 1994: 41). These immigrants have changed the demographic face of Asian America. As of the 1990 Census, there were more than a million and a half Chinese Americans; nearly as many Filipinos; about eight hundred thousand each of Japanese Americans, Asian Indians, and Koreans; six hundred thousand Vietnamese; two hundred thousand Hawaiians; and nearly a million other Asian and Pacific Islander Americans (U.S. Bureau of the Census, 1991).

Although most non–Asian Americans view all these immigrants as part of a common Asian group, most of the immigrants perceive themselves in their ethnic specificity. They may recognize that they are lumped together by White Americans, but few Vietnamese immigrants sense that they themselves have much in common with Filipinos or Koreans. Most of the new immigrants, whether they live in New York's Chinatown, Monterey Park, or Duluth, see themselves as ethnically distinct and racially fairly pure. Theirs are monoracialist world views.

Only a small minority of the immigrant generation intermarry, despite the disappearance of barriers from the White side, although the rates of intermarriage are higher than for previous generations of Asian immigrants. Their children are another matter. There is considerable evidence that, except for such tightly knit groups as the Hmong, intermarriage is a prominent fact of community life among the American-born of each of the Asian American groups. In that generation, not just Japanese, Chinese, and Filipino Americans but Koreans and Vietnamese are broadly accepting of intermarriage. And increasingly, in all the Asian communities, there are places for multiracial people.

Coming Together: Asian American Panethnicity After the 1960s

The Asian American Movement

The Asian American movement of the late 1960s and early 1970s was an emphatically monoracialist enterprise. That is, it was about the construction of a single racial identity out of ethnic specificities that were formerly disparate. In West Coast inner-city neighborhoods in the 1950s and 1960s, there grew up a generation of Chinese, Japanese, and (to a lesser extent) Filipino Americans who had known each other from childhood, who had experienced a common Orientalization from Whites, and who did not harbor their parents' antagonisms toward one another based on Asian politics. These young Asians were the first generation to attend college in large numbers, mainly West Coast public institutions, in the latter 1960s. There they encountered an environment politicized by the Civil Rights and Black Power movements and mounting opposition to the Vietnam War.

In that environment was born a movement for a common Asian American identity—what Yen Le Espiritu (1992) calls a "panethnicity"—much like the common Native American panethnicity that has emerged at various times out of individual tribal identities. William Wei (1993: 42) describes the process:

> As an ethnic-consciousness movement, the Black Power movement made Asian Americans realize that they too had been defined by European American attitudes and dominated by an Eurocentric culture. They had to rethink who they were and re-create their own cultural identity, forging distinct Asian ethnic group identities into a pan-Asian one. The foundation for this unique identity was their experience as Asians in America—a common history of oppression and resistance that would serve as the basis for a "bold culture, unashamed and true to itself."

Some varieties of Asian Americans were closer to the center of this enterprise than others. The American-born were more central than immigrants, for it was in their formers' common experiences in the United States—indeed, in their relationships to one another—that the Asian American identity was born.[6] And within this group it was really Chinese and Japanese Americans who stood at the center, with Filipinos a marginal group, and other varieties of Asian Americans, such as Koreans and South Asians, not even on the map (see Figure 1-1).

Multiracial people of Asian ancestry were part of this map only insofar as they had earned membership in one of the constituent Asian American groups, and, in an often highly politicized atmosphere, insofar as they were willing to eschew connections to other identities.[7] Thus, in the mid-1970s, as part of a full-life commitment to the Chinese community, a Chinese-White law student in San Francisco served on his school's Asian law caucus and, after graduation, formed a small firm with three other lawyers, one Japanese and two Chinese (all monoracial). By contrast, another mixed law student, who had not grown up in Chinatown and who did not marry an Asian spouse, was not accorded a similar place in the Chinese community and did not have the same degree of acceptance in Asian American circles. However, because part-White Filipinos were seen as Filipinos by the Filipino community, they were allowed a connection to the Asian American movement on much the same basis as unmixed Filipinos.[8]

Pan-Asianism a Quarter-Century Later

At the beginning of the twenty-first century, one finds in place a similar hierarchy of Asianness, with Chinese, Japanese, and Korean Americans at the center, and the American-born slightly more central than the immigrants, but with increasing recognition of

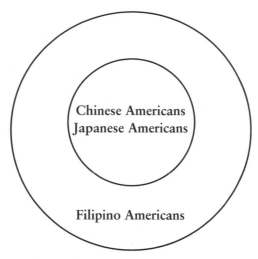

FIGURE I-I. Centrality and marginality of Asian American groups, 1970s

the diasporic quality of all the Asian groups. Vietnamese and Filipino Americans inhabit the second tier of Asian America, followed by other Southeast Asians and South Asian Americans (see Figure 1-2).

The places of multiracial people in this Asian American hierarchy are more fluid, and less dependent on the Asian group to which they may be attached. In the last half-dozen years, mixed-race Asian Americans have been so active, and so insistent on a place in Asian America, that regardless of their specific ancestry they might be placed together

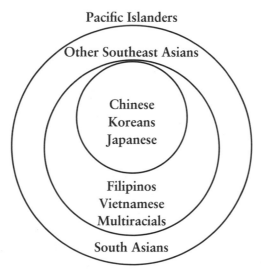

FIGURE I-2. Centrality and marginality of Asian American groups, 1990s

as a multiracial group in the second tier along with Vietnamese and Filipinos. As the in-group definition has been broadened to include Asians of many national origin groups, the simple, binary nature of categorizing has softened, and there has been a greater willingness to include multiracial Asian Americans in the mix. For example, in 1997 an entire issue of *Amerasia Journal* explored the theme of multiraciality (Houston & Williams, 1997); such an event would have unthinkable a dozen years earlier.[9]

It is also worth noting that the situation is now a bit different for another, growing group of mixed-descent Asian Americans: those who have more than one Asian ancestry yet no non-Asian ancestry. Informally at least, monoracial Asian Americans seem to regard such people as more Asian than people whose mixed ancestry includes non-Asian parentage. It is in some ways an affirmation of the strength of the relatively new Asian American panethnicity that for a couple of decades Japanese and Chinese Americans have been marrying each other. There is an assumption in some writings that the children of such intra-Asian intermarriages will be more Asian than people with one parent who is White, Black, or Latino (Espiritu, 1992: 167–168; Shinagawa & Pang, 1988; Kibria, 1997; Lee, 1997; Fong & Yung 1995–96). No one has yet studied this population formally to find out if such assumptions hold true.

Part of the Lump? Pacific Islanders and Asian American Ethnicity

For a long time White Americans have put Pacific Islanders in the Asian American Census category, and for about two decades some Asians have reflexively included Pacific Islanders in their formal definition of Asian Americans. Thus one reads often of the "Asian Pacific community" and finds the name "Pacific Islander" appended to many an Asian American catalogue and institution. And the University of California, Santa Barbara, offers Asian American Studies credit for courses on Hawaiian music and Pacific Islander Americans. Most White people do not think that Hawaiians, Samoans, and Tongans are Asians, but they do not think about Pacific Islanders much, and the Asian category has seemed a convenient place to put them. It is worth noting that in the 2000 Census, Pacific Islanders have a category of their own, although their numbers are so small that they are not likely to gain a spot on the ethnic studies map unless it is as honorary Asians (U.S. Office of Management and Budget, 1997). Even so, on the diagram of Asian America shown in Figure 1–2, Pacific Islanders occupy the tier farthest out, and while Asian Americans have not been unwelcoming to Pacific Islanders, they often do not seem to know exactly what to do with them.

For the present discussion, Pacific Islander Americans are worth contemplating because, even more than Filipinos, Pacific Islanders are conscious of themselves as a people of multiplicity. Throughout the Pacific, people have been moving around from island to island, to Aotearoa and Australia, to Hawai'i and America, for two hundred years. Almost everyone has ancestors or other relatives who have married people from other islands, Europeans, Americans, or Asians. Almost everyone is conscious of an element of mixedness in themselves, even as they embrace one or more of their binary identities. The grounds on which a person may claim membership in one group or another consist of practice (Do you act Samoan? Do you know *fa'aSamoa*?), place (Is there a Tongan place with which you identify?), and family connection (Are there Fijians who claim you as kin?) (Spickard & Fong, 1995).

But many Pacific Islanders go beyond such binary identity-claimings to acknowledge and embrace their ethnic multiplicity. This consciousness of multiplicity can constitute a third cultural (or at least identificational) space, where mixed people identify with other mixed people, not on the basis of their constituent ancestral parts, but on the basis of their very mixedness. Such a third space is the basis of the multiracial student groups that appeared on many campuses in the 1990s.

I leave you with a love story of such a third-space couple and their encounter with the binarily constructed racial environment in Japan. Akebono is one of two *yokozuna*, or grand *sumo* champions, in Japan, and a star of the opening ceremonies of the 1998 Olympic Games in Nagano. Once he was Chad Rowan, a Samoan American growing up in Hawai'i. In February 1998 he announced his engagement to Christine Reiko Kalina, a secretary at the U.S. Air Force base in Yokota, west of Tokyo. Kalina is the daughter of a Japanese woman and a White American father. There was much grumbling in the Japanese press that the match was unsuitable: she was not really Japanese (i.e., she grew up in the United States, could speak Japanese but not write it well, and had a non-Japanese father). Some of the criticism seemed to stem partly from the Japanese public's only grudging welcome to foreign *sumo* champions, even though those individuals, like Akebono, took on Japanese identities and citizenship. But consider: this is an ideally matched third-space couple, although they share no elements of ethnicity. He is a Samoan from Hawai'i taking on a high-level Japanese identity in Japan. She is a multiracial Caucasian-Japanese woman living in Japan. Both are culturally and identificationally mixed by background. Both are displaced by current location. Both are barely tolerated by the Japanese public, viewed as essentially outsiders who have usurped places that rightly belong to unmixed, Japan-born, ethnic Japanese. The press's criticism to the contrary, they are a perfect match (Efron, 1998).

Notes

1. There was one part of the U.S. mainland—the South after Reconstruction—where the situation approximated that in Hawai'i. There, Chinese men entered plantation labor contracts in a multiracial society that bore structural similarities to Hawai'i. A significant number of these married African American women, just as Chinese men of the same era were marrying Hawaiian women in the islands. In subsequent generations, two Chinese populations grew up in the South: a group of purely Chinese ancestry, and a segment of the Black population that acknowledged Chinese ancestry (Loewen, 1971).

2. Much more has been written in White-derived social commentary about the Hapa-Haole (roughly translated, "half-White") population, because such people were important to the islands' power structure and to the maintenance of colonial domination. But such a focus overlooks the equally pervasive connection between Hawaiians and Chinese.

3. Eric Yamamoto (1995) overemphasizes the Japanese element (see also Okamura, 1995).

4. See also Spickard and Fong (1995).

5. Nor did they perceive the diversity within the Italian and Jewish communities (Sarna, 1978).

6. Note that the immigrants—both the parental generation and the new immigrants—saw themselves and were seen by the American-born as more central to the various national ethnic groups.

7. Mixed-race Asian Americans were often seen in the most intensely politicized period as sell-outs by definition, as more White than Asian, as White wannabes, as people whose lives and values were contiguous with people of this description: "They have rejected their physical heritages, resulting in extreme self-hatred. Yellow people share with the blacks the desire to look white. Just as blacks wish to be light-complected with thin lips and unkinky hair, 'yellows' want to be tall with long legs and large eyes" (Uyematsu, 1971).

8. The relative acceptance of part-White Filipinos by the Filipino American community is rooted in the centuries of mixture that took place in the Philippine Islands between native Filipinos and other groups, such as the Spanish and the Chinese. The fact that the early Filipino American community was exceptionally multiracial is probably another contributing factor.

9. The openness to hearing the voices of multiracials also is due to the increasing consciousness in nearly every Asian community of the high rate of intermarriage and the fact that the future face of every Asian community is significantly interracial (Spickard, 1996).

CHAPTER 2

Possibilities of a Multiracial Asian America

Yen Le Espiritu

I often say proudly that I am *all* Vietnamese. But this statement is not quite true. My family has always been much more multiracial and multiethnic than this simple declaration acknowledges. Although I have always claimed that our family was 100 percent Vietnamese, my fifth auntie recently told me that my paternal great-grandmother was of Chinese descent. Since the age of twelve, I have been raised by both my Vietnamese mother and my white American stepfather—a relationship that has not only nurtured my personal growth but has also taught me much about the possibilities and realities of cross-racial families. As an adult, I now revel in my own multiethnic family: my husband is Filipino, and my young children are learning about both their Vietnamese and Filipino heritages as well as the more abstract "Asian American" grouping. I begin my discussion of multiracial Asian America with this personal history because it illustrates the ways in which many Asian Americans insist on monoraciality and fail to see the multiracial and multicultural realities in our everyday lives. In this essay, I argue that Asian America, by definition, is multiracial and that this multiraciality provides us the critical space to explore the strategic importance of cross-group affiliation—not only among Asians but also with other kin groups.

Asian America: A Multiracial Community

In an analysis of multiracial households in the United States, D. Eggebeen, K. Chew, and P. Uhlenberg (1989) report that a significant number comprise a person of some Asian ancestry through marriage, birth, and/or adoption. Since the 1960s, the increased presence of Asian American multiracial families—spawned by the substantial increase in the numbers of Asian Americans who marry non-Asians, of multiracial Asian Americans, and of Asian-descent children adopted and raised by non-Asian parents—has challenged the presumed monoraciality of the various Asian American communities. By the 1970s, the numbers of Asian Americans—particularly Chinese and Japanese Americans—who married outside of their respective groups and then had children were so large that Asian American communities were forced to begin to reconsider the question who is Asian American (Spickard, 1997: 49). It is estimated that in the post–civil rights era, approximately half of all U.S.–born Chinese and Japanese Americans are married to whites (Jacobs & Labov, 1995). A 1990 California survey found that 25 percent of Asian-ancestry children in the state were the product of both Asian- and European-descent parents (U.S. Office of Management and Budget, 1995). The Japanese American community has the highest rate of interracial marriage and of multiracial children. According to the 1990 Census, there were 39 percent more Japanese-white births than monoracial Japanese American births that year (U.S. Bureau of the Census, 1992). The prominent presence of Asian-descent multiracials has spawned a growing public discourse by and about multiracial people in the art and literary worlds, and in the academies (Houston & Williams, 1997).

The contemporary interest in multiracial Asian America is both critical and long overdue, forcing us to explore "notions of boundary-creation, boundary-bursting, and boundary-expansion" (Houston & Williams, 1997: ix). But, Asian-descent multiracial peoples are not a new social phenomenon. Asians in the United States—and also in Asia, Europe, and Latin America—have long created, burst, and expanded racial boundaries, even when it was illegal to do so. Prior to the 1960s, Asian men in the United States, like African American men, were viewed as threats to white racial purity and in certain states were forbidden to marry white women. But although antimiscegenation laws existed, interracial families abounded. Some couples simply entered into common law (not state-recognized) marriages, while others traveled to states without antimiscegenation laws to marry (see Williams-León and Nakashima, Introduction). The end of World War II witnessed an increase in the number of Asian American multiracial households as Japanese, Korean, and Filipina wives of non-Asian servicemen joined their husbands in the United States and as children from Asia, often of mixed parentage, were adopted by American families (Chan, 1991: 140). It is also critical to move beyond the "white-yellow" axis and recognize the multiracial households created by Asians and their "non-white" partners. For example, in pre–World War II California, where many Asian and Mexican immigrants labored together in the fields, Asian men often had Mexican partners (Takaki, 1989: 310–311, 341). Despite the long history of racial blending between Asian Americans and other persons of color, these multiracial families have received relatively little scholarly attention, because they do not threaten the border between whites and nonwhites (Root, 1992a, b).

Besides legislating against miscegenation, the state—as represented by the U.S. Bureau of the Census—has routinely disregarded the reality of interracial families and multiracial individuals. The Census classification of multiracials has been arbitrary and inconsistent—often reinforcing the existing racial hierarchies and/or reflecting the Census Bureau's administrative needs rather than the population's perception of meaningful identities. Through the categories it uses to count and classify ethnic and racial groups, the Census has often legitimated the hypodescent rule, bolstered the claim of white racial purity, and imposed an arbitrary monoracial identity on individuals of mixed parentage. As an example, the 1920 Census stipulated that "any mixture of White and some other race was to be reported according to the race of the person who was not White" (U.S. Bureau of the Census, 1979: 52). Prior to the 1960 Census, racial classification was obtained by the enumerator on the basis of observation. Given the racial "ambiguity" of multiracials, many of these individuals were often misclassified. The 1890 Census schedule epitomizes the problem of misclassification. This Census instructs Census takers to

> be particularly careful to distinguish between blacks, mulattoes, quadroons, and octoroons. The word "black" should be used to describe those persons who have three-fourths or more black blood; "mulatto," those persons who have from three-eights to five-eights black blood; "quadroon," those persons who have one-fourth black blood; and "octoroon," those persons who have one-eight or any trace of black blood. (U.S. Bureau of the Census, 1979: 28)

Beside the racist undertones of these instructions, it is doubtful that these blood-quantum distinctions can be made by mere observation. Not until the 1980 census were enumerators no longer allowed to enter race by observation.

In 1976, the U.S. Office of Management and Budget (OMB) issued a memorandum— Statistical Policy Directive No. 15— requiring all federal agencies to use only the following categories in program administrative reporting and statistical activities: "American Indian or Alaskan Native, Asian or Pacific Islander, Black, and White." (U.S. Equal Employment Opportunity Commission, 1977: 17900). Because this directive instructed Census takers to mark only one category of racial identification, it forced multiracials to choose between the racial identities of their parents, thereby perpetuating the invisibility of multiracial populations. In the past decade, multiracial advocacy groups have consistently challenged the racist tradition of hypodescent embodied in the "single-race checkoff" policy. In June 1993, the Association of MultiEthnic Americans (AMEA), the first nationwide group of its kind in the United States, testified before the Census Subcommittee of the U.S. House of Representatives and proposed that the Census Bureau add a multiracial category under which multiracial people could mark all racial categories that apply (Fernandez, 1996: 25). The growth and activism of the mixed-race movement forced the federal government to launch a review of the race and ethnicity categories. After four years of heated debate, the Clinton administration's thirty-agency Census task force rejected the proposal to create a separate multiracial category, arguing that it would generate yet another population group and add to racial tensions. Instead, in July 1997, the task force proposed that mixed-race Americans for the first time be allowed to "mark one or more" racial category when identifying themselves for the Census and other government programs. By allowing people to mark as many racial categories as they want, the new proposal would remove from Census forms, the "Other" category, which nearly 10 million Americans marked in 1990, making it one of the fastest growing categories. This growth can be explained in part by the increase in the number of multiracials who marked "Other" as an alternative to the monoracial categories (McKenney & Cresce, 1992).

Multiracial Asian America:
Negotiating Race, Gender, and Class Boundaries

In spite of the prominent presence of multiracial households in Asian America, Asian Americans have historically denied the interracial reality of their communities. Upholding the myth of ethnic and racial purity, the Asian American community has been as guilty "of stereotyping and oppressing, of mythologizing and dominating" Asian-descent multiracials as has white America (Spickard, 1997: 45). Prior to the 1960s, most Asian Americans shunned interracial couples and declared that multiracial people of Asian descent could not be Asians (Spickard, 1997: 45). For example, the Japanese American community often discriminated against mixed individuals through blood-quantum requirements in Japanese American sports leagues and Cherry Blossom Queen pageants (Ropp, 1997: 4; King, 1997: 117).

Although the exclusion of multiracial Asians is often couched in racial terms, their treatment has not been uniform but instead has varied according to the racial derivation, class background, and gender of the multiracial. Replicating the hierarchical American racial system, Asian American groups are least accepting of Asian-descent multiracials who are of African heritage. As V. H. Houston and T. K. Williams (1997: vii) state, the product of the interracial union is "considered even more frightening if its multiracial composition includes African ancestry." Concurring with this assessment, Paul Spickard (1997: 55) contends that only in rare instances of famous accomplishments "are Asian communities willing to treat mixed people of African American parentage as insiders." This hostility toward AfroAsians reproduces U.S. racial rankings that place African Americans—and therefore multiracials of African heritage—at the bottom of the social scale. Legally and socially, multiracial people of African American descent have been forced by white Americans to identify only as black and have been raised almost invariably in the black community (Davis, 1991).

The "largely traumatic and dehumanizing" experience of Vietnamese Amerasians provides another example of the combined effect of race *and* class on the community acceptance level of multiracials (Valverde, 1992: 146; see also Spickard, 1997: 52–53; Root, 1997b: 30). In a society such as Vietnam, which values racial purity, the Amerasians were treated as virtual outcasts from birth. But this rejection can also be traced to the racial and class origins of the Amerasian. Although all Amerasians were marked as different and inferior, black Amerasians (*my den*) encountered the most discrimination (Valverde, 1992: 147). The presumed social and economic background of the Amerasian's parents also affected his or her status. In the eyes of most Vietnamese, every Amerasian in Vietnam was the child of a Vietnamese bar girl or prostitute and an American G.I. Thus these biracial children also bore the stigma of immorality, illegitimacy, and the underclass. The role of class becomes more evident when one compares the experiences of Eurasians (children of French and Vietnamese parents) and Amerasians. Although both groups were racially mixed, the Eurasians of the French colonial era seldom faced the same degree of hostility as did the Amerasians of the later period. During the French colonial era, marriages between Vietnamese women and French men were not infrequent. Due to the high status of French colonial officials and to the fact that most Vietnamese women who married French men came from distinguished families, these couples and their children were often accepted in both French and Vietnamese societies. The mestizos (half-Filipino and half-Spanish) in the Philippines provide an analogous example. During the Spanish rule and for a few decades thereafter, the mestizos were not ostracized but instead occupied positions of power and economic advantage over the rest of the "unmixed" Filipino population (Pido, 1986: 21).

Gender ideologies also affect the (mis)treatment of multiracial Asians. One of the most common stereotypes of interracial couples and mixed-race people is that they are sexually immoral. Because women's cooperation is critical for the maintenance of racial purity, the charge of immorality applies much more frequently to women than to men. Women who choose interracial relationships—thus violating cultural norms and racial boundaries—are often presented as sexually "loose" and reduced entirely to sexual beings (Frankenberg, 1993: 87). The myth of the immoral is compounded for the daughters of interracial couples. As the product of an immoral union between immoral people, multiracial women are "consistently imaged as extremely passionate and sexually promiscuous" and are likely targets for sexual objectification and abuse (Nakashima, 1992: 168). The plight of Vietnamese Amerasians provide a case in point. Because the larger community assumes that the mothers of these Amerasians were cheap bar girls, they place the same stereotype on Amerasian girls and women. As a consequence, these women are labeled and treated as prostitutes, often having been raped or sexually abused in Vietnam or in refugee-processing centers (Valverde, 1992: 158).

In another manifestation of patriarchal ideology, multiracial Asians are deemed more "Asian" when their father, rather than their mother, is Asian. During World War II, when multiracial people of Japanese ancestry were incarcerated along with persons of full Japanese ancestry, the U.S. War Relocation Authority (WRA) judged each Amerasian's racial affiliation on the basis of the gender of the non-Japanese parent. Because WRA officials believed that children were more dominated by their fathers than by their mothers, Amerasian children who had Japanese fathers and non-Japanese mothers were not allowed to return to the West Coast, while those with Japanese mothers and non-Japanese fathers could (Spickard, 1997: 47–48). Similarly, C. L. Nakashima (1996: 85) suggests that having an Asian surname, which indicates patrilineal Asian heredity, seems to play an important role in the level of acceptance a mixed-race person experiences. The policy for classifying babies at birth is also gendered. Until 1989, multiracial children of two parents of color were assigned the race of the father. (Reflecting hypodescent laws, biracial babies with a white parent were assigned the racial status of the nonwhite parent.) Since 1989, the new standing policy directs that all infants are given the same race as their mothers (Waters, 1994).

Asian American Panethnicity and Multiracial Asians

Asian American panethnicity has its roots in the racialization of Asian national groups by dominant groups as well as in responses to those constructions by Asian American themselves. Largely on the basis of race, all Asian Americans have been lumped together and treated as if they were the same. The racialist constructions of Asians as homogeneous and interchangeable have spawned important alliances and affiliations among ethnic and immigrant groups of Asian origin. Adopting the dominant group's categorization of them, Asian Americans have institutionalized pan-Asianism as their political instrument—thereby enlarging their own capacities to challenge and transform the existing structure of power. Though powerful, pan-Asianism is not unproblematic: it can mask salient divisions, subsume nondominant groups, and create marginalities—all of which threaten the legitimacy of the pan-Asian concept and bolster (however inadvertently) the racist discourse and practices that construct Asians as homogeneous. For example, some Asian American subgroups have accused the more established Chinese and Japanese Americans in pan-Asian organizations of monopolizing the funding and jobs meant for all Asian Americans; the dissidents complained that newer and more impoverished groups were simply used as window display (Espiritu, 1992).

In the post-1960s, faced with the substantial increase in the numbers of multiracial Asians and the corresponding explosion of multiracial consciousness, pan-Asian organizations were challenged to expand their boundaries and to consider multiracial Asians as fellow ethnics (Spickard, 1997: 51). However, like other nondominant Asian American subgroups, multiracial Asians have charged that pan-Asian organizations have largely ignored or marginalized multiracial concerns. Even today, few Asian American studies programs in the country incorporate multiracial issues into their curricula, and few Asian American organizations have Amerasian representatives in their leadership circles. An example of the slighting of multiracial Asians occurred at a 1988 Asian Pacific American alumni meeting at UCLA, when the then-president of the Asian American alumni organization refused to appoint an Amerasian to the organization's advisory board because he did not believe that the experience of "Hapas" constituted a significant part of the Asian American experience (Houston & Williams, 1997: x). Asian American inability—or unwillingness—to see multiraciality was also evident in the 1990–91 protest of the hit musical *Miss Saigon,* when Asian American activists and communities demanded that the lead role of the Eurasian pimp go to an Asian instead of a white actor. As Spickard (1997: 51) points out, lost in this bitter protest was the fact that an Asian rather than a person of mixed ancestry was being suggested for the role of the Eurasian.

The interests of panethnic groups and those of multiracial groups have also collided over how best to classify and count multiracials in the federal Census. Since the late 1960s, possible affirmative action benefits have provided a material incentive for various Asian American subgroups to organize along pan-Asian lines. As Congress, federal judges, and public officials turned to Census counts to monitor access in housing, education, employment, and other areas vulnerable to discrimination, ethnic activists became increasingly involved in the politics of Census enumeration. In the early 1970s, influenced by the protests from the African American community, Asian Americans and Latinos pressed the Census Bureau for better coverage of their respective communities, which included a significant proportion of new immigrants (Anderson, 1988: 221–226). Although actual affirmative action benefits are vague, ethnic activists believe that the larger the official count of their group's members, the greater the advantage the members have in these programs (Lowry, 1982: 54). In June 1976, after considerable pressure was exerted on the Census Bureau, the Asian Pacific American Advisory Committee for the 1980 Census was created. In an overall effort to increase the total count of Asian Pacific Americans, the committee fought hard to increase the number of Asian Pacific American categories listed in the race item so that fewer or no Asian Pacific groups would have to be enumerated as "Other" (Census Advisory Committee, 1979: 9). They recommended instead that the following write-in responses be recoded as "Other Asian" and counted as "Asian American": "Asian (Asian American), Asiatic, Bangladesh, Burmese, Cambodian, Ceylonese, Eurasian, Indonesian, Javanese, Laotian, Malayan, Mongolian, Okinawan, Oriental, Pakistani, Siamese, Thai, Yellow" (Census Advisory Committee, 1979: 16). Designed to increase the total count of Asian Pacific Americans, this catchall category includes the multiple levels of Asian American identifications: from regional (e.g., Okinawan) to national (e.g., Laotian) to panethnic (e.g., Asian American). It also claims the offspring of mixed parentage (e.g., Eurasian) as one of its own. The expedient nature of this (and similar) claim(s) angered many Amerasians who charged that "Asian American political activists want to take ownership of Amerasians because it is politically propitious and advantageous to do so" (Houston, 1991: 56).

The debate over the classification of multiracials in the 2000 Census provides another example. Denouncing the government's past attempt to wedge mixed-raced Americans into one rigid racial category, multiracial advocacy groups favored adding a mixed-race category to the 2000 Census under which multiracial people can check all the boxes that apply. However, most civil rights groups argued instead that such a category would dilute the numbers of people who identify with a particular race and cause their respective communities to lose hard-won gains in civil rights, education, and electoral arenas (Hernandez, 1996: 29; Nash, 1997: 23). This argument, however, denied the possibility of multiple affiliations and instead poses the interests of multiracials—the right to claim their full heritage—as oppositional to the civil rights needs of Asian Americans— the possible loss of political clout that is tied to numbers. These critics were generally more supportive of the Clinton administration's "check one or more" proposal because it was perceived to be less likely to reduce the total count of their respective groups (Fiore, 1997). As of this writing, it is still unclear how federal agencies will tabulate the new racial formation, particularly what they will do with the overlap. Until more is known about how federal agencies will use the new racial formation, it is difficult to gauge how civil rights policies will be affected (Barr & Fletcher, 1997).

The "acceptance" of multiracial Asians is also fraught with racial biases. Often, multiracial individuals are expected to prove their allegiances and feelings of connection to the ethnic community in order to be accepted as "real" Asians (Ropp, 1997: 6). The expectation that multiracials actively identify with their Asian side is premised on monoracial models of race and community; some Asian groups, for example, will accept multiracial Asians only if they renounce or suppress their non-Asian background (Spickard, 1997: 51). This conditional acceptance perpetuates the racial biases and boundaries set by white America in that it does not allow multiracials to assume multiple identities simultaneously or situationally. This pressure, whether overt or unspoken, forces many multiracial individuals to prove that they are more truly "ethnic"—more knowledgeable and attached to the culture, history, and/or political interests of their Asian side—than monoracial subjects (Nakashima, 1996: 84). An example of this "real/fake" dichotomy is Houston's (1991: 54–55) claim that Amerasians like herself, who have a native Asian parent, are "more richly grounded in Asian culture and custom" than many of the "pure-blooded" Asian Americans. For many multiracial, multiethnic individuals, their political identification with their minority parent's ethnic group can become all-consuming. For example, in a study of multiracial Japanese Americans, Amy Iwasaki Mass (1992) found that they actually had a higher degree of affiliation and identification with the Japanese American community than their monoracial counterparts. In another study of mixed-race Japanese Americans who participated in the Cherry Blossom Queen pageant, Rebecca Chiyoko King (1997: 121) reported that mixed-race candidates "exhibit" their Japaneseness by using ethnic "markers" or "cues" such as language, behavior, ethnic names, or dress to convince other people of their ethnic authenticity. In so doing, they challenge the presumed link between race and culture and claim that they can be "very Japanese" culturally and yet be part-Japanese racially. On the other hand, their desire to present themselves as only Japanese (at least in this setting) leaves intact the presumed desirability of monoraciality. In their demand to be included in the traditional ethnic community, the multiracial project may be more focused on contesting specific racial/ethnic boundaries that would exclude them and less on challenging the overall system of race itself (Ropp, 1997: 6).

Possibilities of a Multiracial Asian America

The above discussion suggests that Asian American panethnicity is a highly contested terrain on which Asian Americans of different racial, cultural, and class backgrounds merge and clash over terms of inclusion. In an essay on Asian American cultural politics, Lisa Lowe (1991: 28) argues for the Asian American necessity "to organize, resist, and theorize as Asian Americans," but also warns against "the risk of a cultural politics that relies upon the construction of sameness and the exclusion of difference." The presence of multiracial individuals and their families reinforces, extends, and complicates the assumptions behind the pan-Asian concept. Although the contemporary presence of racially mixed people is unmatched in this country's history, I argued above that Asian America has long been multiracial. Thus, multiracial Asians remind us of the diversity of our *origins:* being Asian in the United States—and in many parts of Asia—includes an inherent reality of mixed race (Houston, 1991: 55). This reality defies attempts to group Asian Americans into a static, closed, monolithic, and monoracial panethnic category. Instead, it forces us to acknowledge that Asian America has long been a multilingual, multicultural, transnational, and transcultural community. As such, the presence of multiracial Asians challenges us to forge our *destinies*—to build a pan-Asian grouping that is open, dynamic, and plural. Because Asian American inter-racial families and Asian-descent multiracial individuals claim multiple affiliations, their lives also remind us of the interconnections of race, gender, sexuality, and class and challenge us to engage in community-building across diverse groups.

Community-building—within and across groups—is critical in our ongoing efforts to destabilize the dominating hierarchies. But as Martin Manalansan (1994: 59–60) reminds us, community is "not a static, closed, and unified system," but embodies both "a sense of dissent and contestation along with a sense of belonging to a group of cause." The Asian American community provides *one* site from which all Asian Americans can change the direction and structure of race relations in this country. This site will be effective only when it recognizes the multiracial and multicultural reality of Asian America. As an acknowledged multiracial community, the Asian American community can join other kin communities in a frank and open discussion of the meaning of race—one that would reconfigure not only the hierarchies within Asian America but also the logic of U.S. monoracial categories.

CHAPTER 3

Servants of Culture: The Symbolic Role of Mixed-Race Asians in American Discourse

Cynthia L. Nakashima

Recently produced genetic evidence indicates that Thomas Jefferson, who "fathered" our Declaration of Independence, also fathered at least one of the children of his "mulatto" slave Sally Hemmings. Public discussion of how this revelation reflects on Jefferson's morality and on his views of race and race mixing is interspersed with intriguing comments about how America has "always been a multicultural society" and nothing is "more American" than having "mixed blood."

In the many years that I've been thinking about, reading about, and writing about people of mixed race,[1] the aspect of the subject that I've always found most fascinating is the discourse on multiraciality itself. Borrowing from postmodern considerations of culture, a "discourse" can be defined as a system of communication and representation that is (generally) highly regulated, and that is largely responsible for the production of a society's knowledge about a given topic (Foucault, 1980b; Butler, 1993; Osajima, 1995). Discourse in contemporary society tends to be strongly related to institutions and other structural entities, and it can include not only the written and the spoken word, but also visual imagery and other less obvious forms of communication. (Watching cartoons with my nine-year-old daughter alerts me to just how much discourse can be communicated visually!)

A lot can be learned about a society by analyzing its various discourses, and discourses on mixed race are revealing of definitions of race, ethnicity, heredity, culture, and community as well as the power structures that underlie those definitions. In societies that define these concepts in terms of mutually exclusive categories, multiracial people threaten to destabilize meanings and boundaries (as well as structural hierarchies), and so require careful consideration and discussion. Very often, institutions step into the discourse and construct rules or laws in an attempt to fit mixed-race people into the categories. (Nakashima, 1992; Van Tassel, 1997; Wright, 1997). On the other hand, social groups that have less rigid understandings of these concepts seem to spend much less discursive time and energy on the subject of multiraciality (Spickard & Fong, 1995; Van Tuyl, Chapter 18).

Interestingly, the same societies that find multiraciality so disruptive also consistently look to the mixed-race person for a space for the exploration of issues of race and ethnicity. Therefore, oftentimes the discourse on multiraciality is highly symbolic, with the mixed-race person being much less the subject of honest inquiry than a functional representative of a social issue. This becomes especially true and increasingly necessary when the population finds that its racial/ethnic meanings and boundaries are in crisis because of social, political, and/or economic changes, such as increased international contact, changing racial demographics, or a rising outmarriage rate (Elfenbein, 1989; Young, 1995; King, 1997).

In this chapter I will consider the representative role that mixed-race people of Asian/other descent have served in American discourses on race and ethnicity during three periods: (1) the late 1800s–early 1900s, the days of the "Yellow Peril," when anti-Asian sentiment reached its zenith; (2) the 1980s, when a declining America watched a rising Pacific Rim with both admiration and hostility; and (3) the 1990s until the present, when debates about multiculturalism and affirmative action have abounded.

Hybrid Subjects, "Tragic Mulattos," and Other Servants of Culture

The symbolic role of mixed-race people has had a long and varied history. Robert J. C. Young (1995) argues that during the nineteenth century, when the European colonial powers were integrating into a globalized imperial capitalist system, England experienced an identity crisis that was projected onto the subject of mixed-race people, who came to embody the dislocations, the incompatibilities, and the confusions of the time. According to Young, the British fascination with miscegenation and hybridity was characterized by a simultaneous attraction and repulsion.

In many cultures, mixed-race women in particular have been viewed with this combination of attraction and repulsion, and seem to be especially useful as a symbolic representation of race and ethnicity (as well as gender and sexuality). The "tragic mulatto" archetype, who is generally female, has played an important function in American culture for the past two centuries (Berzon, 1978; Bogle, 1989; Elfenbein, 1989; Zack, 1993; Streeter, 1996; Sollors, 1997). Considering why the "black/white woman [is] pivotal to the enforcement of racial boundaries" in the United States, Caroline Streeter (1996: 307–308), for example, concludes that

> the maintenance of racial difference within the context of compulsory heterosexuality relies on woman's role as both biological and cultural reproducer. . . . . The twin specters of hypodescent and antimiscegenation laws compose the pillars of the metaphoric gate that sep-

arates whiteness from blackness. The black/white woman is the symbolically charged gate-keeper of this boundary.

Again, the importance of the Black/White woman as gatekeeper becomes more or less pronounced depending on the social context. The "tragic mulatta" character was common in abolitionist literature, became less visible for a while, and then reemerged during Reconstruction as the Black/White boundary was disrupted with the dismantling of slavery (Elfenbein, 1989). Judith Wilson (1991) found a similar emergence and reemergence of images of miscegenation in paintings done directly before and after the Civil War.

Perhaps the mixed-race woman does her most intense symbolic labor by participating in beauty contests. From Rebecca King's (1997; chapter 13) discussion of pageants in the Japanese American community, and Jan Weisman's (1996a) research on the discourse in Thailand surrounding pageant participants, it is clear that dilemmas about racial and cultural definitions are projected explicitly onto the bodies of mixed-race women contestants. "What is essentially Thai?" and "What is authentically Japanese American?" become legitimate questions when asked by institutions seeking to find a single representative for an entire culture, community, or nation. And, in both cases, recent social changes have prompted a reevaluation of group identity (Weisman, 1996; King, 1997).

The Tragic Eurasian of the "Yellow Peril"

The "mulatto" is not the only mixed-race figure in American culture. The "half-blood" Native American–White character was a staple in nineteenth-century literature (Scheick, 1979) and early twentieth-century film (Stedman, 1982), and depictions of Mexicans, especially in the "conquest fiction" of the Mexican-American War period, emphasized their status as "half-breeds" (Pettit, 1980). Similarly, "Eurasians"[2] made frequent appearances in late nineteenth and early twentieth-century fiction (Kim, 1982; Wu, 1982). As William Wu (1982) points out, mainstream fiction about Asians between 1850 and 1940 was typically of the "Yellow Peril" genre, reflecting certain social, economic, and political concerns of (especially West Coast) Americans. The Yellow Peril refers to the idea that Asian countries and Asian immigration posed a threat to the United States and to White Americans, and ranged from the White working class's fear that Chinese immigrants would lower wages to the government's anxieties over Japan's growing political and military power (Saxton, 1971; Takaki, 1989; Chan, 1991; Okihiro, 1994).

An important theme in Yellow Peril fiction is the interracial love affair that ends tragically, often with the White character contaminated with a deadly disease, or one of the lovers dead by murder or suicide (Wu, 1982). The Eurasian character is an extension of this idea, and also ends up dead much of the time (Kim, 1982). But before his or her untimely demise, the Eurasian, because of his or her proximity to and intimate knowledge of both Asians and Whites, is an especially persuasive witness to the racial and cultural superiority of Whites over Asians, and of the "unassimilability" of Asians into mainstream America.

The Eurasian characters of Yellow Peril literature wish desperately that they were White. This is consistent with what Judith Berzon (1978: 140), in her study of the "tragic mulatto" in American fiction, calls "white narcissism" and defines as the persistent "assumption that the mixed blood yearns to be white and is doomed to unhappiness and despair because of this impossible dream." In the 1922 story "The Daughter of Huang Chow" by Sax Rohmer (author of the Fu Manchu series), a young Eurasian woman lives with her father, a rich and powerful Chinatown leader. Because she has had very little contact with White people since her (White) mother died when she was a child, she at first does not recognize how vile her Chinese father is. It is only by comparing him with the White men in the story that she comes to see the truth, but before she can escape from her father and Chinatown, she is killed by a mysterious deadly spider that her father keeps for murdering his enemies.

Another Eurasian who yearns to be White is the amazing Henry Johnson in Wallace Irwin's 1921 novel, *Seed of the Sun*. In his first scene, he describes himself as a "chimera," which he defines as

> the dragon's tail of the Orient fastened to the goat's head of Europe . . . a very unsatisfactory beast . . . . All the time the European goat in me is striving to butt forward, the dragon's tail is curling round some ancient tradition and pulling me back. (Irwin, 1921 [1979]: 39)

Irwin, like Sax Rohmer, specialized in racist anti-Asian fiction, and *Seed of the Sun* is a fascinating example of Yellow Peril paranoia. The title of the book is a double entendre; with the "seed" of the "sun" refering both to the farming industry in California and to the reproductive "seed" of Japan, the land of the rising "sun." Throughout the book, the Eurasian Johnson acts as a translator and informant for the White characters, ultimately revealing the plot of the Japanese immigrants to invade America via interracial marriage:

> They have already borrowed your telegraph instruments, your educational systems, your military equipment, your advertising methods. They have borrowed your brain, but they cannot change their bodies without one thing—intermarriage. Don't you see? Four feet six wants to become six feet four. Then Japan will have everything. (Irwin, 1921 [1979]: 38)

It is important to remember that the very year that Irwin's book was published, 1921, the United States government passed a law called the "Ladies' Agreement," which cut off the immigration of "picture brides" from Japan (Takaki, 1989). It was passed in response to anti-Asian forces on the West Coast who wanted to stop the formation of settled Japanese families with American-born children, since only American-born Asians could legally purchase land. Irwin, who was very much a part of the anti-Asian discourse in California, must have feared that Japanese bachelors would look to non-Japanese (especially White) women as mates since they could no longer bring wives from Japan.[3] The highlight of his book is a speech made by a Japanese baron to his fellow expatriates:

Small as we are in numbers here, let us see to it that our race shall increase. Seed of Yam-ato, germinate anew! Beget, beget, beget! While the Emperor permitted it, it was well that you brought wives from the homeland—young wives, and fertile. And now it is more impor-tant still that we marry into this American stock. Prove your race equality in the blood of your children. Choose white women if you can. Where this is not practicable, marry negroes, Indians, Hawaiians.

Do not fear that our race shall be lost in such a mingling of blood. The blood of Japan is immortal, because it is descended from the sun goddess, Amaterasu. Plant it where you will, Yamato's seed shall never die. Even unto the tenth generation Japanese with blond skins and blue eyes will still be Japanese, quick with the one God-given virtue—loyalty to empire and the Emperor. (Irwin, 1921 [1979]: 183)

But not every American who worried about Asian immigration imagined insidious plots of invasion. Many academics, politicians, and social commentators who pondered the "Oriental problem" were more concerned that by allowing another non-White pop-ulation into the country, the United State was setting itself up for social problems like the ones it was having with Blacks and Indians (Takaki, 1989; Okihiro, 1994). An important question in this discussion was whether Asians could become part of the "melting pot"; a crucial aspect of assimilability was the possibility and probability of intermarrying with the dominant group, the goal being that any distinctive ethnic fea-tures would eventually disappear so that the group would become fully "American." Was it possible for Asians to "melt" into real Americans, culturally and physically? Some, like scholar Sidney Gulick (1914) argued yes and offered photographs of people of 50 percent Japanese and 50 percent White heritage next to those of people with 25 percent Japanese and 75 percent White heritage as proof of a gradual shift in Eurasians toward a European phenotype. Many more argued no, especially those involved in the Yellow Peril hysteria (Takaki, 1989; Okihiro, 1994). One such naysayer was James D. Phelan, principal political speaker in the anti-Japanese movement and mayor of San Francisco. In 1900 he declared that the Japanese

are not bona fide citizens. They are not the stuff of which American citizens can be made . . . They will not assimilate with us and their social life is so different from ours, let them keep at a respectful distance. (quoted in Wilson & Hosokawa, 1982: 121)

Phelan must have still believed this in the early 1920s, when he was a U.S. senator who "based his campaign on attacks against the Japanese" (Wilson & Hosokawa, 1982: 128). It was around this time that Senator Phelan donated to the University of California at Berkeley graduate library a 1921 novel by John Paris called *Kimono*, an extremely anti-Japanese book that firmly professes the unassimilability of Asians. One of the ways that it does this is by introducing a psychotic Eurasian character, Yae Smith, who is described as "a bundle of nerves and instincts, partly primitive and partly artifi-cial, bred out of an abnormal cross between East and West, and doomed from concep-tion to a life astray between light and darkness" (Paris, 1921: 61) After the highly sexualized Yae causes the death of one of her lovers and a shoot-out between two more, she destroys the marriage of an Englishman and a Japanese woman—both by seducing the husband and by showing the couple how immoral and dangerous their marriage is. The narrator of the story explains to the reader that

> it is not for us to condemn Yae, . . . but rather should we censure the blasphemy of mixed marriages which has brought into existence these thistledown children of a realm which has not kings or priests or laws or Parliaments or duty or tradition or hope for the future, which has not even an acre of dry ground for its heritage or any concrete symbol of its soul—the Cimmerian land of Eurasia. (Paris, 1921: 112)

Very soon after the publication of Paris's novel, the anti-Asian forces responsible for Yellow Peril propaganda had an enormous victory in the passage of the 1924 Immigration Act, which put a complete stop to Asian immigration into the United States (Takaki, 1989).[4]

The Super-Eurasian of the 1980s

The 1980s were a time when the Eurasian returned to Americans as a cultural tool for the exploration of race, ethnicity, and culture. But the relationship between the United States and Asia had changed significantly since the early part of the century, and thus the Eurasian of this decade was a very different beast.

Growing political and social conservatism and economic insecurity characterized the United States of the 1980s. Mainstream Americans were losing faith in the "American Dream," and the nation seemed to be losing its position as the world's leader (*Newsweek,* 1988; Takaki, 1989). At the same time, it was a period of growing prosperity and political power in Asia, especially in Japan. The media often placed these two trends in relation to each other, as *Newsweek* (1988: 3) did in its cover story on "The Pacific Century: Is America in Decline?":

> It is fashionable these days to talk of America in decline. Trade deficits, the falling dollar and waning global influence are seen as signs the American Century is ending. But that erosion is only relative to the rise of a handful of Asian countries—Japan, the so-called "four tigers" and, increasingly, China—that are remaking the global economic landscape.

Faced with the possibility of Asian dominance of the world economy, Americans became fascinated in every aspect of the Pacific Rim: business, education, childrearing practices, philosophy, religion, art and design, food. College students began to choose Asian language courses over European languages, sushi bars grew in popularity, and movie stars explored the teachings of the Buddha. As Americans have always found it difficult to conceptually separate Asians in Asia from Asian Americans, the discourse on Asia's success often included discussion about the educational and economic successes of Asian Americans (Takaki, 1989; Okihiro, 1994). Asian Americans became known as a "model minority" of academic and economic superachievers, while other Americans (especially other people of color) seemed to have rapidly declining test scores and standards of living (Browne, 1986; Butterfield, 1986; *Time,* 1987). The media demanded to know: "What accounts for Asian students' success?" (Browne, 1986).

The depictions of Eurasians in American culture during this decade reflect the American love/hate relationship with Asia. Alongside a newfound appreciation of Asians and Asian culture was a return to a Yellow Peril–style anxiety over the threat of Asian competition and invasion (Takaki, 1989; Okihiro, 1994). Likewise, together with an abundance of clichéd depictions of Eurasians as "the best of both worlds" was a more interesting exploration of supposedly "American" and supposedly "Asian" characteristics, and how they compared to one another.

Nowhere is this more extreme than in the series of popular best-sellers by Eric Van Lustbader. In his adventure/suspense/romance novels, Van Lustbader presents male Eurasian main characters that embody the "best of both worlds" while working through American anxieties and hostility toward Asia (Van Lustbader, 1980, 1984, 1985, 1986). He pieces together what he seems to view as the best characteristics of White American men—physical size and racial phenotype, charm, adventurousness and bravery—and pairs them with the best characteristics of Asian men—intelligence, persistence, a strong work ethic, and knowledge of Asian culture and language. His Eurasian superheroes travel comfortably between Asia, Europe, and the United States; have frequent sex with both Asian and White women; and always defeat the (usually Asian) bad guys.

A remarkably similar Eurasian superhero is the lead character in the 1984 film *The Adventures of Buckaroo Banzai: Across the Eighth Dimension*. Buckaroo is a Eurasian who "looks" White (the actor Peter Weller plays the role) but has the "brains" of a Japanese. As it says in the preface to the movie, he is a "brilliant neurosurgeon, . . . [who] roamed the planet studying martial arts and particle physics, collecting around him a most eccentric group of friends, those hard-rocking scientists The Hong Kong Cavaliers." Ultimately, Buckaroo and his "Team Banzai" must save the Earth—not from an Asian invasion this time, but from an alien invasion.

The flip side of the Super-Eurasian is the "worst-of-both-worlds" villian in Marc Olden's (1988) novel *Oni*. This Eurasian, Viktor Poltava, is the illegitimate son of a sadistic, alcoholic Russian man and a poor Japanese woman. His father had murdered his mother, then committed suicide in prison. Viktor was raised by his Japanese grandmother (who was semicrazy and practiced witchcraft) in a Japan replete with xenophobia, schoolyard bullying, and the kind of academic pressures that caused his classmates to commit suicide. In Olden's Eurasian we see the culmination of a violent interracial heritage and the "worst" of supposedly Asian cultural and social traits. It is no wonder that with this background and in this environment, Viktor became a sexually perverted sadist and murderer.

It is significant that Eurasian characters developed in the 1980's tended to be male, created by male writers. While there are some female Eurasian characters from this period, they tend to be much less interesting—usually a "best-of-both-worlds" combination of Asian and European physical traits, paired with the same old search for an identity that has been the hallmark of mixed-race characters in American fiction and film for the past two centuries (Dickason, 1987; Davis, 1989). It seems that American men in particular felt the need to explore the duality of their admiration and their competitive hostility toward Asia. Perhaps, too, the maleness of these characters imbued them with the power (economic, political, physical, sexual) that was central to the discourse on American-Asian relations at that time.[5]

A "Cablinasian" in a "Color-Blind" America

The 1990s and the beginning of the twenty-first century have proved to be a watershed period for Americans of mixed race. The discourse on multiraciality is now no longer limited to one-dimensional characters in films and novels, but also includes real people, speaking in their own voices, in what has been called a multiracial movement that has entered the mainstream dialogue on race and ethnicity (Nakashima, 1996; Root, 1996; Spencer, 1997). But the inclusion of mixed-race people in the dialogue does not mean that they are no longer being used as symbols of cultural dilemmas. On the contrary, the growing voices of multiracials have offered a bounty of representational possibilities for Americans. In fact, these days just about every political and ideological camp utilizes mixed-race people in support of their arguments. The single best illustration of this is golf prodigy Tiger Woods, who in 1996–97 became perhaps the busiest symbolic tool in the history of fictional or nonfictional mixed-race characters. The biggest difference today is that the characters like Tiger can finally participate in the discourse to some extent.

The discussion about race and ethnicity in the 1990s began with one that had started in the latter 1980s, when demographers announced that, by the middle of the twenty-first century, Whites would no longer be the majority racial group in the United States. For the most part, the mainstream media tried to react cheerfully to news of the "browning of America" by stressing that America's strength is in its diverse people, that we are a nation of immigrants, and that we must explore and appreciate our "multicultural" heritage.[6]

People of mixed race were thus presented as a positive version of a multicultural America—a new, more colorful sort of "melting pot," where racial groups do not separate and segregate, but marry and have babies (Smolowe, 1993; Rodriguez, 1995, Jacobs, 1997).

The representation of mixed-race people as the "children of the future" sporting "global identities" has continued, manifesting itself in advertisements that take advantage of the wide marketing potential of the "W.U.R.E." ("woman of unidentifiable race or ethnicity") (Page, 1996), and in fictional and especially science fictional characters that use multiraciality as the racial expression of an Everyman (Prager, 1995; Freeman, 1996). As one marketer explains, "At a time when young people are buying corporate conceptions of 'alternative,' ethnic ambiguity confers both individuality and a sense of shared values" (Leland & Beals, 1997: 60). This juxtaposition of unique and universal is packaged and sold in the Nike television advertisement where faces of young people of a variety of racial phenotypes are flashed, one by one, each of them saying, "I am Tiger Woods."

But shortly after bumper stickers began to remind Americans to "Celebrate Diversity," many expressed the concern that the nation has become "too obsessed" with race, that an emphasis on diversity is "divisive," and that there needs to be a more unified "American" identity (Okihiro, 1994; Peterson, 1995; Cose, 1997). By the early 1990s, the dialogue was driven more and more by social and political conservatives and neo-conservative scholars, complaining about the oppressive nature of "politically correct" language and thought (D'Souza, 1991; Henry, 1993; Hu-Dehart, 1996a; Takagi, 1996b). According to Gary Okihiro (1994: ix),

> pluralism and diversity, many argued, only served to divide and fracture the nation. The debate over the nature and primacy of Western civilization and its canon of "great books" on college campuses, they warned, was just the leading edge of a coming chill that threatened the "disuniting" of America.

Also in the university, postmodern and poststructuralist thought has challenged some of the ideas of multiculturalism, although from a very different perspective from the conservative critique. Postmodern discussions of race and ethnicity call attention to the "totalizing" and "essentializing" treatment of racial and ethnic identity, experience, and history that often characterizes multicultural discourse (Lowe, 1991; Anthias & Yuval-Davis, 1992; Spencer, 1993; Awkward, 1995). By adhering to the dichotomous categories of African American, Asian American, and so on, multiculturalism tends to place single, unifying definitions around groups of individuals, validating ideas of essential differences. These categories also put certain identities and experiences at the center of the definitions, while those outside of the center are considered marginal and/or inauthentic. People of mixed race, as well as gays, lesbians, and bisexuals, have served as illustrative examples for the postmodern projects of "deconstructing" categories, "problematizing" identities, and "disrupting the master narratives" (Bucholtz, 1995; Ginsberg, 1996).

The act of deconstructing racial categories is one area of postmodern discourse that has entered into the mainstream dialogue on race and ethnicity. When the highly controversial book *The Bell Curve* by Richard J. Herrnstein and Charles Murray was published in 1994, the question of genetic differences between racial groups was reviewed in the media (Cose, 1997). The February 13, 1995, issue of *Newsweek* was dedicated to challenging not only *The Bell Curve* but the racial category of "Black." The magazine argued that claims such as Herrnstein's and Murray's are based on outdated notions that view racial categories as scientifically sound, when in fact science itself sees them as mere "social constructs" (Morganthau, 1995). Indeed, shortly after the *Newsweek* article was published, geneticists at the American Association for the Advancement of Science's annual conference announced that they had confirmed that the racial categories are biologically meaningless (Begley, 1995; Noguchi, 1995).

Newsweek attributed this "assault on racialist thinking" to the growing population of mixed-race people and to the recognition that the traditional categories, based on the "one-drop rule" of heredity, are no longer acceptable to many Americans (Morganthau, 1995). But others wonder if America's recent "retreat from race," as Dana Takagi

(1993) has called it (or, "the postmodern conspiracy to explode racial identity," as Jon Michael Spencer [1993] has termed it), is mostly a movement away from social programs designed to assist people of color in structural integration (Wright, 1994; Noguchi, 1995). The newest chapter in the attack on multiculturalist ideologies has been the appropriation of the term "color-blind" by the conservative discourse (Cose, 1997). While operating on the assumption that racism is wrong,[7] these new proponents of a "color-blind society" argue that race-conscious policies (i.e., affirmative action) in education, employment, and voting are discriminatory and violate the civil rights of certain Americans based on race (Peterson, 1995; Cose, 1997).

Interestingly, those who espouse a color-blind agenda seem especially fond of arguing that interracial marriage and multiracial people support their position. They generally do this in one of three ways (Horner, 1995; Jacobs, 1996; Hoppe, 1997): (1) the growth of a racially mixed population is proof that racism is on the decline and that race matters less and less (which means we don't need affirmative action); (2) the growth of a racially mixed population makes traditional racial categories outdated and inaccurate (which means we should stop using categories, especially for programs such as affirmative action); and (3) racially mixed people are able to manipulate racial categories, thus making race-based policies easily corruptible (which means we need to dispose of affirmative action).

In a 1996 article in the *San Jose Mercury,* Joanne Jacobs draws on all of these arguments as she expresses her support for the California Civil Rights Initiative (CCRI), otherwise known as Proposition 209, the anti-affirmative action proposition that became law a month after her article.

> The system of racial classification in this country is starting to break down, but it will take a generation. I see the future in our wedding pictures: Li marries Schmidt, Kelly weds Rodriguez . . . . It seems to me that the debate over race-based affirmative action is based on categories and ideas that are in flux . . . . To paraphrase the Wicked Witch of the West: We're melting. Meanwhile, affirmative action has created opportunities for gamesmanship. The big winners are people who look white, so they don't have to put up with casual bigotry, but have a claim to minority status . . . . I think the only hope is for Ryan Li-Schmidt to grow up and marry Nicole Kelly-Rodriguez. (Jacobs, 1996: 7b)

The debate over racial classification models for the U.S. Census is where all of these issues—diversity, multiculturalism, the questioning of racial categories, affirmative action, and color-blindness—have been projected onto the subject of people of mixed race,[8] or rather onto one particular person of mixed race, Tiger Woods. Actually, mainstream America and its hero Tiger entered into the debate quite late. For several years the discussion took place primarily between organizations representing multiracial families and individuals, and civil rights organizations such as the NAACP (National Association for the Advancement of Colored People), the National Urban League, the National Council of La Raza, and the National Asian Pacific American Legal Consortium. The mainstream media mostly stayed out of it, except to report—from an outsider perspective—this disagreement occurring within the communities of color.

But all of this changed when, in April of 1997, golfer Tiger Woods won the Master's tournament at the age of twenty-one, signed several multimillion dollar endorsement deals, and went on the Oprah Winfrey show announcing himself to be a "Cablinasian"—a neologism referring to his Caucasian-Black-Indian-Asian heritage. Suddenly, the discussion over racial classification had exploded into a national debate.[9] On May 5, 1997, both *Newsweek* (Leland & Beals) and *Time* (White) ran lengthy articles about Tiger and "his multiracial generation." African American and Asian Amerian periodicals such as *Ebony* (1997) and *AsianWeek* (Guillermo, 1997) carefully scrutinized each of his statements on his ethnic and racial identity. Oprah ran a second show on Tiger, this time focusing on the controversy over his "Cablinasian" identity. At a summit on volunteerism a few days after the first Oprah show, Colin Powell was questioned by the media about his reaction to Tiger's racial/ethnic identity and his opinion on a "multiracial" category on the Census.[10]

With this "mainstreaming" of the debate around multiracial identity, the mixed-race organizations found that mainstream America was usually sympathetic to Tiger and his "multiracial generation." In fact, the perceived enemy in this struggle had shifted from the government and its Census to the civil rights organizations and their greed for numbers and power and set-asides (*San Francisco Chronicle*, 1997; Jacobs, 1997). Positioning themselves as champions of individual rights, many Republican politicians, such as House Speaker Newt Gingrich, came out in favor of a "multiracial" category for the Census (Eddings, 1997). Most of this conservative support, however, including Gingrich's, was undoubtedly motivated by the desire to use the category to upset social programs such as affirmative action by diluting numbers and making tabulation unruly. A few, like James Glassman (1997) of the American Enterprise Institute and political commentator George Will (1997), openly admitted to this.

Conclusion

Ironically, this country's first Census was supervised by Thomas Jefferson himself in 1790, when the racial categories were "free White males," "free White females," "other persons" (which included free Blacks and "taxable Indians"), and "slaves" (Wright, 1994). We can only wonder if Jefferson was able to recognize the fluidity in these classifications, as reflected in his own family.

On October 29, 1997, the U.S. Office of Management and Budget (OMB) announced the decision to allow Americans to check more than one racial/ethnic category on the 2000 Census and rejected the option of a separate "multiracial" category, stating that it would "add to racial tension." The OMB's policy was presented as a compromise between those lobbying in the interests of people of mixed race and the traditional civil rights organizations. But in actuality, no compromise was needed: In June 1997, a coalition of mixed-race organizations, such as the Association of MultiEthnic Americans and Hapa Issues Forum, had been in dialogue with the NAACP and the Japanese American Citizens' League and had released a statement that they were *not* in favor of a separate multiracial category, but rather preferred the multiple-check model.

Multiracial people and hybrid identities continue to destabilize racial and cultural boundaries and hierarchies as the dominant society struggles to manage these populations and their identities. Fictional mixed-race characters, under full control of their authors, have served as a site for the exploration and resolution of social dilemmas. But in the drama of the racial classification debate, the attempt to use mixed-race characters to dismantle race-based policies was ultimately thwarted by the real people who can and do speak for themselves.

Notes

1. In this chapter, I use the terms "race," "mixed races," and "multiracial" with the full recognition that each of these concepts is socially constructed, not scientifically concrete. My use of the terms "Asian" and "Asian American" is limited to East and Southeast Asian ethnicities, as the representative roles of South Asians and Pacific Islanders in American culture are beyond the scope of my research.

2. The Eurasian, who, by definition, is the racial/ethnic combination of European (i.e., "White") and Asian, acts as a symbolic representation of the interaction between Whites and Asians. For this reason, Eurasian characters, as opposed to Afro-Asian, Latino-Asian, or Native American–Asian characters, have had a much stronger presence in mainstream literature and film. An important exception to this is the recent interest in golf superstar Tiger Woods (see n. 9 below).

3. There were, of course, antimiscegenation laws in California at this time, which prohibited the marriage of Asians and Whites. Still, interracial couples could and did find ways around these laws. For example, some traveled to a state without an antimiscegenation law in order to obtain a marriage certificate. Others simply lived as a married couple without legal recognition. One indication that American women were, in fact, marrying Asian men at this time is the passage of the Cable Act of 1922, which stripped a woman of her American citizenship if she married an immigrant Asian.

4. The 1924 act ended immigration from all Asian countries except the Philippines, then an American territory ("won" in the Spanish-American War). In 1934, Congress passed the Tydings-McDuffie Act, which changed the status of the Philippines to a commonwealth and put an end to Filipino immigration (Takaki, 1989).

5. The discussion of gender, sexuality, and the representation of Asians and of people of mixed race is much more complex than that which is offered here. For example, while power was central to the discourse on American-Asian relations in the 1980s, Asian men and Asian culture were frequently portrayed as asexual or effeminate (Okihiro, 1994).

6. However, a strong undercurrent of anti-immigrant attitudes that began to develop at the end of the 1980s and continued throughout the 1990s led to a series of legislative attempts to limit immigration and naturalization policies and immigrant rights (Nelan, 1993; Ellison & Martin, 1999).

7. This is not to say that all Americans agree that racism is wrong. Recent years have also seen a significant rise in White supremacist organizations, who still firmly believe in the genetic superiority of White Christians, and who are very much opposed to interracial marriage, mixed-race people, and a multicultural America (Winant, 1997).

8. Although I am focusing on the representative role of people of mixed race in mainstream America, multiraciality has played such a role in communities of color as well. In the debate over

racial classification, the assertion and exploration of mixed race identities have been conflated with the movement for a "multiracial" box on the Census, and is often portrayed—by individuals and institutions within the communities of color—as politically naive at best or disloyal at worst (Wright, 1994; Norment, 1995; Frisby, 1996; Hu-DeHart, 1996b).

9. When Tiger Woods objected to such labels as "the great black hope," which recognized only his African American heritage, all of America took a great interest. The fact that he is a mixture of several racial/ethnic heritages, and that he describes himself culturally and ethnically as Asian and Black—two "minority" identities—seems very important. If he, like so many other American athletes and entertainers, were only Black and White or Asian and White, it is doubtful that his identity assertions would have received such an enormous amount of mainstream attention. This is because it was Tiger's Asian heritage (as embodied by his lovingly devoted mother, who is from Thailand and is phenotypically Asian) that was being "denied" to him, a situation that falls outside of America's established tradition of denying "Whiteness" to those who are mixed.

Societal hypodescent rules did initially label Tiger as "Black," but once he publicly objected to this, the mainstream media seemed to respond positively. It was members of the African American community who were most resistant to Tiger's mixed-race, Black-Asian identity. And it was this resistance that fascinated the mainstream media, and that made him and the "multiracial" Census category an opportunity for social and political conservatives to attack minority interests.

10. It is interesting that reporters would have asked for Powell's opinion on these issues at an event that had nothing to do with the subject of race. Powell has openly admitted to having a multiracial family history, but consistently identifies himself as an African American when questioned by the media, as he did on this occasion.

CHAPTER 4

"The Coming of the Neo–Hawaiian American Race": Nationalism and Metaphors of the Melting Pot in Popular Accounts of Mixed-Race Individuals

John Chock Rosa

The topic of mixed-race Asian Americans and Pacific Islanders is not entirely new. In the early part of the twentieth century, European American sociologists, anthropologists, and community leaders made efforts to describe various factors that were then contributing to the intermarriage of peoples in Hawai'i.[1] The Chicago School of Sociology and other social analysts, for example, saw Hawai'i as a kind of "racial laboratory" (Adams, 1937: v) where "outstanding race studies" (Du Puy, 1932: 118) could be conducted. These studies from the 1930s, and popular accounts based on them in decades since, have promoted Hawai'i as a model for multiethnic communities on the continental United States (Du Puy, 1932; Gulick, 1937; Shapiro, 1953; Little, 1952; Michener, 1959; Fuchs, 1961).

Since the early decades of the twentieth century, politicians, community leaders, missionaries, social scientists, and others have consistently touted the islands as a racial paradise (Hooper, 1980). More specifically, Hawai'i stands out from other places in the United States as a geographic and symbolic site where "East meets West"—a meeting ground where international relations can be brokered between Asian nation-states and European and American powers. From a domestic perspective, early social scientific studies have also examined how "East" met "West" within the geography of urban Honolulu: sociologists like Robert E. Park (1926, 1937, 1938) and his students Romanzo Adams (1937) and Andrew Lind (1938) studied Honolulu as a multiethnic setting that was home to immigrants from Asia, their second-generation descendants, and increasing numbers of bi- and multiracial children. After charting the increasing rate of intermarriages in Honolulu, one popular account even proclaimed "the coming of a Neo–Hawaiian American Race"—a single, unified people of Asian and Native Hawaiian descent (Gulick, 1937). I shall examine how in the 1920s and 1930s the Territory of Hawaii came to be seen as a testing ground for the mixing of Asian Americans, Native Hawaiians, and Whites. I focus specifically on early popular and scholarly accounts about Hawai'i, and explore how they have contributed to the image of Hawai'i as a racial paradise where intermarriage and mixed race people live and flourish. I argue that in many ways, the logic behind these early accounts in Hawai'i has prefigured the writings about people of mixed ancestry seen in mainstream national magazines of the 1990s.

The Melting Pot in Hawai'i and the Continental United States: A Metaphor in the Service of Nationalism

Beginning in the early nineteenth century, an elite class of American businessmen and missionaries living in the islands played a central role in popularizing Hawai'i as a physical and social paradise (Hooper, 1980). To a great extent, the paradisal myth of Hawai'i that emerged was a derivative of several myths that were already a part of American thought. In one sense, the idea of Hawai'i as a physical paradise corresponded rather directly with the European discovery of America and the subsequent perception of the new continent as a "Zion in the wilderness," an ideal setting for a utopian social world. In a similar sense, the view of Hawai'i as a social paradise echoed an earlier view of America as a land free from European prejudices, where people of almost all backgrounds could live together in harmony (Hooper, 1980: 185–186). This view of America, expressed by J. Hector St. John de Crevecoeur (1782 [1981]: 70) during the Revolutionary period and transformed over the decades into the myth of America as a "melting pot," was carried over into promotional literature for Hawai'i written by American missionaries and business interests.

While the image of a melting pot has long appealed to many European Americans, in the case of Hawai'i some wondered how differences in culture, language, and religion would be resolved. Albert W. Palmer (1924: xiii), a minister of the Central Union Church in Honolulu, was only one of many who took their stay in the islands in the early twentieth century as an opportunity to comment on Hawai'i and its future, asking:

> How will it all come out? Will Hawaii at last be American or Japanese? Will it be Christian or Buddhist? East and West are meeting here—which will prevail? Or will each learn something from the other? Will they meet to fight and snarl at one another or to appreciate and understand each other to the helping of the world?

Palmer's questions in the 1920s were also a kind of social science discourse. Well before the construction of the East-West Center at the University of Hawai'i, before strategic discussions of the "Pacific Basin," and before international business talk revolving around catch phrases like the "Pacific Rim," European Americans on the continent perceived a need to study the interactions of races and cultures in the "crossroads of the Pacific."[2]

Social Scientific Accounts: The Chicago School of Sociology in Hawai`i

In the first decades of the twentieth century, European American social scientists from the Chicago School of Sociology were beginning to see Hawai`i as the frontier in race relations. Robert E. Park, a founding member of the school and a pioneer in the study of race and race relations in the United States and in the Pacific, introduced Frederick Jackson Turner's concept of the frontier as a central element in the study of race relations and applied it to Hawai`i. Combining his theories of a racial frontier and a race relations cycle, Park (1926) found Hawai`i to be a unique social situation in time and space where peoples of diverse cultures and Native Hawaiians are brought together and intermingle:

> In the Hawaiian Islands, where all the races of the Pacific meet and mingle on more liberal terms than they do so elsewhere, the native races are disappearing and new peoples are coming into existence. Races and cultures die—it has always been so—but civilization lives on.

By 1934, Park saw the exciting, multicultural atmosphere of Hawai`i as an opportunity to extend his concept of racial frontiers to a worldwide setting. Hawaii's geographic isolation and location at the "crossroads of the Pacific" made it a perfect research site to study the interactions of peoples from around the globe and the place of the islands in a modern world economy, in a setting where

> all the peoples of the world have come together in an association more intimate than is possible in regions less insular and less isolated by surrounding seas; the processes of assimilation and acculturation, characteristic of port cities and metropolitan communities elsewhere, have been going on at a rate that has made the Islands the most notable instance of a melting-pot of the modern world. (Park, 1938: xii)

Captain James Cook's arrival in the islands in 1778 had hastened and radically altered social development in Hawai`i—but Park and Lind hoped that the archipelago's remoteness in the middle of the Pacific would continue to serve as a buffer against the transmission of racial prejudice and other Old World social ills. Hawai`i was a perfect testing ground for social experimentation.

Toward the end of the 1930s, the focus on Hawai`i had also come to question more explicitly the results of racial mixing. The "intermingling of the races"—even on the most intimate and personal of levels—was now seen in a favorable light. Lind (1938: 304), for example, viewed "racial amalgamation" to be the "final solvent of the cultural barriers and the best index of assimilation." One year earlier, Adams had published an extensive study that addressed the mixing of racial groups more directly. In *Interracial Marriage in Hawaii*, he provided a statistical and descriptive history of the "amalgamation, *A Study of the Mutually Conditioned Processes of Acculturation and Amalgamation*" or mixing, among Native Hawaiians, White missionaries, and immigrants from Asia and the West Indies who had come to labor on sugar plantations. He saw the intermediary population of "mixed-bloods," in Hawai`i or any society, as one that could potentially function to mediate race relations. As long as law and public opinion allowed interracial marriage, he argued, "the hybrid population resulting from mixed marriages serves freely as a liaison group between the parent races" (Adams, 1937: 85).

Park and his students Adams and Lind all understood "race" as a matter not of biology but of historical conditions that were fluid and flexible. For the most part, their social scientific studies focused not on biology but on the interchange of goods and people—matters of commerce and immigration. Influenced by the Chicago School's thorough understanding of the nature of capitalism, Adams and Lind focused on economic exchanges, labor, and needs, and how these factors served to alter the demographic composition of frontier locales like Hawai'i.

A Popular Account of Mixed-Race Individuals in Hawai'i: Sidney Gulick's *Mixing the Races in Hawaii* (1937)

Remarks on mixed-race individuals in Hawai'i reached a peak in the 1920s and 1930s, when the "intermingling" of population groups sparked attention both in the islands and on the continental United States. Dr. Sidney Gulick, a clergyman who had been involved in fighting against Japanese exclusion on the mainland, was one of those who took an interest in the increasingly mixed population of Hawai'i. He expressed an extremely positive outlook in *Mixing the Races in Hawaii: A Study of the Coming of the Neo–Hawaiian American Race* (1937: v):

> Here a poly-racial, polychrome, poly-linguistic, poly-religious and thoroughly heterogeneous population is being transformed into a homogeneous people, ethical, social and religious ideas and ideals, putting into practice with remarkable success the principles of racial equality, and maintaining a highly effective, democratic form of government.

Although less empirically based and less incisive than the works of Lind and Adams, Gulick's book was widely read and has had a lasting impact on popular notions of Hawai'i. For example, one can see traces of his work in James A. Michener's best-selling novel *Hawaii,* published over two decades later. As Michener (1959: 973) wrote in his historical fiction, even after World War II had brought the United States and Japan into direct conflict with one another,

> in 1946, . . . a group of sociologists in Hawaii were perfecting a concept whose vague outlines had occupied them for some years. . . . they suggested that in Hawaii a new type of man was being developed. He was a man influenced by both the west and the east, a man at home in either the business councils of New York or the philosophical retreats of Kyoto, a man wholly modern and American yet in tune with the ancient and the Oriental.

Michener called this new creation the "Golden Man"—an update of Gulick's "Neo–Hawaiian American Race."

The studies by Lind and Adams argued for a careful look at demographic trends, charting changes in immigration policy and stressing the need to accurately record and predict the impact of the successive waves of immigrants and their descendants entering the labor force. Gulick's book, on the other hand, was more sensationalistic. He barely scratched the surface of demographic changes in the islands. Instead, he employed physiognomic metaphors to describe the population as a whole and spent a curious amount of time focusing on the facial complexion of Hawai'i residents from the East and West. In his opinion, youths of Asian descent who were born in Hawai'i and raised under the influences of Western culture showed visible signs of the "Occidental type of facial expression—vivacious, frank, open and self-revealing." Such expressions were a welcome change to the "mask-like" Asian facial expression that was "stolid, stoical, reserved and puzzling" (Gulick, 1937: 4).

Embedded in Gulick's (1937: v) prose was a strong view of race as a biological construct: "The races are actually growing together—fusing biologically. . . . a new race is in the making. . . . The physiological characteristics of the new race will be a mixture of Hawaiian, Caucasian and Asiatic, while its psychological, social, political and moral characteristics will be distinctly American." His remarks also reveal his hope that new civic values in this territorial outpost of the United States would forge citizens who were distinctly American. Gulick thus combined a racial thinking typical of the nineteenth century with the well-worn metaphor of the melting pot into a fervent nationalism that praised the mixed-race population of early twentieth-century Hawai'i. He ultimately offered his book as an "effort to describe the various factors that are 'weaving' the poly-racial elements of the population of Hawaii into a single unified people—the Neo–Hawaiian American race" (Gulick, 1937: v).

For the most part, Gulick was a man with socially progressive views, as evidenced by his extremely positive attitude toward the mixing of the races and his disdain for racial prejudice. But he was also influenced by the ideology of eugenics. Gulick's enthusiasm for race mixing also included discussion of the possibilities of a "super-race" in Hawai'i. Even more frightening was his endorsement of the use of involuntary sterilization of those deemed socially undesirable. In one of the final paragraphs of his book, Gulick discusses how "students of the racial problem" in Hawai'i were seriously considering this sort of genetic engineering. He referred to Dr. Nils P. Larsen, at one time a physician advising the Hawaiian Sugar Planters' Association and then Medical Director of Queen's Hospital, who wrote: "If the Territorial Government should promptly adopt measures for eliminating the poorer stock (criminals and imbeciles) from each of our races and prevent them from breeding, we would then have a real opportunity for producing something very striking in the direction of a super-race" (Gulick, 1937: 211).

Popular Accounts of the 1990s: *Time* Magazine and the Continuing Metaphor of the Mixed-Race Individual

Comments in the 1990s on the increase in interracial marriages and children of mixed race show how the dialogue on matters of mixed race has changed very little. Intrigue about facial complexion, the strongly held belief in race as biologically determined, and speculation on the physiognomic effects of interracial marriage have persisted without serious discussion as to whether these questions are warranted. In the fall of 1993, *Time* magazine published a special issue on "The New Face of America" that used computer morphing technology to show the probable outcomes of mixing seven different racial/ethnic groups. Superimposed on this grid of forty-nine possibilities was a large photograph of a computer-generated female face that was designated as the "symbol of the future, multiethnic face of America." A description from the editor explained the tinkering behind this now well-known cover image:

> The highlight of this exercise in cybergenesis was the creation of the woman on our cover, selected as a symbol of the future, multiethnic face of America. A combination of the racial and ethnic features of the women used to produce this chart, she is: 15% Anglo Saxon, 17.5% Middle Eastern, 17.5% African, 7.5% Asian, 35% Southern European and 7.5% Hispanic. Little did we know what we had wrought. As onlookers watched the image of our new Eve begin to appear on the computer screen, several staff members promptly fell in love. Said one: "It really breaks my heart that she doesn't exist." We sympathize with our lovelorn colleagues, but even technology has its limits. This is a love that must forever remain unrequited. (*Time*, 1993: 2)

Apparently, in 1993 *Time* magazine and continental Americans were just then noticing the phenomenon of racial mixing that had been common in Hawai'i since the early twentieth century and had become increasingly visible on the mainland in the last half of the century. But mainstream America seemed to need to be persuaded that the results of interracial unions could be actually quite appealing, as the *Time* staffers admittedly "fell in love" with this imaginary woman.[3]

Such desire for "mixed-race" individuals, one could argue, still contains an emphasis on racial purity as its stated objective. In the *Time*'s 1993 special issue, as in Gulick's discussions of the "Neo–Hawaiian American Race," the image of the melting pot proposes the forging of a new race out of a conglomeration of immigrants old and new. This representation of racial mixing in the body or face of one individual is not uncommon. In 1932, for example, when the U.S. Department of the Interior and national newspapers placed intense scrutiny upon Hawai'i as a result of the interracial Massie rape case,[4] a federal report entitled *Hawaii and Its Race Problem* sought to ameliorate fears about the degree of interracial mixture that was then occurring in the islands. Compare *Time*'s comments in 1993 with the remarks made about Hawai'i in 1932:

> It seems safe to conclude that the ultimate Hawaiian American will come to rest at a point that represents the mean blood of his veins. On the basis of the present population he, therefore, will be something near one-third Japanese, one-fifth Filipino, one-ninth Portuguese. . . . His women will be known around the world for a peculiar beauty found no place else. (Du Puy, 1932: 115, 117)

In both of these popular accounts, special emphasis is placed on the numeric value of each racial type, even though the numbers themselves do not directly correspond to any demographic ratios found in U.S. Census statistics for the decades in question. Both commentaries also assure readers that these mixtures—particularly the women—will possess incomparable beauty. These accounts can be read as a curious brand of nationalism in support of the dominant metaphor of an American melting pot in which racial and ethnic difference are to be technologized to beauty and purity through assimilation.

In commenting on the *Time* cover photo, racial theorist David Theo Goldberg (1997: 60) has noted that, as usual, no Native American variables were used in the computerized image, thus overlooking the history of the indigenous peoples who inhabited the continent before contact with the West. By comparison, in the early twentieth century Adams was one of very few sociologists—even among the Chicago School—who understood that Native Hawaiian interactions with other peoples were historically different from the general intermixture of immigrant peoples elsewhere in the United States and around the world (Persons, 1987: 92–95).

Conclusion

The intrigue posed by perceived facial complexion, biological composition, and the physiognomy of "race" has not disappeared in the United States at all. In fact Robyn Wiegman (1995) has argued that the category of American citizenship has often relied on a modern, visible economy of race that focuses on skin color and the body. Studies of mixed-race Asian Americans and Native Hawaiians tell us to be careful of any research that seeks to essentialize race as a biological construct. In many respects, Adams's *Interracial Marriage in Hawaii* of 1937 is a model for current studies of mixed-race individuals, for he carefully charts demographic trends, without dwelling incessantly on the individual body as the site of biological mixture, or speculating on the probable "psychological confusion" that mixed-race individuals are expected to endure.

Issues of mixed-race Asian Americans in multiethnic communities—at the outset of both the twentieth century and the twenty-first—have forced mainstream Americans to consider the limits of a simple Black-versus-White paradigm of race relations in the United States. As this essay has shown, however, attitudes toward mixed race seem to have progressed very little when one looks at popular press accounts like *Time*'s special issue of 1993. Picturing the melting pot of America in the face of one individual has been a nationalistic metaphor of assimilation since the early Republic and is embedded in the racialized founding of the United States. Assimilating the feared "other" through intermarriage and intermixture is a solution that many have sought to technologize over the decades, whether by calling for eugenics or by employing computer technology to forecast the "New Face of America." We are not likely to escape biological notions of race anytime soon, but we should at least be aware that the ways in which mixed-race individuals have been discussed—as well as the existence of mixed-race individuals themselves—are far from new phenomena.

Notes

1. In 1992 the State of Hawai'i passed a legislative measure encouraging the proper usage of the Hawaiian language in the naming of state organizations, streets, and so on. In keeping with

standard practice in Hawai'i, I use the proper '*okina,* or glottal stop, whenever possible, unless the quote or organization does not use it. The possessive adjective "Hawaii's" is an English-language term, so the '*okina* is not used in such cases.

2. For a concise account of the history of this East-West discourse and its various permutations, see Connery, 1995.

3. A few scholars of race and the media have commented on this vexing cover photo. See, in order of their appearance, Rogin, 1996; Goldberg, 1997; and Berlant, 1997.

4. In the Massie case of 1931–32, Thalia Massie, the twenty-year-old White wife of a naval officer stationed at Pearl Harbor, alleged that she had been raped by a "gang of Hawaiians" one September night in Waikiki. Two Native Hawaiian men, two Japanese Americans, and one Native Hawaiian–Chinese man were charged with the crime. The initial rape case resulted in a mistrial, but before a retrial could be convened, one of the accused—Native Hawaiian Joseph Kahahawai—was kidnapped and killed by a group that included Grace Fortescue (Thalia Massie's mother) and Thomas Massie (her husband) in January 1932. The Massie-Fortescue group was found guilty of manslaughter in May 1932. Under enormous federal and public pressure from the continent, Governor Lawrence Judd shortened the group's ten-year prison sentence to one day, fearing that Hawaii's status as a territory might be stripped in favor of a commission-form of government headed by the U.S. Navy.

Section II

Navigating Sociocultural Terrains of Family and Identity

The second section of this volume delves into how multiracial identity is experienced, presented, and lived among multiracial Asian Americans. The social and ecological context within which racial and ethnic identities are experienced, performed, and therefore transformed becomes the platform upon which the identity of multiracial Asian Americans are acted out and eventually enacted as part of a socially recognized group identity.

In popular discourse, literature, and the social sciences, mixed-race people have been definitively and problematically characterized as either products of interracial procreation or mere extensions of their monoracial parent groups. This characterization has translated into mixed-race people being viewed and treated as perpetual children whose disjointed and fragmented either-or identities are made valid only in relationship to their parents' ethnic, gendered, and (mono-)racialized identities. As a result, most multiracial people were socially and structurally constrained to limit their ethnic identification to a forced choice of one heritage *over* the other in order to avoid suffering personal, social, and even political marginalization. However, despite these structural arrangements, multiracially organized Eurasian, Afroasian, and part–Native Hawaiian communities have historically existed as ethnic groups and viable communities in the United States and around the world (Gist & Dworkin, 1972; Brinsfield, Chapter 16; Espiritu, Chapter 2; Rosa, Chapter 4; Van Tuyl, Chapter 18). As social interactions with multiracial Asian Americans have increased in people's personal lives (family, peer groups, workplace, schools) and in public venues (popular culture, mass media), and as social depictions of their identities have become commonplace, multiracial Asian Americans *may* sustain themselves as an aggregate group, with culturally defined features and ethnic rules, in the monoracial Asian American imagination beyond the "perpetual children" or "monoracial extension" molds.

The chapters in this section illustrate how the sustenance and persistence of a multiracial Asian American identity are contingent upon how multiracial Asian Americans navigate the terrains of family, culture, generation, community, and other social arrangements at the microexperiential level. How do multiracial people create their social realities and actively engage in the development of their racialized and gendered multiple identities? The gendered and racialized multiethnic identity among mixed-race Asian Americans is mounted and sustained through social performance, management, and presentation of their identities throughout their life time. What factors, then, come to influence and inform how mixed-race Asian Americans live and sustain their identities?

Much of the discourse on racial minority status has emphasized socially imposed labels and identifications based on the criteria of gene frequencies and their arbitrary demarcations. Ethnic designations and boundaries, on the other hand, have been treated as stemming from ingroup markers and self-definitions based on cultural characteristics. The phenotypical ambiguity of Asian-descent multiracial individuals and their lack of a socially and politically recognized group status have often left them in a racial and ethnic "no man's land" (Thornton, 1983). Yet, these perspectives have often failed to explain the complex interactive processes between socially imposed identities and self-definitions. Thus, the formation and articulation of identity, in which the meanings of race and the functions of ethnicity are continually undergoing generational changes, necessitate the *agency* of the individuals and groups who will wear their badges of ethnicity.

According to Maria P. P. Root (Chapter 5), multiraciality, as an extension, reinscription, and reification of racial processes, illustrates how social factors matter in the shaping of one's multiracial identity. She elaborates, "so much of the racial identity process is a parcel of a larger development process influenced by family environment and by gender." Root's examination, based on the Biracial Sibling Project findings, emphasizes how race, influenced by gender, class, and generation, continues to play in the identity formation of biracial individuals, and leads to the conclusion that "racial construction is dynamic and informed by many different aspects of an individual's lived experience in a particular historical era and a gendered body."

Curtiss Takada Rooks's essay (Chapter 6), based on an ethnographic study of Asian American families in Alaska, found very little differentiation between multiracial Asian American and monoracial Asian American families in cultural practices, ethnic identification, and community participation. Those differences that do occur, he explains, can be largely attributed to generation status effects.

In Chapter 7, Christine C. Iijima Hall and Trude I. Cooke Turner explain how variegated biracial identity development is in contrast to monoracial identity. They write that "the process of identity development and identity choice for American biracials is a heterogeneous one that depends on several factors, including racial groups of parents, physical characteristics, cultural knowledge, and geographic location." They further elucidate the variations among biracials who are "Asian-minority" and those who are "Asian-majority," defying the traditional ways in which researchers have approached the subject of multiracial identity.

Michael C. Thornton and Harold Gates (Chapter 8) focus on a particular Asian-minority combination, the "BJAs," or Black Japanese Americans. Their work, employing data collected from Thornton's 1983 study, remains unique "in its effort to examine the range of identities among Afro-Asian Americans and to place this experience into a context beyond the individual, both socially/politically and familially." Much like Hall and Turner's approach, Thornton and Gates's focus on the BJAs serves to unhook and thereby decenter the hinges of Whiteness in discussions of multiethnic and multiracial identity. Furthermore, they critique previous studies on multiracial identity in which researchers' emphasized "personal internal dynamics" and focused on adolescent and young adult populations.

The multiracial movement (Nakashima, 1996; Root, 1996) has demonstrated that prescriptions for and definitions of identity undergo changes as social and political boundaries shift, and that boundaries shift as definitions alter and people's realities change. Walter T. Anderson (1999: 5), notes that more and more writers are now referring to the trend of "regaining the features of the world before the modern nation-state was invented" as a kind of "new medievalism," or ways of being that border-crossing peoples practice and enact. He expounds on this concept:

> The world [is] changing—with much difficulty and bloodshed along the way, of course—into a place that is no longer neatly divided along geographic lines or by any other clear boundaries. It is becoming a world in which people have more options about where to live, how to define who they are, what to identify with. (Anderson, 1999: 5)

Certainly, as the chapters in this section illustrate, multiracial Asian Americans have been integrating this "new medievalism" into their identity formation processes, even though Asian-descent multiracial people possess different qualities and experiential specificities that involve minority-minority biraciality (Thornton and Gates; Hall and Turner); geographic location, cultural practices, and community participation (Rooks); and variations in generation and Asian backgrounds, family dynamics, and gender (Root).

These essays highlight the complex dimensions and multiple ranges of Asian-descent multiracial identity, as well as the intersecting axes upon which multiracial Asian American identity rotates, shifts, and transforms. As personal and social aspects of this identity collide, interact, influence, and inform, Asian-descent multiracial individuals actively propel them into motion and demonstrate that multiraciality complicates and diversifies "race" as we know it. And indeed, these essays all punctuate that the whole of multiracial identities is often greater than the sum (Hall and Turner).

CHAPTER 5

Factors Influencing the Variation in Racial and Ethnic Identity of Mixed-Heritage Persons of Asian Ancestry

Maria P. P. Root

The first significant cohort of mixed-race Asian Americans was born in the Korean War era between World War II and the Vietnam War, on the doorstep of the modern civil rights movement. Reflecting the interplay between societal structure, politics, and economic agendas, the emergence of the Amerasian in the U.S. conscience has been tied to either war or labor needs, thus making it easier to objectify these products of interracial unions. "*Where are you from?*" was asked as frequently as "*What are you?*" Thought of as "war babies" regardless of the marital status of their parents, this cohort suffered from the same stereotyping as children from black-white marriages, as assumptions were made about unstable and illicit relationships propagating unwanted offspring.

Although international marriage continues, usually involving foreign brides rather than grooms (Thornton, 1992b), the contemporary cohort of mixed-race Asian Americans usually has two American-born parents. This demographic change stems from the growth of the Asian American population since 1965 and the tendency toward intermarriage that increases with each generation (Kitano et al., 1998). American culture is not foreign to the contemporary generation's parent. However, although being a later-generation Asian is correlated with greater structural assimilation, this parent may also be isolated from an Asian American community and not have extensive means of reinforcing cultural knowledge and its subtleties.

The increased variability in the origins of multiracial Asian Americans and growth of this population in a post–civil rights era have spawned an array of identities; including Asian American, Eurasian, Afroasian, Amerasian, Japanese American, *hapa,* black, white, Jewish, Indian, Filipino, Punjabi, mixed, and Vietnamese American. I have suggested (Root, 1998c) that racial and ethnic identity formation must be considered in historical and generational context, as the factors governing the boundaries and meanings of race and racial interaction change over time and are regionally driven. M. Omi and H. Winant (1986) argue that historical projects about racial categorization, fueled by economic and political agendas, promote racial formation and its transformation. With the repeal of antimiscegenation laws and the movements toward ethnic self-identification associated with the civil rights movement, the claim of multiple identities or integrated identities is naturally extended, but with a subversive twist in notions of multiplicity. Asian American communities currently grapple with the largest proportion of persons of mixed descent (King, 1997).

This chapter discusses a portion of preliminary findings from the Biracial Sibling Project (BSP), a community interview study conducted by Maria Root in Seattle, Washington, in 1997 and 1998. Washington, the only state on the West Coast without antimiscegenation laws, experienced a significant amount of racial mixing. Its sizable Asian American communities, particularly Chinese, Filipino, and Japanese, make it an appropriate setting for the study of broader issues of identity.

Siblings were recruited as a way of minimizing some of the flaws inherent in the "snowballing" techniques often necessarily used in recruiting biracial people for research (Root, 1992b). Whereas the initial respondent was likely to have had an interest in a study that sought "biracial" and "multiracial" siblings, his or her sibling might not have been someone for whom such labels resonated. Thus, the pool of participants had a greater chance of including persons who do not necessarily identify racially or ethnically as mixed.

This study sought to reach a better understanding of three interactions: (1) how different racial and ethnic combinations may influence identity formation; (2) how gender, race, and ethnicity interact in the context of mixed race; and (3) how generation affects the development of identity. Although the larger study, the results of which are not reported here, was not limited to persons with Asian ancestry, this paper discusses only participants with Asian ancestry.

Methods

Siblings were recruited using an ad placed twice in a weekly employment paper and a press release picked up by small community newspapers throughout Washington State. To be part of the study, the siblings had to be over eighteen years of age, one sibling had to be willing to participate, and they had to share the same biological parents, although it was not necessary for them to have grown up in the same household. Participants completed questionnaires and two two-hour, semi-structured interviews each, separately from one another. The framework for written and oral questions was based on the Ecological Framework for Understanding Variation in Identity Development (Figure 5-1; see also Miller, 1992; Stephan, 1992). Each participant was paid sixty dollars. Among those who responded to ads, 86 persons (or 43 pairs of siblings) met the criteria and were sent questionnaires. Interviews have been completed for 57 persons. Of these persons, 24—14 women and 10 men—have Asian ancestry. The sample of 57 participants averaged 26.7 years of age; the average age among the Asian Americans was 26.1.

Results and Discussion

The interview results are discussed below according the three goals of the study, which explored the interactions of racial and ethnic combination, gender and racial combination, and generation by racial combination. But before these results are presented, it is important to examine a broad finding that was relevant regardless of the racial combination: the influence of the family environment upon identity development.

Family Environment

In a leading study of the experience of persons of Asian ancestry, G. K. Kich (1982, 1992) observed that the presence of both parents and extended family influences the identity process. Furthermore, he as well as T. K. Williams (1992) noted that the absence of a parent can have a large effect on identity, in part due to the child's interpretation of the reasons for and meaning of the absence. In Williams's study of Americans of Asian ancestry on military bases in Japan, for example, such an absence, particularly of African American fathers, left some participants identifying more with a general sense of being American (and Japanese) but not necessarily African American. For the first cohort of Amerasians, family strife, particularly when it ended in divorce, often became coded in a conflict of loyalties between nationalities in which culture was embedded.

Family environment exerted some critical influences on development in general in this study. Positive family environments allowed for a safer exploration of the world and the individual in relationship to other people. The family also provided a place of refuge when peer interactions were difficult. Being able to feel loved, not having to attend much to parents' emotional needs, and not worrying about the stability of parents' relationships were associated with more integrated identities, regardless of the racial mixture. Furthermore, family environments in which race was talked about overtly provided tools to decode and challenge stereotypic messages about race. On the other hand, family environments that were fraught with conflict, violence, or abandonment appeared to derail the general process of individuation (Root, 1998a). In turn, these influences were associated with a confusion of family instability or trauma with race or ethnicity.

Color Coding   A child may "color code" abandonment, cruelty, instability, and psychopathology within the family to race or ethnicity unless the child is old enough to have accrued exposure to enough people of different races or at least the races of his or her parents (Root, 1998a). If the child does not have this experience and is left to his or her own devices, the insidious stereotypes provided by society may provide the template for attributions. In this case, the individual may experience difficulty embracing the heritage to which negative attributions have been made.

The process by which this differentiation is achieved may be constructive or destructive (Root, 1998c). In *constructive differentiation,* a push away from the reference point is absent, and thus differences can be observed and interpreted less defensively. *Negative differentiation* results from a desire not to be the same as someone. However, it does not provide a template for what one is moving toward. Often trauma is at the root of pushing away from what is seen as negative.

Exposure and Isolation.   Because ethnic and racial identification represents a symbolic attachment to a group, exposure to the group is critical to forming this attachment. In a study of multiracial Asians of college age in Honolulu, C. W. Stephan (1992) concluded that exposure to the ethnic environment is neither a necessary nor sufficient condition for identity formation. The findings of the BSP reinforce this conclusion. By using a methodology that involved sibling pairs, it was shown that individual differences also drive this process (Figure 5-1). Some of these differences seem to fall under the category of personality, while others develop through opportunities for friendship or other association in the environment. For example, one sibling could go to an almost exclusively white school, while just two years later a family move may dictate a very different environment for another.

Exposure to different groups of people and to different family members can provide a cultural context for understanding personality, culture, and behavior. Such exposure becomes particularly important if there is marked family instability or marital strife. If the family rarely socializes with the Asian relatives, the children have fewer opportunities for developing a breadth of interpretation of their ethnic experience. An affirmation of ethnicity may also come from participating in community activities. However, if the family lives where there are few Asians, then the opportunity to develop such an attachment does not exist. There may be no negative feelings, but there may be no positive feelings either. Accordingly, the isolated person may become more likely to develop a symbolic ethnicity, which M. C. Waters (1990) defined as the luxury of choosing to affiliate distantly with a group because it gives a person a sense of uniqueness. However, this choice is not imposed by outsiders and has no costs. Thus, it is the ironic way of satisfying the American quest for both belonging and for individuality.

For example, third-generation Asian American sisters with Filipino origins on their mother's side and a white European heritage on their father's grew up isolated from any Asian American community. The younger sister, age twenty, noted that they did not live in an area that had many Asians. In fact, she remembers knowing perhaps only one other Filipino family during her childhood. Their exposure to Filipinos was limited to their mother and to the families of her older brother and sister, whom they visited in California during the summer. Both of these older siblings had been born and raised in the Philippines, whereas their mother had been born and raised in the United States. It was during these visits that they would be exposed to Tagalog, a Philippine dialect, and more Filipino foods than they had at home. These aunts and uncles, however, were very strict. Because of their limited exposure to other Filipinos, the sisters could not determine how much of their own conflict with their mother was due to her as an individual and how much to their cultural differences. The older sister observed that they both acknowledged their Filipino heritage and found it interesting, although this statement had an air of detachment to it. Neither sister identified with it and had not really considered her racial or ethnic position in America. Whether either would be accepted by

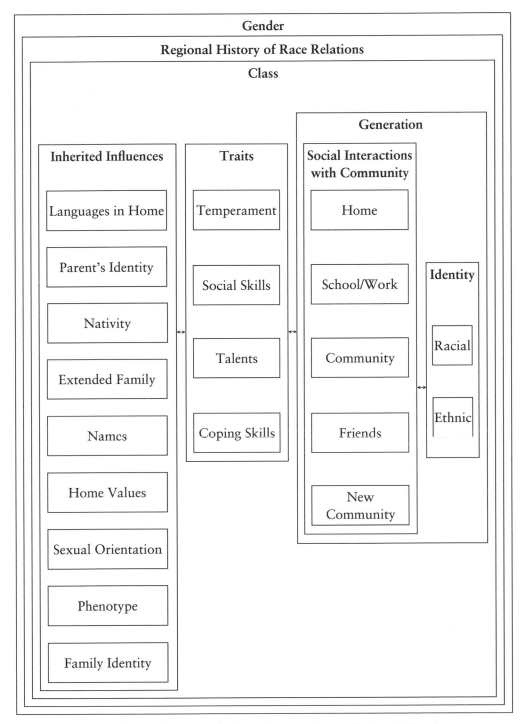

FIGURE 5-1. Ecological framework for understanding variation in identity development

Filipinos in general or be accurately perceived as such was not an issue, since neither sister ethnically identified as Filipino. Much like some of the European counterparts who are no longer part of ethnic communities, their current exploration and sometimes identification as Filipino may be an expression of symbolic ethnicity (Waters, 1990).

In contrast, three of the four other pairs with Filipino ancestry in the study had much greater degrees of attachment to being Filipino and to being identified as Filipino. These pairs all had access to Filipino American communities and thus were able to place some of the cultural practices in their home in context. However, unlike the two sisters, they did experience frustration and rejection at not being accurately identified as Filipino.

In summary, isolation has multiple outcomes. While it allows some persons to live a life in which little overt racial construction is imposed upon them, it leaves others feeling like outsiders. Isolation for multiracial persons of Asian ancestry can also promote a symbolic practice of Asian American ethnicity. At some level, these individuals perceive no repercussions for making such a choice, but, if their social context should change (for example, if they move to a community with a stronger Asian American presence), their symbolic ethnicity may be questioned. Symbolic ethnicity may be possible for multiracial Asians because of the phenotypic ambiguity. It also has a generational difference, which will be discussed below.

Generation

The meaning of being a person of mixed heritage with Asian ancestry today appears to be vastly different than it was for the cohort of persons born in the era of the Korean War, possibly because of the growth in the Asian American population and historical changes that resulted from the civil rights movement (Root, 1998b). These two cohorts are distinguished in three important ways. First, the younger cohort generally has two American-born parents. Because they did not meet in the context of war, certain stereotypes about their children do not abound. Second, intermarriage was legal for the parents of the younger cohort, whereas it often was not for the older group. Third, with increased time in this country and the repeal of laws barring marriage to Asian nationals, intermarriage increased among the Asian American population (Kitano et al., 1998; Shinagawa & Pang, 1988), which has led to a large number of mixed-race persons who have similar Asian heritages (see, e.g., Cauce et al., 1992).

The first cohort experienced an America that had had little exposure to Asian Americans, except for crises involving economic security, which meant Asians and Asian Americans were not distinguished from one another. Like their Asian-ancestry mothers, the offspring were often viewed as foreigners and not Americans. Because most persons in this cohort were used to being asked, "Where are you from?," they often were the first to define the meaning of being Asian American. By contrast, many of their mothers had some ambivalence about declaring themselves American, much less Asian American. This cohort also came of age when the ethnic pride movements swept the country in the 1960s and 1970s and usurped the power to determine the terminology desired for their group.

In contrast, the contemporary generation grows up more often than not with two American parents, with the one with Asian ancestry having already forged some understanding of her or his social location as an Asian American. Whereas this parent is still more likely to be the mother, this cohort has an increasing number of Asian American fathers, a change with subtle and not-so-subtle implications for being accepted by the Asian American community. In groups that are still very patrilineal, having an Asian American father may make acceptance a bit easier, particularly through surnames.

Although Erikson (1968) and P. Weinrich (1986) may argue that ethnicity requires the congruence of the self with the group to which one perceives belonging, this association is now being challenged by some mixed-race people, as was very apparent in the BSP. Some of the younger people identified racially as white, not perceiving the boundaries as being so absolute or mutually exclusive; they had not absorbed the hypodescent rules that were imperative for maintaining the racial order more prevalent among an older generation. Thus, some of the mixed-race persons, like many white persons, said they had not thought much about race. Simultaneously, other participants described a symbolic identification with their Asian heritage that had an element of choice to it and that often promoted a positive uniqueness about themselves that suits the American struggle for individuality. However, the more an individual identified with his or her Asian heritage, the more likely he or she was to racially identify as mixed or both rather than white. Whiteness was reserved to persons who displayed no attachment to their Asian heritage except through some symbolic and distant interest. This occurred when they had grown up isolated from an Asian American community or relatives. For example, a white/Japanese man of twenty observed that being part Japanese added a unique twist to him. However, he tended to think of himself not as an Asian American but rather as a white American with Japanese heritage.

One explanation for this finding may be that Asians and Asian Americans have been viewed more favorably by mainstream society than some other minority groups, and thus there is less need to keep boundaries so rigid. Another reason may be that the contemporary generation of Asian Americans, whether of mixed heritage or not, has not faced as much overt racism as the first cohort. The ethnic community, which once reminded people of their difference, can now be a place in which to affirm a positive sense of ethnicity, which is a common phenomenon in racial identity models based upon monoracial populations (e.g., Atkinson et al., 1979; Cross, 1991; Helms, 1990).

Black and White Still Matter

This study allowed for a comparison of the degree to which whiteness versus blackness affected the process of identity development. A clear finding arose from the four persons of Asian and African ancestry: people, including the Asian American community, construct a person of African descent differently and more inferiorly than persons of European heritage. Those persons with Asian and African American parentage suffered more rejection, more lack of recognition, and less acceptance by other Asian Americans, particularly first-generation Asians. This finding arose from narratives that discussed parents', relatives', friends', and friends' parents' reactions to them. Some particularly poignant experiences were related to dating. For example, a young man, born of a first-generation Korean mother and an African American father, described how his mother, identifying him as Korean, wanted him to marry a "nice Korean girl." However, even though he was raised to have knowledge of and participate in Korean culture, he experienced overt rejection when some of his mother's peers saw him as black only and therefore an unsuitable suitor for their daughters.

Furthermore, whereas study participants who were Asian and white sometimes identified racially as white while still acknowledging their Asian heritage, those participants who were Asian and black tended to identify as both racially. Such choices are rooted in the historical construction of race in this country. Members of the first cohort, products of a society shaped by hypodescent and recovery from war, seldom identified as white. But whiteness was more accessible to the second group, possibly as a result of the contemporary challenge to race, the growing number of mixed-race persons, the nature of the relationships into which they were born, and Asian ancestry having moved from a caste status to a class status. Some of them unconsciously equate "American" with "white," and typically feel they have access to both since they have two American-born parents, one of whom is white.

But those persons who are Asian and black still experience hypodescent in both society at large and the Asian American community (Davis, 1991). Whereas some persons might be tempted to interpret the tendency of those persons with this dual heritage to identify with both groups as a way of negating their African ancestry, it is more likely that they have indeed had exposure to both cultures. By contrast, persons of white ancestry rarely still have an ethnic link, by behavior, rituals, or beliefs, to their European heritage (Polish, Scottish, French, etc.). Thus, whiteness is simply a race, rather than an ethnicity. When whiteness has an ethnicity attached to it, such as Jewish or Italian (particularly if the ethnic parent is first- or second-generation American), there seems to be a greater tendency to embrace whiteness as a race to which an ethnicity has been attached in a nonsymbolic way. The decision of persons of African and Asian heritage to identify with both seemed to meet with less resistance from both Asian and African American age peers than for the previous cohort. However, the pressure to choose loyalties and affinities, particularly from African American peers, was still present. Participants of African and Asian heritage who identified mostly as African American or black tended to do so because of multiple influences, including neighborhood, schools, availability of relatives, and general treatment by society.

Finally, participants with black and Asian ancestry indicated that they received less negativity from the African American community than if they had been mixed with European heritage. This observation is consistent with the historically based suspicion toward black-white persons. By contrast, these persons were certain they received more negative reactions and barriers to identifying with their Asian heritage from the Asian American community than if they had been a European Asian mixture.

However, although this study showed that racial combination does matter, phenotype did not clearly drive identity choices, as other research has indicated (Hall, 1980;

T.K. Williams, 1992). Still, interpretation of phenotype as having African heritage did result in more severe and negative interactions with people.

Gender and Race

Whiteness seemed to exotify young women of Asian American descent, but blackness did not seem to do so to the same degree. European features provided an advantage that distinguished them from both their white and Asian American peers. The mixture also allowed these women to conform to more conventional standards of attractiveness, which have not valued strong ethnic or racial features that are different from European. The mixing was also advantageous for some young women who did not fit the stereotyped petiteness of Asian American heritage.

For black-Asian American women, being black seemed to subsume their Asianness in the eyes of the outsider. These women felt that they were allowed more breadth for being assertive than their Asian or white peers. However, they also had some doubts about who their partners would be. They felt that white men were less accessible to them, and that black men might prefer black women, mixed white-black women, white women, and then them. This observation suggests that these women felt less real power in being able to choose their partners.

Black–Asian American women, in contrast to their European–Asian American counterparts, were more often challenged as to whether they are authentically black or black enough (Root, 1998a). Neal-Barnett (cited in DeAngelis, 1997) suggests that pilot studies of social anxiety among black teens and adults show that parenting practices that minimize the role of race are correlated with increased social phobia, since they leave children of African American heritage without the tools for coping with racial realities, such as teasing for "acting white." Although hazing exists within the Asian American community, it is evidently not as severe. Driving this process seemed to be peer competition for boys' attention and a narrow definition of African American identity, solidarity, and attachment to the ethnic group.

Blackness seemed to be used to construct a certain type of masculinity for Asian black males that whiteness did not. The two young black Asian men in the study mentioned several issues that are consistent with how young black men are stereotyped and constructed in America. First, they talked about how, if they had phenotypically ambiguous features, white persons particularly were less comfortable with them when they learned that they were also black or that they identified solely as black. They consciously used their ability to arouse this discomfort, based on the threat of violence or danger, to construct their sense of masculinity.

Stereotypes of blackness also had a masculinity associated with sexuality that stood in stark contrast to the stereotypes of Asian American men, which has emasculated them. For example, a young white–Asian American male talked about having some worry about his genital size in his first sexual relationship because of the jokes and stereotypes about Asian American men having small genitals in contrast to their other male peers.

In summary, racial combination does make a difference, and gender interacts with racial combination.

Conclusion

The preliminary findings from the Biracial Sibling Project strongly suggest that the construction of Asian heritage and its subsequent meaning in the experience of mixed race have changed since the Korean War era. One of the most significant changes is that for many persons of mixed Asian and European ancestry, whiteness as a racial identity is now accessible. Furthermore, Asian American identity seems to be more symbolic for the contemporary cohort (Waters, 1990), an option that did not exist for the earlier group. The process of thinking about one's racial self now seems less fraught with the angst experienced by the first cohort, who were often constructed as foreigners. Nevertheless, race still does matter, particularly in combination with black or white. Participants who have African American roots appear to have had harsher racial experiences, although these experiences do not predict how individuals will racially or ethnically identify themselves. So much of the racial identity process is a parcel of a larger development process influenced by family environment and by gender. Whiteness for women seems to increase a sense of attractiveness, whereas blackness for young men is used to construct a masculinity that depends on people's stereotyped fears. Although preliminary findings, the results that are emerging from the Biracial Sibling Project verify that racial construction is dynamic and informed by many different aspects of an individual's lived experience in a particular historical era and a gendered body.

CHAPTER 6

Alaska's Multiracial Asian American Families: Not Just at the Margins

Curtiss Takada Rooks

Within Asian American studies, as in most academic treatments regardless of discipline, multiracial families and their multiracial children have been examined as marginal to Asian American ethnic communities, as well as to the "other," non-Asian racial and ethnic communities. While the marginalization and exclusion of multiracial Asian American families by individuals and institutions cannot be denied, the pivotal nature of multiracial families in the formation of Asian America must be acknowledged.

Historically, many of the first Asian American communities comprised multiracial households. In New York (Tchen, 1990), Louisiana (Cohen, 1984), and Mississippi (Loewen, 1988), Chinese immigrant marriages to Irish and Blacks mark the formation of some of the earliest recorded Chinese American families. As J.K.W. Tchen (1990: 165) states, "that the Chinese adopted Anglo names, married Irish women, and had children in New York tends to indicate this was a settling as much as sojourning population." Chinese men also formed families and fathered children with indigenous populations in Hawaii and Alaska (Rooks, 1997: 79). Chinese pioneer immigrants were not alone in multiracial family formation in the United States during the late 1800s and early 1900s. Asian Indian men married Mexican women, forming communities in California's Imperial Valley (Leonard, 1992), while in the 1920s Japanese men married Eskimo women throughout western Alaska (Rooks, 1997). For the most part the records of these pioneer Asian American families have been lost. However, we do know that rather than playing marginal roles, these families were core participants in the development of the local and ethnic economies of the areas in which they resided.

During the closed-door period of Asian immigration, from 1924 to 1965 (Hing, 1983; Takaki, 1989; Chan, 1991), multiracial Asian American families comprised the largest single group of Asian immigrants (Thornton, 1992a) and in some locales, such as Junction City, Kansas, they were the majority of the Asian American population. This was particularly true between 1945 and 1965. These families and their multiracial Asian American children represent a segment of the contemporary Asian American population whose contributions to the building of Asian America has been virtually ignored and hence little understood. In contemporary Asian America, multiracial families continue to play vital roles in the formation and retention of ethnic and panethnic Asian American communities, particularly outside of the traditionally Asian American urban strongholds.

The data for this discussion come from a larger research project, conducted from 1991 to 1993, in which I sought to understand the post-1980 formation and development of Asian American ethnic communities in three Alaskan locations: Anchorage, Kodiak, and Nome. The discovery of the core membership of multiracial families in Alaska's Asian American ethnic communities was in a sense serendipitous, because the study was not focusing on multiracial Asian American families or individuals, although I was trying not to exclude these groups from my research. While I had not intended, nor expected, to find anything special about multiracial Asian American families per se, as a multiracial Asian American, I wanted to write them into the ethnography of Alaska's Asian American communities. Instead, I discovered that multiracial households were indeed important catalysts in the affairs of ethnic Asian American communities in contemporary Alaska. In some instances, ethnic populations and community organizations may not have formed in their absence.[1]

In this chapter I examine Alaskan Asian American multiracial families from two perspectives. First, I look at the roles they played in post-1980 immigration patterns and ethnic community formation among Asian American populations in Alaska. In this way the inclusive, or exclusive, character of Alaska's Asian American ethnic communities can be assessed. Second, I look at the day-to-day practices of the multiracial households, because it is here that multiracial Asian American children learn their worldview. This perspective also allows for the testing of several theoretical positions regarding multiracial families, assimilation, and ethnic/cultural change. Through a comparison of multiracial and monoracial households, the direction and type of ethnic/cultural change are analyzed.

Multiracial Asian American households have played a pivotal role in Alaska's Asian American communities. Within the Korean, Filipino, Southeast Asian, and Japanese American ethnic communities, Asian immigrant partners in interracial marriages served as anchors in family and ethnic resident chain migration. Multiracial Asian American families served as sponsors for family and refugee migration to Alaska, and they also recruited sponsors—institutions and persons, non-Asian and Asian—to assist Asians in immigrating to the United States and settling in Alaska. Asian American community leaders and community residents informed me that this has been particularly true of the Southeast Asian (Vietnamese and Laotian), Korean, and Filipino American communities. The account of the origin of Nome's Vietnamese American community serves as a case in point.

Since the early 1980s, Vietnamese Americans have comprised the largest Asian American ethnic community in Alaska's Norton Sound region. At its largest in the mid-1980s, the Vietnamese American population reportedly numbered around 110 in a village of roughly 3,000–4,000 persons. The migration history of Nome's Vietnamese American population is traced to three Vietnamese American women, married to non–Asian American spouses who were Nome residents.

In the early 1970s, a European American businessman returned to Nome from Vietnam with a Vietnamese wife. The couple had three multiracial Asian American children, each born in Nome. Soon after the arrival of the first couple, two more European American male residents returned to Nome with Vietnamese wives. Each couple had children born in Nome, now the home of three multiracial Vietnamese American families. Following the fall of Saigon in 1975, the Vietnamese wife of the first man to return to Nome went to a Florida refugee relocation camp in search of family members. Unable to locate any, she walked up to a fenced-in area where a number of Vietnamese men who had yet to find sponsors for their relocation in the United States were milling about. She yelled, "Who wants to go to Nome, Alaska?" Several seemed interested, and she informed them that there were job opportunities in Nome and that the people of Nome were friendly. A handful responded. Taking their names, the Vietnamese woman returned to Nome and informed the other Nome Vietnamese wives, along with several local business owners, about the Vietnamese men in Florida who needed sponsors. Together, the multiracial families of the Vietnamese women and a local businessman sponsored the immigration of four Vietnamese refugee men to Nome. From this core group an ethnic community began to form as they used local and personal resources to sponsor the immigration of family members and friends to Nome. Each new Vietnamese migrant brought additional kinship links and other social networks in Vietnamese American communities throughout the United States as well as in Vietnam. Additionally, several of the Vietnamese men met and married Alaska Native women in Nome, thus forming a new generation of multiracial Asian American–Alaska Native families.

Along with anchoring the migration of Vietnamese to Nome, the original multiracial Vietnamese American families assisted in their adaptations and adjustments. Moreover, they created an ethnic communal atmosphere as they informally brought Vietnamese residents to their homes for social gatherings and for the celebrations of Vietnamese and American holidays.

Nome offers a clear example of the impact of multiracial Asian American families on the local community. Similar accounts hold true for each of the various Asian American ethnic groups in Kodiak and Anchorage (Rooks, 1997). Asian American ethnic communities in Alaska recognize and appear to value the presence of multiracial Asian American households, whose members are not shunned and in fact hold a variety of leadership positions in local Asian American ethnic organizations. For example, in 1992, the principal of the Anchorage Korean language school; co-principal of the Anchorage Chinese language school; and several members of the boards of directors of the Filipino, Chinese, and Japanese American ethnic organizations were Asian American spouses from multiracial families. Several non–Asian American (both European and African American) spouses were also active in the Asian American ethnic communities, serving as board members in ethnic organizations. Sunday school teachers in ethnic churches, and assistants in a variety of ethnic celebrations hosted by ethnic organizations.

The multiracial Asian American children were also active in Asian American ethnic organization activities. During the 1992 Chinese New Year's celebration of the Alaska Chinese Association, multiracial Chinese American children represented 50 percent of the children performing the tambourine dance and other holiday entertainments. Thus rather than separating themselves from the Asian American ethnic communities, the interracially married Asian Americans and their multiracial families have carved out pivotal positions within their ethnic communities.

Multiracial family members have also been instrumental in developing relations among Asian American ethnic communities, as well as between Asian Americans and non–Asian Americans. In Anchorage, the Asian Cultural Center (ACC), a pan–Asian American organization founded in 1983, was created by a coalition of leaders from the Filipino, Japanese, Korean, and Chinese American communities. Over half of the founders were spouses from multiracial Asian American families. From 1991 to 1993 over half of the ACC board—who are representatives from the various Asian American ethnic organizations—again were members of multiracial Asian American families. The Asian Cultural Center serves as the primary organization providing education and outreach to non–Asian Americans about Asian and Asian American culture, and is the only pan–Asian American collaborative in Anchorage.

Ethnographic observation of Alaska's Asian American ethnic communities conflicts with social science theory on the role and purpose of interracial marriage. Let us look at a basic outline of existing theory, and then turn to a comparative analysis of multiracial Asian American household data for empirically warranted challenges to this theory.

Over the past forty years, social theorists have asserted that interracial marriage of minority-group members to majority-group members is a sign of assimilation (Gordon, 1964; Kitano et al., 1984). This is marked by the movement of the minority-group member toward the majority group and by the majority group's acceptance of the minority group. By extension, the practices, beliefs, and values of minority-group members who marry interracially and biculturally should be distinct from those of monoracial households, as multiracial households become more and more like the majority, or dominant-culture, households. Most of the earliest studies of Asian American multiracial households concerned themselves with the potential pathology of such unions, focusing on divorce rates, acculturation, or assimilation (Connor, 1976; DeVos, 1977; Cheng & Yamamura, 1957).

More recent analyses of interracial marriage in the Asian American community follow one of three basic approaches. The first is traditional, assessing divorce rates and assimilation in attempts to explain retention or loss of ethnicity (Fugita & O'Brien, 1991). The second seeks to explain interracial marriage as the part of a larger internal colonization of Asians and other minorities by the United States and Western European countries. This approach recognizes interracial marriages as the result of internalized racism on the part of the minority partner and oppression on the part of the dominant-group partner (Spickard, 1989). In this view, interracial marriages are problematic at best and pathological at worst. The third sees each multiracial/interracial household as dynamic, creating a unique blended culture (Williams, 1992; Thornton, 1983).

Given the widely accepted theory of interracial marriage within U.S. social inquiry as advanced by Gordon and others, two hypotheses can be tested:

1. Multiracial and monoracial Asian American households will differ on traditional ethnic behaviors and practices.
2. Multiracial Asian American households will behave more like "American" monoracial households than monoracial Asian American households.

This analysis reviewed 291 household interviews of Asian American (169), European American, Alaska Native, and African American respondents. Of the 169 Asian American respondents, 125 are married; 48 of those marriages are interracial. Among the 48 interracial couples, 39 (81%) are married to European Americans (see Table 6-1).[2]

The analysis in this section examines traditional ethnic practices, kinship, social networks, and well-being measures of Asian American respondents who are in interracial marriages in comparison to Asian American respondents who are in same race and ethnic group (monoracial) marriages (i.e., Asian married to Asian). Interracially married Asian American respondents were found to be significantly different from monoracially married Asian Americans in two of eight domains (ethnic food consumption and native-language use) on nine of thirty-eight measures (see Table 6-2).

Asian American multiracial households in Alaska on the whole demonstrated few significant differences from Asian American monoracial households. Moreover, the evidence suggests that it is the non-Asian spouse that is affected by the traditional ethnic practices of their Asian spouse and that movement occurs from majority to minority practices. This is particularly true of the first-generation spouses, as the non-Asian spouses engage in a variety of ethnic practices as participants and leaders.

On the whole, Asian American multiracial households vary little from their Asian American monoracial counterparts. Where differences do occur, an analysis of generational status either accounts for the variation or demonstrates parallel phenomena between multiracial and monoracial Asian American households.

TABLE 6-1.   Racial background of spouses of Asian American respondents in interracial marriages

	Number	Percentage
Alaska Native	3	6.3%
Asian American	1	2.1%
Europeean American	39	81.3%
African American	3	6.3%
Hispanic/Latino	1	2.1%
Biracial	1	2.1%
Total	48	100.0%

TABLE 6-2. Eight domains of traditional ethnic practice and well-being measures

Traditional ethnic and subsistence food consumption: 6 measures
Asian (native) language usage: 5 measures
Kinship networks: 4 measures
Informal social networks: 4 measures
Ethnic community networks: 4 measures
Non–Asian American community involvement: 4 measures
Well-being: 9 measures

There are no significant differences between interracially and monoracially married respondents in six of the eight domains. Respondents from multiracial Asian American families celebrate ethnic holidays, reside in the same communities in which some of their kinspersons reside, interact with those persons on regular bases, visit and are visited by relatives and friends, join and participate in ethnic organizations, participate in the local community, and demonstrate well-being measures at the same rates as Asian Americans in monoracial households.

Asian American multiracial and monoracial households did demonstrate significant differences on the frequency with which Asian ethnic foods were consumed (both annual and recent consumption) and with which Asian languages were used. These differences were expected inasmuch as the presence of a non-Asian partner affects food choices and language uses within the household. It was not expected that either partner would adopt wholly and completely the ethnic foods of the partner.

It was my observation that eating the foods from the two ethnic traditions within the family was often a protracted form of sharing and intimacy. For example, in a Korean and African American family, the African American father often cooks "soul food" so that his wife and children can share in the foods that marked his growing up and that bring him pleasure. He and his wife are particularly mindful that their children know both cultures. However, these meals are not made up exclusively of "soul food." Side dishes are often Korean cuisine, and on occasion "soul food" augments Korean meals. In this case, appreciation of and participation in both cultures are deemed important by both partners of the interracial marriage.

Eating of Asian ethnic foods is important to Asian American multiracial families, as is the consumption of the ethnic foods of the non-Asian spouse. However, the eating and preparing of Asian ethnic or nonethnic foods are not seen as mutually exclusive practices. Both practices occur, sometimes in the same meal.

The difference between multiracial and monoracial Asian American households on annual and recent Asian ethnic food consumption is significant. Despite the difference, Asian American multiracial households continue to consume ethnic foods at high rates. Ethnic foods make up half or more of the foods consumed annually by 61 percent of the respondents, and 75 percent of the annual diets of 42 percent of the respondents. Consistent with these yearly consumption rates, 72 percent of the interracially married respondents reported having eaten ethnic foods during the two days prior to the interview, and 88 percent of them had had the food prepared by someone in the same household.

In accounting for the variation between Asian American multiracial and monoracial households, generational analysis revealed that as generation status increased, the differences between the two groups decreased. That is to say, second-, third-, and fourth-generation Asian multiracial households were far more likely to eat and prepare ethnic foods in the same proportions as their monoracial counterparts. Only among the first generation were the differences in eating ethnic food behaviors clearly significant.

While Asian American multiracial household ethnic food consumption lags behind that of Asian American monoracial households, it differs markedly from that in non-Asian monoracial households. For example, no European American monoracial households reported annual diets consisting of more than 50 percent Asian ethnic foods, and only 22 percent had eaten Asian foods in the two days prior to being interviewed. Clearly, Asian American multiracial households and European American monoracial households show no signs of similarity with regard to Asian ethnic food consumption.

Asian language use was the other domain in which significant difference was found. First, Asian American multiracial families do not have as many native Asian–language speakers residing in the household as monoracial families do (45% versus 96%). And second, fewer multiracial families use Asian languages in the home at least some of the time than their monoracial Asian American counterparts (48% versus 92%). These results hold for generational analysis. The results come as no surprise, particularly if the non-Asian spouse does not speak the Asian language. In these households, English becomes the commonly spoken language, although, as indicated, Asian languages are sometimes used. Generally, this usage refers to greetings, practical everyday phrases such as "I'm hungry" or "Are you hungry?," terms of affection, and admonitions for unruly children.

Generational status influences both the Asian-language home use and Asian-language use with friends. Home use of at least some Asian-languages increases to 55 percent for first-generation Asian multiracial households versus only 13 percent for the second, third, and fourth generations, when generation status is partialed. Reduced home use of native Asian–language use was found among Asian monoracial households as well, decreasing from 97 percent to 40 percent between the first and later generations. This dramatic decrease demonstrates a generational effect. Consistent with these findings, interracially married first-generation respondents were less likely to consider their children bilingual than monoracially married respondents, but no second-, third-, or fourth-generation respondents considered their children bilingual, regardless of interracial marriage status.

As with home Asian-language use, generation status accounts for variation in Asian-language use with friends between Asian interracially and monoracially married respondents. Among first-generation, married Asian American respondents, no difference is found among interracial and monoracial groups, with both reporting rates of use with family and friends of 95 percent or greater. Second-, third-, and fourth-generation married respondents did demonstrate significant differences.

Asian American multiracial households differ little from their Asian American mono-racial counterparts on most of the traditional measures used in this study. Where differences do occur, generational status accounts for much of the variation. Ethnographic observations of Alaska's Asian American communities find that Asian American multiracial households are intimately involved in their respective ethnic communities and in pan–Asian American collaborative efforts. They participate actively in ethnic organizations, religious institutions, and community ethnic holiday celebrations. In a review of household data on traditional social science variables, we can address the issue of assimilation among Asian American multiracial households. The data do not support the hypothesized move by Asian American multiracial households toward the American group and loss of similarity with monoracial Asian American households. Rather Asian American multiracial households in Alaska retain ethnic identity and practices, and expose their children to their Asian heritage as well.

The ethnography of Asian American communities in Nome, Kodiak, and Anchorage reveals that Asian Americans from multiracial households have been central to the migration and formation of those Asian American communities. In virtually each Asian American ethnic group, members of multiracial Asian American households hold formal and informal leadership positions, participate actively in ethnic community events, and serve as anchors in the chain migration of Asians and Asian Americans to Alaska. Analysis of individual household practices demonstrated that multiracial Asian American households differ little from their monoracial Asian American counterparts. The ethnographic and empirical findings of this study call into question a priori assumptions of marginality of multiracial households in ethnic communities and the long-held assimilationist notions of U.S. social inquiry. Perhaps we should look to the center, rather than the margins, to understand fully the role of multiracial families in Asian America.

Notes

1. I suggest that the roles played by multiracial families in the development of Asian American ethnic community infrastructure in urban settings are also more instrumental than necessarily reported or understood. For example, a cursory look at the list of prominent Asian American scholars and writers reveals that a number of them are members of multiracial families, have non-Asian spouses, or are children of interracial couples. Among them are Sucheng Chan, Velina Hasu Houston, Ronald Takaki, Franklin Odo, Gary Okihiro, Janice Mirikitani, Frank Chin, and contributors to this volume.

The data were gathered over twenty-six months beginning in January 1991 and ending in March 1993. A multimethod approach encompassing archival research, participant observation, key informant, and household interviews was employed. Household data ($N = 291$) were gathered in three primary periods of field work: winter 1992, summer 1992, and winter 1993. Participant observation was conducted throughout the entire time. I continue to maintain contact with the Asian American community members. This study was supported by a National Science Foundation Dissertation Enhancement Grant and a University of California Regents Dissertation Fellowship.

Throughout the 1980s and early 1990s, Asian Americans were the fastest-growing ethnic/racial population in Alaska. Moreover, their growth was consistent and persisted during periods of economic downturns, when non–Alaska Native populations were declining at extremely quick rates (Rooks, 1997: 11–13).

This narrative is paraphrased from a series of interviews I conducted with the informant, her ex-husband, the non-Vietnamese spouse of another Vietnamese bride, and other long-term Nome residents.

In winter 1992, the local Catholic church assisted a Vietnamese American woman in sponsoring the immigration of her sister's family to Nome. The assistance of local churches and business persons greatly enhanced the ability of Nome's Vietnamese American community to recruit, sponsor, and support newcomers.

This is not to say that individual Asian Americans do not hold prejudices against interracial marriages. They do. However, as a community, Asian Americans do not deny these family members of interracial Asian American households the opportunity to participate in community events and organizations.

In all, 198 variables were analyzed (see Rooks, 1997: Appendixes I, IV). Statistical analyses of univariate, bivariate, and multivariate relations were conducted. Frequency, Goodman and Kruskal's gamma (γ), and the significance of difference statistics, z-scores, and *chi* square were utilized. Where appropriate, means and modes were the central tendencies used. Nonparametric multivariate analysis utilizing multidimensional scaling techniques allowed for interethnic and interracial comparisons.

2. Two criteria were imposed to determine the statistical significance of relations when comparing two or more items (e.g., ethnic or racial populations, generational status, study sites, and research waves). The relationship in question had to yield a *gamma* of 50% reduction of error or higher and a z-score or *chi*-square significance of $P < .05$ or better. Statistical significance for this study required both conditions to be met. While conservative, these strict criteria guard against overestimating the strength of relationships among variables and allow for greater confidence in empirically warranted generalizations derived from the statistical analysis.

Annual diets: P .001, γ .52

Meals eaten 2 days prior to the interview: P .03, γ .52

$$P \text{ .00}, \gamma \text{ .94}$$
$$P \text{ .00}, \gamma \text{ .89}$$
$$P \text{ .05}, \gamma \text{ .93}$$

CHAPTER 7

The Diversity of Biracial Individuals: Asian-White and Asian-Minority Biracial Identity

Christine C. Iijima Hall
Trude I. Cooke Turner

Introduction

Studies on mixed-race identity have primarily focused on Black-White biracials. Consequently, most research has failed to address the differences between minority-majority[1] (with one White and one minority parent) and minority-minority (with two parents from different minority groups) biracial individuals. Instead, biracials have been viewed as a homogeneous group having similar experiences and similar psychological processes for identifying themselves as racial beings. Except for their mixed-racial heritage, however, American biracials constitute a heterogeneous group with varied social and psychological experiences. The within-group and between-group factors that influence racial identity of minority-minority and minority-majority biracials will be examined in this article, with specific attention given to Asian-Whites and Asian-minorities, since these combinations have been increasing dramatically over the past two decades (Fujino, 1997; Standen, 1996). In fact, in 1989 the number of mixed-race Asian births outnumbered those of monorace Asian births in the United States (*USA Today,* 1992). The majority of these mixed-race births were Asian/Asian American[2] and White.

Minority-Minority and Minority-Majority Biracials

Research and publications conducted on biracial Americans through the early 1980s primarily focused on biracials of minority-majority backgrounds—mainly Black-White (Buttery, 1987; Herring, 1992). Later studies on biracials have become more "colorful" to include other racial groups who have intermingled with Caucasians. Research on Asian-White individuals began to add to the wealth of literature about biracial diversity (Grove, 1991; Kich, 1983; Murphy-Shigematsu, 1987), as did works on Latino-White (Salgado de Snyder et al., 1982) and Native American–White (Wilson, 1992) that began to surface during the latter 1980s and early 1990s.

It was not until the early 1980s that U.S. research began to study the biracial identity development of individuals of minority-minority decent. C. Hall's (1980) work on the racial identity of Black-Japanese biracials was the first large study on minority-minority biracial identity in the United States. Hall's findings gave the psychological community new insight into working with minority-minority individuals. Later in the decade, B. L. Wilson (1986) studied the cognitive development and racial understanding of four–eight-year-old Asian-Black biracial children.

Subsequent research has examined minority-minority biracials less frequently than minority-majority biracials, although the necessity for such work has been noted in a number of sources (Grover, 1989; Hall, 1996; Ramirez, 1996; Wilson, 1986; Grove, 1991; Kich, 1983, 1992; Murphy-Shigematsu, 1989; Salgado de Snyder et al., 1982; Wilson, 1992). There is also the need to investigate the differences between minority-minority and minority-majority identity development patterns. By virtue of the hypodescent "one-drop rule," anyone with minority blood is viewed as a minority, thereby ignoring a minority-majority individual's possible choice of identifying with the majority group. Individuals with "two drops" of minority blood—each of a different type—would undoubtedly be viewed as minority, but which one? Thus, minority-minority biracials may encounter different social experiences than minority-majority biracials. In addition, these experiences may differ even further depending on the particular minority backgrounds. That is, the social experience for the Asian-Hispanic biracial may differ markedly from that of the Asian-Black biracial and so on. These social experiences may influence racial awareness and ethnic identity choices.

Mixed-race individuals have felt the pressure to "choose sides" throughout their lives (for multiple readings see Root, 1992a, 1992b, 1996). In the United States, most biracial individuals have had three identity options—to identify with the paternal racial group, with the maternal racial group, or with both groups in some way. Although choosing between parental groups is difficult for all biracials, the issues affecting this choice may be different for minority-minority and minority-majority individuals. As discussed, the minority-minority individual does not have to choose between being a member of a minority or a majority group. Because these individuals already belong to two minority groups, their social standing in American culture is usually minority (Leslie et al., 1995). While many alliances of color have been formed over the past thirty years, the bond of being a minority in the United States is not always consistent, and many ethnic minority groups have historically been at odds. Incidents have occurred such that Asians are in conflict with African Americans, Hispanics vie for power with Blacks, and Native Americans feel betrayed by ethnic brothers/sisters in the struggle for recovery. Thus, the individual of minority-minority mixture may have some complicated issues of belonging to two minority racial groups who have been at odds. Identification with one may cause difficulty for inclusion with another (King & DaCosta, 1996). For example, in many cities in the United States, African Americans and Koreans have been in conflict. A biracial of mixed Black and Korean heritage may be seen as a "traitor" if s/he chooses to identify with one group over the other.

The minority-majority biracial individual may have similar issues of complicated choices. S/he must contend with the traditional minority versus majority controversy. The minority-minority biracial will at least be identifying or affiliating with a U.S. racially oppressed group with which there may be some commonalties. For the minority-majority, however, the choice between identifying with the oppressor or the oppressed may be a more difficult one.

How does a biracial individual decide on a racial identity? How does an individual of minority-minority heritage choose between the two minority groups? What does the minority-majority biracial do? What are the mechanisms, factors, pressures, and processes affecting these choices?

Racial Identity

As the theories of monoracial identity suggest, individuals come to understand themselves as racial beings through encounters with other groups who have different racial heritages than their own (Cross, 1971; Parham & Helms, 1985; Speight et al., 1996). Each group has its own set of behaviors, rules, attitudes, and beliefs. Racial identity is thus defined as the adoption of the beliefs, attitudes, and behaviors of a group and the development of an affinity, loyalty, and feeling attached to membership within it (Casas & Pytluk, 1995).

In 1997, T. Cooke examined the racial/ethnic identity of American biracial individuals. As part of her dissertation data collection, she surveyed 74 American biracials of both minority-majority and minority-minority heritage. We will report on 34 of these respondents who were Asian-White and Asian-minority. The Asian groups represented were Japanese, Chinese, Filipino, Samoan, Korean, Thai, Vietnamese, East Indian, and Pacific Islander. Twenty-two of the respondents were Asian-White (7 male, 15 female), and 12 (6 male, 6 female) were Asian-minority (10 with Black heritage, 2 with Hispanic). Their ages ranged from 18 to 59; the females averaged 28.75 years of age, and the males 35.46. Recruitment of the participants was conducted by using referral and "snowballing" methods, contacting biracial support organizations and campus-based student organizations, and sending announcements over computer listserves and websites.

Cooke measured the respondents' ethnic identity by mailing a revised version of J. S. Phinney's (1992) Multigroup Ethnic Identity Measure (MEIM), known as the Cooke-Hall Biracial Identity Assessment Scale (BIAS) (Cooke, 1997). Phinney's scale, designed for monoracial individuals, asks respondents if they agree or disagree with statements such as, "I have a lot of pride in my ethnic group and its accomplishments." The revised Cooke-Hall scale allows an individual to respond to such statements twice—once with regard to his/her father's ethnic group and once with the mother's ethnic group. A biracial identity was identified when there was no significant difference between the score on the total father's scale and the total mother's scale. In addition, Cooke asked each respondent if s/he possessed any physical characteristics that might be "identifiers" to his/her racial heritage. (These are discussed in the following section, Factors Affecting Ethnic/Racial Identity.)

Cooke found no significant difference in how strongly her Asian-minority respondents identified with their mothers' heritage versus their fathers' heritage on the BIAS. Thus, her Asian-minority respondents displayed a biracial identity. The majority of her Asian-White respondents, however, did not report biracial identities. Instead, they identified significantly more strongly (P < .06) with their mothers' racial group than their fathers' group.

Delving deeper into the finding that Asian-White respondents identified more strongly with their mothers' heritage, it appears this significant difference occurs primarily among individuals with Asian mothers and White fathers (N = 14 of 22). Respondents with White mothers and Asian fathers showed no significant difference in their identification with their mothers or fathers. Perhaps the ethnic mother's role is more powerful in the identification process, since women have traditionally been the conveyors of culture (Miller & Miller, 1990; Zack, 1996).

Overall, however, the majority of Cooke's respondents had some identification with at least one minority component of their heritage. These results are consistent with past research on biracial identity. For example, J. B. Mar (1988) reported that Chinese-White couples stressed the Chinese culture more than the White culture, and J. M. Oka (1994) similarly found that parents of Japanese-White biracial children preferred their children to exhibit traditional Japanese American values and behaviors. In addition, all of B. Standen's (1996) Korean-White respondents felt that being Korean was very important to them, while only 50 percent felt that being White was very important. Similarly, Hall (1980) and Wilson (1986) found most of their minority-minority respondents identifying with both minority cultures.

These results demonstrate the powerful effect of a racial minority status in the United States. That is, most biracial individuals will have some identification with their ethnic minority heritage. Those biracials with two minority parents are more apt to identify with both minority heritages, since society may not force them to choose one minority group over another, as was shown with the Asian-minority biracials in Cooke's study.

The powerful effect of the "one-drop rule" on minority status is further demonstrated with Cooke's Asian-White respondents, since most identified to some degree as a minority. That is, the respondents with Asian mothers and White fathers tended to identify more with their mothers. In addition, since there was no significant difference between identifying with their mothers' or fathers' heritages for respondents with White mothers and Asian fathers, by operational definition these individuals are biracial. Thus, these respondents found a way to be both Asian and White; that is, they were still identifying as an ethnic minority but not as strongly as those with Asian mothers.

About the same time Cooke was conducting her research, T. H. Mukoyama (1998) was also working on her dissertation, which closely paralleled Cooke's study of the difference between Asian-minority and Asian-majority mixed-race individuals. But whereas Cooke chose to modify Phinney's Multigroup Ethnic Identity Measure, Mukoyama used it in its original form. As a result, Cooke measured how subjects felt about both of the racial groups of which they were a member, while Mukoyama examined their overall attitude to their biracial heritage.

Mukoyama surveyed 54 Japanese-White Americans and 32 Japanese-African Americans. She found the majority (76%) of her respondents felt their biethnic/biracial heritage had enough salience in their lives for them to spend some time exploring their heritages. The Japanese-White and Japanese-African Americans, however, differed in their ethnic identification. Parental support among her Japanese-African American respondents was shown to promote a higher sense of ethnic identification than with her Japanese-White American respondents. This was further displayed in the finding that more Japanese-African American respondents (40.6%) than Japanese-White respondents (27.8%) participated in activities that explore and embrace ethnic heritage.

In addition, Mukoyama found a sex difference in ethnic identity choice. Her male respondents identified monoracially at a higher rate (51.7%) than her female respondents (28.1%). This was especially true with her Japanese–African American male respondents. Mukoyama's explanation of this was that biethnic males may have more societal pressures that promote monoethnic identification, while women may be freer to cross ethnic/racial boundaries. Cooke did not find a sex difference in terms of biracial versus monoracial identity.

Further, Mukoyama found that parental support of biethnic identification correlated with self-esteem ($r = .35$, $P < .01$). Overall, her entire sample scored highly on the self-esteem measure, managed life stressors effectively, and were well-adjusted.

Thus, Cooke's and Mukoyama's findings demonstrate how the development and choice of ethnic identification vary between Asian-White and Asian-minority individuals. The experiences of these individuals differ on many dimensions that may lead to the differences in ethnic identity choice.

Factors Affecting Ethnic/Racial Identity

Phinney's (1992) and Cooke and Hall's (Cooke, 1997) scales view ethnic identity as a social identity characterized by four attributes: self-identification, which is the identification with a particular group; ethnic behaviors and practices, which include one's activities that are similar to those of a particular group; affirmation and belonging, which reflect the extent one feels attachment to, pride in, and affinity with a group; and ethnic identity achievement, which is the extent one has delved into the meaning of one's group affiliation and has internalized membership within it. Thus, racial identification with a group involves multiple dimensions.

Other researchers (Hall, 1980; Stephan, 1992; Winn & Priest, 1993) found similar psychosocial factors that influence the identity development of mixed-race individuals—cultural knowledge/experience/affinity with their groups, physical characteristics, family attitude and teaching about racial differences, social/peer influence, geographic location, sociopolitical attitudes, age, and acceptance/nonacceptance by and of either ethnic group. Let us discuss two of these factors in more depth—cultural knowledge/experience/affinity and physical characteristics—with respect to Asian American biracials.

Cultural Knowledge

Aspects of a culture may include language, music, history, and customs. Knowledge and adherence to these cultural indices are believed to be important in the development of ethnic identity of monoracial and biracial individuals (Hall, 1980; Kich, 1982; Murphy-Shigematsu, 1987; Phinney, 1992; Salgado de Snyder et al., 1982; Stephan, 1992). However, the "Americanized" version of a culture may be difficult to describe and measure. That is, language, history, and food are fairly constant in an ethnic culture over time, but music, social practices, and family structure may amorphize. Therefore, what are the cultural norms for twenty-first-century Asian Americans? These norms may differ from those of the traditional, native Asian country. The same can probably be said for African American, Hispanic, and European American cultures. Thus, it is difficult to measure the cultural knowledge/affinity/identity of ethnic Americans using scales based on the native culture. For example, the Ethnic Identity Questionnaire (Matsumoto et al., 1973) and the Suinn-Lew Self-Identity Acculturation Scale (Suinn et al., 1987) test adherence to the Asian culture by asking respondents about their food, language, and other lifestyle preferences (e.g., "A good child is obedient," or "I especially like Japanese food"). However, an individual may not answer toward the Japanese end of the scale and thus be seen as acculturated, yet may identify strongly as a Japanese American.

In fact, Amy Iwasaki Mass (1992) suggests that cultural knowledge and strength of affiliation/identification with a group are not necessarily correlated. She found that although her sample of Asian-White biracial individuals had less cultural knowledge, they still identified as Asian. Hall (1980) likewise found that her participants identified strongly as being both Black and Japanese regardless of the amount of knowledge they had about either culture. This, again, shows that cultural knowledge is not the only predictor of ethnic identity (Phinney, 1992). One can have less cultural knowledge and still have a strong internalization of group membership.

The findings of Mass and others, however, do not deny that cultural knowledge may aid in the individual's acceptance by a group or comfort with that group. That is, interaction with and acceptance by a particular group usually requires some knowledge of its language, food, customs, and so on. However, this does not necessarily guarantee acceptance by the group. An individual may learn about the Asian, African American, Native American and Chicano culture but still not know how to feel comfortable with these particular groups. Hall (1980) and others (T. K. Williams, 1996) have found that many mixed-race people feel they are not completely accepted by either of their racial groups due to their mannerisms. However, this nontotal acceptance by the group does not preclude the racially mixed person's identification or internalization with the group.

For example, a Korean-Black biracial woman who was adopted by a White family (McRoy & Hall, 1996) respected and had knowledge of her African American and Korean cultures, but her mannerisms were not the same as those of other African American students at her university, who shunned her for not "acting Black."

But what is it to act Black, White, Asian, Hispanic, or Native American? What are the rules for inclusion? Group membership can be measured by behavioral cues (Mitchell, 1990; Salgado de Snyder et al., 1982), but what are they? The knowledge, affiliation, behaviors, and internalization of membership of two racial groups apply to the biracial individual. However, in the past century minority groups have tended to have more defined expectations and less variance in the behaviors that define group membership than Whites (Helms, 1990; Landrine & Klonoff, 1994). For example, Hispanics, African Americans, and Asians have traditionally defined in-group behavior with language, religion, dress, familial activities, and holidays.

Overall, racial and group membership rules appear to be more widely discussed with minority-minority biracials whose heritage includes two groups that emphasize language facility and recognition of cultural cues (Comas-Diaz, 1994; Hall, 1980; Salgado de Snyder et al., 1982). While both factors are seen as indicative of group membership in minority-minority as well as minority-majority groups, the dual minority may be expected to be more culturally aware of both cultures (Twine et al., 1991). For example, the minority-minority individual who is of African American and Asian Indian descent, although raised in the United States, will be expected to be able to communicate comfortably using both "Black English" and an Indian dialect.

In contrast to minority groups, what is White culture, and how does someone "act White"? "White" has come to mean middle-upper-class behaviors and the absence of an accent (Doss & Gross, 1994). Many educated and professional people of color have been accused of "acting White" due to these criteria. This perhaps was operating with the Korean-Black woman mentioned earlier.

The "White" cultures include the many European and other Caucasian ethnic groups who have come to the United States, such as Italians, Israelis, Jews, Swedes, and Irish. Americans with these ethnic heritages may have the knowledge and practices of these groups and feel affiliation and identification with them. In addition to race, religion can also affect White identity. For example, N. Zack (1996) believes Jewishness may take precedence over White racial heritage. With the diversity movement, more Caucasians are beginning to discover their ethnic and religious roots, and thus the definition of White is becoming broader and more diverse.

The amount of cultural knowledge needed for inclusion and identification can be affected by other factors. Many people have stated to the authors of this chapter that the mixing of races has "diluted" the Asian cultural knowledge of the biracial Asians. However, it is more likely that generational factors are influencing this change, for research has shown that each generation loses some of its native culture (Matsumoto et al., 1973). This would be true of the Asian biracial's Asian-born parent *and* non-Asian parent. For example, a young Asian-White student whose mother is a Swedish immigrant has expressed a great affinity for the Swedish culture.

Biracials with at least one immigrant parent may also experience the additional discrimination of being new to the United States (Williams, 1992). Many ethnic American cultures shun their immigrants. Since many Amerasians are themselves immigrants, refugees, or children of U.S. military men left behind after a war, they may encounter additional discrimination and trauma. A study by J. F. Newell (1991) showed the primary cause of psychological stress among Vietnamese Amerasian youth was the lack of knowledge of their American fathers and mixed-race discrimination.

Discrimination of biracials can emanate from many groups. The Asian-White individual may encounter racism from Whites for being Asian and from Asians for being White. Also, not all minority groups are accepting of other groups. Thus, the Asian-minority biracial individual may experience racism from other minorities.

The amount of discrimination toward mixed marriages and biracial individuals may also differ by geographical areas (Hormann, 1972; Johnson & Nagoshi, 1986). Whether a biracial individual is accepted versus subjected to racial hostility will most likely affect how that person feels about him- or herself. For example, Cooke (1997) interviewed a twenty-five-year-old Asian-White female who felt comfortable with her dual ethnic heritage because for many years she had lived in Hawaii and California, where interracial relationships are common and more accepted.

Geographic location may also affect the amount of culture available to the mixed-race individual and thus his or her racial identity. If a core group of Asians, Whites, other people of color, or other mixed-race individuals is available to the biracial person, that person may be more apt to experience more of his or her culture, have more positive experiences, and be more accepting of his or her racial background (Anderson, 1993). In fact, Mukoyama (1998) found a strong correlation between self-esteem and growing up in an ethnically diverse neighborhood with her sample of biracial Asians.

Research has indeed found a strong correlation between ethnicity of neighborhood/friends and ethnic identity (Hall, 1980; Larson, 1995; Lloyd-Tarrisyna, 1989). Thus, an Asian-White individual may feel more comfortable if there is a critical mass of Asians or Whites in his or her community and identify accordingly. For example, one of the male Asian-White respondents in Cooke's study identified more as White since he lived and went to school in Southern White towns. His "dating and social activities were concentrated within the Caucasian community. He never dated a female who was not Caucasian. . . . He attends a [Southern] Baptist church that has a predominant Caucasian membership" (Cooke, 1997: 73–74). Similarly, in the present study an Asian-White female said she had little knowledge of her Asian background "not due to personal motivation, but [to] lack of access to information, people, and resources, etc."

Physical Appearance

Physical appearance tends to have a particularly strong influence on racial identity or social and personal experiences, since racial group membership, orientation, allegiance, and loyalty are measured by physical cues (Mitchell, 1990; Salgado de Snyder et al., 1982). A biracial individual who resembles one racial group over another may be accepted by that group more readily. If his or her identity is somewhat masked by no particular delineating racial features, it may be more difficult to be accepted by or identify with the group. Some of the physical cues for racial membership are skin color, hair texture and length, eye and nose shape, height, and weight distribution (Hall, 1997). For example, a twenty-five-year-old Asian-White female respondent from Cooke's research was repeatedly mistaken for Chicana — "People always thought I was part Hispanic"—because of her hair, eye, and skin color (Cooke, 1997: 75). Similarly, in the present study, a twenty-seven-year-old East Indian–Black female said people assume she is "Spanish because I have straight hair."

To investigate some of these physical racial cues, Cooke's Asian biracial respondents were asked to identify which of their physical characteristics they consider to be ethnic. All thirty-four respondents listed at least one physical feature that cued their ethnicity/racial background. For the Asian-White group the most common was eyes (87% females, 70% males), followed closely by hair color (40% females, 70% males), skin color (30% females, 57% males), and nose (30% females, 43% males). Height was not mentioned by men but was mentioned by 30 percent of the females. The most common physical identifier listed by Asian-minority respondents was skin color (66% females, 50% males), hair color/texture (50% females, 66% males), eyes (66% females, 33% males), lips (33% females, 50% males), and nose (33% females, 16% males.)

Thus, it appears all the respondents believed they possessed at least one physical racial identifier. It also seems that most of the identifiers can be seen as the more traditional ethnic-minority racial characteristics. That is, eyes were the most dominant feature listed by Asian-White respondents and were listed prominently by Asian-minority respondents. Eyes, of course, are one of the major attributes that distinguish an Asian phenotype. Skin and hair color, the next most commonly cited characteristics, are also traditional ethnic cues for minorities (especially African Americans). Thus, the respondents were quite aware that their physical characteristics delineated their racial/ethnic heritage.

Skin color played a more dominant role for Asian-minorities, which is consistent with most of the research (Spickard, 1989). While the variation in skin color within racial groups is diverse, each group is usually able to identify its own members (Hall, 1980; Standen, 1996). In addition, each of the American minority groups has its own rules of color, whereby lighter-skinned individuals are considered more appealing than darker-skinned individuals (Comas-Diaz, 1994; Funderburg, 1994; Haizlip, 1994; Morganthau, 1995; Russell et al., 1992) This makes for interesting combinations of skin color and acceptance of biracials by different groups. For example, an Asian-Hispanic could have differential acceptance in both of his/her racial groups depending on the lightness or darkness of skin color, since the Hispanic culture also prefers lighter skin (Comas-Diaz, 1994). An Asian-Black individual may be more accepted in the African American community for being light-skinned but not as accepted in the Asian community for being too dark. This was mentioned by many of Hall's respondents in her 1980 study.

Adding to this complicated equation of skin color are the different standards of beauty for men and women. In the United States, stereotypically preferred females are petite, light-skinned and passive—similar to the physical and social image of Asian women

(Hall, 1995a, b, 1997). However, once this perfect image is mixed with another, not-so-accepted image, the status may change. Thus, the Asian-White female may be more acceptable in the U.S. culture than the Asian-Black. For men, the preferred male image is larger, more aggressive (but not violent), and darker (but not too dark) (Welsing, 1991). The Asian-White male may not possess all these qualities, but the Asian-Black male may have many of these and thus be preferred by all racial groups. Many of Hall's (1980) Black-Japanese male participants reported their popularity with women due to their exotic looks and muscular body stature. The Asian-Hispanic male may have an added social image of being strong and in control (Lopez-Baez, 1997), thus making him more attractive.

Conclusion

Previously held assumptions about biracial identity suggested that American biracials experienced similar patterns of identity development, much like those outlined in monoracial theories. However, this chapter demonstrated that, unlike the experience of monoracial individuals, the process of identity development and identity choice for American biracials is a heterogeneous one that depends on several factors, including racial groups of parents, physical characteristics, cultural knowledge, and geographic location. Cooke's data on Asian-minority and Asian-majority individuals are a new addition to the growing body of research on biracial identity.

While recognizing the heterogeneity of experiences and identity development of biracials, the reader must also remember that Asian biracials may have different biracial experiences from those of other minority-minority and minority-majority mixtures. Since Asians are seen by White America as the "model minority" (Sue 1975), individuals of mixed Asian ancestry may be more accepted than other minority individuals. Asian-White individuals may thus be the most acceptable of the Asian mixtures to the Asian and White communities (as seen by the increase in Asian-White interracial dating and marriages); Asian-Black may be the least acceptable to the Asian community (Spickard, 1989).

A new generation of biracials who understand the depth and breadth of the biracial experience appears to be emerging (Houston & Williams, 1997). They tend to identify with both parental groups in ways that interact and intersect in multiple ways (Thornton, 1996). As one student, Bruce, explained, being biracial does not mean that he is *half*-Black and *half*-Japanese but rather, as many other biracials have said, is *all* Black and *all* Japanese. However, this student found many people have difficulty with this concept, arguing that the whole cannot be greater than the sum of its parts, and that the total must add to 100 percent. His answer to this lack of understanding is to ask, "What percentage of your love is given to your father, and what percentage is given to your mother?" Most would not say, "50 percent to each." Thus, this student analogizes that love, as with ethnic identity, cannot be measured by conventional mathematics; it is not a zero-sum gain issue.

Notes

1. The term "minority" is used herein to represent U.S. people of color—African Americans, Asian Americans, Latino/Hispanic Americans, and Native Americans/American Indians. Although "people of color" is currently the preferred term, the authors ask the reader for understanding, since it was easier to use the terms "minority" and "majority."

2. This chapter will not address the issue of inter-Asian interethnic individuals, such as Korean Chinese, Filipino Japanese, etc.

CHAPTER 8

Black, Japanese, and American: An Asian American Identity Yesterday and Today

Michael C. Thornton
Harold Gates

As we write this chapter, the U.S. Office of Management and Budget has decided to incorporate into the 2000 Census a "check one or more" format for identifying one's race. With this development we have officially begun to deal with the implications of a growing multiethnic population in the United States, and this is a good thing. But as we rush toward institutionalizing a new "racial" category in government documents and perhaps elsewhere, the need to clarify what it means to be multiethnic/multiracial looms ever larger. The present volume leads us to explore one aspect of this phenomenon: the long-ignored experience of multiethnics of Asian ancestry.[1]

When significant numbers of this particular population began to conduct self-reflective research in the 1980s, they encountered decades of inquiry riveted on their parents, mostly Asian women who had married American men following World War II and the Korean War. In contrast, work on the offspring from these unions was nonexistent until the late 1970s, with interest on multiethnics instead centering on Black-White mixtures, Asian mixtures in the Asian context, or Eurasians. The theoretical footing to these works was the most negative aspects of the "marginal man" thesis (Park, 1928; Loewen, 1971). As products of two ill-crossed people, multiethnics were condemned to live in antagonistic worlds, where mental health was impossible. They manifested ambivalent attitudes, inferiority complexes, hypersensitivity, and a conformist nature. Newer research, however, focused the discussion very differently. As a result, previously disabled and marginal personalities became well-rounded, and cosmopolitan in perspective—the ideal for the next century, the "multicultural person" (Thornton, 1996).

To date what has driven much of this inquiry about multiethnics generally and of those with Asian ancestry particularly are political agendas, for multiethnics remain a group used to prove a point: they represent a debate over the consequences of tearing down racial walls. In attempting to essentialize the multiethnic experience (suggesting that it is good or bad), researchers consistently, and with few exceptions, ignore that this group embodies the human experience first and foremost. As such they "often experience the same events differently. Similarly, multiethnics may have a positive or negative encounter with multi-ethnicity [;] that [*sic*] individual, moreover, may have a positive and negative experience with his/her status at different points in time" (Thornton, 1983: 108). In the rush to essentialize this experience and to identify its key ingredient, the field remains too focused on a narrow range of experiences, and as such we've ignored the multiplicity of multiethnic life. Our fixation on personal aspects of group identity has meant that we ignore the larger process, starting with one's family, and progressing to greater independence from family and finally to the place at which ethnic identity fits into all of our other multiple identities. In short, this field of inquiry is stuck at the adolescent stage of the life course of multiethnics.

In this chapter, we assess the current state of work on multiethnic people who have Asian ancestry, but especially those with an African American heritage. This particular part of the field has lagged behind other work on multiethnic Asian Americans. To suggest how we might expand the area, we will mine an early effort by the first author. It remains one of the only studies of Asian American multiethnics that has incorporated major discussion of social context, including parental influences.

Literature Review

The past two decades have witnessed a phenomenal growth in research on so-called mixed racials. During the 1990s a number of popular texts appeared, including *Miscegenation Blues* (Camper, 1994); *Black, White, Other* (Funderburg, 1994); *American Mixed Race* (Zack, 1995); *Racially Mixed People in America* (Root, 1992a); *The Multiracial Experience* (Root, 1996b); *The New Colored People* (Spencer, 1997); and "No Passing Zone" (Houston & Williams, 1997). In contrast to their predecessors, these works commonly move beyond caricature to explore various dynamics within this experience. Nonfiction story-telling by mixed authors (Alexander, 1991; Haizlip, 1994; Jones, 1994; Nunez, 1995; See, 1995; G. Williams, 1995) enhances discussions across ethnic and racial combinations. The popularity of this subject is further witnessed by a growing number of college courses, especially those incorporating Asian Americans in the discussion (Williams et al., 1996).

Concomitant to the more traditional avenues of inquiry, the Internet has also become a prodigious site of debates over Asian American multiethnics; "Amerasian" webpages are popping up all over. Indeed on these pages we often see that groups ignored elsewhere are given an avenue to express their own concerns and views. Discussions of such topics as "Being Blackanese" (Uehara-Carter, 1996) and "Blasian and Jewish" (Polk, 1997) are common, as is talk of bewilderment about one's identity, how others treat multiethnic identity as exotic, and the struggle to come to terms with being both Black and Asian. This dialogue speaks of identity as a negotiation process.

Research on Asians of multiple heritage, while lagging behind these more popular discussions, has nonetheless moved to a new level of sophistication over the past few years. Whether involving gayness (Kich, 1996; Allman, 1996) or romantic tribulations (Twine, 1996), emerging work has begun to incorporate issues beyond racial/ethnic identity and, when focused on identity, to move beyond a narrow understanding. We see that multiethnics vary in their sense of being different from their monoracial counterparts, while purposefully using racial ambiguity to survive an otherwise hostile world. This latter phenomenon is particularly intriguing, for it moves us to viewing identity as situational, changing with context, which is a very different view from earlier interpretations that considered similar positions as pathological (e.g., T. K. Williams, 1996; Kich, 1992). However, the most significant development in this research has been to broaden prevailing notions of Asianness to include others, such as multiethnics, who were previously ignored in the Asian American category.

The theme of much of the work on multiethnic Asians has been described as following either the equivalent or the variant approach (Thornton & Wason, 1996). The equivalent approach views the process of identity development as being similar for everyone (Cauce et al., 1992). For example, Grove (1991) compared identities of mixed White–Asian Americans with those of their White counterparts. He found similar identities, the main difference lying in the fact that multiracials had to figure out where they fit racially. Other research suggests that how individuals handle the ambiguity appears to differ by gender, with males revealing higher racially desirable traits, and females being more likely to be extroverted than their monoracial counterparts (Johnson & Nagoshi, 1986). Works taking the variant approach suggest that multiethnics of Asian heritage are not to be seen as a separate and distinct group, but to be acknowledged as having access to all sides of their heritage (Mass, 1992; T. K. Williams, 1996; Standen, 1996; King & DaCosta, 1996; Stephan & Stephan, 1989, 1991). But emerging research intimates that this community is diverse in perspectives, and includes those who try to fit into traditional ethnic/racial communities, those who wish to form a multiracial community, and those who try to dismantle dominant racial ideologies and group boundaries to reach across humanity (Nakashima, 1996). The idea of multiple experiences among multiethnics is gaining credibility.

Nonetheless, despite this explosion in exploring the multiethnic Asian American experience, the research literature remains bogged down with substantive limitations (Thornton, 1996; Thornton & Wason, 1996). Three of these problems will be addressed here. First, reflecting the history of bipolar/dichotomous schemes that clearly delineate people into mutually exclusive categories (Daniel, 1992a), the term "mixed race" continues to refer mostly to Asian-White mixtures. Few works examine minority-minority bonds, such as Latino-Asian or Black-Asian mixture (e.g., Hall, 1980). Second, while the social context of identity has drawn some attention, we still know little about how primary groups fit into the process of identity formation. Thus how friends or parental upbringing influence identity is rarely examined (for exceptions see Root, 1996a). Third, we have only begun to explore how multiethnic identity is related to bonding with or distancing from other racial/ethnic groups in one's environment. Which groups are of potential importance is in part related to the ethnic/racial mix of the person involved (Thornton, 1996).

The focus of this chapter is on Afro–Japanese Americans, or what the first author termed "BJAs" (Black, Japanese, and American) in his dissertation. The dissertation came out of a struggle for personal identity, an attempt to understand his Japanese and Black heritage, and it was just as narrow as many of the works we have criticized here. It was limited in that the view taken was to examine a link with Asia and not Asian America (the first author would have never thought of himself as an Asian American then). It was also hindered in that its focus was on racial/ethnic identity and not others. But where it remains unique is in its effort to examine the range of ethnic identities among Afro-Asian Americans and to place this experience into a context beyond the individual, both socially/politically and within the family context.

The Informants

The interviews for this study were conducted in 1982–83. Collected via a "snowball" technique, the first author interviewed sixty-one adult informants in Kansas, Washington, D.C., Michigan, and Massachusetts. Included were thirty-five offspring of Black-Japanese parents, who at the time ranged in age from twenty to thirty-three. Also included in the study were their parents, thirteen married couples. (For more details see Thornton, 1983.) The discussion below highlights parental influences on ethnic identity and the dimensions to identity among the Black Japanese Americans.

Parental Influences

For the parents it was important that their children learn to value hard work, and to be neat and clean, polite, dependable, and independent. Socializing them to be popular, religious, and aware of their racial heritage was immaterial. These views were held by 66 percent of the parents. Racial heritage was the least important of a list of twenty-six socialization values presented to the parents. Some explanations offered for this state of affairs were: "That is something he will learn about on his own when he gets older"; "There is nothing to teach him, life will do it"; and "That sort of thing is not significant for Blacks who are mixed. They will have it easy. Anyway, they will learn later when they are teenagers."

To examine how these feelings about race were related to the socialization process more generally, the parents and their offspring were both asked about how much they liked several racial/ethnic groups: Black Japanese Americans, interracial children as a group, Japanese, interracial marriages, Japanese Americans, Americans, Whites, White Japanese Americans and Blacks. Informants were asked to evaluate how they felt with a scale that ranged from 1 (like very much) to 4 (dislike very much). Responses were consistent along gender lines. The mothers and daughters felt similarly about all the groups, feeling relatively close to them all. Nonetheless, there existed a hierarchy to these feelings of closeness. Both felt closest to mixed-heritage groups and Japanese: BJAs, interracial children, Japanese, and interracial marriages. At the bottom of the list were Whites, Japanese Americans, and Blacks. Overall the mothers felt less close than the daughters to all the groups, but especially to Japanese Americans, Whites, Americans, and Blacks.

The fathers and sons too resembled each other in the groups they liked. Highest on the list were BJAs, Japanese, and interracial children. With the exception of White-Japanese Americans, fathers and sons had the same preferences. For the sons, at the bottom were White-Japanese Americans, Japanese Americans, and White Americans. For the fathers, at the bottom were White Americans. Blacks were in the middle of the list for both fathers and sons. Overall the sons were less close than the fathers to all groups.

While space precludes examining why Blacks are viewed ambiguously by the parents and therefore their children (for more detail, see Thornton, 1983: chap. 3), it is sufficient to say that many of the parents held views of Blacks that reflected this ambiguity: "Blacks would rather sleep or gamble than work"; "Black people, I'm sorry to say, can't do anything well or for long; they are their own worst enemies." These were opinions from fathers, but these views were often mimicked by the mothers.

Identities: Black, Japanese, and American

The attitudes of the adult children seem to mirror those of the parents when it comes to identifying the significant reference groups, which appear to be people of mixed-heritage and Japanese. Bonds with Blacks are problematic. To explore how these reference groups fit into their identities, we will examine more closely the adult children's perceptions of important reference groups and what they believe these groups feel about them. We will then explore their choice of ethnic label and canvass dimensions of ethnicity among this group of mixed-heritage Asian Americans.

Respondents were asked to describe how much they had in common with Blacks, Japanese, and BJAs, the three groups most ostensibly tied to their own heritages. They describe a range of bonds with each group. Thirty-two percent said they had "a lot" or "much" in common with Blacks, while 40 percent felt similarly toward Japanese, and 78 percent felt similarly toward BJAs. Thus most did not feel a special link with either of their parental groups, but felt especially estranged from Blacks. Reflecting their ambiguity about their parental ethnic groups and their own place in society, when asked about the groups with which they felt most comfortable, 62 percent said Whites, 23 percent Japanese and Whites equally, 14 percent chose Blacks and Japanese. No one said they felt most comfortable only with Blacks.

To examine further why they distance themselves from their parental groups, a similar question was asked about what informants believed Blacks and Japanese felt about them. Generally they felt both groups did not accept outsiders. Blacks were seen as being strongly pro-Black and disliking everyone else. Japanese were seen as especially disliking multiethnics. While the informants saw themselves as accepting of Blacks and Japanese, they believed this feeling was not reciprocated by these other groups.

When asked to choose an ethnic label, Black (51%) was the first choice, then biracial (37%) and Japanese American (12%). Given their ambiguous feelings toward Blacks, it is surprising that Black was the most common choice. Perhaps it merely reflects an appreciation of the social convention that labels them Black. The evidence thus far suggests that, for most of the informants, it is more a descriptor than an accurate reflection of their bonds with other Blacks.

Dimension I

How BJAs understand their place in the social landscape is determined by their mode of consciousness, of which there appears to be two general dimensions: Dimension I (American and biracial) and Dimension II (black and multiethnic). Dimension I is what we describe as semi-intransitive, or dominated by outside forces. In this stage one is quasi-immersed in one's own experience; things are not seen in social context but in personal circumstance. Typically a person at this stage often attributes social outcomes (e.g., economic success) solely to individual abilities. Two types of Dimension I identities arise out of the interviews: American and biracial.

American Those in this category (14% of informants) possessed little substantive knowledge of Black or Japanese culture or people. In most cases the knowledge they did have was communicated as a disparaging view of Blacks but a neutral stance toward Japanese. Americans typically point to some problem inherent to the Black experience:[2]

> Living in the ghetto on welfare, talking Black talk, instead of English . . . standing on street corners huckin' and jivin' or standing on the corner harmonizing are not things I care to learn about. (p. 136)

> Blacks don't believe in working, they like welfare. They are lazy and just drink, gamble and sleep, among other things. They're all not like that, but a lot are. (p. 137).

> I don't know why people are proud to be Black. You are what you are. How can you be proud of a color you have nothing to do with, especially when all they do is steal and take welfare. They take money when all can work and stop having kids. (p. 138)

Respondents in this category claim not to have experienced a racial/ethnic identity crisis since race meant little in their lives. If they encountered discrimination, it was not from Whites. This in part explains why they feel most comfortable around them. In contrast, they often felt that Blacks disliked them, would often treat them unfairly, and made them uncomfortable. Ultimately, these informants saw life in individualistic terms, where personal initiative explained most of one's position in life. This stands in contrast to their description of Blacks not as individuals but as a category of people. Not surprisingly, they also felt that social constraints did not negatively affect their lives: "I'm tired of hearing about people, especially minorities, blaming society or the government for all their problems. They have no one else to blame but themselves" (Thornton, 1983: 138).

Biracial   Biracials (57% of the informants) resemble the American identity in most ways, except for having expanded knowledge of Black and Japanese people (although it still is little beyond caricature), and have gone through a reassessment apparently galvanized through school. Many biracials have also developed a growing appreciation of the role social factors play in affecting one's life, although race still served a relatively unimportant role in theirs. They understood that social structures and social constraints exist, but these were seen unclearly, in that they were not seemingly linked to other peoples' actions. As a result biracials still held a blame-the-victim mentality.

For them, too, their experiences with Blacks have been mixed. Typically, they have tried to interact with them but claim they were rebuffed. Unlike those with the American identity, biracials like to believe that they are equally drawn to Blacks and Japanese but have been unsuccessful at building a link with them because members of these groups do not accept them for who they are:

> I am a Black American, and Japanese. I don't want to be White, as some would claim. I probably feel most comfortable with Whites, however, because they "hear" different things from the statement that I am Black and Japanese. I think Whites hear that I am saying I am, and want to be, unique. In some ways this may be easier for them, given that I am unique anyway, being the only Black, or whatever, in a group of Whites. They see no or little connotations because race is of little significance to them. I mean that in their own lives they seldom think of themselves as Whites. Whether that distinction plays a part in other aspects of their lives is another matter altogether. Blacks hear from that statement that I want to be better than they; . . . they hear that I feel I am better. To some degree this is understandable, but I am not a "Tom" as such an analysis would imply. (p. 184)

Biracials move beyond the cultural caricatures held by those with American identities. Most claimed knowledge of Japanese culture. Some had taken classes on Japan or in the language. But their range of knowledge was not typically very extensive. Standard responses to a question about what they knew about Japanese culture were: "They are polite"; "They take baths often, use chop-sticks and are noted for their politeness"; "We celebrated Boys' and Girls' Day for awhile"; or "Japanese eat fish products, bow a lot, take their shoes off when they enter the house."

They were also asked to identify Japanese traits they saw in themselves. These ranged from none to what many identified as typically Japanese qualities, such as being "hardworking," "quiet and shy," "polite," or organized and considerate. Common responses to this question were: "I believe that cleanliness is heavenly; everything should be in its own place"; and "Don't complain, do what you do best and you will make it. Be conscientious, polite and considerate of others and you will get far" (Thornton, 1983: 136).

Knowledge about Black culture was also more extensive with this group, with 87 percent having some opinion on the issue, such as, "I know about Black foods, for example chitterlings, hog-maws—they taste terrible. Some history, music and African New

Years called Kwanza." It was the exception not to have taken a class or read some book on an aspect of Black culture or history. "I know mostly about Black history 'cause I took some classes. I know about some Black leaders but that's about all" (Thornton, 1983: 136).

Dimension I to Dimension II: Issues of Transformation

Biracials and Americans still see themselves as disconnected from Blacks and other reference groups in their world. What separates Dimension I (American and Biracial) from Dimension II (Black and Multiethnic) is the experience of a significant identity crisis, a stage in their lives where their racial/ethnic heritage overwhelms other aspects of their being, leading them to question who they had thought they were. Very much like the stages of identity described by other authors (e.g., Cross, 1991; Kich, 1992), this reassessment of one's identity involves the informant becoming a subject instead of an object. For most of them there was an attempt to comprehend the themes of the historical and social epoch in which they live, for these condition one's view of the world and level of consciousness.

For P. Freire (1973), the transition from one dimension to the other can be described as moving from, in the relationship between Whites and people of color, what he called a "culture of silence." This silence entails the directive ability of Whites as the majority, and a dependent or controlled capacity of minorities. This dependency leads to the latter interjecting into their own identities cultural myths and lifestyles of Euro-America and producing a dual identity, a being not of self:

When I was growing up, I tried to look White, I guess. I used hair straighteners, avoided the sun—wore hats and long sleeves even when it was hot. I was always afraid someone would find out that I was Black. I thought Black women were, while not ugly, not as attractive as Whites, who were also better looking than Asians. The only problem was, was that I was not White. I would even avoid Black music. I felt I was on a treadmill, though I never questioned it until recently. (p. 191)

It got to the point when I said I have to stop being so concerned with what others thought about my being Black. (p. 128)

One day (really one year) I came to the realization that I was Black and Japanese whether I liked it or not; that was fact. But I realized I was not really Black and Japanese, only in a genetic, biological sense. I was not politically, identity-wise, a Black man or a Japanese man—I was more American, which means White middle class. When I finally came to the realization what that meant—that I was "White"—for who I was, I was angry yet glad. I now better understood who I was and who I want to be. The choice was mine. (p. 128)

I said hey!, this is really silly, Blacks are no worse or better than other people. Why should I be ashamed of that? (p. 128)

I had gone to schools until high school all White, except for me. I wondered what Blacks were like and what going to school with them would be like. I know I was prejudiced, so I was also interested in finding out more about me. I—during high school—transferred to a mixed school to find out. I stayed at a friend's house in the area to be eligible to do it. I lasted only one semester. I found I was really afraid for my safety. The school was very cliquish with Blacks on one side and Whites and Hispanics on another. I didn't want to be confined to any one group. But when I made White friends, I was told to leave them by Blacks; they threatened me, but didn't want me as one of them either. So I left. (p. 129)

The transition initially involved fitting in-between the groups. For some it stemmed from a desperate need to be wanted, to be part of a recognized group, albeit at times one different from one's parent group:

I was always painfully aware of my surroundings. I would constantly examine how people looked at me to see if they disliked me or even could tell I was mixed. (p. 125)

I would lie about what I was because I didn't think they would accept me for what I was, because I was Black. I would ask them what they thought I was. They thought I was Hawaiian. So I said, when they asked, my mother was Japanese and my father was Hawaiian. (p. 125)

I would talk "Black" when with Blacks and normal with others. The Black talk was "giving five" or saying "I'm hip" and other stereotypes I heard. I was never comfortable doing it; but I didn't feel comfortable not doing it either. At least if I did it, it made me appear more Black than I was. At least I think it did. (p. 125)

I knew this one bi [biracial] girl who was really pretty. She wanted to run for high school beauty queen. Ya know you can't run as a beauty queen but as a White, Hispanic or Black beauty queen. She wasn't any of the first two, so if she ran she would have to run for Black queen. So she did. But the Black girls got mad cause they said she wasn't Black so she couldn't run. They threatened her on the phone, said they would get her. But she still ran anyway and won. She was really brave. I think most of it was cause she wasn't a member of a racial clique and didn't act Black. (p. 125)

While the informants typically termed such an experience a "crisis," many revealed that such a word was actually a misnomer, for on average this "crisis" occurred over a period of years, ranging from three to four to over twenty and still in progress at the time of the interview. For most this transition began at the age of thirteen, which also is concomitant with the voyage into adolescence. So to the normal adolescent course of searching, groping, synthesizing, and questioning was added the dilemma of forming a multiethnic identity. Ultimately different things led them to a new identity:

I was tired of flipping back and forth, back and forth. I had to decide. (p. 124)

I was afraid to go out 'cause inevitably someone would ask "What are you," which usually only meant one thing to me. . . . "What race was I?" I had no choice but to change. (p. 124)

It wasn't so much a conscious change; it happened over time. As I found out more about myself, it seemed the less I knew. Then I found that I was comparing myself to a White-Western image. Then I started on the road I'm still on; I was able to find out who I was, not who I was told I was. (p. 124)

While at home it never really bothered or concerned me. When I went to college, it started to hit home. It was a period of Black Pride and anti-White and anti-Black feelings. I was thrown into the middle. 'Cause I lived in military environments, this was very strange to me. At first, I would identify as mixed; if asked I would not say Black, but Indian and Japanese. It was, ironically enough, after I fell in love with a White girl who was very much into things in African history, that I first started to form a real identity—one with Africa. (p. 124)

The naive, transitory stage of Dimension I can degenerate into a fantasized consciousness with its somewhat irrational view of the world. Or it can develop into critical consciousness, where one interacts with the empirical world, constantly testing and reshaping ideas. This is the essence of Dimension II.

Dimension II

Freire (1970a,b) would describe Dimension II as an altered, semi-intransitive state, when there is a noticeable rift between reality and what one had once believed to be reality. There is a transition from a fatalistic world in which the dominant culture and ideals found in Dimension I remain unquestioned, to a world in which one begins to distinguish what was not clear previously. This consciousness is inseparable from acting on reality. The entire process involves transforming one's worldview from being or existing in or being determined by the world as an object, to being with the world and going beyond mere existence to critical reflection and the transformation of one's environment as a subject (Freire, 1973, 1972a,b). There are two aspects to this dimension of Black–Japanese American identity: Black and multiethnic.

Blacks (14%)   Those at this stage actively strive to be Black, to associate primarily with Blacks (and at times with Whites and Japanese), to read Black history, and to frequent Black-owned stores and businesses. While they have no hatred of Whites, informants in this category are skeptical about them. Blacks have a seemingly better understanding of Japanese culture, although it too remains superficial; they identify with the Japanese in more abstract ways that are not that much different from those seen in people who hold biracial identities. While more moved to this dimension as part of a process of changing their identity, most feel that their position here is rather stable. For them race is extremely important, and they are thus very much oriented toward Black America, an attitude missing in biracials and Americans. They also comprehend the role of social constraints on their own and Black existence. For many of them who had been in Dimension I, this means that they withdraw from a world previously their cornerstone; they have entered another world. As one woman said of her previous habit of dating only White men, that was "in my other life" (Thornton, 1983: 137). Others expressed similar feelings:

I'm Black and sink or swim with the Blacks in America. (p. 131)

I'm Black too, so by definition [I] have Black attitudes, and must feel for Blacks. (p. 131)

I have historical links and some family ties to Black America.

We are all oppressed people. I am Black because I choose to be. And therefore what happens to Black people concerns me.

Black people are my people; they are my family. So as I would do for a family member in distress, so I would do for a brother. (p. 137)

Multiethnics (15%)   The essence of the multiethnic identity is that it remains in flux out of choice. The informants attempt to create a link with all three parts of their heritage—American, Black (some with Africa, some with a domestic focus) *and* Japanese (rather than Japanese American). They usually have a good knowledge of Africa, Black America, and Japan, although again, the last one is least well developed. They are very aware of the role economics, politics, and other social forces play in their lives, and thus see themselves in the same boat as other people of color.

> I used to believe I could be an American: blend in and be no different from everyone else. But, for me, what I was doing was laying the blame on myself and other people like me for successes or failures. So, Blacks were poor 'cause they were too lazy to join in the process. Japanese were better 'cause they were the "model minority." Now of course, I realize there are other societal factors to consider as well as other realities: Japanese have only partially made it, 'cause many are poor still. The pretty picture of America painted for me when I was younger is now starting to peel. (p. 164)

Nonetheless, many make the point that although they have come a long way in their thinking, their earlier "wrong-minded socialization" remains. Some talked about how they still preferred light-skinned partners, which they saw as stupid and unnecessary. As another said:

> everyday (well almost everyday), I find some way that I'm still distorted in. I find class and color related prejudices I still possess. At this stage, these are the most difficult of any I have had to face. How do you convince yourself that light-skin (it used to be White, so I am making progress) that light-skin is no more preferable than Black? I'm progressing but it creates a serious dilemma for me because I don't feel I can marry until it is solved. So maybe I will never marry. (p. 141)

Another also talked about how difficult it is to choose one's identity:

> If I identify as a Black Japanese American, that causes problems. . . . First, I don't know what that is exactly, or which, if any, group should be paramount. Second, others won't accept me as such, 'cause they want me to be one or another. They, . . . especially Blacks, want me to "prove" that I am Black and not a "Tom." I assume that this means that I do "Black" things, but I don't know what these things are, except to be with Blacks all the time. But this is unnatural to me; it is artificial, since I was brought up among many races. Trying to bring all these identities into one is made even more difficult because Blacks and Japanese have little contact and most refuse to have anything to do with each other. (pp. 164–65)

Multiethnics also have a more complex understanding than the other groups about their Asian heritage:

The Japanese are like one big family: the father—at least until WWII—was the emperor. The remainder of the nation was like his children. All relationships are vertically oriented, very much governed by protocol, status, roles and positions.

There is a relationship, that is pretty rigid, between elders and those younger, between teachers and students, and between even brothers and sisters, men and women. It shows up in their language and how they interact. (p. 135)

What was evident among those who identified with Black culture, but not among those who felt similarly about Japanese culture, was a political bonding that took various forms and included issues of minority status, common heritage, and group solidarity:

I understand being a minority.

I'm stereotyped too. I face it everywhere I go.

I face discrimination because of how I look, my color, my facial features, my hair, everywhere I go.

All minorities encounter similar treatment—it's all bad and due simply to the color of one's skin. (Thornton, 1983)

Conclusion

New work on Asian-heritage multiethnics has begun the process of moving beyond the one-dimensional discussion of racial identity to include other aspects of their lives. Nonetheless, the primary focus of this work has revolved around issues of off-Whiteness and identity with a psychological emphasis, or the internal dynamics of this experience. That Whiteness is highlighted in the emerging work is an artifact of the racial/ethnic heritage of those entering the field over the past few years. That this trend has also been linked to the very personal emphasis on researchers' own internal dynamics has meant that much of the work has focused on Asian American–White multiethnics who are in late adolescence–early adulthood.

Adolescence is a time of finding one's place by concentrating on one's individual identity development. However, with the emphasis on internal dynamics that arises from breaking from parental bonds and becoming one's own person, it is easy to miss the important role that other adults ("old people") and contexts play in one's life. While much of the newer work, which centers around this search for identity and self-definition (see Hall 1996), offers important insights, it ignores the forces that lie outside one's control and often influence that development.

The first author's dissertation (Thornton, 1983) suggests that we multiethnics are not as much our own persons as we may believe, for our parents' views on what it means to be multiethnic remain intact, as does the influence of other reference groups inside and outside our ethnic heritage. This lack of focus on family, historical, and social contexts remains an important limitation to work on multiethnic Asian Americans. Many important paths remain unexplored, especially the issue of minority-minority mixtures and family context (see, e.g., Comas-Diaz, 1994). But slighting minority-minority intersections avoids the current debate about the inadequacy of treating race and ethnic relations in White-versus-other terms, while ignoring the role of family denies our humanity. By minimizing these contextual concerns as we try to reveal the range of experiences among multiethnics, we run the risk of creating another set of stereotypes. We should expect more of ourselves.

Notes

1. Throughout this chapter, we employ the term "multiethnic" to refer to people who are racially *and* culturally (i.e., ethnically) mixed. In order to begin deconstructing the concept of race and acknowledging that mixed-racial-descent peoples of Asian backgrounds have rich cultural heritages and affiliations, we avoid applying the term "multiracial" or "racially mixed" to the subjects of our chapter. Rather, they are "multiethnics of Asian ancestry."

2. The following displayed quotations from informants, as well as the subsequent ones in this chapter, are from Thornton (1983). The page numbers in parentheses refer to that source.

Section III

Remapping Political Landscapes and Communities

On August 15, 1912, a German citizen named Albert Henry Young was denied the right to become a naturalized American citizen by federal District Court Judge Cushman of Washington state. As stated in the ruling, although Young had complied with all of the requirements for naturalization, he was not eligible "for the reason that he was not a white man." But, Albert Henry Young *was* of European heritage—his father was German. The problem was that his mother was Japanese, and, as ruled by Judge Cushman:

> In the abstractions of higher mathematics, it may be plausibly said that the half of infinity is equal to the whole of infinity; but in the case of such a concrete thing as the person of a human being it cannot be said that one who is half white and half brown or yellow is a white person, as commonly understood. (In *re Young*, 195 F. 645, 645–646 [W. D. Wash., 1912])

Fast-forward to October 29, 1997, when the U.S. Office of Management and Budget announces its decision to allow Americans to classify themselves as belonging to multiple racial/ethnic categories on the 2000 Census. This ruling came only after long and intense debate, led largely by organizations representing multiracial individuals, such as the AMEA (Association of MultiEthnic Americans), and traditional civil rights organizations, such as the NAACP (National Association for the Advancement of Colored People), Urban League, National Asian Pacific American Legal Consortium, and National Council of La Raza.

Dealing with the rights and status of mixed-race people has been an ongoing problem for Americans. "Who are they?," "Who should we allow them to be?," and "What do they mean to the rest of us?" are important questions in a society that has so much invested in the concept of race.

Throughout this volume we consider the significance of context to the lived experience of being mixed race. In the context of the contemporary United States, asserting a multiracial heritage frequently means engaging in the public struggle to define and control mixed-race people's identification and representation. In the third section of this book, we will consider several situations in which multiraciality becomes a site of both public and private contestation and negotiation. Considered is the variety of ways that multiracial people present and represent themselves in the public setting, and the anxieties and debates that so frequently develop in response.

Chapter 9, by Daniel A. Nakashima, looks at the subject of personal names as both public representations of people's racialized selves and personal representations of people's private identities. The testimonies of the individuals whom he spoke with show that multiracial people often become proactive in naming themselves, "with the goal not of 'staging' a false identity, but of representing themselves in a way that is closer to how they actually identify."

Chapter 10, by Darby Li Po Price, also looks at the presentation of self and how it interacts with the public's expectations and assumptions in the comedy industry in Hawai'i. Price finds that Hawai'i is both a multiethnic heaven and a multiracial hell, making multiraciality and multiethnicity a commodity that can be used both to critique and to uphold racist ideology.

Chapter 11, by Kieu Linh Caroline Valverde, and Chapter 13, by Rebecca Chiyoko King, focus in on the politics of identity for multiracial Asian Americans in two specific ethnic contexts. The multiracial Vietnamese men and women in Valverde's article make active choices about the ways in which they present themselves, mindful of the expectations, assumptions, and biases of their ethnic community. As she describes, mixed-race people in the Vietnamese American community tend to be from either very privileged or very underprivileged backgrounds. Therefore, a complex hierarchy of characteristics is used by community members to determine the class status of multiracial Vietnamese.

King looks at the presentation of self by mixed-race women who are involved in beauty pageants in the Japanese American community. She demonstrates how competing models of beauty, and definitions of what is authentically and essentially Japanese, are projected onto and struggled over at the site of multiracial women's bodies. Both Valverde and King find that the multiracial people in their studies are keenly aware of how this process of classification operates and have developed creative strategies for controlling its outcome.

Presentation of self and the politics of identity become even more complex with individuals and communities who are defined not only by race and ethnicity but also by sexuality. Teresa Williams-León, in Chapter 12, looks at gays, lesbians, and bisexuals of multiracial Asian descent, a group of individuals who are "multiply marginalized" in their many communities. She finds in this population that there are many "themes of convergences" among the negotiations, navigations, and performances of racial/ethnic identities and sexual identities, and that there is much to be learned by those who travel in multiple "no passing zones."

Finally, in Chapter 14, Cathy J. Tashiro considers how the racialized identification and classification of multiracial people are issues not only of politics, but also of physical health and medical care. She looks at the inconsistencies inherent in the medical system, which adheres to racialized categories as if they were biologically sound, and the multitude of ways in which this affects people of mixed race. Tashiro contends that the field of medicine and society in general need to "negotiate a space from which to consistently challenge the basis of racial classifications as reflecting a fundamentally racist epistemology while simultaneously giving every attention to the very real effects of racism on specific populations."

CHAPTER 9

A Rose by Any Other Name: Names, Multiracial/Multiethnic People, and the Politics of Identity

Daniel A. Nakashima

'Tis but thy name that is my enemy;
Thou art thyself, though not a Montague.
What's Montague? it is nor hand, nor foot,
Nor arm, nor face, nor any other part
Belonging to a man. O, be some other name!
What's in a name? that which we call a rose
By any other name would smell as sweet;
So Romeo would, were he not Romeo call'd,
Retain that dear perfection which he owes
Without that title. Romeo, doff thy name,
And for that name which is no part of thee
Take all myself.

WILLIAM SHAKESPEARE, ROMEO AND JULIET, ACT II, SCENE II

The Tao that can be told is not the eternal Tao.
The name that can be named is not the eternal name.
The nameless is the beginning of heaven and earth.

LAO TSU, TAO TE CHING

Introduction

On Sunday, August 18, 1996, in the heat of California's battle over the anti-affirmative action bill Proposition 209, the *Los Angeles Times* published an article by Scott Collins that reflects the political struggles that people of multiracial/multiethnic backgrounds often face when trying to identify themselves ethnically. Entitled "Playing the Name Game: Newscasters with Anglo-Sounding Last Names Are Switching to Ethnic Handles. It Gets Them Work—but Some Ask if It's Ethical," the article focuses on a small number of cases in which multiracial/multiethnic television news personalities have changed their professional names to indicate their Asian or Latino ethnic heritage: David Johnston became David Ono, switching from his father's surname to his mother's maiden name; Cathy Warren became Cathy Warren-Garcia and then Cathy Garcia, again, using her mother's maiden name; Gordon Gary became Gordon Tokumatsu, utilizing his grandmother's maiden name. As reflected in its title, the article claims that their new "ethnic" surnames are responsible for the broadcasters' occupational success. However, the newscasters themselves argue that their changed names didn't get them any jobs, but only brought them more attention and exposure. As Garcia said, "I think it (an ethnic-sounding name) helps in the very first stage of a job search, getting a news director to see your [audition] tape."

Interestingly, regardless of the fact that the people in the article had not fabricated new surnames but only switched to matrilineally derived family names, Collins shows how their choices have met with suspicion and harsh criticism from people in the news industry. For example, Chris Williamson, a White reporter from KTVL-TV in Medford, Oregon, is quoted as saying that name-changing is "almost like [a journalist] staging a story . . . . We all know TV can be a very shallow business at times. There are lots of people who have done this for surface reasons and not substantial reasons." Henry Mendoza, a member of the Chicano News Media Association and a former news director at KBAK-TV in Bakersfield, California, is described by Collins as a "vocal critic of name-changing" who would like to see news directors devise authenticity tests for those asserting ethnic surnames. According to Collins, Mendoza "blames both reporters and broadcast executives 'who play affirmative action as a numbers game. . . . There's what I consider unscrupulous intent on both sides.'"

A few weeks after the *Los Angeles Times* article appeared, Emil Guillermo, a columnist for the weekly periodical *AsianWeek,* wrote a follow-up piece on the issue, lamenting the fact that his "full-blooded" Chinese American friend (the person who had originally shown him the *Times* article) has been unable to find work as a newscaster, while ethnic posers like Ono and Tokumatsu have had success. He writes:

> The *Times* article was an eye-opener to me. No wonder people hate affirmative action. When people start playing loose with the rules, there is no integrity. Yeah, I know Carey [*sic*] Grant was really Archibald Leach, but we're talking about journalism here. Change a name? Would reporters stage a story too? But as long as it's okay for now, and since we really want an Asian American anchor back on CBS, why don't we just demand that Dan Rather's name be changed to Dan Fung. (Guillermo, 1995: 5)

Although multiracial identities are becoming more acceptable in the eyes and minds of many Americans (Bucholtz, 1995: 360), racial discourse in the United States still tends to demand that a multiracial person choose a single group with which to belong. As Michael Omi and Howard Winant (1994: 54) explain, in the United States, "classificatory standards . . . have imposed an either-or logic on racial identity." In other words, to be more than one race is like having your television both "on" and "off" at the same time—a metaphysical impossibility. In light of Collins's and Guillermo's articles, this kind of binary thinking extends beyond the site of ethnic labels to the realm of personal monikers as well. A Johnston cannot be an Ono. A Warren cannot be a Garcia.

The postmodern theorist Jean-François Lyotard (1984: 15) wrote that "even before he is born, if only by virtue of the name he is given, the human child is already positioned as the referent in the story recounted by those around him, in relation to which he will inevitably chart his course." David Johnston and Cathy Warren, like many multiracial/multiethnic people in the United States, were born into a dominant culture with a patriarchal naming tradition, and are expected to identify with the cultures and histories of their fathers' ethnic groups. Simultaneously, they are expected not to identify with any other ethnic groups, including their mothers'.[1] But, like David and Cathy, multiracial people have the opportunity to change the course of their "racial" destinies—to rename their affiliations by changing their personal names.[2] In doing so, they risk being accused of unethical behavior, of opportunism, and of a fraudulent attempt to "pass" for people who they are not.

What one calls oneself, personally as well as ethnically, is thus a site of political struggle, where conventional racial classifications can be transgressed, accepted, or ignored. Though a mere combination of words, the personal name can be an important site for the negotiation of the private and public selves. In *Feminist Practice and Poststructuralist Theory,* Chris Weedon (1987: 23) writes that

> we need to view language as a system always existing in historically specific discourses. Once language is understood in terms of competing discourses, competing ways of giving meaning to the world, which imply differences in the organization of social power, then language becomes an important site of political struggle.

Nowhere in America is the political struggle over language more intense than in the discourse about race, and for no group of people is the struggle to name the world more hotly contested than for multiracial people.

"What's in a Name?" Race, Ethnicity, and Identity, That's What

According to Omi and Winant (1994: 59), "we utilize race to provide clues about *who* a person is" (emphasis in original). We assume that if we can classify a person by his or her race or ethnicity, we will know something about that person's true self. One of the ways that we perform this classification is via a person's name. *The Ultimate Baby Name Book* states that

> naming is the first task of speech through which we differentiate one person or thing from all others. . . . Throughout the world, each child is assigned a sound or series of sounds that will be his or her name. Because that name is a part of the language of the child's parents, it imme-

diately identifies the child as belonging to a particular society. So our names identify us both as individuals *and as members of a group*. (Consumer Guide, 1995: 1 [emphasis added])

In a diverse society, we read names as signifiers not only of one's individual identity and membership in a particular family, but of one's membership in a particular racial, ethnic, and/or cultural group. Very often, when reading the name of a multiracial/multiethnic person for racial and ethnic clues, challenges arise both for the "reader" and for the multiracial/multiethnic person being "read." The "reader" might be confused by a name that does not "match" with the person's physical appearance or mannerisms, whereas the multiracial person might feel that his or her name is not an accurate reflection of his/her race, ethnicity, and identity.

Generally, in the United States surnames are derived patrilineally. This means that a person's last name usually represents only his or her father's family's ethnicity—and even then, only one branch of that family. Adoption, divorce, and births outside of legal marriage can disrupt the patrilineal naming structure, sometimes bringing in surnames that are not representative of an individual's ethnicity at all.[3] And, of course, in a society where married women are expected to take on their husbands' surnames, the majority of adult women spend much of their lives with last names that are not reflective of their family lineages. Therefore, a surname is by no means a reliable reflection of a person's ethnicity.

A more complete nominal representation of a person's ethnicity is dependent upon his or her "given names"—specifically, his or her first and middle names. However, everyday practice usually excludes the casual use of middle names, and first names are oftentimes chosen from the dominant language of the country where the person resides. Consequently, in the United States, a person will often have a recognizably "American" first name, while his or her more "ethnic" middle name remains hidden from everyday exposure. Another common naming practice is to give a child a name that can be pronounced as "ethnic" at home and as "American" outside of the home. Thus, as much as personal names can signify the ethnic origins of individuals, the rules of naming in the United States often provide inaccurate clues as to the person's racial and ethnic identity. Also, as none of us has any input on the names we are given at birth, personal names can run counter to how we identify, publicly and/or privately. Compounded with a racially ambiguous phenotype, a multiracial/multiethnic person's name can serve to confuse more than to clarify ethnic identity.

To explore the issue of names, ethnic identity, and multiraciality, I interviewed six people—three women and three men—each of whom has multiracial/multiethnic Asian heritage. At the time of the interviews, in the fall of 1997, all of the subjects were in their twenties and thirties and resided in southern California. With their permission, I have chosen to reveal the names of my subjects rather than give them pseudonyms, because of the importance of their actual names in the discussion.

During the interviews, I inquired as to how the subjects identify themselves ethnically, how they are identified ethnically by others, and how their names operate (or do not operate) as ethnic signifiers. This chapter is far from being an exhaustive and definitive discussion of the relationship between multiracial/multiethnic people and their names. For one thing, I have collected no data on people, like myself, who are multiracial but have an Asian surname. Nonetheless, this small sample reveals a range of diverse experiences surrounding names and ethnic identity.

Raced, Race-ing, Remembering: Multiracial/Multiethnic Individuals Talk About Their Names

In "Race-ing and Being Raced: The Critical Interrogation of 'Passing,'" Teresa Kay Williams (1997: 64) considers how multiracial/multiethnic people both "'do race' and get 'race done to them.'" That is to say, multiracial/multiethnic people navigate a racial existence where, in some instances, they identify themselves and their ethnicity to others—and in other instances, people classify them with no real interest in how they identify themselves. I found this to be very true of the individuals whom I interviewed, particularly with respect to their personal names. During her interview, Karla Kaori Stine gives examples of how others read all three of her names as signs of race/ethnicity/culture:

> And then they—I don't know how they—people make this leap. But they do. A lot of people make this leap. They see my name, . . . somehow they think I am from Maori. Yeah, because it looks like "Maori." And I don't know why they would think that, because my name looks like "Maori," I would be Kaori from Maori [laughs]. I don't know how they—but they do . . . They really are like, "Oh, does that mean you're from Maori?" I found that so many times, seriously. So, a lot of people think I am from Maori.
>
> So, my last name is Stine which is really weird because everyone thinks I'm Jewish. So then they really get confused. People always misspell Karla with a "C" and Stine they always spell, "E-I-N." . . . And people get Karla, like if they just, if I say my name is Karla, and they don't know me, . . . sometimes they think I'm Latina. Like, then, that's just confirmation that I'm Mexican. Like they thought I was Mexican, my name is Karla, "Oh, Kaaarrrla." So I have . . . the Mexican first name, the whatever middle name—Japanese middle name and the Maorian middle name—and the Jewish last name.

Thus Karla's first and middle names both function to solidify people's predetermined guesses about her racial/ethnic background—guesses that are probably based on Karla's phenotype, which is often read as Latina or Pacific Islander. Meanwhile, her last name, identified by others as Jewish, often confuses people, because it fails to support a hypotheses built on her appearance. Actually, Karla Kaori Stine is not Jewish, Latina, or Pacific Islander. When asked how she identifies herself ethnically, she responds, "I identify myself as . . . I guess I could say I'm a Hapa. But if people ask me just off the street what I am, I'll say, mostly I'll just say that I'm Black and Japanese. Yeah, just to simplify things."

"'Tis but Thy Name That Is My Enemy": Being "Raced" by Names

Debra J. Saunders (1998) has reported a relationship between "ethnic-sounding" names of political candidates and people's voting patterns. According to her, some poll analysts think that certain candidates have garnered fewer votes simply because of their names—in other words, they've suffered racial and ethnic discrimination based on how they appear on paper. For example, Saunders cites cases where Asian and Latino candidates, identified as such by their "ethnic" names, have received fewer votes than their White colleagues with similar voting records.

And, as names are not always reflective of people's ethnicities, a person can experience this "paper" prejudice toward groups of which he or she is not a member. Saunders (1998: A12) tells of a losing candidate, Coleman A. Blease, who might have experienced this sort of prejudice: "Some believe that Blease, who is white, lost votes because his name sounds black." Karla Kaori Stine shares a story of how she experienced a similarly negative reaction to her supposedly Jewish last name:

> I once was doing a paper on, I don't remember what the paper was on, I mean it had something to do with Black issues. I was calling the Nation of Islam. I was talking to this guy and everything was going well. I was getting information from him and he asks me what my name was and just, you know, clueless, I was like, "Oh, my name is Karla Stine." And the guy hung up on me. And I didn't know what was up until I realized, "Oh, he probably thinks, like, I'm some Jewish, White person." You know like it—I mean, there's a slight chance that that isn't true. But I think it was, 'cause he heard my last, . . . because my last name is very obviously Jewish . . . , if you just hear it.

The possibility of being ethnically and racially misidentified based on how his name appears on paper concerns John-Clay Keola Morris, especially in terms of his future career in medicine:

> I know there are people who are very concerned about the ethnicity of their doctor. They do not want to see a Black doctor. They do not want to see a Hispanic doctor. They don't want to see a woman doctor. Hopefully, in the next twenty years that will change. Um, and, sure, it may be awkward for people if they see that they're going to get Doctor Morris, and they meet me . . . and they look at me and they're the type of person that categorizes—that have thick lines between Asian and Caucasian groups. So, that may be an issue, and I haven't figured out what I'm going to do about it.

When asked to describe his ethnicity, he says:

> If I had to describe it succinctly, it would be, umm, Hawaiian/Japanese/Caucasian, because I identify most with those three cultures. If you count Caucasian as a culture [laughs], which it really isn't. But, uh, Hawaiian/Japanese/American.

"O, Be Some Other Name!": Race-ing Yourself with a Name

To prevent misunderstandings, multiracial/multiethnic people will sometimes employ a middle name or a mother's maiden name to make visible a part of their background that would have otherwise remained hidden behind conventional usage of one's first name and patrilineal surname. Like the newscasters in the *Los Angeles Times* article, most of the individuals whom I spoke with have considered ways to attempt to affect how others "race" them by their names. Steven Masami Ropp had, at one point, considered changing his last name from his father's name to his mother's maiden name (Suwa):

> I thought about changing my last name. Umm, I probably most seriously considered it in college, as an undergrad. I guess I felt like—in particular at that point it was like—I think that I was going through my own identity process and thinking about who I was and wanting to be . . . . I felt like I grew up in the community, but then people didn't always . . . see me as being Japanese American or being part of the community. People assume that I wasn't. And I felt like I wanted them to know that I was Japanese American. Because, as I said earlier, a lot of times they couldn't tell. So I felt like if I change my last name to my mother's maiden name, then maybe people would, you know, have an easier time seeing me as being Japanese American.

Steven eventually decided not to change his last name, partially because of the hassle of a legal name change and partially because he felt that his mother's maiden name might not be effective in signifying "Japanese" to others. Instead, he began to use his middle name, Masami, to indicate his connection to his Japanese American family and to the community that he grew up in. As he explains,

> When I first started to do it [use Masami], I was doing stuff in Asian American Studies, and I think I did recognize that, well, I felt like that, umm, I consider myself to be Japanese American but sometimes people don't know that. And so, if I put the name, then it gives them a clue.

Using personal names to give people "clues" about ethnicity is described by other interviewees as well, as Karla Kaori Stine describes:

> Actually, I started really using my middle name. I never did before. . . . I guess because I want people to know that I'm part Asian or part . . . I've always been, you know, . . . on any document, "Karla Stine." And at UC Berkeley, . . . everything you have has your middle name on it. . . . And I kind of got used to that and I liked that. I mean, everything I have says, "Karla Kaori Stine," 'cause that's the way they do it at school. . . . But, like, even this past summer, when I was applying for positions, no matter what the position was, it always said Karla Kaori Stine. I had my whole—my full name. And then . . . especially working with Asian groups . . . I used my whole, I made them use my whole name. [You use it with Asian groups to indicate . . .] That, yeah, . . . I'm part Asian. But . . . now, for just, like, all purposes, I guess, . . . Karla Stine seems so, it seems lacking. . . . I mean both for my own purposes and for identification purposes, in order to be identified correctly. . . . And, of course, there's going to be tons of people who will see my middle name and won't realize that it's a Japanese name. But there will be tons of people who will. So, yeah, I think, even just for the people who will know, just to give them a clue. . . . Again, sort of, um, put it out there from the beginning for them.

"And for That Name Which Is No Part of Thee": Remembering One's Past Through One's Name

When I was growing up, I wrote, "John Morris". . . . And now I write my full name. [Why did you change?] Why did I . . . ? I think because more people started to address me as John-Clay. Um, and, as I grew older and had more experiences in Hawaii, I felt more of a connection towards the island, and I saw it as something very significant in my life. And, it's something I'd like to stay attached to. . . . And, if I don't sign my name—I'm not going to ever forget it— . . . but, um, it would make me feel that I still have some connection to that, even though I don't live in Hawaii and I don't belong to a Hawaiian club. But, that may be something I'd like to do when I get older.

John-Clay Keola Morris began to use his "ethnic" middle name when his ethnic identity started to shift. He explains that using his middle name is a means to remember his Hawaiian past and feel his connection to his history in Hawaii. Here, an ethnic name is employed less as an indicator to others than as a personal pathway toward recognizing and honoring one's cultural heritage.

Names are also used to remember certain family members. For example, Steven Masami Ropp's middle name is derived from the first name of his grandmother, Masae, to whom he is very close:

That name, you know, has significance for me in terms of my connection to my family, . . . not only my family, but, specifically, my grandmother. And, umm, you know, I feel like it is, sort of, my connection to being Japanese American . . . having a Japanese middle name. . . . Given my specific circumstances, the name, you know, does have some meaning for me.

Joseph Jiro Clayton is also named for a family member who has special significance for him. His middle name, Jiro, means "second son" in Japanese, but was given to him, a first child, because his uncle Benny Jiro Iha was the only member of his mother's family who didn't disown her when she married an African American. Thus, Joseph says when asked if his name fits him,

Yeah, it's me. Um, the Japanese, you know, part, they don't normally see it. All they know is my center initial is "J." Whenever I sign anything, my legal signature is "Joseph J. Clayton." And, I always insist on that . . . because, yes, there is that, that Japanese, you know, part. And, so, if they ask, I tell them. But normally they don't ask. They . . . no one really knows why I insist on that center initial, but I always do.

"Thou Art Thyself, Though Not a Montague": Concluding Remarks on Naming and Mixed Race

I would like to baptize myself under a new name, a name more like the real me, the one nobody sees. Esperanza or Lisandra or Maritza or Zeze the X. Yes. Something like Zeze the X will do.

SANDRA CISNEROS (1984: 11)

Our names, being the gift of others, must be made our own.

RALPH ELLISON (1995: 192)

Maria P. P. Root (1992: 7), in her book on multiracial people in the United States, writes:

Whereas one of the breakthroughs of the civil rights movement was empowerment of American racial minority groups by self-naming (Helms, 1990), this process is just beginning among multiracial persons. In essence, to name oneself is to validate one's existence and declare visibility. This seemingly simply [*sic*] process is a significant step in the liberation of multiracial persons from the oppressive structure of the racial classification system that has relegated them to the land of "in between."

Each person's name is a construction of meanings that are relevant both for that person and for others. Many multiracial/multiethnic people find that they are not satisfied with the meaning that their name effects. Some of these people become proactive in naming themselves—attempting to "race" themselves before they are "raced" by others. All of the people whom I interviewed described times in which they have employed middle names, maiden names, or pseudonyms, with the goal not of "staging" a false identity, but of representing themselves in a way that is closer to how they actually identify. For some respondents, this has meant asserting a name so that their ethnicity is more visible to others. For others, utilizing a name or an initial functions as a symbol for their private remembering of family and ethnic heritage. By presenting and concealing parts of their names, multiracial/multiethnic people attempt to gain some control over the process by which they are racially and ethnically categorized. But in a society intent on policing its racial and ethnic borders, these people—people like the newscasters, people like the ones I spoke with—are frequently viewed as illegal aliens, crossing into territory in which they do not belong and are not welcome.

Notes

Acknowledgments: The author would like to express his utmost gratitude to the respondents who shared their stories as well as their time to make this chapter happen. Ten thousand pages could not have captured their thoughts and feelings, and I hope these few pages do them justice. Also, a big shout-out to Carlos Lemus and Jason Howard, who read early drafts of this paper and helped me to shape it. And, most of all, all my love and thanks to my sister, whose patience is beyond my comprehension. Thanks, everybody.

1. The meanings of race, ethnicity and culture often overlap in the United States, and are used more or less interchangeably throughout this paper.
2. The same holds true for so-called monoracial people. Think of how Malcolm Little changed his last name to X, thereby charting a new course against the practice of using a surname inherited from White slaveowners.
3. There are many other circumstances that can disrupt the patrilineal naming traditions of mainstream American culture. Slavery, for example, has left a legacy of surnames that are not derived from family relations. Immigration, too, has left many Americans with names that were taken as a means toward a swift assimilation or that were given to them mistakenly by immigration officials.

CHAPTER 10

Multiracial Comedy as a Commodity in Hawaii

Darby Li Po Price

Hawaii is a chop suey nation—Portagee, Pake, Buddha Head, Sole, Kanaka, Haole[1]—all mixed up. Nobody is in the majority here. We are all part of at least one minority group. Some of us are part of several minority groups. And we all laugh at ourselves. This is healthy.

—DE LIMA, 1991B: V

Comic celebrations of mixed race run counter to the dominant conception of mixed-race identity as a tragic situation (Price, 1997, 1998). Drawing upon extensive ethnographic research and interviews, this chapter analyzes the mediation of multiracial identities among comedians of partial Asian and Pacific Islander descent in Hawaii. What role does multiethnic humor play in the conception of Hawaii as a "multiethnic paradise"? How do cultural, national, political, and economic forces shape performances of ethnicity? Why are certain identities in comedy privileged over others? How do Hapa (multiracial) comedians subvert or cater to dominant racial paradigms and relations?

Theories of Ethnic Humor

Theories diverge on whether ethnic humor functions as an expression of hostile aggression toward groups (Dorinson & Boskin, 1988) or creates a sense of "we-ness" that melts differences and tensions between them (Lowe, 1986). Paradigms of race and ethnic relations that conceptualize ethnicity in terms of separate groups vying for power often view mixed marriages and mixed offspring as the natural butts of jokes due to their ambiguous status on the periphery of established groups (Davies, 1990). However, multiethnic identities are given a central rather than peripheral status in ethnic humor in Hawaii, where no one group is the majority and interracial marriage is widely accepted. Approaching humor from a multiethnic perspective can challenge dominant conceptions of racial and ethnic identities based on clearly demarcated, binary, singular, and fixed entities.

Establishing "We-ness" in a Multiethnic Paradise

> We in Hawai'i buck the common sense when we celebrate those among us whose ethnicity, contrary to common-sense appearances and claims, is not clear. This cherished paradox is reflected in the widespread intermarriage and the total lack of stigma attached to the ethnic or racial in-betweens, the "hapas" as they are called. The "hapas" are also represented in the local jokelore when in making fun of crosses between stereotypes we demonstrate the idiocy of taking ethnicity seriously: "What do you get when you cross a Portagee with a Pake? Someone who saves all his money, but can't remember why." (Blake, 1996: 8)

Ethnic joking is credited for promoting good-humored relations between groups in Hawaii. According to comedian Pat Morita (1985), "laughter or aka aka in Hawaii is called the best medicine necessary on an island with mixed ethnic groups." Ethnic identities are routinely ridiculed to undermine beliefs that any group is superior. According to comedian Frank De Lima (De Lima & Kolohe, 1980), "our ability to laugh at the absurdity of setting any one race above another is an excellent defense against bigotry." University of Hawaii professor Fred Blake (1996: 7) believes humor about various ethnic groups contributes to a cohesive "in-group" local identity that dissolves intergroup animosities: "The joking is 'interethnic' in that each group takes its turn as the butt of a joke. The joke is not so much on a particular group as it is on all the groups. The joke is on the thing that separates local people into different groups, that is to say, the joke is on ethnicity itself."

Integrated worksites, neighborhoods, and families in Hawaii have resulted in a relatively high degree of familiarity across ethnic groups (Takaki, 1983). Supposedly, this prevents the residents of Hawaii from taking ethnic stereotypes seriously. De Lima, perhaps the best known of Hawaii's tourist-trade comedians, utilizes stereotypical representations of ethnic groups in his act, where he makes such statements as, "Chinese like ramen, Japanese like Kikomen, and Filipinos like Doberman" (quoted in Robello, 1995). He describes the close relations among people of different ethnic groups as being conducive to the enjoyment of local ethnic humor: "A lot of us are mixed ancestry, grew up in neighborhoods where we had grandma and grandpa with accents. Very few of us grew up without liking this local humor" (quoted in Robello, 1995).

And yet some residents of the islands do not appreciate this kind of humor. According to De Lima, those who place their specific ethnicities above a collective local identity are most critical of his jokes: "There are all these people coming in who think of themselves as specifically ethnic, for example, 'Filipino' instead of 'Hawaiian.' These newcomers have the most problems with my humor" (interview, 1996). But some of De Lima's critics are not "newcomers"; a comedian of Native Hawaiian ancestry, who wishes to remain anonymous, feels that De Lima "is not doing culturally Hawaiian comedy because, while Hawaiians commonly make fun of themselves in their humor, they don't superficially play the stereotypes" (interview, 1995).

Still, many would argue that the social and cultural environment in Hawaii is such that residents don't take ethnicity as seriously as they do on the mainland. In fact, "political correctness" is viewed by some as a mainland cultural standard that is being imposed upon local culture. But the ability to laugh at ethnicity does not seem to translate into a decrease in the importance of ethnicity in Hawaii. While some scholars believe ethnic jokes hasten "assimilation" and "Americanization" by discouraging ethnic differences (Lowe, 1986), jokes about multiethnicity in Hawaii often celebrate a pluralistic maintenance of ethnicity. For example, comedian Rap Reiplinger (1995) asserts that his multiracial identity is a microcosm of Hawaii's:

> Me, I'm living proof of the people of Hawaii. You know what my nationalities is: Huh? Well, just by looking what your think? Huh? I'll tell you. Me I'm Hawaiian, Chinese, I'm Japanese, I'm Portuguese, I'm Haole, I get Puerto Rican, I get Spanish, oh I got all of them pieces jammed up inside of me.

Establishing ancestral ties to many ethnic groups is often utilized by comedians as proof of an authentic "local" identity. It can also function as a precursor to the telling of jokes about multiple ethnic groups and combinations. Interestingly, comedians of multiple ancestries seem to have greater license to joke about groups beyond their own heritage, perhaps because they do not clearly belong to any one group.

Challenging Multiethnicity Through Humor

In a "multiethnic paradise," a Hapa comedian can use humor to challenge notions about race and ethnicity. Mocking dominant beliefs or expectations about people of mixed descent is a common theme among comedians of mixed heritages. One common stereotype of Hapas is that they are the "best of both worlds." As a playful counterpart to James A. Michener's (1959) description of multiethnic Hawaiians as the "Golden Men," De Lima (1991b: 96) combines Asian, Polynesian, and European names to create unsavory Hapa "characters Left Out of James Michener's Novel About Hawaii: Kimo Therapy, Saimin Legree, Terry Yaqui, Pua Ting, Lei Down, Masa Kerr, Lynn Ching, Kim Chee, and Mo Chee." Such unappealing "Eurasian" names are incongruous with the common image of Hapas as beautiful people.

Challenging the major tenets of the dominant racial paradigm, such as the binary classification of White and non-White, or the rule of hypodescent, can provide grounds for mixed-race humor. Comedian Andy Bumatai, who is of German, French, Hawaiian, and Filipino heritage, believes common language about race is more damaging than jokes: "I was once described as non-White, which is a subtle way of saying White is the norm, and non-White not the norm . . . Language is more dangerous than ethnic jokes. [This is seen,] for example, [in] saying 'minority' for non-Whites when Whites are the real minority" (interview, 1995). As a reflection of his multiethnicity, the cover of his 1994 audio recording *Andy Bumatai: Stand Up Comic 1984–1994* features his face in Escher-style fragmentation. Both Hawaiians and mainlanders who classify him according to the racial binary of "White" and "non-White" are the targets of his humor. He recounts the irony of a Native Hawaiian woman in Georgia who called him "White" to insult him and said to him, "How come you talkin' li' dat bro? . . . Bust out da pidgin . . . Aw, you jus wan haole" (Bumatai, 1994). Then, during a film audition in California he encountered covert racism from a woman who had a card with "non-White" written in under his name:

> I asked, "What is this 'non-White' thing?" She was like, "That's not official or anything, that's just my personal notes. So don't worry about it." It's interesting to be categorized by what you're not, because here [in Hawaii] we categorize so strongly by what you are. Only because it's easier. The "not" thing is very strange. Imagine if we did it that way: "Hey, bro, you know Charlie, the guy who's not Chinese, Filipino, Samoan, or Portagee?" "No, I don't know him. What else isn't he?" (Bumatai, 1994)

When Bumatai tells the woman that "it's interesting to be categorized by what you are not," she becomes upset and says, "Well, you're not White, so you might as well face it!"

Ironically, when Bumatai returned to Hawaii, the local "moks" with whom he had grown up wanted to know why he had been going to the mainland and asked, "What you be gettin' White?" His response is:

> Yes, I'm trying to face it. It's like living in the middle of one of those Escher paintings. You know those paintings. You know those paintings where it starts off like a bird and it finally turns into a fish and right in the middle you don't really know what it is? That's like me in there—going aaahhh!!! (Bumatai, 1994)

In addition to expressing frustration at being erroneously racialized on both the mainland and Hawaii, Bumatai discusses the politics of race and ethnicity when he tells of initially enjoying career success as a local favorite, then being accused of selling out when he moved to Los Angeles for a few years.

Simplifying Multiethnicity and the Marketing of Comedy

Spickard and Fong (1995) found that multiethnic Pacific Islanders in Hawaii frequently simplify their reported ethnic backgrounds, omitting certain aspects of their heritage. In these simplifications, European heritage is the most likely to be omitted, Asian heritage second most likely, and Pacific Islander heritage least likely. Similarly, most comedians of partial Hawaiian descent market themselves as "Hawaiian." One likely reason is that, in Hawaii there is a certain prestige in being able to claim Native Hawaiian heritage. But a second reason is that comedians in Hawaii find that both mainlanders and locals are more interested in them and their comedy if they present themselves as

"Hawaiian." Comedian Bo Irvine, who is of Portuguese, Filipino, Scots, and Hawaiian descent, observes that people never paid much attention to him until they found out that he was part Hawaiian. "Then," he says, "all of a sudden, they thought I was cool and wanted to talk to me" (interview, 1995).

A good illustration of how multiethnic identity can be simplified according to situation is the career of comedian Andy Bumatai, who is of German, French, Filipino, and Hawaiian descent. Bumatai's *All in the Ohana* television show, which aired in 1980, featured Bumatai as all five members of a pidgin-speaking native Hawaiian family torn by generational and cultural differences, and brought together in their struggle to keep their land (Harada, 1981). Yet, the widely circulated local fact book *Fax to Da Max* (Simonson et al., 1985: 104) includes "Andy Bumatai (née Bumatay) Comedian/Actor" under the category of "20 Filipinos who made good." Simultaneously, the promotional material for the television series *Marker* describes "native Hawaiian, Andy Bumatai [who] portrays Pipeline, the loopy local" (Online, 1995). Bumatai explains that "I'm like an ethnic chameleon. [Having] . . . many different backgrounds . . . is an advantage. . . . Most places I go, there is a group that will embrace me" (interview, 1995). Still, he has expressed mixed feelings about how people often identify him according to his non-European ancestry and overlook his European heritage.

Comedians can assert their Hawaiian identity in a variety of ways, such as by referring to their ancestry or to their "local" upbringing, by expressing a certain political ideology, by speaking pidgin English, or by using a "Hawaiian"-sounding name. Frank De Lima establishes his Hawaiian ethnicity through his local birth, upbringing, and Hawaiian ancestry. On his first album, *Frank De Lima Presents a Taste of Malasades* (1978), he introduces himself as having been "born on the rugged slopes of Punchbowl Crater to humble parentage of mostly Portuguese descent," and explains that he "became well-versed and knowledgeable in the customs of island cultures" through his "frequent contacts with Japanese and Chinese neighbors and by watching the Filipino fiesta" every weekend. According to De Lima, "the Hawaiian came naturally, of course, by ways and means of pure Kanaka blood having been transfused down through his genetic heritage, three-quarters pint." In his *Frank De Lima's Joke Book* (1991b), he further establishes his Hawaiian identity for his mainland audience by using a photograph of himself in a Hawaiian shirt on the cover and in the chapter "Da Mixed Plate," which opens with his song "I'm Local."

Not wanting to be pigeonholed as an "ethnic comedian," Andrew Bumatay adopted the stage name of Andy Line during his first year as a stand-up comedian in 1976–77 (Ursul, 1977). Then, influenced by the resurgence in local ethnic pride, which became a major cultural movement in the 1970s, he switched his last name to Bumatai to make it appear more Hawaiian. Bumatai won strong local support through humor that asserts ethnic pride and Native Hawaiian causes: "I'm one-quarter Filipino. My father is Filipino/Hawaiian . . . . He loves to clean his yard but he no mo' land" (Pescador, 1995).

A firm pro–Native Hawaiian position and anti-*haole* stance have made comedian Bu La'ia a favorite among locals. La'ia has a penchant for political satire, and gained local celebrity status through his parodic campaign for state governor (although it was only a joke, he received 5,784 votes). In fact, "Bu La'ia"—a pidgin pronunciation of "Bull Liar"—is a name he invented for the campaign to make a statement about the credibility of politicians. Jacques Yerby (personal communication, 1996) asserts that "the current king of comedy is Bu La'ia. He's a pretty high blood quantum Hawaiian and is funny as hell." Recognizing the importance of "blood quantum" for establishing Hawaiian identity, La'ia (1995a: 105) makes an imaginative multiracial Hawaiian autobiographical comment when he says, "Bu La'ia was born to Papa La'ia (who claims to be Duke Kahanamoku's son) and Mother Teresa." Acknowledging "blood quantum" as a site for questioning authenticity, he emphasizes a desire to be identified as Hawaiian over his other heritages. La'ia (1995a: 42) writes: "You an' five thousand oddah people like inquire about da same thing. How much Hawaiian am I. OK, one mo' time: Bu La'ia is 100 percent Hawaiian, 10 percent Chinese, 5 percent Haole, an' 3 percent Samoan."

Despite assertions that culture is more important than race in Hawaii, comedians find themselves judged in large part on the basis of their racial ancestry and phenotypic features. La'ia's "Hawaiian" image is visually enhanced through photographs on his book and tapes that feature him with black hair locks and a missing front tooth. However, the hair is a wig, worn over his own short brown hair, and the "missing tooth" is actually black ink applied over a real tooth. In his comedy, La'ia also makes references to his "puka teeth" (teeth with holes in them) and long locks. His persona of a pidgin-speaking, homeless, underclass Hawaiian underdog contrasts with his actual background as an articulate Stanford University graduate. According to comedian Kehau Biajo (interview, 1996), "while some believe La'ia plays up to the worst image of Hawaiians, and are critical of his coarse, low-class Hawaiian image and militantly anti-*haole* stance . . . [others] . . . give him credit for dealing with issues such as sovereignty, government, or social injustice in ways that other comedians won't touch."

Multiethnic comedians who appear to be phenotypically White must make an added effort in asserting their Hawaiian heritage. For example, the back cover of Kent Bowman's fourth record *No Talk Stink!* explains:

> This album is a product of Bowman's French Quarter (the other three quarters are Hawaiian, Scottish and English).
>
> When he made his first recordings in pidgin English, Bowman managed to preserve a certain amount of anonymity behind cartoon album jackets . . . Now, for the first time, it seems to him to be reasonably safe that his face and all (almost) be put on public display on the front of an album. No longer will he find himself in situations like when he went "to the country" one time to entertain at a benefit: a covey of Hawaiian ladies took one look and said loudly, "as not heem, as a ******* haole!"

In short, Bowman had avoided revealing his physical appearance (as well as making references to his ancestries) on his first three records, because he assumed he would be labeled a *haole*. Only after he became well-established as a local comedian, through recordings of his pidgin-English humor, was he willing to show photos of himself and discuss his ancestry.

Euro-American Domination in a Multiethnic Paradise

There is a whole agency that perpetuates that ethnic crap—that aloha crap. When anything starts with something like "aloha"—it's a false creation used to sell a Hawaii that never was for the tourism industry. (comedian Andy Bumatai, interview, 1995)

Here in Hawaii the ethnic melting pot can be more of a boiling pot—it's a veneer of niceness—which is very Asian—but an undertow of racial tension. (comedian Jaz Kaner, interview, 1995)

While race relations are generally viewed as being less polarized in Hawaii than on the mainland, many note rising levels of intolerance, hate crimes, and racial/ethnic inequality (McLaurin, 1993). Some argue that these contemporary social problems are extensions of the European and American hegemony and racism that has dominated the islands since the inception of colonial relationships in the early 1800s (Odo, 1993). While contemporary Euro-American domination may not be as openly authoritarian as it was in the past, the political economy of tourism dominates the livelihood of the islands. H. K. Trask (1990: 11) writes that the fact that Hawaii has "6 1/2 million tourists annually—over 30 for every Native Hawaiian"—creates "a hostage economy where tourist employment means active participation in their own degradation." In colonial times, the missionaries were known to prohibit the use of native languages as well as the most humorous feature of hula comedy—overt sexual references. Today, Hapa comedians are rewarded for presenting their identities and their humor in ways that appeal to tourists' desires.

The tourist-based economy of Hawaii strongly influences what types of comedy are commercially viable. Most comedy clubs are housed in large hotel complexes in Honolulu and cater primarily to Euro-American tourist audiences. Tourism inhibits the expression of local and Native humor, in that a mainland audience is unable to understand or appreciate pidgin language, local cultural references, and local perspectives. In addition, in order to appeal to mainland tourists, comedians must tone down the political, pro-Native, and anti-Caucasian sentiments that are a common part of local and Native Hawaiian culture.

In fact, comedians who are openly critical of tourism and Euro-American domination of the islands have been blacklisted from the tourist-oriented clubs. Bu La'ia and Andy Bumatai were banned from the Honolulu Comedy Club, according to comedian/club manager Bo Irvine, for "personal and political reasons" (interview, 1995). And I saw comedian La'ia have his microphone turned off in midperformance and be told to leave the stage at another club for saying, "Why don't you go home, fuckin' *haole?*"

Comedians with local sensibilities find that audio recordings offer a more conducive market for their material than do the comedy clubs. Local socioeconomic, cultural, and political issues are expressed more freely in comedy records, tapes, and CDs (some come with a "Ha'aole Advisory—Local Lyrics" sticker), as heard in songs such as the 2 Local Boyz' "Home in Da Housing," the 3 Local Boyz' "Me So Hungry," Augie Tulba's "Illiteracy Hotline," and Bu La'ia's "Hawaiian Sovereignty Song."

Tourists seem to prefer comedians who can represent Hawaiian-ness without being "too" Native Hawaiian. While audiences may be reluctant to accept comedians who look "too White" as authentically Hawaiian, partial Caucasian ancestry can serve as a point of identification between multiracial comedians and Caucasian audiences. As comedian Mel Cabang explains, "I tell *haoles* in the audience so they won't feel bad I'm part *haole*. I'm Portuguese—that's *haole*—and Pilipino, so I'm a '*jalepino*' [pronounced "*haole-pino*"]" (quoted in Robello, 1995). Multiracial comedians with Caucasian appearances can assert Pacific Islander ancestry to bridge the gap between Caucasians and Islanders. Comedian Bill Sage jokes, "Most people don't realize I'm Samoan. It's because I'm albino. My favorite Samoan/Irish pub [is] right down on Merchant Street—OataPali's. Like for Christmas they sing 'It was the night before Christmas and all through the Pali, we got plenty corn beef, and oh my golly!'" (quoted in Robello, 1995).

Freddie Morris was an immensely popular local ventriloquist and musical comedian, greatly loved for his abilities to bring Moku Kahana, his "Native Hawaiian" dummy, to life.[2] When Morris first began working clubs, he presented himself as a local Hawaiian, accompanied by a White dummy with red hair and freckles named Archie. Under the advice of his manager, Morris switched roles with Archie and replaced him with the darker Moku:

I needed a Hawaiian dummy because I didn't look Hawaiian enough. Although I would explain we both grew up in Hawaii, neither of us looked Hawaiian enough to be speaking pidgin. Besides, people had difficulty understanding pidgin anyway . . . . I had to learn to enunciate. People hear me now and say, "You don't sound like you're from here, you have an accent." It's because I had to learn. (interview, 1996)

Having four teeth knocked out and his guitar broken by an offended audience member taught Morris to become tactful in his act. By speaking through Moku, he found that he was able to get away with more socially and politically critical comments than if he had said them on his own.

As the regularly featured comedy act at Don Ho's Waikiki Beachcomber Hotel, Morris began with, "I'm one-quarter Japanese, and Italian, German, French, and a little bit of Cherokee American Indian, and I grew up in Hawaii." Identifying his mixed heritage gave him the license to joke about different ethnic groups, particularly the Japanese. Comedian Jaz Kaner explains that "Freddie Morris gets away with doing all kinds of impersonations of Japanese because he's part Japanese" (interview, 1995). Hapa jokes about the Japanese are viewed by some as a response to their rejection by the Japanese in both Hawaii and Japan (Spickard, 1997). But jokes about the Japanese can also create a bond between comedians, locals, and tourists from the mainland, through the venue of American nationalism.

Morris prefaced his jokes about the Japanese by saying, "My ex-wife was Japanese; that's why I hate the Japanese." He would tell the waitress, "Bring Ed a drink, put it on the tab of the Japanese guy that owns the hotel, and tell him thanks for bombing our harbor." Stuffing a large potato in the crotch of his pants, Morris joked, "I used to be Japanese, but I quit because I found that [pointing to his crotch] was a problem." Morris's manager, Bernie Harrison, recalls that "people liked the Japanese jokes, especially when he put on the glasses with the Japanese eyes," and "they always laughed when he stuck the potato down his pants" (personal correspondence, 1998).

Conclusion

Ethnic comedy in Hawaii can both transcend and play upon the tensions that exist among racial/ethnic groups. These tensions are a reflection of the fact that Hawaii itself is both a multiethnic paradise *and* an ethnic boiling pot. In this kind of complex environment, multiethnic comedians are able to use their humor and their identities in many different ways: for example, as evidence of Hawaii's greater tolerance for diversity and intermarriage, as a way to critique racial inequality and to challenge racial ideology, and as a license for making fun of a wide variety of racial/ethnic groups. In the final analysis, regardless of how a comedian uses his or her multiethnicity in his/her humor, the celebrated status of mixed heritage in Hawaii's jokelore is an enormous contrast to America's historical marginalization of multiracial identity as only a "tragic" situation.

Notes

1. Portagee = Portuguese; Pake = Chinese; Buddha Head = Japanese; Sole = Samoan; Kanaka = Hawaiian; Haole = Caucasian.

2. Morris suffered from a fatal seizure disorder. Before his death in September 1998, he and other comedians performed at a concert held in his honor. The show is available on video and CD as *Hawaii's Comedy Stars*. (Quiet Storm, Kaneohe, Hawaii).

CHAPTER 11

Doing the Mixed-Race Dance: Negotiating Social Spaces Within the Multiracial Vietnamese American Class Typology

Kieu Linh Caroline Valverde

Introduction

Growing up mixed race within the Vietnamese American community,[1] I have come to realize that I occupy a particular space that simultaneously incorporates a Vietnamese American experience with that of a separated/marginalized "other" within that experience. This "space" reflects my history as an immigrant from Viet Nam and as a second-generation mixed-race woman (having a Spanish/Vietnamese mother and a Vietnamese father).

All of my life, I have been confronted with "What are you?" questions, both from Vietnamese Americans and from other Americans. I have found that, although these questions seem innocent enough—just a curious passerby, wanting to place me somewhere, anywhere—they are deliberately chosen to assist in that person's classification of me. In the Vietnamese American community, people depend on the "What are you?" questions not only to racially categorize a multiracial person, but also to place him or her within a social class hierarchy.

I, and others like myself, have learned to negotiate our identities within the complex class typology that exists for multiracial Vietnamese within the Vietnamese American community. I liken this dynamic labeling process to a dance. How have we complied with and how have we resisted such classifications?

In this paper, I will explore the mixed-race class typology that exists in the Vietnamese American community, and will consider how Vietnamese multiracials negotiate and create a social space for themselves in this environment of multiple categorizations. While many studies have looked at the mixed-race experience in terms of racial classification, no one yet has looked at the class dimension of "What are you?" encounters (T. K. Williams, 1996).

Methodology

As a Vietnamese multiracial living in the San Francisco Bay area for over twenty-five years, I have had the opportunity to participate in and observe the daily interactions of Vietnamese Americans within their communities here. These communities (i.e., San Jose, Oakland, and San Francisco) constitute the second largest cluster of Vietnamese Americans in the United States, who now number over 1 million.[2] I have also lived in Viet Nam, both as a child and again as an adult, in 1993, 1996, and 1999. There, I was exposed to the mainstream Vietnamese society as well as to expatriate subgroups, which included some mixed-race Vietnamese from the United States.

Over the course of ten years, beginning in 1990 and ending in 2000, I conducted ethnographic interviews with over thirty Vietnamese American multiracials living in the United States and Viet Nam, thirteen of which will be highlighted in this paper. With the exception of one subject living in Seattle and one in Viet Nam, all of the respondents either reside in the San Francisco Bay area or consider it to be their "home base." Some of the interviews took place in only one meeting, whereas others were conducted on numerous occasions over the ten-year period. The character of the interviews ranged from formal and structured to personal conversations. Some took place in English, others in Vietnamese, and some in both languages. In this paper, I consciously maintain the subjects' speaking style with only some minor editing for clarification. I have translated all Vietnamese interviews into English. I have changed the names of all the subjects to protect their identities.

What began as an exercise in self-exploration in order to better understand my place within and outside of the Vietnamese American community gradually transformed into a research venture that has spanned two continents and a decade of investigation. This chapter, then, is the culmination of that venture—a personal as well as a theoretical ethnographic endeavor to uncover a particular dynamic interaction between Vietnamese Americans and Vietnamese multiracials.

Identifying the "Social Dance" of Classification and Acceptance

The majority of adult Vietnamese multiracials in the United States are immigrants and/or refugees from Viet Nam (DeBonis, 1995; Freeman, 1995). However, this does not make them any easier to categorize than any other group of Asian Americans. It is most accurate to think of them as people in a state of heterogeneity, hybridity, and multiplicity, as developed by Lisa Lowe in *Immigrant Acts* (1996). In other words, Vietnamese multiracials are not a homogeneous group but rather a product of historical and contemporary influences (hybridity),[3] differing in gender, sexuality, class, history, time of entry into the United States, level of English proficiency, and amount of education (heterogeneity). They are also constantly negotiating for power within the structures of patriarchy, capitalism, and the state (multiplicity).

Although I have just argued that Vietnamese multiracials are by no means a homogeneous group, there are important experiential similarities in their attempts to establish a connection with the Vietnamese American community. Because, phenotypically, Vietnamese multiracials often cannot blend into the Vietnamese American community, there exists some resistance to their complete acceptance by Vietnamese Americans.

A typical first encounter between a multiracial Vietnamese and a monoracial Vietnamese American might go something like this: the Vietnamese American will identify the Vietnamese multiracial as mixed because of his or her physical appearance. The person will, then, ask the multiracial Vietnamese a series of questions to place him or her along a class line. Where the mixed race person fits in the Vietnamese American class typology will determine his or her level of acceptability into the community. "Acceptance" in this case does not mean that the Vietnamese American might consider the Vietnamese multiracial to be the same as a "pure Vietnamese," but only that the person might be accepted into the community as someone who is "different" or "novel." All of this hinges on whether the mixed-race person's difference is determined to be of the good sort or the bad sort.

In return, a Vietnamese multiracial can directly affect his or her class standing and, thus, acceptability within the Vietnamese American community by carefully choosing the information that he or she discloses and withholds. Negotiating one's class position as a multiracial Vietnamese requires familiarity with the class typology, a complex structure that reflects the historical past and contemporary social norms. These encounters between Vietnamese multiracials and monoracial members of the Vietnamese American community can be described as a dance—the Vietnamese American individual leads with a series of questions, and the multiracial in turn engages the lead with some spins, dips, turns, and even sidesteps.

The Multiracial Vietnamese American Class Typology

Discussions of mixed-race populations have tended to simplify them as either a privileged people who benefit from the "best of both worlds" or a severely disadvantaged group who represent the "worst of both worlds" (Nakashima, 1992). But in the historical context of postwar Viet Nam and the postwar Vietnamese diaspora, there is a recognition of a greater complexity within the multiracial Vietnamese population. Specifically, mixed-race Vietnamese represent the continuum from economically, socially, and politically disadvantaged to extremely privileged. And while they have tended to cluster at either extreme, there is a growing population of Vietnamese American multiracials who are somewhere in the middle.

The following is my description of the three most common types of multiracial Vietnamese Americans, as imagined by the Vietnamese American community. In evaluating and classifying people into these categories, the community utilizes gross generalizations and stereotypes. The categories themselves both reflect and solidify the Vietnamese American community's highly contextualized social class hierarchy.

1. *Amerasians:*[4] They currently live in, or have lived much of their lives in, Viet Nam. If they are in the United States, they came well after the fall of Sai Gon (1975), usually as part of the U.S.–sponsored Amerasian Homecoming Act of 1986, which allowed roughly twenty-thousand Amerasians and their family members to enter the United States as immigrants with refugee benefits (Valverde, 1992). This group of mixed-race Vietnamese are generally assumed to be poor and uneducated.

2. *Multiracial Vietnamese:* They were either born in the United States or came at a very young age. Some of this group are the children of legalized marriages between Vietnamese women and American men who left Viet Nam prior to the fall of Sai Gon. Others arrived in 1975 as part of the first wave of Vietnamese refugees, which represents a generally more privileged group of Vietnamese Americans, who have enjoyed a more successful adaptation to the United States than have other refugees.

3. *Cosmopolitan mixed-race Vietnamese:* These are the children of diplomats and/or upper-class families who had the opportunity to leave Viet Nam at any point before, during, or after the war. They are frequently well educated and have experienced international travel and/or residency, and now live in the United States. Oftentimes, these mixed-race Vietnamese have French backgrounds and/or are second-generation Vietnamese multiracials.

On a hierarchy of class and social status, Vietnamese Americans tend to place "cosmopolitan mixed-race Vietnamese" on top, "multiracial Vietnamese" in the middle, and "Amerasians" on the bottom. In my experience, Vietnamese Americans perceive all multiracials between the ages of twenty and thirty-five as "Amerasian," until proven otherwise.

Ten Questions for the Purpose of Classification

With over two decades of observing the dynamic movements of this typological dance between monoracial and multiracial Vietnamese Americans, I have found ten permeable elements that participate in determining a mixed-race individual's place in the community's class hierarchy. These elements, based on gender, geography, personal attainment, culture, phenotype, and other markers of physical appearance, shape the ways in which Vietnamese multiracials are perceived, processed, and classified by the Vietnamese American population. How one fits into these categories determines one's class standing, and consequently, one's treatment within the community.

In this section, I will describe this questioning process and will discuss the repercussions of the various answers that are available to the mixed-race person. The voices of Vietnamese multiracials, many of whom are cleverly adept at answering for a desired effect, illustrate how truly complex and multifaceted this process can be.

Question 1: Are You Male or Female?

As in most social encounters, Vietnamese Americans first observe the gender of a multiracial person, then proceed to make their assessment. In general, male multiracials are regarded as more acceptable than females, according to a Vietnamese patriarchal mindset in which men and boys rank above women and girls (Ta, 1984).

But, in addition to this general male privilege, in the Vietnamese American community male multiracials are less likely to be seen as the products of purely sexual relationships than are female multiracials. While mixed-race women are often considered beautiful, they are hyperobjectified due to their non-Asian features and eroticized based on stereotypes of mixed-raced individuals as oversexed (Nakashima, 1992; Valverde, 1992).

Brigitte Trang Renier, a Vietnamese/French graduate student who came to the United States from France after high school, remarks on the objectification of Vietnamese multiracial females in the Vietnamese American community:

> When I first lived in Vietnamese community [as an adult], I was considered exotic. When people saw me, they always said, "*Dep qua* [very beautiful]," and my looks became the focus of conversation. But this [my looks] wasn't enough for them [the Vietnamese Americans]; I still had to prove to them that I was more Vietnamese than the Vietnamese. For this reason, I didn't even date for two years. However, it was difficult [to prove myself], especially within my own family. Even when I talked to male or female relatives, I was seen as perverted because of my French blood. It was hard for me as a woman.

Question 2: Is Your Father or Your Mother Vietnamese?

Mixed-race Vietnamese who have Vietnamese fathers are accorded a higher status than those with Vietnamese mothers, mostly because there is a higher probability that the person was conceived outside of the Viet Nam War context, and is therefore not an abandoned Amerasian. Vietnamese men who have met and married European and American women have often done so while studying or working abroad. Thus, they are assumed to be from privileged backgrounds. Intermarriages between Vietnamese men and non-Vietnamese women also challenge the stereotype of mixed-race Vietnamese as the products of illicit affairs between "bar girls" and GIs (Valverde, 1992).

Many Vietnamese multiracials recognize this bias and answer questions accordingly. Of those whose mothers are Vietnamese, some simply avoid disclosing this information, if at all possible. Those with non-Vietnamese mothers, on the other hand, often highlight the point. Charles Pham, a lawyer and native of California, is very conscious of this issue when he answers the question, "What are you?":

> I would always answer that my dad is Vietnamese and my mother is Russian Jew. I answer this way because I want people to know who I am and that my mother is not a slut.

Similarly, Deeloan Hotran, American born and a recent college graduate, recognizes the greater entree available to those with a Vietnamese father, and thus openly discloses her parents' ethnicities to the community:

Most Vietnamese people ask me if I'm Vietnamese. I answer that my father is Vietnamese and my mother is Indian. I do this so that the person can understand better. I know that one reason I can get away with my activism is because my family—grandfather, father, and uncles—are very involved in the community. Because of that, they [the Vietnamese community] cannot really criticize me.

Question 3: *Were You Born in Viet Nam or Outside of Viet Nam?*

For multiracial Vietnamese, it is considered higher status to have been born outside of Viet Nam than in Viet Nam. Again, this is because of the distance that it puts between the multiracial person and the Viet Nam War. In the aftermath of the fall of Sai Gon in 1975, Viet Nam experienced enormous economic hardship and political remaneuvering. Failed developmental experiments resulted in establishing it as one of the poorest countries in the world. While the entire population endured years of poverty and hardship (Marr & White, 1988), the Amerasians also faced extreme economic and social discrimination because of their status as the descendants of the enemy—the Americans (Valverde, 1992).

In this historical context, multiracials who seem "less Vietnamese" are assumed to be of higher status, and those who were born outside of Viet Nam seem the "least Vietnamese" of all. Gavin Robinson, an Amerasian man who arrived in the United States in 1984 as a twelve-year-old (which is before most Amerasian immigrants arrived), is constantly aware of the subtle differences of looking and acting more "American" than "Amerasian," and of how they affect a mixed-race person's treatment in the community:

> They [Vietnamese Americans] are curious about my mannerisms. Most of the Amerasians I grew up with are very skinny. The ones that come later dress a certain way. They dress better now. It's a dilemma to the Vietnamese [Americans], because I look like a White kid. It doesn't fit their idea [of how an Amerasian should look], so they are curious. If I'm a skinny, dark Amerasian, they would not be that curious. It's how much you've adapted to the American way of life.

Question 4: *What Is Your Occupation?*

In the United States, if you have a prestigious career, you have a better chance of being treated well by others. This is certainly true in the Vietnamese American community (Freeman, 1995).

For Amerasians in Viet Nam, there has been very little opportunity for economic mobility. Many Amerasians, without supportive families, left home and tried to make a living in urban areas such as Ho Chi Minh City (formerly Sai Gon). This contributed to the prejudice against them, because people saw homeless Amerasians, roaming the streets and making money in a variety of suspect ways. Consequently, Amerasians came to be referred to as "*bui doi*" (dust of life), which is a name also used for the homeless, "troublemakers," and rebellious individuals (Valverde, 1992; DeBonis, 1995). This bleak situation left the Amerasians with little hope for a better life.

Having lived in Viet Nam until her late teens and now residing in the United States, Janet Tran clearly understands how her image as a successful lawyer has gained her acceptance within the Vietnamese American community:

> How they [Vietnamese Americans] perceive me now is because of my title [lawyer], but that's not who I am. Before, when I had no title, I was treated like a nobody. When I began working for the social services, people came to me when they needed me for something. When I was in the marketplace and spoke Vietnamese, the Vietnamese [Americans] didn't treat me very well. Now that I'm a lawyer, I get a lot of respect. So, it's my title, not me. It's not my goal to have titles to be accepted, but it helps to have these titles. I get accepted into the community easier.

Question 5: What Is Your Educational Level?

Again, in all segments of society, it is prestigious to have a high degree of education. But for multiracial Vietnamese, being highly educated is a direct challenge to the stereotypes of Amerasians as naturally dumb and ignorant.

In Viet Nam, discrimination has kept the Amerasian population largely undereducated. In the early school years, the bullying and teasing of multiracial children have been commonplace, inflicted not only by other children but by teachers as well. This has led many Amerasians to opt for quitting school altogether. At the high school level, the Vietnamese government has systematically kept Amerasians from advancing as part of an overall harassment of anyone with ties to the old government or to the United States (Valverde, 1992).

Economics are another reason why many Vietnamese Amerasians lack an education. Amerasians are overrepresented in single-family, female-headed households, which tend to have fewer financial resources. In Viet Nam, where an education is regarded as a luxury, many Amerasians have had to leave school early because of a lack of funds (Valverde, 1992).

Having gone to school since coming to the United States, Gavin Robinson realized that his education would bring him recognition with his family in Viet Nam:

> I left the country [of Viet Nam] at 12 but I didn't know how to read. The teacher beat me and made it difficult. I felt I was stupid in Viet Nam because that's what people told me. So, when I went back to Viet Nam, I showed my family in Viet Nam that I was studying in Ha Noi. And now they think I'm smart. The family doesn't remember that they treated me badly and they treated my [monoracial] Vietnamese sister better.

Johnny Quoc Hoang, who arrived in the United States in 1992, believes that education and economic mobility is one way to attain equality in the United States. He has encouraged other Amerasians like himself to follow his example of hard work:

> I realized that I still needed to get ahead. I decided to study to be a technician. I first got a job as a [product] tester, then continued to work full-time while going to school full-time. During this period, I only slept four hours a day. I now have a certificate as a technician and am working on a B.S. in computer science. I attend Evergreen City College and plan to trans-

fer to San Jose State University. I now work full-time and go to school four hours a day to keep up with English. I get tired a lot but I know this is what I must do to better myself. I tell other Amerasians that this is the land of their fathers so it is their country too. They have to keep trying to improve themselves so that they have less of a chance to fail.

Question 6: Are You "Eurasian"[5] or "Amerasian"?

In the Vietnamese American community it is considered better to be Eurasian (i.e., French/Vietnamese) than Amerasian (American/Vietnamese). This is because, although Viet Nam was once a colony of France and went to war with France, the Vietnamese have a high regard for French culture. Americans, on the other hand, are seen as having very little culture—only financial and military might (DeBonis, 1995). For example, although Brigitte Trang Renier is from a working-class family in France, the historical connection between Viet Nam and France raises her class status within the Vietnamese American community: "Older [Vietnamese American] gentlemen like to speak French with me. I think it gave me more status [knowing French and] being Eurasian."

Question 7: Do You Speak Vietnamese?

Interestingly, compared to how monoracial Vietnamese Americans are judged, for a multiracial Vietnamese American it is considered more prestigious to have poor or nonexistent Vietnamese-language skills. Once again, this has to do with the assumption that a Vietnamese multiracial who is "more American" is from outside of the war context. The exception to this is if the mixed-race person is very young—in his or her early twenties or younger—and is therefore too young to be a product from the war. In this case, a multiracial person who can speak Vietnamese well is admired for maintaining his or her Vietnamese culture, even though he or she had other options. This attitude holds true for those young multiracials who actively set out to learn Vietnamese, such as college students.

Janet Tran, who is fluent in Vietnamese, recognizes the assumptions about multiracials who do and do not speak Vietnamese:

> When they [Vietnamese Americans] know that you speak Vietnamese, they think you are Amerasian. That's why it's better not to speak Vietnamese or have limited knowledge of Vietnamese. It's even considered cute to speak in broken Vietnamese, but not the other way around.

Gavin Robinson, however, views his Vietnamese fluency as beneficial for his interactions in the community, largely because Vietnamese Americans often identify him as White rather than Amerasian:

> I would use my Vietnamese because it would give me access to things. I do it [speak Vietnamese] at restaurants all the time. I'm fluent in Vietnamese, but I have a third-year writing level. It takes a few moments for them to figure it out. I am conscious of using Vietnamese. I get really excited because I want to impress them. I like watching them surprised.

Hanh Kantor, who was born in the United States and now works in Viet Nam for nongovernmental organizations, believes community acceptance depends on one's mastery of Vietnamese:

> I used to take my grandmother to *Tet* [New Year] things and temple. They [Vietnamese Americans] would say, "Why is she different?" My grandmother said, "She's American." I felt kind of bad that I wasn't accepted but I'd still like to work with the [Vietnamese American] community in the future. I'm open to it. People [like Vietnamese Americans] probably don't think you can relate to them unless you know the language.

She adds, "I think most [Vietnamese] people [living] in the United States draw the line between Vietnamese who know Vietnamese and Vietnamese who don't. And I don't know if it's a malicious thing or if it's a natural thing, but they do make the divide."

There is a stereotype in the Vietnamese American community that the accent from the northern region of Viet Nam represents "proper" Vietnamese speech. Those who speak with this accent are often seen as being well schooled and belonging to good families with high class standing. I have observed many Amerasians attempting to fake the northern speech patterns in order to appear more educated.[6]

Question 8: How "Americanized" Do You Look?

Specifically, do you wear clothes that can be easily identified as having a U.S. or western influence? As mentioned, the more "American" one looks, the further distanced he or she is from the "child of war" stereotype. Charles Pham, who is six feet tall and has dark, curly hair and light eyes, remarks on how he is never mistaken for an Amerasian from the war context: "With my style of dress and the way I look, I never get mistaken for being [an Amerasian] from Viet Nam. Plus, speaking fluent English doesn't hurt either."

However, for young Vietnamese multiracials, wearing traditional Vietnamese clothing can act as a cultural badge for the purpose of being identified as Vietnamese. Deeloan Hotran explains how she sometimes makes a conscious attempt to look "more Vietnamese" to authenticate her heritage:

> When I decided to run for the Vietnamese Student Association [VSA] president position, I had good friends say they would not vote for me because I'm mixed. When I made the VSA speech, I wore an *ao dai* [Vietnamese traditional dress]. What better way to promote Vietnamese culture? I'm involved with my Vietnamese family and Vietnamese culture and Vietnamese politics. How much more Vietnamese do I have to be [to be accepted by Vietnamese Americans]?

Question 9: Are Your Non-Asian Features More "White" or More "Black"?

Vietnamese multiracials who are perceived as having "European" features are generally treated better in the Vietnamese American community than those perceived as having "African" features. This is due to a racist and classist ideology that is a combination of pre- and postimmigration stereotypes and beliefs (DeBonis, 1995; Valverde, 1992).

Steven DeBonis (1995), in his collection of oral histories of Amerasians and their mothers, suggests that Vietnamese racism against Blacks stems from the French colonial period, when North African members of the French army were stationed in Viet Nam. These troops were reputed as having been especially brutal pillagers and rapists, and therefore there is an association between Africans and brutality. This was probably compounded by the colorism that has long existed in Viet Nam, whereby dark skin represents the peasantry, laboring in the sun, while light skin represents the idle rich.

Some Vietnamese immigrants have exported these ideas to the United States, where they were then combined with the American stereotypes of African Americans. Because media images of African Americans as poor, uneducated, and criminal are very similar to the Vietnamese stereotypes of Amerasians, Vietnamese Americans can be especially unaccepting of Afro-Amerasians. Loan Nguyen, a single mother of two who works in a variety of menial jobs, laments about the injustices she has endured due to her dark skin color: "I think it would be easier if I were White Amerasian. I see their lives and I see mine and I know things would be easier for me if I were light. Vietnamese people hate me; they hate my color."

It is common for Afro-Amerasians living in the Vietnamese American community to have internalized the racist attitudes that persist, especially if they follow traditional Vietnamese ways of thinking. Trac Nguyen, a college student and part-time nightclub singer, relates an incident where his manager (a Vietnamese American woman) told him to change his look:

> She told me that I look like "the devil" on stage. She asked me to put on some makeup to change my look. I felt bad at first because I know it's due to my dark skin. But, I had to agree with her criticism, because I think I do look better with a little makeup."

Question 10: Do You Look "Healthy," and Are You Attractive?

Often, a monoracial Vietnamese American will attempt to judge a multiracial's class standing based solely on his or her physical appearance. If the person looks "healthy" (i.e., tall and fit), he or she is likely to be perceived as being American-born and thus of a higher social class. Recently arrived Amerasians, having lived for years in one of the poorest countries in the world, often appear malnourished in comparison to their American-born or longtime-American counterparts.

Along with those who look "healthy," Vietnamese multiracials who are considered to be physically attractive experience many more positive interactions within the community. However, while it gains attention, being considered handsome or beautiful does not translate into acceptance as a community equal, for, as mentioned, attractive female—and even male—Vietnamese multiracials tend to be sexually objectified by the Vietnamese. And yet, Daniel Bousque, who has lived most of his life in expatriate communities throughout Asia, doesn't mind this kind of acceptance: "I don't mind being called 'exotic.' It's better than being called nothing—bland."

Observations and Analysis

Multiracial Vietnamese, as illustrated by my interviews, tend to be very aware of the class typology for mixed-race people that exists in the Vietnamese American community. They are also quite familiar with the assumptions and the stereotypes used to categorize them into this typology. How they react to the classification system—how they "maneuver during the dance"—varies from person to person, and from situation to situation.

The phenomenon called "passing" is a behavior that seems both resistant to and in compliance with dominant ideology (Daniel, 1992b; Ginsberg, 1996). Some of the people to whom I spoke attempt to manipulate the standard perceptions of Amerasians, multiracial Vietnamese, and cosmopolitan mixed-race Vietnamese by "passing" from one group to another. For example, some Amerasians attempt to "pass" as Eurasians in order to better their class standing. Inversely, sometimes a more privileged multiracial Vietnamese will "pass" as an Amerasian in an attempt to debunk the prevalent stereotypes of them in the community.

A few of the mixed-race people in my interviews feel that "passing," even when it occurs accidentally, is dishonest and shameful, and so go out of their way to exhibit their racial/class background. Van Binh Knight, a young Amerasian college student and activist, explains his opinion on the subject:

> I identify as Vietnamese Amerasian, not *Hapa*. It's class for me. "*Hapa Haole*" means "half-White" [in Hawaiian], so it's exclusionary. "*Hapa*" refers to people [whose parents] met in college or other privileged scenarios. When I say I'm "Amerasian," it brings in the military factor, so it's a very political term. "Amerasian" is a bit more inclusive. I answer [that I am a] "*nguoi lai*" [person of mixed heritage] with Vietnamese people.

These examples serve to illustrate the complexities of class manipulation in the Vietnamese American context. Although they find it frustrating at times, Vietnamese multiracials show a sophisticated understanding of their various options, and generally make informed and conscious choices in their presentation of self. In the process, they sometimes find that they do have alternatives to their identity affiliations—alternatives that can free them, to a certain extent, from the labels and classifications. For example, Duyen Kantor attempts to challenge the conventional categorizations by manipulating the Vietnamese language in her answer to the "What are you?" question:

> I guess in Vietnamese it's easier [to evade the question by answering], "*My goc Viet* [American with Vietnamese roots]." I like it when [race] is not an issue. I like it when I go to the market and bargain and have whole conversations before they [Vietnamese from Viet Nam] say, "Hey, why are you speaking Vietnamese? Oh, are you . . . ?"

By using a fairly obscure and racially ambiguous term—*My goc Viet*—for mixed-race people, Duyen leaves it to the other person to make sense of her identity. Essentially, she walks away from the responsiblity of having to explain her existence.

Tuan Tran, who came to the United States in 1989 and served as the coordinator of an Amerasian group in San Jose, California, also reflects on terminology and his identity:

> Sometimes I say I am "Vietnamese," sometimes "American," sometimes I say "half-Viet-namese." I am a permanent resident now, and it's better to be a part of the mainstream com-munity—which also includes the Vietnamese community. We need to have an open mind.

The language that Tuan uses to express his identity reflects a combination of ethnicity, race, and legalistic terms associated with citizenship. The issue of being or not being "American" seems to be much more important to the Amerasians than it is for other mixed-race Vietnamese. This might be because, in Viet Nam, Amerasians are told that they are "Americans" and belong in the United States. Many have internalized this fic-tive national identity, only to be disappointed when they arrive in the United States and find that they are not "American" at all (Valverde, 1992).

Another alternative to "dancing the dance" is to avoid the Vietnamese American community entirely. This option is available primarily to the multiracial Vietnamese and cosmopolitan mixed-race Vietnamese, as they are much more independent of the com-munity's resources, and are therefore able to look elsewhere for a sense of belonging and acceptance. Harmony Jones readily admits that she is not yet ready to delve into her Viet-namese heritage. However, she very much embraces her gay[7] and mixed-race realities:

> I identify as gay first. It's such a relief to not deal with race by focusing on sexuality. But, in all my bios, I state that I am a poet of mixed-race heritage. I'm influenced by individuals who have showed me that having a "mixed" identity transcends the experiences of White/Asian mixes. Different mixed people can have similar experiences.

Conclusion

Although the process of categorizing mixed-race Vietnamese by the Vietnamese Amer-ican community is informal and occurs somewhat covertly, Vietnamese multiracials are astutely aware of its existence. In fact, the testimonies of the people whom I have inter-viewed show that many have developed conscious strategies for maneuvering within the typological hierarchy. Many do this in order to achieve the best possible class position for themselves, while others prefer to react against it for a variety of social, political, and personal reasons.

Having "aired the dirty laundry" of a community that I consider myself very much a member of, I would like to say that it has not been my purpose to chastise the Viet-namese American community, nor to criticize Vietnamese multiracials who do not resist the typology. Still, I do believe that any classification system that sets out to discrimi-nate against people based on race and class needs to be problematized. Hence, I hope this article has shed some light on a rarely discussed topic, and will encourage people to consider the mixed-race class typologies that, I suspect, exist in other Asian Ameri-can communities as well.

Notes

1. I broadly define "multiracial Vietnamese" and "mixed-race Vietnamese" to include any individual who has both Vietnamese and non-Vietnamese heritage. This can include people whose non-Vietnamese heritage is considered "Asian" (i.e., Asian Indian) according to American categories of race. I am not so much concerned with what an individual's non-Vietnamese heritage is, but with whether other Vietnamese recognize that person as "*lai*" (mixed) based on his or her phenotype.

My definition of the "Vietnamese American community" includes anyone with Vietnamese heritage living in the United States, including those of mixed race. For the purposes of this paper I refer to "Vietnamese" and "Vietnamese Americans" as "monoracial" populations, although I recognize that there is much ethnic diversity within these categories. For sociolinguistic integrity, I utilize the spellings "Viet Nam" and "Sai Gon."

2. According to the 1990 U.S. Census, there were 614,547 Vietnamese living in the United States at that time, with 84,662 residing in the San Francisco Bay area alone. By 1994, the National Congress of Vietnamese in America estimated that the Vietnamese American population was at 900,000 nationally (Freeman, 1995). Today, it is estimated that there are over 1 million Vietnamese Americans living in the United States, with approximately 200,000 living in the Bay area.

3. Although Lowe's use of the term "hybridity" is metaphorical, in the context of this discussion we can consider its literal as well as its figurative meanings.

4. When the Viet Nam War ended in 1975, more than thirty-thousand Amerasian children were left behind, with no support from the U.S. military or government. As a result, the Amerasian experience in Viet Nam has been largely traumatic and dehumanizing. They've endured Communist persecution because of their connections to America, racial prejudice because of their phenotypic distinctions from the mainstream, and class prejudice becasue of their status as an impoverished and uneducated population. Cumulatively, these factors have sentenced Vietnamese Amerasians to a marginal status in the most negative of senses (Valverde, 1992).

5. At the end of the first Indochina War, France and Viet Nam negotiated the issue of Vietnamese Eurasians. The French government offered them French citizenship at age eighteen, and provided "repatriation" and educational opportunities to those who wished to live in France (Trautfield, 1984). Some of these Eurasians married French citizens and other Europeans, and have produced subsequent generations of Vietnamese multiracials in Europe. In contrast, when the Viet Nam War ended in 1975, the United States showed no intention of recognizing Amerasians as an American responsibility. (Valverde, 1992). This is consistent with America's treatment of Amerasians in Japan after the Occupation (see Murphy-Shigematsu, Chapter 17) and throughout Asia.

6. However, a northern Vietnamese accent can sometimes be considered a negative characteristic in the Vietnamese American community, as it is also associated with being a Communist or Communist sympathizer. But because there were very few Americans in northern Viet Nam at the time of the war, this stereotype is not applied to Amerasians.

7. Unfortunately, I am unable to expand on issues of sexuality and its relationship to identity in this chapter. I should note that a substantial number of my respondents identify as gay or bisexual.

CHAPTER 12

The Convergence of Passing Zones: Multiracial Gays, Lesbians, and Bisexuals of Asian Descent

Teresa Williams-León

Introduction

QV Magazine, a gay Latino publication based in Los Angeles, placed several models on its cover who appeared to challenge some of its readership's conceptualizations of "Latino" and "Hispanic" (1998a, b) (see Photo 12-1). The magazine's Internet guest logs and message boards vigorously debated what was meant by "100% Latino" (www.qvmagazine.com). As part of this discussion, readers argued whether Asian Latinos were "authentically" mestizo and could properly represent Latino gay maleness. It was the Asian in the overall Latino equation, rather than the European, indigenous, and African, that seemed to provoke the fiercest contestations of Latino authenticity. It was murky as to what legitimated being 100 percent Latino, yet it was quite clear which specific ancestral mixtures of Latinos were deemed "authentic." That is to say, Asian ancestry seemed to disqualify one from being authentically or legitimately Latino. Despite their differing views, *QV Magazine* respondents articulated a number of racial and ethnic significations in grappling with what it meant to be Latino: first names and surnames, national origins, ancestry, phenotype, cultural practices and knowledge, community involvement, political awareness, and even employment. The magazine's cover models, whose ethnic legitimacy was being tested and contested because of their unusual names or Asian ancestry, were thrust, unbeknownst to them, into traverse spaces of liminality and marginality by the readership in which voluntary and involuntary racial "passing" and "outing" had become a contested social reality among the publication's predominantly gay Latino audience. Hence, multiply marginalized groups (in this case, Latino and gay male), who occupy "borderland spaces," too have consciously and inadvertently practiced disassociation and exclusion of individuals by con-

PHOTO 12-1. Questions about Latino authenticity were vigorously debated on *QV Magazine*'s on-line message board after *QV's* cover model ("Louie") graced the now sold-out "Faith" issue in the summer of 1998. (Courtesy of *QV Magazine*.)

structing inconsistent rules of demarcation, even among those with whom they share aspects of their collective identities.

This chapter interrogates how Asian-descent gay, lesbian, and bisexual (GLB) multiracials map out and negotiate their converging "passing zones" of race and sexuality. Secondly, it illustrates how Asian-descent GLB multiracials perform their social identities and develop strategies of negotiation and navigation within and across social boundaries, transforming their "passing zones" into "no passing zones" (Houston & Williams, 1997).[1] Finally, this essay explores the parallels of racial and sexual indeterminacy in the lived experiences of Asian-descent GLB multiracial individuals and posits the interrelationship between the sociopolitical constructs of race and sexuality.

Multiraciality and Sexuality

Race and sexuality have often been treated as fundamentally different in experience, in motivation, and in cause. As the public debate around gays in the U.S. military unfolded in 1992–93, for example, heterosexual peoples of color and White gays and lesbians often found themselves on the opposite sides of this issue. While White gays and lesbians dominated "the gay perspective," and illustrated the similarities between racial minority and sexual minority statuses, heterosexual people of color, with powerful representatives like General Colin Powell, maintained and defended the separateness of race and sexuality. Needless to say, Asian Americans were completely absent in the entire public debate.

Concealment of identity, ambiguous outward appearance, or issues of voluntary disclosure of sexuality have been argued as distinguishing sexuality from the more obvious and commonsensical markers of "race." As Dana Takagi (1996a: 25) has explained, "There is a quality of voluntarism in being gay/lesbian that is usually not possible as an Asian American. One has the option to present oneself as 'gay' or 'lesbian' or alternatively to attempt to 'pass,' or to 'stay in the closet,' that is, to hide one's sexual preference." Race and sexuality are often organized, positioned, and displayed differently, yet the parallels between the two are more evident than ever when examined within the framework of multiraciality.

Due to the phenotypical ambiguity of many Asian-descent multiracial people, it is not uncommon for racial identities to be presented, manipulated, and performed (King & DaCosta, 1996; Williams, 1996, 1997). Multiracial people "do" race, and also get race "done" to them (Williams, 1997). Multiracial people are often talked about as "passing" for one racial group or another. When actor Dean Cain, who played Superman on the television show *Lois and Clark,* disclosed his Japanese ancestry in *Yolk Magazine* in the summer of 1995, did he make a conscious decision to exit the "racial closet" and change his "racial uniform" (Takaki, 1989)? He did not have to volunteer this information about his racial lineage, since his "vaguely ethnic" appearance and Anglo surname have been socially and publicly coded "White." When Andrew Cunanan, a gay Filipino–European American spree-killer, became one of the FBI's "Ten Most Wanted" in May of 1997, he was described as a "master [of] disguise" and a "chameleon," who could pass for Jewish, Latino, and Italian. Despite his ethnically Filipino surname, Cunanan's phenotypical ambiguity and openly gay sexuality identified him as White.

Over the years, scholars have conducted empirical studies with Asian-descent multiracial individuals to explore and examine the complexity of their multiple racial identities (Hall, 1980; Kich, 1982; King, Chapter 13; Thornton & Gates, Chapter 8; Murphy-Shigematsu, 1987; Ropp, 1997; Williams, 1992, 1996, 1997; Yoshimi, 1997). In many of these studies, ethnographic interviews are a major source of the data used to ascertain the richness of the lived realities of multiracial peoples. These works challenged the idea that social problems and psychological pathology were innate and essential components of multiracial identities. We have learned from these accounts how structures have imposed various forms of limitations on and/or provided a series of advantages to multiracial peoples. These interview-based studies have illuminated that "race" is an ever-changing construction wrought with layers of contested meanings. Furthermore, they have revealed that the personal identities and social realities of Asian-descent biracials boldly contest and innovatively transgress either/or, monoracial constructions of race in which multiracial people create and sustain "no passing zones—critical spaces of resistance and empowerment" (Williams, 1997: 64). Although (hetero)sexuality is at the core of how racism manifests itself psychologically, socially, economically, and politically, rarely have these studies examined how gay, lesbian, and bisexual sexuality informs multiracial identities and the larger discourse on multiraciality in general.

Heterosexual mate selection, dating, and marriage have been treated as important predictors of ethnic identification due to the intimate, personal, and emotional investment of these primary group relationships that may eventually become institutionalized. In her 1990–91 study, Francis Twine (1996: 304) found that the (hetero) dating choices of multiracial people directly corresponded to shifts in their racial identity in which they "identified their attraction to romantic partners from a preferred racial background as an expression of their allegiance to a specific racial community."

In a 1992–93 pilot study on biracial individuals of various backgrounds I conducted in California, I found a significant number of respondents who openly discussed their gay, lesbian, and bisexual sexualities without my direct solicitation (Williams, 1996). This was a far cry from the results of the interviews I conducted in 1988 with Eurasian and Afroasian biracials in a U.S. military environment in Japan. At that time, I had assumed the exclusivity of their heterosexual orientation, and, in retrospect, the interviewees all responded accordingly (Williams, 1992). In the 1988 sampling, the majority of the forty-three respondents stated they "preferred" to date other biracials like themselves. Dating was presumed to be heterosexual courtships. I explained:

> While the older Amerasians (25–35 years) said they had no preference in the selection of friends, they still seemed to associate "naturally" with other Amerasians. Those between the ages of 16 and 24 clearly stated that they "preferred" other Amerasians as friends and dates. When asked to identify the ethnic makeup of their close friends, most of them reported (a) half Japanese or *haafu,* (b) Euro-Americans, (c) Japanese, (d) Americans of color.
>
> More than half of the Amerasian respondents (26 of the 43) were dating or married to other Amerasians with a similar upbringing. Bilingual communication, cultural familiarity, and physical attractiveness were the top three reasons Amerasians gave for preferring "their own kind" as dating and marriage partners. . . . Intimacy and comfort, according to many of the respondents, were easily and "naturally" established with people of "their own kind."
>
> Among this sampling, the awareness of Amerasians and/or racially mixed individuals like themselves as possible and even desirable mates existed. A sense of being an ethnic group of their own or having something in common with other Amerasians and racially mixed American persons thus had been imprinted in their consciousness by the time many of them reached ages to select their friends, dates, and marriage partners. (Williams, 1992: 289)

Nowhere in the 1988 study did I mention sexuality—heterosexual, gay, or bisexual. However, questions around dating and marriage had assumed exclusive heterosexuality. Looking back, how many respondents were perhaps further silenced and/or "othered" by these heterosexist assumptions? How did the gay, lesbian, and bisexual Eurasians and Afroasians in this study—if any—find creative ways to answer these questions without disclosing their sexuality? Thus, during this interview process, there may have been gay, lesbian, and bisexual Eurasians and Afroasians who had few or no options but to enter "passing zones."

Lisa Lowe (1991) and Takagi (1995) have problematized the assumption of Asian American homogeneity and primordial ethnic orientation (Espiritu, 1992). In the same way scholars are now questioning whether a monolithic Asian American identity exists, a solely race-based and ethnicity-focused multiracial identity can no longer drive the discourse on multiracial identity that compartmentalizes one's human identity into separate and often disjointed parts. Most of the racial discourse, be it monoracial or multiracial, while acknowledging and even celebrating multiple racial and ethnic identities, is framed within the contexts of compulsory heterosexuality and institutionalized heterosexism. In fact, multiracial identity has been exclusively linked to and defined by interracial *heterosexual* sexual relations between a man and a woman of different racial heritages, in many ways fostering "hyper-heterosexuality" among multiracial individuals.

As Asian Americanists debate the expanding complexity and diversity of Asian America (Hirabayashi, 1998), the most often (but not exclusively) discussed marginalized groups within Asian American communities are Asian Americans gays, lesbians, and bisexuals *and* multiracial Asian Americans (Okihiro, 1994; Houston & Williams, 1997; Fong, 1998). Rarely have Asian-descent multiracials who are gay, lesbian, and bisexual been the subject of Asian America's "doubly forgotten."

L. Hutchins and L. Kaahumanu (1991), in *Bi Any Other Name: Bisexual People Speak Out;* Maria P. P. Root (1996a) in *The Multiracial Experience: Racial Borders as the New Frontier;* and Velina Hasu Houston and Teresa Kay Williams (1997), in "No Passing Zone: The Artistic and Discursive Voices of Asian-Descent Multiracials" (*Amerasia Journal*) were perhaps among the first works on multiracial identity to address and include images and writings about gay, lesbian, and bisexual sexuality as an integral component to multiracial identities. Karen Maeda Allman (1996: 279) has explained how "race, gender, and sexuality exist as a sort of unstable triad; shifts in one create disturbances in the other two." She elaborates:

> I used to wonder why I have so often felt preoccupied with issues of boundaries and of identity. Why am I still startled when someone asks, yet again, *What are you?* Are you (fill in the blank racial/ethnic group, usually an incorrect one)? It can't be! Are you sure? Are you a woman first or a person of color/Asian American first? If this is a lesbian group, why do you keep talking about race? We are all women here!
>
> An Asian American professor, one with whom I had often spoken about our shared experiences with racism on our campus, once told me, "You can pass for white any time." I had to stop myself from immediately running to look at myself in the mirror, and I must confess that I spent a lot of time scrutinizing my appearance in the following weeks. Had my features suddenly shifted, perhaps in the middle of the night, when I was sleeping? She seemed to think that my Asian heritage was something hidden within me, a secret that only she could see, and that racism was something I could choose to experience or not. I wondered if perhaps my lesbianism somehow "whitened" me in her eyes. . . . "How does one negotiate a multiple situated identity if race, gender, and sexual orientation are taken for granted as so separate and boundaried?" (Allman, 1996: 277–278)

George Kitahara Kich (1996) has examined the parallels of race and sexuality by focusing on biraciality and bisexuality as units of analysis. He has explained that both racial and sexual identity have been "charted among the landmarks of biology and behavior, of self-awareness and relatedness, and of belongingness, and differentiation within which everyone navigates" (Kich, 1996: 267). Thus, the discourse on the complexity and expansivity of socially constructed identities among Asian-descent populations necessitates the inclusion of gay, lesbian, and bisexual multiracials.

June Jordan (1998: 440) has illustrated the inextricable nexus between race and sex, and moreover between multiraciality and multisexuality, as she articulated the politicization of "the middle ground":

> I need to speak on bisexuality. I do believe that the analogy is interracial or multiracial identity. I do believe that the analogy for bisexuality is a multicultural, multiethnic, multiracial world view. Bisexuality follows from such a perspective and leads to it as well.

Lani Kaahumanu, a self-described "mixed-race bisexual woman of color," spoke about racial and sexual "passing zones," which she called "the middle ground," in a speech at the Gay and Lesbian March on Washington in April of 1993:

> Like multiculturalism, mixed race heritage and bi-racial relationships, both the bisexual and transgender movements expose and politicize the middle ground. Each shows there is no separation: that each and everyone of us is part of a fluid social, sexual, and gender dynamic. Each signals a change, a fundamental change in the way our society is organized.

In the 1993 article "Tune in, Come Out" (cited in du Plessis, 1996), made the connection between "multiculturalism" and "multisexualism." Michael du Plessis (1996: 42) argued, in "Blatantly Bisexual: or, Unthinking Queer Theory," that this racial, sexual middle ground is "not a neutral zone in between, but a highly politicized terrain, in which identities can nevertheless come together." Thus, the identities and realities of GLB Asian-descent multiracial people are compilations of negotiations between and among passing zones and middle grounds, or overlapping spaces of resistance and creation.

Method

This chapter explores the identities of Asian-descent GLB multiracials, or those gay, lesbian, and bisexual individuals who possess two or more socially distinct racial and ethnic ancestries in which one of them is Asian. The chapter is based on unstructured, qualitative interviews with 18 openly GLB Asian-descent multiracial individuals between the ages of eighteen and thirty-eight: 1 Asian-Asian (1 Japanese-Filipino); 4 Asian-Latinos (2 Japanese–Mexican Americans, 1 Chinese-Salvadorian, 1 Filipino-Mexican); 8 Asian–European Americans (2 Filipino–European Americans, 1 Vietnamese–European American, 1 Korean–European American, 4 Japanese–European Americans); and 5 Asian–African Americans (2 Japanese–African Americans, 2 Filipino–African Americans, 1 Chinese–African American). These 18 respondents consisted of 8 gay men, 1 bisexual man, 2 bisexual women, and 7 lesbian women. There were 5 more GLB biracial respondents whom I interviewed, but their interviews are not included here because they are not of Asian-descent.

Qualitative interviews and field studies (such as attending GLB and/or multiracial conferences, forums, and functions) are useful methods that allow the researcher to see, experience, and understand the social world from the perspective of the interviewees themselves (Thornton, 1983; Emerson, 1988; Williams, 1992; Yoshimi, 1997). Furthermore, field methodology maintains the social context in which the respondents experience their lives with minimal presupposition and outside imposition by the researcher.

The emphasis of the initial interviews was on the multiple *racial* aspects of multiracial respondents' identities. In addition to their dual racial realities, these eighteen GLB Asian-descent multiracial interviewees also shared and discussed their nonheterosexual sexuality, its influences on how they experience and negotiate their multiraciality, and the struggles of integrating it into their multiple identities. Furthermore, the GLB multiracials also expressed an acute awareness of how their gender experiences as men and women were also informed by both their biraciality *and* their GLB sexuality. Certainly, the heterosexual multiracial individuals also talked about their gender and sexuality. However, the major difference in the discussion of sexuality between heterosexual multiracials and their GLB counterparts is that heterosexual multiracials tended to possess a "taken-for-granted" understanding of their sexuality because their heterosexuality had not been "othered," although heterosexual multiracials often understood how a racist society has racialized their (hetero)sexuality as well as their parents'. From the vantage point of the heterosexual multiracial respondents, stories and explanations about their parents' interracial unions, their boyfriends, their girlfriends, their potential marriage partners, and their attractions and desires are not seen as fitting into the realm of sexuality. By contrast, the GLB biracial respondents had a conscious awareness about the roles race, gender, and sexuality interactively played in their lives and how they shaped their complex identities.

Which One Are You? Which Race Do You Date?

The faulty question "So, with which group do mixed-race people identify (more)?" has been addressed by a growing number of multiracial scholars (Root, 1992a). The follow-up question that attempts to ascertain biracial identity development and the social positionality of biracials has been, "So, whom do mixed-race people date and marry?" A Japanese–African American lesbian explained the dating and marriage questions she is often asked:

> They ask me how my parents met and what it was like for them getting married. . . . Asians, Black people, White people, everyone asks, "How the hell did a Black man and an Asian woman ever get together?" . . . But, then I get asked, "So who do you date?" When they ask this, I know they are implying race—like which race do you prefer and all. But for me, I'm so busy thinking of ways to deflect my sexual orientation that it becomes very stressful, but being mixed, you know, you get asked those questions—about your parents and about who you date. As a lesbian, being asked these questions by strangers—especially when I know they are coming from a heterosexual point of view—I find the questions really intrusive. I

try to find ways to transfer my attractions toward women to make them sound like I'm talking about men, which means I have to think about how a particular racial group is gendered.
It's more than just changing pronouns from "she" to "he."

As an extension of one's racial (and gender) identity, questions about dating and marriage partners are often raised (Williams, 1992; Twine, 1996). Perhaps it may be implied
that if multiracial individuals of Eurasian ancestry tend to date and marry European
Americans, then they have rejected their Asian minority self, taken on the racial identity of the dominant society, and chosen the course of straight-line, Anglo-conformity
(M. Gordon, 1964). After all, outmarriage to the dominant White racial group has been
treated as the surest indicator of structural assimilation by sociologists like Robert Mer-
ton and Milton Gordon. On the other hand, if multiracial individuals of Afroasian
ancestries exclusively date Asian Americans, it may be perceived that they are denying
their African ancestry, opting for the more favorable minority identity—in this case
Asian—or even rejecting the hypodescent rules that define them as exclusively Black
(Davis, 1991; Root, 1992a, 1996; Williams, 1996, 1997). One Japanese–Mexican
American gay man explained:

> I identify as Chicano and Latino, and so naturally I find myself going out with Latino men.
> I think the Asians and Japanese people in my family and the ones I know take that [dating
> Latino men] as part of my Mexicanness. Like, he's Mexican so why wouldn't he want to
> date Mexicans? I suppose. It's just matter-of-fact.

Thus, interrogating the mate choices of biracial individuals is often an attempt to gauge
one's measure of ethnic identification within a heterosexist, racist social structure in
which compulsory heterosexuality is demanded and interraciality is discouraged of all
romantic sexual unions.

The racial, ethnic, and gender influences of biracial individuals' mothers and fathers
are often put forth to explain dating preferences and marriage choices. What these questions and views say is that conscious and unconscious dating and mating decisions
reveal something racially significant about one's identity. However, the important dating and marriage questions have been framed from a heterosexist vantage point.

The Racial-Sexual Formula

Individuals learn to become members of society through the lifelong process of socialization; they learn who they are through social interaction. Charles Cooley (1902) used the
metaphor of the looking glass to discuss how the self is produced, constructed, and
informed by others' perceptions and impressions. Identity development is an interactive
process between an individual's concept of self and the evaluation one receives from the
"generalized others" and "significant others" (Mead, 1934).

Erving Goffman (1959) likened the social world to a theater where human beings are
actors who manipulate, manufacture, and foster their many selves. Through the socialization process, one quickly learns society's views and expectations (generalized others)

of what it means to be gay, straight, bisexual, male, female, White, Black, Asian, Latino, and so on. Throughout one's life course, one continues to be informed on how to perform his or her various identities "on stage." Barry Thorne (1994: 35), for example, has illustrated how elementary school children are marked according to gender early on. The boy/girl dichotomies established in school form a social line of demarcation that can be introduced or used to reinforce differences at any given moment in the ongoing life of school children. The society has a social formula for how one is to present oneself. The presentation of one's outward racial-sexual selves then is viewed by and responded to contextually by the generalized others. Through this interactive process, one learns how to be a gendered, sexualized, racialized being. As Ruth Hubbard (1995: 49) has summarized: "each of us writes our own sexual script out of the range of our experiences. None of this script is inborn or biologically given. We construct it out of our diverse life situations, limited by what we are taught or what we can imagine to be permissible and correct."

Until recently, the generalized others' conceptualization of multiracials and GLBs has either been nonexistent or, when available, sorely negative and pathological. In a society that has not constructed a healthy, normalized social formula for "othered" groups such as multiracials and GLBs, many have had to navigate through unchartered waters without a working compass (Omi & Winant, 1986). Many of the interviewees discussed how they had to "figure out" their identities and "act out" their social uniforms without any script to follow. As one respondent explained:

> Okay, so now that I finally figured out that I wasn't crazy, that I was just a guy attracted to other guys and yet sometimes I still desired women and that I wasn't just Black but I was Black and Asian, I felt relieved. I guess you could call it like a personal liberation. But man! For a while I was trying to be everything and everyone, or should I say I was trying to "do" everyone, but not everything [laughs]. I dated Black girls to prove I was Black and had the goods to please my African sisters. I dated Asian girls to please my mom. I dated Black guys to be Black. I dated White guys. I dated Latin guys. No one ever told me how a Japanese-Black bisexual man was supposed to be like. Really, you have to find your own path. It might've taken me longer, maybe, because I'm bisexual and mixed, but we get through life and it's one big figuring out game. I wish my life came with a script so it would've been easier.

Allman (1996: 286) has explained how interracial families "contain opportunities for many permutations, confusions, and working out of racialized gender roles, engendered racial identities and multiple sexualities." A Japanese–European American bisexual respondent discussed how her interracially, heterosexually married parents provided her with a racial and sexual formula after which to pattern her own identity:

> Yes, I identify as mixed, Hapa, whatever you want to call it. I'm both Japanese American and White American. I'm also part-heterosexual. I arrived at this conclusion at an early age because I saw my White mom and my Japanese dad around in my house. They are interracial, and they are a heterosexual pair. I could understand who I was and how I was to be by looking at my parents; even though they weren't physically mixed like me, they were "mixed" by marriage. But as I came to understand my bisexuality, my parents' [heterosex-

ual] relationship became a strain, like a reminder of my difference. The fact that they were interracial became obsolete.

By being the product of an interracial marriage, this respondent was taught "who" she is (i.e., Japanese and European American). By being the product of a heterosexual marriage, she was shown "how" she is to be (i.e., to interact relationally to men and women in a heterosexual manner or as a heterosexual). However, her parents' lives offered her no social script to follow when it came to the lesbian aspects of her bisexual desires and attractions.

A Filipino–European American gay man also put forth how, lacking a social formula, he had to "figure it out" for himself who he was.

Which one was tougher [being gay or being mixed]? I can't really answer that in the way the question is framed. I mean, it's almost like being mixed and being gay assumes that I'll be fucked up. . . . Being mixed might've been a little easier because I grew up with other mixed kids. But I did have friends who were mixed, so it wasn't like there weren't other mixed kids around. I didn't feel like an alien Martian or something because I was mixed. There were lots of us around. . . . The hardest part was not knowing what my same-sex attractions were all about. I had to figure it out on my own. You learn real quickly that whatever attractions you're feeling as a gay child—and I didn't know what "gay" was back then, even though I knew I was a mixed child—those gay feelings made you feel real bad. And before I knew it, I hated those feelings, but they were there. It's not until I became a young adult that I was able to understand what it all meant. But no one taught me, no one told me, and there were no role models or books or manuals I could turn to and read and say, "Hey! Okay, that's what I'm feeling. That's how I'm supposed to be."

Another Japanese–European American gay man, who—for the most part—"passively" passes as a member of many different racial groups and as a heterosexual, explained how he came to understand and "settle into" his identity without a social formula:

I knew I was gay since I was three or four, and I knew I was half-and-half since about that time too. No one really told me what being gay was or being half-Japanese was all about. I just realized it through, I guess, just from daily living. Because I learned that gay people were "fags and sissies" and wanted to become girls, I thought I'm not really gay. I've always behaved stereotypically straight—whatever that means. I'm not feminine. I didn't play with dolls. I loved sports. I had guy friends growing up and we did guy things. I teased girls. I fought with other boys. So, I always felt confused about my attractions for guys. I felt some confusion for being mixed, like am I more Japanese or am I more American, but I settled into my racial identity pretty smoothly by the time I hit high school. I've been totally mixed since high school. . . . It's taken a little longer to settle into my gay identity. I mean, like finally figuring out that you can be masculine and be gay, that the two aren't mutually exclusive. Some people say that I'm passing for being straight. I'm not conscious of it. I'm just who I am and people impose their ideas of what is straight and what isn't onto me. I guess I do it too, but, yeah. . . . When I tell people I'm gay, they think I'm playing with their minds. When I tell them my race, a lot of people say, "Get outta here!" . . . They don't believe me.

The notion of passing—be it intentional or unintentional—reifies the social line of difference between gay and heterosexual, between men and women, and among socially defined racial groups. On one hand, intentional passing—especially for the more privileged status group—suggests that the "passer" is adhering to the strictly enforced boundaries and contributing to the maintenance of an oppressive racial-sexual hierarchy and reaping the benefits of a privileged status. On the other hand, if one is unintentionally passing because the "generalized others" misread racial and sexual cues and impose the society's formula onto the biracial and/or GLB individual, then the "passer" could arguably be said to cross, subvert, and transgress rigid lines of social demarcation based on race, gender, and sexuality (Daniel, 1992a; Williams, 1997)

Much like the Asian–European American who connected gender roles with sexual orientation, a Japanese–Mexican American lesbian also indicated how she came to understand her identity, although her phenotype and gender projections contradicted societal expectations:

> I feel more Mexican. My Japanese grandparents cut my father off when he married my mother so we were raised with my Mexican relatives mostly. I have a lot of Asian features so Mexicans think I'm *China* [Chinese or Asian], so I know I'm both even though my loyalty is with the *raza*, you know what I mean? As for my lesbianness, I look and act straight, unlike Laura [her biracial Mexican–European American lesbian cousin]. I'm—I guess you could say—ladylike, feminine, so most people think I'm straight. I'm very "out" about being gay, so when people think I'm straight, I have to clarify that. Sometimes it's bad when other lesbians think I'm straight, because then they won't ask me out, or when straight guys just won't let off on me. But, it's been good for me. My immediate family is so supportive about me being lesbian so. . . . But looking like what you feel you're not is something that I have to really try to make sense of, to myself. When you're told you look more Asian, but you feel more Mexican, or when you're told you look more straight, when you're lesbian, makes me very different from people who look and act like what they really are.

As simultaneous racial-sexual "others," Asian-descent biracial gay, lesbian, and bisexual individuals live and experience "the intersection between two aspects of our multiple self-maps, our sexual identity, and our racial/ethnic identity, and in particular, the experience of identifying as both bisexual and biracial" (Kich, 1996: 264). Thus Asian-descent biracial gay, lesbian, and bisexual individuals who are conscious of having marginalized social realities because they are gay, lesbian, or bisexual *and* biracial, learn to construct new ways of processing the self, to negotiate with the various communities to which they belong and the larger society that are already racially and sexually scripted, and ultimately to redefine a new social positionality that overlaps with all of their identities and incorporates their multiplicity.

When Sexuality and Multiraciality Collide

I participated in an annual conference by, for, and about Asian-descent multiracial university students in April of 1995. A group of gay, lesbian, and bisexual Hapas publicly challenged the organizers on the heterosexist focus of the conference.[2] They explained that just one week prior, they had attended an Asian/Pacific Islander Queer conference that had included a mixed-heritage workshop in which they were able to integrate their truly multiple identities in a way that acknowledged and affirmed multiraciality, gender, and sexuality. They further argued that many of the grassroots multiracial and interracial organizations that emerged in the 1980s and 1990s had failed to question their fundamentally homophobic and heterosexist nature and focus.

The question "What about the children?" is often asked of heterosexual interracial couples considering marriage in order to discourage them from such a "forbidden union." In the 1980s and 1990s, many interracial community organizations were formed out of trying to address this "simple" question. In fact, these organizations became influential forces in advocating and establishing U.S. Census recognition for multiracial people in the year 2000. However, the question "What about the children?" implies that the existence and identity of biracial individuals have been defined by the social relationships between the racial statuses of their parent groups; in other words, biracial children exist because their parents dared to cross taboo racial boundaries (Nakashima, 1992; Spickard, 1989). Interestingly, "the children's" concerns are also raised when gay and lesbian couples are considering having children through artificial insemination, adoption, or other alternative means. People thus instantly become champions of "the children's well-being" when they are vigorously opposing interracial marriages and/or gay and lesbian marriages. Until recently, the identities of multiracials have been viewed, measured, and explained in relation to their parents' racial groups and statuses (Root, 1992a, 1992b, 1996; Zack, 1995), which means they have been treated as "perpetual children." Those organizations that are dedicated to creating a social space for and guaranteeing the political legitimacy of biracial individuals, interracial couples, and the multiracial family have in fact only reinforced and reified the existence of an exclusively heterosexual, middle-class, nuclear (and therefore a heterosexist and classist) interracial family unit, as the Hapas of the 1995 conference testified.

Some of the GLB Asian-descent biracial interviewees shared their disappointments with heterosexual biracials who socially distanced themselves from GLB realities. A Filipino–European American gay man put forth why he did not feel that biracial/multiracial events would be positive for his self-identity:

> I don't think I would feel comfortable going to an all-mixed event now that I'm "out." Before I could lie about being straight, but it's not healthy. Most of the mixed people I know are straight, and they want to have mixed pride. I have mixed pride because being mixed has been a very positive experience for me. See, being mixed, automatically I feel like I'm seen as this "sex symbol." No matter how exploitative it may seem, hey! anytime you're thought of as good-looking, it makes you feel darn good. I don't need mixed pride. I need gay pride. And I certainly don't want to be talked about as, "Oh, another good-looking mixed guy who is gay. Too bad." Straight girls say that to me all the time. Too bad for who?

Being a "dual-minority" mixed-race person as well as a lesbian separated this Japanese/African American woman from most Asian-descent biracial activists who were part-European American and heterosexual at an event she attended:

> Well, I went to this meeting thing for a multicultural-like event. And, we had to introduce ourselves and tell our backgrounds. There were a lot of mixed people; most were like Black and White or Asian and White. That of course, already, was a different experience from mine

because I'm a double minority. Anyway, we were talking about interracial dating and all. . . . It was really interesting because these couples made comments like, "Well, *at least* we're dating and marrying people of the opposite sex, so why do people make such a big deal. It's not like we're GAY or anything!" So, of course, I'm thinking, well some of us are. There's always a pecking order within any group, and people are unaware.

A bisexual Japanese–African American man also reiterated that the subtle homophobic attitudes among heterosexual Hapas kept him from getting involved with multiracial activities:

I like being around other mixed people. It can be really affirming, especially meeting other Black and Japanese folks. But I realize that there is this invisible wall between me and the completely straight folks. I was hanging out with some Asian-White mixes the other day. These two Asian-White guys were joking around. When one guy accidentally sat on the other guy's lap, he said in a real feminine tone, "Ooh! Sorry. I just got a little too close there." And the other guy loosens his wrist to give a so-called effeminate, gay male gesture and responded back in a female voice, "Oh, honey! That's okay." I know these guys don't mean anything really bad, but it's the buildup of these subtle things that says to me that I don't want to be around straight people all the time, mixed or otherwise. This is the kind of thing that throws a wrench in mixed-race solidarity.

When questions of attraction and desire are such fundamental components of multiracial existence and identity, why then is sexuality not addressed beyond the confines of compulsory heterosexuality among biracial individuals in the multiracial movement? One might ask the critical question: are GLB Asian-descent biracials being embraced more by the Asian/Pacific Islander GLB community rather than the Hapa and/or multiracial community at large? If so, why? Although both are marginalized, do Asian/Pacific Islander GLBs have a more expansive and flexible understanding of their multiply marginalized status that allows them to include Hapas in ways that the heterosexual multiracial/Hapa community has yet to?

Multiraciality and Same-Sex Attractions: Themes of Convergences

The interviews of these eighteen Asian-descent biracials have highlighted some of the parallel experiences multiracials and GLBs generally incur as their racial and sexual realities converge. Although many outspoken heterosexuals of color have expressed their outrage on the comparisons made of race and sexual orientation by GLB activists, especially during the push for gays in the military and the legalization of gay marriages or gay adoptions (or most recently in California with Proposition 22, which stated California will recognize only marriages between a man and a woman). However, when examining how biraciality in particular exposes the socially constructed and politically maintained nature of racial identity, the interconnectedness of race, gender, and sexuality comes into focus. Thus, GLB multiracials, who are *both* biracial/multiracial *and* GLB, face an accelerated struggle and complexity with which to integrate their multiplicity amidst marginalization (Hutchins & Kaahumanu, 1991; Lim-Hing, 1994).

From the interviews, several common themes emerged that illustrate the parallels between notions of multiraciality and those of same-sex attractions, in addition to serving as examples of how Asian-descent multiracial GLBs must create and negotiate their personal racial-sexual identities against the backdrop of society's perceptions and constructions of them. Some of these parallel perceptions and experiences that inductively arose from the interviews include the following:

1. *GLBs and multiracials are perceived as hypersexual beings:* GLBs have been defined by sex, and biracials have been seen as the products of illicit, forbidden unions in which sex and (hetero)sexuality define their social perceptions. Stereotypes like the hot, sexy mulatta or the sultry, sensuous Eurasian—"half White purity" and "half colored hypersexuality"—illustrate how race and sex work to fuel racist ideologies, much in the way that the gender and sexuality of peoples of color have been racialized as well (e.g., the Black male rapist, the emasculated Asian male, the hot, passionate Latina). It is no wonder that genitalia have become measuring sticks of one's raciality in a racist, sexist, and heterosexist world. Likewise GLBs in general have been identified as hypersexual and sexually perverted, as their entire existence is treated as if it hinges upon sex and sexual acts, which are almost always described as "abnormal" and "perverse." For monoracial GLB Asians/Asian Americans and Asian-descent multiracial GLBs, these faulty images have often been constructed within sexually repressed, sex-phobic, nonverbal Asian cultures and a sexually repressed Puritanic Anglo-American tradition.

2. *GLBs and multiracials are perceived as emotionally crippled and genetically defective:* Not only are both GLBs and multiracials outside of the norm, but they also have been described by scientists and social scientists as "freaks of nature" who are unable to produce healthy offspring either because they are homosexual or because they are products of interracial sexual unions. In her critique of Madonna's film *Truth or Dare,* bell hooks (1992) points out how Madonna had rather patronizingly portrayed her Latino and Black gay male dancers as "emotional cripples." The hybrid degeneracy theory (Nakashima, 1992) that has long represented the "tragic mulatto" and "Amerasian dust children," for example, has also put forth that multiracials are torn between their parent races and thus doomed to eternal sadness or suicide. In the same way, one respondent noted that GLBs have been perceived as having nothing to look forward to in their sad lives but to grow into lonely old "faggots" and "dykes"or to choose suicide to end their misery.

The insidious connection between race and sexuality can be seen in the view of the multiracial person as the physical embodiment of two lustful people of different races who dared to defy racial taboos to engage in sexual intercourse, *and* the GLB person as the physical embodiment of nonheterosexuality. Thus, GLBs have been identified as (hyper)sexual beings "by nature." Physical defectiveness and deformity have characterized both the multiracial person (as the offspring of interracial sexual intercourse) and the GLB person (as a nonheterosexual who is sexually abnormal and perverse).

3. *Membership legitimacy and loyalty tests are frequently administered to GLBs and*

multiracials: In a racist world, where peoples of color across all sexualities are othered and marginalized, GLBs of color and heterosexual biracials who assert their multiple racial and sexual identities are at best looked upon as suspicious and at worst are fully excluded and denied membership not only into the larger White-dominated society but also into marginalized communities of color (Allman, 1996; Kich, 1996). Race-mixing has been interpreted by some as hurting communities of color because it takes place in the context of White racism, diffusing the minority cultures and decreasing the minority demographics (i.e., group resources) needed to combat the hostility of the dominant society. Similarly, homosexuality has been treated as a "White disease" meant to emasculate men of color and end the institution of family for communities of color. In some ways, Asian American cultures in particular may be prone to interpreting interracial relationships and homosexuality as forms of rebellion against their traditions and acceptance of White, liberal, selfish desires. Thus by dismissing interracial couples and homosexuality as foreign, the burden of proving ethnic legitimacy is placed on interracial couples, multiracial people, and GLBs.

4. *Processes of concealment and revelation often inform the identity development of GLBs and multiracials:* Both GLBs and multiracials are often forced to live in racial-sexual closets during certain periods of their lives, either temporarily, intermittently, or continuously. Both groups must often engage in the individual strategy of "passing" for a variety of racial-sexual groups, depending upon the social and political climate of the times; the racial-sexual peer pressure they face; and the social, economic, and political rewards at stake (Daniel, 1992a; Kich, 1996; Williams, 1997). "Passing," however, is not always an active, conscious choice. Using race, sex, and sexuality as compasses to navigate through their social environment, people often impose a racial-sexual label onto GLBs and multiracials (Omi & Winant, 1986). Unless there are identifiable social cues (which are often inaccurate and stereotypical), people are assumed to be heterosexual, monoracial, and monogendered (male or female). For example, GLB magazines like *The Advocate* have debated whether it is ethical to "out" well-known GLBs. *Interrace Magazine,* a publication for interracial families, featured an issue on "outing" multiracial celebrities, with actress Jennifer Beals on the cover (September/October 1991).

5. *GLBs and multiracials are often discussed within the debate of nature versus nurture:* There are "heterosexual" men who have same-sex attractions and may even engage in sexual activities with other men (e.g., situational homosexuality), but do not possess a conscious, articulated, public identity as "gay men." The identities of these men may be seen as paralleling the racial identification of mixed-race people who have cultivated a monoracial identity for whatever sociocultural reasons, even though their ethnic and/or sexual behavior and/or societal treatment may not always correlate. It is one's articulated identity, *not* his or her specific attractions, behaviors, or genealogical blend, that makes one gay, lesbian, bisexual, and multiracial.

6. *GLB and multiracial activism and visibility have increased:* As GLBs, especially those of color, and multiracial peoples carve out their social spaces, assert their rightful claim in the racial-sexual landscape, and fight for human and civil rights, their visibil-

ity will only continue to grow. Furthermore, GLB multiracials themselves will begin to challenge the separate GLB and multiracial movements—whose goals are in fact amicably intertwined—and will critically interrogate why either or both have not included them. It is not uncommon today to have GLB and multiracial identity panels at Asian American community events and academic conferences. The activism and visibility of GLBs and Asian-descent multiracials—many of whom are both—are manifestations of "no passing zones" (Houston & Williams, 1997), where marginality is transformed into empowerment and self-definition.

Conclusion

In Renee Tajima-Peña's critically acclaimed film *My America: . . . Or Honk! If You Love Buddha* (1997), she takes her audience on a cross-country journey from locations of the Asian American past into its present. After reviewing Asian Americans' tumultuous twentieth century, filled with exclusionary immigration policies, the World War II internment of Japanese Americans, the Civil Rights Movement, the Yellow Power Movement, the anti-Vietnam war protests, post-1965 immigration, debutante balls, and pro–affirmative action student rallies, Tajima-Peña offers a glimpse into the future. Tajima-Peña presents her own marriage to a Mexican American man, as well as the transnational, multiracial identity of a South Asian Indian–German lesbian, as examples of what the new millennium may hold.

On February 15, 1993, at the sixth annual Black Gay and Lesbian Leadership Forum conference, the keynote speaker, bell hooks, challenged heterosexual African Americans, who had championed civil and human rights for many generations, to expand their "fight for freedom" to include *all* African Americans. Speaking on behalf of gays and lesbians, she put forth poignantly: "If I can not share the truth of my existence, then how can you know or love me? And most importantly, how can you work for freedom on my behalf?" bell hooks's words powerfully resonate as a self-critique for heterosexually identified Asian-descent multiracials (and Asian Americans in general) who work politically and educationally on behalf of all Hapas for civil rights, social acceptance, and new conceptualizations of Asian Americanness.[3]

Asian-descent GLBs who live and operate in a variety of "passing zones" have much to offer Asian American communities, as Tajima-Peña forecasts in *My America*. Knowing and loving all of our community members, as bell hooks spoke, benefits all and brings liberation to our groups as a whole, regardless of how small they are in number or how invisible their members may be. When passing zones meet and converge, forming amorphously boundaried spaces of liminality, possibilities for transgressing one-dimensional prescriptions of identity and mapping new ways of being emerge. These converging passing zones, which become no passing zones "of resistance and empowerment in which Asian-descent multiracials define their composite identities, express their critical authenticities, and mark their social existences" (Houston & Williams, 1997: v, xi), encapsulate the active identities of peoples who transfigure multiple marginalities into something else (Anzaldua, 1987; Saldivar, 1997). As all of the communities to which Asian-descent GLBs belong by birth, by affiliation, and by identification come to see their social realities and struggles for liberation inextricably interlocked with multiracials, with Asian Americans, with GLBs, and with individuals who are "all of the above," human beings as a collective social entity will move incrementally closer to the praxis of inclusive politics and shared emancipation (Williams, 1999).

Notes

Acknowledgments: I dedicate this chapter to "Louie"—my teacher, my brother, my best friend—for providing a pioneering example of how to live across many *fronteras,* for claiming our Latin/Spaniard heritage openly, for catapulting racial and sexual multiplicity into new and uncharted areas of discourse, and for taking risks to soar to higher horizons. I thank Tracy Jay Williams, the University of California at Berkeley's M.A.P., Karen Maeda Allman, Cynthia L. Nakashima, and Michael Omi for their helpful feedback, comments, and critiques.

1. The term "no passing zone" was coined by playwright Velina Hasu Houston. In 1997 it became the title of the special issue of the *Amerasia Journal* focusing on writings by and about multiracial Asian Americans. While Houston applied the concept of "no passing zone" to an Amerasian character in her play *Broken English,* describing it as "a state of being in which she embraces all of her racial identities in a composite multiracial identity," the author of this chapter interpreted it as "a space of resistance and empowerment in which Asian-descent multiracials define their composite identities, express their critical authenticities, and mark their social existences" (Williams, 1997: 64). The author wishes to acknowledge Houston for her conceptual contribution to the title of this chapter.

2. Since the public criticism in April of 1995, this particular organization has had workshops on sexuality and has been making steps toward including GLB issues. Just as multiracial people (as a critical mass) have challenged monoracial communities to include and embrace multiracial issues as their own, GLB multiracials are now offering alternative paradigms for understanding multiple identity constructions and presentations.

3. As Asian Americans grapple with issues of multiplicity, diversity, and expansion, in addition to recognizing biracial and GLB Asian Americans, they have often discussed the need for also including deaf Asian Americans, immigrants and monolingual Asian-language speakers, poor and working class Asian Americans, disabled Asian Americans, and so on in their discussion.

CHAPTER 13

Mirror, Mirror, on the Wall: Mapping Discussions of Feminism, Race, and Beauty in Japanese American Beauty Pageants

Rebecca Chiyoko King

As I enter the grand ballroom on the night of the San Francisco Cherry Blossom Queen Pageant, I feel my throat catch and I try to breathe deeply as the nervous energy is palpable and voices rise louder and louder in a poor attempt to contain their excitement. As I sneak through the service entrance and slide quietly through the black velvet curtain to the back-stage dressing area, I am struck by the bright lights that surround the dressing-table mirrors. A long line of Japanese American women, both mixed race and monoracial, sit with stares affixed straight ahead as they consider their makeup, hair, and skin. As I plunk myself down, spinning around on the swivel chair, I begin to notice that some mixed race candidates are putting on heavier eye makeup to make their eyes more almond-shaped, while some consider using brown contact lenses to conceal their blue, "non-Japanese" eyes. Others have dyed their hair a darker shade of black in order to look "more Japanese." Still other monoracial candidates are trying to make their lips look bigger and to make their *daikon* ("white-radish") legs look longer and thinner. Both sets of women are working hard to conform to beauty standards that are difficult for them to obtain, and race has complicated this matter immensely.

Japanese American women contend not only with Western hegemonic notions of beauty, such as big lips and a tall, slim build, but also with counterhegemonic models of beauty that often draw on traditional Japanese American attributes, such as fair skin, almond-shaped eyes, and jet-black hair. Japanese American women have either tried to assimilate and fit in with hegemonic models of beauty in the United States or to create a beauty "difference" that itself has been co-opted by the mainstream as "exotic." Thus far, the theoretical literature on beauty has analyzed these hegemonic and counterhegemonic models in isolation, but has not examined the effect that counterhegemonic models have on hegemonic ones and the negotiation between the two. Hence, theoretically there is no way to understand the dynamic interaction that takes place between different models of the definition and maintenance of beauty for women of color. The experiences of multiracial women (who are both Japanese and white in this instance) offer a place where we can see the interaction of these two models of beauty most clearly, and perhaps develop a third way to interpret beauty as not just "white" or "Japanese American," but as a complex interaction of both. Counterhegemonic models of beauty are, of course, always shaped by hegemonic white models, but there is interaction between the two that could provide a space for new ways to "do" beauty, race, and gender. Beauty is neither a total reproduction of hegemonic norms nor counterhegemonic ideals, but instead is constructed out of an interactive process whereby women negotiate between the two.

The participation of mixed race Japanese American women in Japanese American beauty pageants is not a new phenomenon. Since the 1960s, as an outcome of increasing interracial marriage, there have been multiracial candidates in such community events. In fact, their increasing presence and participation prompted the adoption of "racial rules" (e.g., candidates must have at least 50% Japanese ancestry) to determine who was "authentic" enough to be allowed to represent the local Japanese American community.

This chapter illustrates that the judging criteria and beauty standards in Japanese American community pageants are qualitatively different than those in mainstream contests, such as the Miss America pageant, which are representative of hegemonic white beauty standards. After a brief historical review of the changes that have taken place in the Japanese American pageants over time as they moved from being primarily monoracial to being primarily mixed, I examine beauty construction interactions between the candidates, between the judges, and between the candidates and the community they represent.[1]

Feminism, Beauty, and Japanese American Women

Feminist critiques of beauty have argued that beauty pageants are sexist events that crystallize and perpetuate the highly specific and unrealistic images of beauty promoted by a patriarchal culture (Friday, 1996; Wolf, 1991; Bordo, 1993). They do not, however, examine the impact of these standards on women of color, apparently assuming that all women measure themselves against the hegemonic (white) model of beauty.

This situation can be seen in the beauty industry's attempt to encourage assimilation to white models of beauty by creating products such as skin lighteners and hair relaxers for black women and nose shadow for Asian women (Li, 1992: 32). By failing to recognize the difficulty that Asian American women have in being regarded as beautiful in a white-dominant context, the white feminist critics ignore the diversity of the women that they claim to represent. How then are women of color to negotiate a white model of beauty?

Japanese American women, for the most part, have focused on how they are forced into dominant white models of beauty (e.g., straight hair, light skin) in order to be considered beautiful. Christine C. Iijima Hall (1995a) suggests that because beauty images in the United States are premised on a white majority, the self-esteem of Asian women is harmed as they must constantly try to live up to a white model, with some even going so far as to have surgery to make their eyes look more Caucasian and therefore more beautiful.

However, studies such as Hall's, which focus only on how Japanese American women respond to hegemonic white models of beauty, miss the interplay that goes on between different, sometimes competing models of beauty.

Furthermore, Japanese American women also use their own active and independent models of beauty to undo the "dragon lady" stereotypes of Asian American women and to resist white-dominant models of beauty. While clearly there is some penetration of dominant models of beauty in these community contexts, Japanese American women have constructed alternative and powerful models that have not been sufficiently understood and analyzed.

The hegemonic white models and the alternative counterhegemonic Japanese American models of beauty interact and change over time. For example, in Japan a crooked tooth is often considered cute, and light (i.e., untanned) skin is seen beautiful, but both would contradict hegemonic white American images of beauty. On the other hand, American standards of beauty strongly influence Japanese styles, for example promoting "tea-colored" hair (dying hair to be light brown instead of black).

Other Asian American feminists have, however, warned that, instead of being considered beautiful for their physical "differences," many Asian American women have been exoticized and objectified (Espiritu, 1997). Once again, Asian American women are not seen as agents determining their own beauty. Japanese American women, for example, have been stereotyped as being "hyperfeminine" and attractive primarily for their docile, demure, and obedient characteristics (Espiritu, 1997). In other words, Asian American women either are not "white" enough and therefore are not beautiful, or are "unwhite" and therefore are exotic objects. The challenge for Asian American feminists is to negotiate a space between assimilation and exoticization where they can create and maintain their own images of beauty.

It is the interplay between these two conceptions of beauty that is at work in Japanese American community pageants. Both models—hegemonic white ones, which see height as an advantage, and counterhegemonic Japanese American ones, which value almond-shaped eyes, black hair, and light skin—interact especially in terms of mixed race Japanese American women, because they are constituted as both white and Japanese American.

Mixed race women, particularly those who are both Japanese and white, have struggled to balance these different models of beauty, often finding themselves looking "too white" to be seen as an authentic member of the Japanese American community, and "too dark/different" to be considered "white." Exoticized as a "beautiful mix," they are deemed a "sell out" if they cannot assimilate fully to either model. One place where the struggle for their own definitions of beauty has been publicly observed and commented upon is community beauty pageants. As mixed race women increase their participation in such events, they illuminate the process by which racial and ethnic groups debate their collective identity, the boundaries of the community, and the accompanying gendered expectations. They become the focus of collective Japanese American struggles about how the queens should look as representatives of the community as a whole.[2]

When mixed race Japanese American women started to become their community beauty queens in the 1960s and 1970s, they brought to the fore a debate over who was qualified to represent the community and what characteristics they should have. At the same time, this phenomenon revealed the ongoing tensions between both dominant white and alternative Japanese American models of beauty. Methodologically, these debates regarding mixed race pageant candidates represent an ideal case for studying the interaction of different racial and ethnic models of beauty.

Competing Models of Beauty in Japanese American Pageants

Because beauty pageants are community-driven, they provide a unique opportunity to see how a Japanese American community determines what it should look like, because the appearance of the queen herself is so controversial. For example, in 1982 in Los Angeles, when both the queen and first princess were racially mixed, there was a fierce debate in the *Rafu Shimpo* (a local Japanese/English newspaper) about "half queens." The controversy was ignited by a letter to the editor from Linden Nishinaga (1982), who wrote, "This disproportionate selection and seeming infatuation with the Eurasian looks not only runs [sic] counter to what I consider pride in our Japanese ancestry but also the very idea of Nisei Week itself." The debate continued, as other letters to the editor arrived that disagreed with Nishinaga's position. Clearly not only the queen's appearance but the group's visual definition of itself was at stake.

When there were an increasing number of mixed race queens in the 1980s, the debate roared forward precisely because her appearance was not seen as the "average" in the Japanese American community and therefore was not viewed as representative of it. One of Nishinaga's main arguments in 1982 was that because the majority of the Japanese American community in southern California was not mixed, its queen should not be either. This debate highlights the fact that an important part of being the queen was to be visually recognizable as Japanese American in order to symbolize the community. Social recognition as well as self-definition is necessary to authenticate the mixed race queen as a collective representation.

How then are these competing models of beauty, which have been debated so fiercely within the community, negotiated within the pageants themselves? In the course of my fieldwork, in the Japanese American beauty pageants, I often heard participants and the community volunteers advance three main views about the appropriateness of the mixed race candidates and their favored status. Some argued that mixed race candidates will win because they look more white (i.e., closer to dominant models of beauty). Others, however, disagreed and said instead that mixed race candidates don't win because they don't look sufficiently Japanese American to serve as an accurate visual representation of the community. For example, many people told me that a mixed candidate who was part-Chinese and part-Japanese would do better in the pageant because she was "full Asian," rather than white/Japanese or black/Japanese. Those who took this position support a counterhegemonic understanding of beauty, because they believe that the pageant is a context where alternative images of beauty are invented and reinforced. Furthermore, many of the interviewees argued that the pageants should retain their racialized, blood-quantum rules about who is allowed to participate. In other words, being 50 percent Japanese American is acceptable now, although some felt that if the number falls any lower, the pageants should be discontinued. Finally, still others felt that mixed race candidates win because they look mixed. Many felt that being mixed itself might be an advantage, because mixed people are seen as more beautiful since they are more "exotic" than either monoracial whites or monoracial Japanese Americans. While this point of view substituted a third model of beauty for the dominant and counterhegemonic models, it is one that is racialized and exoticized.

These three arguments thus reflect the tension that surrounds the issue of the incorporation of mixed race members in many Japanese American communities. Mixed race pageant candidates therefore find their bodies to be the catalyst for intense competition among three different models of beauty: dominant white norms, counterhegemonic traditional racial characteristics, and a new exoticization of mixedness. We see this present in the contestants, the judges, and the Japanese American communities themselves.

Racial Shifts in Community Pageants

When the community beauty pageants were first started in 1935 in Little Tokyo in Los Angeles, there were few, if any, mixed race participants and therefore little debate about the racial appropriateness of the queen. Initially the Nisei Week Queen pageant was more of a popularity contest based on votes cast through spending money in Little Tokyo. Later evolving into a more recognizable beauty pageant, the Nisei Week event was often spoken of as a place for Japanese American women to be seen as beautiful on their own terms. In this sense, the pageant was a home for Japanese American counterhegemonic notions of beauty, since mainstream ideas were not available to them. As Ellie Nagata, a queen from that era, told me, "We couldn't be Miss America, not after the war, but at least we could be Nisei Week Queen." Terry Goto, another former Nisei Week queen, said:

> If you think thirty years ago pageants were . . . well, it was a way for young Japanese American girls to get involved in pageants when you are obviously not going to be Miss America. You can't even be Miss California. But, hey, you want to be the prettiest Japanese American girl around—do this pageant.

Nisei Week and other ethnic pageants allowed Japanese American women to reaffirm their own beauty because they couldn't participate in mainstream images of beauty. This "ethnic pride" strategy was operating at the very same time that these same women were buying into the mainstream American idea of beauty pageants. Japanese American patriarchy, in this sense, was a copy, but not an exact one, of the more mainstream patriarchy of the time. The women themselves, though, thought it was "very daring" to take part in the pageant and considered it a feminist move to put themselves "out there" publicly and even risk losing. They saw participating in the pageant as a way to affirm their racial/ethnic identity as well as their identity as women, albeit in a patriarchal institution. At the time, the pageant was clearly dominated by counterhegemonic models of beauty, and the participation of mixed race women might have threatened the existence of this "safe space" to reaffirm Japanese American beauty. However, even though the rules at this point may have allowed mixed race women to participate, few did.

By the 1960s, however, the Japanese American community had an outmarriage rate of 50 percent or higher (Kitano, 1993; Shinagawa, 1994), and more mixed race women started to take part in the community pageants. But their participation was met with some opposition, and, as a result, pageants instituted racialized rules whereby a contestant had to have at least one parent who was 100 percent Japanese."[3] This is an illustration of how "ethnic legitimacy tests"(Root, 1996a) are taken to a "racial" level. Despite these rules, the presence of the mixed race women set off a communitywide argument about their beauty. Still, by the 1990s, their presence in San Francisco and Los Angeles was widely accepted, which raises the question of how the emergence of mixed race candidates has shifted the models of beauty within the pageant.

Negotiating Beauty Within the Pageant

Most of the mixed race candidates were caught between hegemonic and counterhegemonic understandings of beauty. They often explained that although they felt that looking Japanese was an advantage in the contest, they were being simultaneously attacked by the community for looking "too white." Some felt that the mixed race candidates had a better chance because they looked more white. As one mixed race participant said: "The Eurasian woman is much more attractive than the plain Japanese. She is taller and better looking."

One of the first mixed race women to become queen in her community in the 1970s was aware of the comments about her victory. "Some people were saying, well, 'Are we choosing queens based on a Western standard of beauty?' I don't know how much is sour grapes and how much is ethnic integrity." Even mixed race women who felt that they were beautiful in a larger context believed that they were not accepted in the context of the pageant. Sandra Jones, a recent Japanese/white pageant participant, explained that

> mixed kids are more cute, more beautiful, but we are not really Japanese. I have heard of [full] Japanese who want light eyes, curlier hair, bigger eyes. They want it because it is considered cute. But during the pageant, they kept saying to me, "You are so brown; stay out of the sun."

Many full-blooded Japanese, influenced by Western models of beauty, may want lighter or bigger eyes, as evidenced by the prevalence of cosmetic surgery and products to make eyes appear larger (Wagatsuma, 1967; Kaw, 1993; Hall, 1995a). However, in the context of the Japanese American pageant, these ideals may *not* be the desired look. Although Sandra's tan might be an advantage in a more mainstream setting, in the pageant her "brown" skin makes her ugly, as the volunteers remind her.

Many mixed women described themselves as being "caught in between" and spoke of the mixed message they felt they were receiving in terms of beauty. They admitted that media images prioritized a white woman as being beautiful, but they also recognized that looking white was not necessarily always the most desirable thing in all contexts—especially not in the context of Japanese American community pageants. The visibility of the queen as a symbol of the local Japanese American community was racialized to mean someone who looks Japanese. Therefore, those mixed race candidates who did not look Japanese felt they were at a disadvantage in the pageant.

Others argued that not looking Japanese (i.e., looking too white) hurt mixed race women in the pageant. As Terri Nakano, a monoracial candidate, explained about a mixed race fellow participant, "Her age and the fact that she was half held her back. She is just too white looking." Angela Hikomoto, also monoracial, added the following about the same mixed contestant: "What they are looking for is that stereotypical look . . . black hair and the brown almond-shaped eyes, but if you don't have that you don't quite fit, you know?" Sheila Taniguchi, a mixed race candidate herself, said:

> There will be people in the community who will say that she [a mixed race queen] doesn't look Japanese and it is important to them. If it is important how you look, then it has to be a Japanese person racially. You can't really get away from the visual aspect of it.

Thus even though the mixed candidates, especially those who are part-white, may be envied for their more "exotic" look in the larger society, they are made to feel less than authentic in the Japanese American pageants. Many mixed race women also realized that being a mix of two Asian groups—such as Chinese and Japanese—is better than being Japanese and white. As one candidate said: "It is sad that if you are half-Chinese and half-Japanese, that is still better than being half-Japanese and half-Caucasian. You still look Japanese so technically in the pageant it is better."

Judging Models of Beauty

Judges play a critical role in mediating the interaction of the models of beauty. Some candidates argued that Western standards of beauty would still be rewarded in the pageant if there continued to be Caucasian judges.[4] As one participant described:

> They had two actors who were judges. They weren't Japanese so maybe they didn't judge what others considered important, you know, classical Japanese traits. Like maybe they leaned towards big eyes and a voluptuous figure, and maybe the Japanese judges pulled away from that to feature Japanese features.

Another contestant had encountered a similar situation: "Some of the judges are in the movie industry. They are going to choose somebody who is more like the blue eyed blonde. It is whatever looks good to them." Others felt it important that Japanese judges be the majority, because they would assert Japanese American models of beauty. One former judge said that "a lot of people feel that an Oriental judge is better than a Caucasian judge because they look for different things. If you get a Caucasian judge, they go more for the body. An Oriental judge goes more for the face and how she carries herself."

Many people among contestants, judges, and the community at large felt that as long as there were both Caucasian and Japanese/Japanese American judges, the queen would reflect both models of beauty. The assumption being made here is that Caucasian judges are biased toward "white-dominant images and that Japanese judges have a different, Japanese image of beauty. Once again, however, the discussion focused on how to balance the two biases, and not on how to negotiate new images of beauty themselves.

Candidates and the Community

Many argued that a Japanese appearance was prioritized in the pageant because the queen represents the Japanese American community. Kelly Conlan, a mixed race contestant, explained what would happen if she won and went to Japan to represent the San Francisco Japanese American community to the Japanese. "If I win and go to Japan, people in Japan would . . . be curious because I don't look Japanese. I think they would be like, 'Who is she?'"[5] Another mixed race participant asked, "How can you represent the Japanese American community when people look at you and they don't see a Japanese American?"

Specifically, appearing Japanese to others was clearly identified as being important. There was ample evidence that even the mixed race candidates were aware that Japanese images of beauty that contradicted the white hegemonic ones were valued and reinforced in the Japanese American pageants. Cara, a mixed race candidate, explained:

> Also, going back to traditional Japanese beauty being the pale complexion: if you are out there with your California girl tan, that is bad in the pageant. . . . "Dark" to Japanese people means just like it did long ago—you are the peasant class; you work in the fields.

Sheila, a mixed race candidate, has internalized Japanese images of beauty that she applies to herself: "I know this sounds racist against myself but maybe it comes down to how Japanese you look. Japanese people look more natural in a kimono than *hapa* people. Don't you think?" Clearly the way one looks to others became the focus of the debate, and the mixed race candidate's chances for success in the pageant were thought to be highly correlated with how "Japanese" she looked.

Some mixed race Japanese American women have, however, become very popular and prominent community beauty queens. This in turn may be proof that "Japanese" looks may not be valued over other qualities, such as culture, language, or personality. Hence the participation and oftentimes the success of mixed race women may actually serve to undermine the need to look Japanese in order to be a good representative of the

Japanese American community as a pageant queen. Where counterhegemonic models had dominated historically, the definitions of Japanese beauty are now more hotly contested. Many also argued that mixed race women should and do win and go on to represent the reality of the Japanese American community, which is decidedly mixed.

Conclusion

Counterhegemonic models of traditional Japanese American beauty dominated the community pageants historically, but change has come with the increased participation and success of mixed race women. This shift has made the definition of "beautiful" a contested topic. The prior writings on models of beauty, even those by women of color, don't deal with the theoretical complexity needed to understand this case study. By examining Japanese American pageant candidates, judges, and communities, I have shown that mixed race candidates have not been able to create a new, nonexotic, more flexible model of Japanese American beauty. Instead, they have problematized the definitions of Japanese American beauty and have given rise to a debate about them.

Notes

1. This paper is based on a fifteen-month ethnographic and in-depth interview study of Japanese American beauty pageants in Los Angeles, San Francisco, Honolulu, and Seattle. All names have been changed. Many thanks are due to all those who hosted me during my research in these cities. I also thank Teresa Williams-León, Janet Francendese, and Seán Ó Riain for their much-needed comments, and the University of San Francisco Faculty Development Fund and the Irvine Foundation for their research support.

2. In general, all women of color have to struggle against white-dominant models of beauty. I am not trying to argue that they struggle in the same ways or have the same images. In fact, they are quite different. For example, black women are considered "hypermasculine," while Asian women are "hyperfeminine." Each group of women has its own images to battle, but the commonality is that they all are subjected to unattainable white images in addition to the stereotypical racially specific images they must grapple to overcome.

3. These rules were present in all the cities that I studied. In Honolulu, until 1999, a candidate had to be "one hundred percent Japanese" to participate in the Cherry Blossom Queen Pageant. In Seattle the blood-quantum rules have been more flexible. The examples given here are taken from the "official rules" of these pageants in 1995–96.

4. There have almost always been a mix of judges—both men and women, Japanese American and non–Japanese American. In Los Angeles, many of the judges who are not Japanese American have been Caucasians from the entertainment industry. Therefore, some people assumed that since they were white and in the entertainment industry, where mainstream images are valued, they would be looking for mainstream images of beauty in the pageant.

5. All the queens I studied win a trip to Japan and a kimono that symbolizes their link to Japan. They all explained that they see themselves as ambassadors of the Japanese American community while in Japan and that one of their primary goals is to develop stronger ties to the Japanese in Japan. This part of the queen's duties may reinforce what are seen as traditional Japanese models of beauty.

CHAPTER 14

Mixed but Not Matched: Multiracial People and the Organization of Health Knowledge

Cathy J. Tashiro

While I was working on a study of the lives of older mixed-race people of Asian American/White and African American/White descent, I kept a personal journal of events in which race would come up for me in everyday life. This chapter begins with one such event that illustrates many of the issues confronting multiracial people in a health system that organizes information about health risks by race.

Bone Density (or How Race Enters into Everyday Life for the Mixed-Race Person in a Seriously Flawed Health System)

Today I went to the local hospital to get my baseline bone density scan to assess my risk for osteoporosis.[1] I arrived early, but by the time I got through registration, I was late for my appointment. After the registration clerk completed my paperwork, she gave me my papers and told me to go to the osteoporosis clinic on the sixth floor.

I walked to the nearest elevator and pressed six. I got out on what looked like an intensive care unit. I walked down the hall and found an unobtrusive office that said something like "Osteoporosis Center." I stepped into the office to check in (by this time, I was five minutes late). The woman at the desk was on the phone, so she waved me back to the hallway to sit.

While I was waiting there for my appointment, I looked at my registration papers. While I hadn't been asked about my race, next to the race question on the form was typed the letter L. I smiled to myself that the woman who had processed my papers, who appeared phenotypically to be African American, must have thought I was a

Latina. I then mused a bit on what her impression of me might have been based on that identification.

Eventually another woman gave me some more papers to fill out. One of the first questions asked for my race. The choices were White, Black, and Asian. Without thinking much about it, I chose "Asian." I remember thinking that I should pick that to be consistent with what my Asian American doctor had put on my referral form, in which he had identified me as an Asian woman.

The test itself consisted of an enormously heavy piece of machinery passing slowly over my body with an ominous hum, after which a computer printed out the results in the form of a graph. As I was leaving, I asked the woman who conducted the test (whom I guessed was a Filipina) if the results were given according to a person's stated race, and she said they were. "I'm also half-White," I said. "Shouldn't you also analyze my results by averaging them?" "No, no," she said, "it can only be one race."

Risk and Race

In the United States, unlike many other industrialized countries, health statistics are organized by race rather than by socioeconomic status (Navarro, 1990). In certain cases, such as bone density measurement, different norms are used as diagnostic criteria for different racial groups. These norms are based on population averages for people who either self-identify or are identified by the standard Census racial categories. My encounter with the health care system for a fairly routine test raises several issues about the reliability of health information for people of mixed ancestry when it is organized by race. In my one encounter, I was recorded as a "Latina" in the hospital's statistics. However, my bone density values were recorded as those of an "Asian" woman. And the health of my bones, and thus my risk of osteoporosis, was reported to my doctor based on the norms for an Asian woman. Yet I am as much "European American" as I am "Asian American."

When I asked my doctor about the implications of this practice for multiracial people, he admitted that he'd never thought about it. One potential problem he could see could be the denial of reimbursement for treatment by insurance companies. He explained that treatment for osteoporosis is typically initiated when the woman's bone density is 2.5 standard deviations from the norm for young women of her race. Since Asian norms are lower than those of White women, my bone density could theoretically be deemed abnormal and indicate the need for treatment if I were categorized as a "White" woman, but considered within the normal range if I were categorized as an "Asian" woman.

My situation as a multiracial person encountering the health care system is not unique. In the course of my study of older multiracial people, Grace (a pseudonym), a woman of African American/White descent, described the following incident:

> I went in because I thought I was starting premenopause, so the nurse practitioner was checking me out and asking me all these questions, and somehow or other, she either

assumed or asked me if I was African American, and I said, "Yeah." So we've gone through all of this and she asked, she got down to the issue of bones and so forth, calcium, oh, that's right, you don't need to worry about that, because African Americans don't suffer from that. And I said no. I went out of there. I never thought twice. Not one time. So I'm at home, and I'm telling my husband what she said, and I said, "I don't have to worry about this," and he said, "Grace, you're half-White." And I went, "Oh, my God, I totally forgot that."

This quote raises some intriguing questions. Why did the nurse practitioner assume that Grace's social identification as an African American automatically protected her from a physiological problem? Phenotypically, Grace is very light skinned and could probably pass as a woman of Mediterranean ancestry. If she had identified herself as "White," what advice would she have gotten from the nurse practitioner? Why did Grace "forget" that she was half-White? In fact, Grace is more than half-White, as her "Black" father himself had a mix of African, European, and Native American ancestry. What is the meaning of the lower risk of osteoporosis for women of African descent who are mixed like Grace, given that the "Black" population from which her father comes and from which the averages are drawn is already mixed (Polednak, 1989)?

It is well accepted among medical practitioners that Black women, *on the average,* have denser bones than White women (Luckey et al., 1996) and thus a lower risk of osteoporosis. Bone density and risk of osteoporosis for Asian women vary by subpopulation, country of residence, and a variety of behavioral risk factors (Tobias et al., 1994; Huang et al., 1996; Ho, 1996; Lau & Cooper, 1996). But, to quote F. James Davis (1991), "Who is Black?,"[2] and, for that matter, who is Asian? People of mixed ancestry like Grace who identify themselves as "Black" on the Census and other forms are absorbed into data used in research that determines disease incidence and prevalence rates by race. And my data will be entered as those of an "Asian" woman (who was a "Latina" when she checked in!). The data inconsistencies for multiracial people are just the tip of the iceberg of the problems with the way statistical information about race and health is organized. I'd like to discuss some of these problems to put the multiracial issues in context.

The Question of Data Quality

When we are asked to "choose one" on the various forms we complete in the course of our lives, most of us have little inkling that we may be contributing to a vast database of morbidity and mortality statistics organized by race. When health data is gathered by race, it is almost always done so based on the standard Census racial groups (White, Black, Asian) and "Hispanic" ethnicity. Thus, the health profiles of people of mixed racial backgrounds have historically been effaced.

In 1970, nearly 88 percent of the U.S. population was racially identified as White; by 1990 one out of every four persons was a member of a racial or ethnic minority group (McKenney & Bennett, 1994). Traditionally, epidemiologic studies that have included female and non-White subjects have been rare (Jones et al., 1991). Now we are in an era in which inclusion of female and minority subjects is a condition for much of federally funded health research, based on the requirements of the National Institutes for Health Revitalization Act of 1993 (P.L. 103–43). While this has opened the door for very much needed attention to the particular health issues of racial and ethnic minorities, a multitude of issues arise when race and ethnicity are used as variables.

One important issue is how well the current racial and ethnic categories function as the basis for health statistics. The Census population totals for the racial and ethnic groups are commonly used as the denominators for incidence and prevalence rates of diseases within populations. The Federal Statistical Policy Directive No. 15, issued by the U.S. Office of Management and Budget (OMB) in 1978, currently provides the basis for Census racial and ethnic categories. It stipulates that federal agencies collect and present data on at least four racial groups, namely "American Indian or Alaska Native," "Asian or Pacific Islander," "Black," and "White," and on one ethnic group, "Hispanic." The OMB categories were implemented to meet the need for civil rights monitoring and for other legislative and agency reporting. The directive is clear that the categories are social, not biological classifications.

In 1993, the OMB began collecting recommendations from the public regarding revisions to the racial and ethnic categories. On August 28, 1995, they published the "Interim Notice of Review and Possible Revision of OMB's Statistical Policy Directive No. 15: Race and Ethnic Standards for Federal Statistics and Administrative Reporting," which summarizes testimony gathered at several public hearings on racial/ethnic classifications for the year 2000 Census. Out of this voluminous testimony, perhaps the most contentious issue was the growing demand for a multiracial category. To get a sense of the dimensions of this situation, the report states that whereas in 1960 there were approximately 150,000 interracial marriages, in 1990 there were about 1.5 million. In 1990, 4 percent of couples reported that the partners were of different races or that one was of Hispanic origin. Such households had about *four million* children. Granted that probably not all of these children are of mixed heritage, as these households may include children from previous unions of the parents, still the numbers are undoubtedly greater than the two million that the report indicates is the population size necessary to merit inclusion as a separate category. Although the 2000 Census did not include multiracial designation, respondents were permitted to check more than one racial category. Other federal programs will be required to adopt the revised standards no later than January 1, 2003.

We don't yet know the full impact the OMB decision will have on the organization of public health statistics. If nothing else, the documented existence of a multiracial population will hopefully cause people who use this data to question their assumptions about the relationship between race and health status.

We do know that there are inherent problems with the reliability of data based on the existing racial and ethnic categories. For a category to be useful for research purposes, it must be replicable, that is, it must show reliability and consistency with repeated measures (Hahn & Stroup, 1994). In a study on infant mortality and racial classifications, Robert Hahn, Joseph Mulinare, and Steven Teutsch (1992) discovered major inconsistencies between the race recorded at birth and at death for U.S. infants born from 1983 through 1985 who died before the age of one year. This was particularly pronounced for infants of races other than Black or White, of whom 43.2 percent had a different race recorded at birth and at death. The authors found that when infant mortality rates were calculated using consistent racial definitions at birth and death, the rates were lower for Whites and higher for all other racial groups. The increase in mortality rates was particularly pronounced for American Indians, Chinese, Japanese, and Filipinos.

For infants born to parents of different races, the problems with correct and consistent identification are compounded. Prior to 1989, the race on a newborn's birth certificate was determined by the race of the parents. An infant with one White parent was assigned the race of the non-White parent. If neither parent was White, the child was assigned the race of the father. Since 1989, the race of the mother has been indicated as the child's race on the birth certificate (Hahn et al., 1992). This raises obvious problems when the child's parents are of different races.

Even when individuals are self-reporting their race, responses are inconsistent over time. For example, 34.3 percent of household members reported different ethnic identities to the U.S. Bureau of the Census in March 1971 and March 1972, and 41 percent of respondents identifying as "American Indian" in a reinterview study had reported themselves as "White" in the 1980 Census (Hahn, 1992). Individuals' identification with a particular racial or ethnic group can fluctuate over time as a function of changing social conditions. Social movements, for example, can change individual and collective identities and identifications (Espiritu, 1992; Nagel, 1994).

In addition to the inconsistencies in the categories applied to and chosen by individuals, there have been major inconsistencies in the terms themselves. For one thing, no single racial classification scheme has been used for more than two Censuses since 1800 (Goldberg, 1997). Also, the Census categories have been inconsistent with each other; they have reflected an illogical mix of national origin, tribal affiliations, and physical characteristics to distinguish groups. The ambiguity over what really constitutes "race" is reflected in the contradictory and confusing construction of the racial and ethnic categories. Race is conflated with ethnicity, nationality, culture, and language. For example, the current categories subdivide Asian "race" by nationality or country of origin, while doing the same for Hispanic "ethnicity."

Finally, while Census counts of racial and ethnic groups are used to determine rates of various illnesses by population, there are differences between the Census format and other surveys that form the bases of public health surveillance. These include different data collection methods, different content and format of questions, and different criteria for inclusion in racial and ethnic categories. In some health surveys, "race" and "Hispanic origin" are combined. Categories may vary by agency; for instance Medicare uses "white" and "all other races" or "white," "black," and "all other" (Hahn & Stroup, 1994).

In summary, the problems encountered when attempting to classify people by race foreground the inherent contradictions of the entire structure of the racial classification system, the meaning of race, and the problems with racializing health research and data.

Conceptual Problems

The 1995 edition of *A Dictionary of Epidemiology* defines race as "persons who are relatively homogenous with respect to biological inheritance" (Last et al., 1995: 139). Although the lack of a biological basis for race has been established in science for decades (Dubinin, 1956; Livingstone, 1964), and although there is more genetic heterogeneity within than between the groups we call "races" (Barbujani et al., 1997), the belief in race seems to have a power and life of its own. This belief is reinforced by everyday experience in which race is one of the most fundamental characteristics organizing social experience in the United States (Omi & Winant, 1994). Nowhere are the contradictory messages about what race is and isn't more apparent than in the arena of health research, which provides the foundation for standards of medical practice.

Health care professionals and researchers are not immune to belief in the everyday "knowledge" about race that is promoted in the greater society, as demonstrated by the outdated definition in *A Dictionary of Epidemiology*. In fact, the ways that race is treated in health care research reveal the larger society's contradictory thinking about race. In addition, disease and illness have physical, biological manifestations, which makes medical and public health literature particularly prone to bias toward genetic interpretations of variations in health and illness patterns among different populations. The fact that people who do health care research conduct their work "scientifically" simultaneously obscures the degree to which they are affected by the biases of the larger society and affords their work a legitimacy that further reinforces those biases in the public mind.

I have found Pierre Bourdieu's (1977) concept of *doxa* to be a useful framework for analyzing the reproduction of scientific knowledge about race in context. *Doxa* is a society's body of knowledge for which there is no consciousness of alternative knowledge. It is the type of knowledge that is taken for granted. It includes the role that dominant classes play in maintaining control over the boundaries of the "thinkable." While there have been diverse scientific perspectives on race, *doxa* offers insight into why the *dominant* science of the last several centuries has, by and large, reflected the racial worldview[3] of the dominant classes in society. Our knowledge of race is *doxic* knowledge. On the one hand, science is a recognized authority in the realm of formal knowledge. Science appropriates for itself the role of the avant-garde in the production of knowledge. Yet scientists are subject to all the unconscious biases, the prevailing *doxa,* of the society. If those biases are unrecognized, scientists have the power to reinforce and legitimate them.

The concept of biological differences between the races in the United States developed in the context of slavery and colonialism. For example, Nancy Krieger (1987) provides a vivid account of medicine's justifications for slavery, which were based on the "biological inferiority" of Blacks. Much research on racial variations in health is based on a genetic model that emerged in the late eighteenth century. According to this model, race is a biological category. The genes that determine race are linked to those that determine health, and the health of populations reflects their inherent biological robustness. This heritage is still present in current thinking on race. David Williams, Risa Lavisso-Mourey, and Reuben Warren (1994: 27) rightly point out that treating race as biological is less threatening to the status quo. "If racial or ethnic differences in health result from innate biological differences, then societal structures and policies that may be involved in the production of disease are absolved from responsibility and can remain intact."

There are numerous instances in which flagrant bias has contaminated "scientific" perspectives on racial differences (Gould, 1981). A good example is the scientific support provided by early geneticists for the belief in the dangers of race-crossing. Charles Davenport, the first American scientist to focus on human genetics, alleged that cross-breeding between races was ill-advised, because combining the different characteristics of the parents would lead to disharmonious results in the offspring (Provine, 1986). For example, crossing a tall race with a short one would yield children with either large frames and small organs or small frames and large viscera. This extremely mechanical view of heredity seems ridiculous now, but was accepted as scientific wisdom for decades.

It is encouraging that prominent voices from medicine and science are emerging to contest these deeply held prejudices about the nature of race. On April 9, 1997, the President's Cancer Panel convened a meeting of experts on "The Meaning of Race in Science." Dr. Harold P. Freeman (1997), the chairman of the panel, summarized its main points in his letter to the president:

- Race as used in the United States is a social and political construct derived from our nation's history. It has no basis in science or anthropology.
- Biologically distinct races do not exist. Indeed, there is no evidence that they have ever existed in the recorded history of the human community.
- Neither is there a genetic basis for racial classification. . . .
- Racism, rooted in the erroneous concept of biological racial superiority, has powerful societal effects and continues to influence science.

But If Race Isn't Real, Why Are There "Racial" Differences in Health Status?

We have reviewed the problems with the quality of health knowledge organized by race and heard from some experts that race doesn't exist. But what about sickle cell anemia, pleas for racially matched bone marrow donors, and elevated rates of black hypertension and infant mortality? We are inundated with such information, which seems to confirm the existence of race as a meaningful biological category. Does a constructionist view of race break down when we have to deal with flesh and blood? To properly address this question, we need to briefly visit population genetics and determine what aspects of human genetic differences *are* real.

Our current racial classifications derive from eighteenth-century European conceptions of how to organize human diversity (Schiebinger, 1993), which were inextricable from the prevailing social attitudes toward the "less civilized," darker-skinned people Europeans encountered in colonial projects. Although present knowledge of population genetics and physical anthropology provides alternative ways of categorizing people, *no* scientific system of categorization corresponds to current racial classifications.

An alternative way of organizing people by genetic characteristics is based on the concept of "breeding populations" (Molnar, 1983), which are those that have been breeding in relative isolation, due either to geography or to culturally imposed restrictions on marriage. As a result, they have developed certain common genetic traits that are distinctive to their population group. The size and configuration of breeding populations are much smaller than "racial" groups or nations. Examples include remote villages, tribes, and religious enclaves whose members are prohibited from marrying outside the group. "Genetic drift," or increasing genetic differentiation, increases with isolation, resulting in differences between small, isolated groups. This diversity amongst groups makes generalizations about larger population units like "races" and nations problematic.

Another way of classifying populations is by clinal distribution, which locates the geographical range of human genetic or morphological characteristics. Clines map these characteristics. Clinal mapping can be done for many types of human variations, including skin color and hemoglobin S, which is responsible for sickle cell anemia. As with breeding populations, populations that are organized by clinal distribution bear little resemblance to our traditional "racial" boundaries. For example, although sickle cell anemia is viewed as a "Black" disease in the United States, the clinal distribution of hemoglobin S covers parts of Africa, the Middle East, southern Europe, and Southeast Asia. It has been widely hypothesized that the sickling of the red cells arose through natural selection as a protective response to malaria (Molnar, 1983; Bowman & Murray, 1990). People who are sicklers are less likely to die from malaria than people with normal hemoglobin. The clinal distribution of hemoglobin S falls within the distribution of malaria across the globe. Thus, the propensity to have hemoglobin S is not restricted to people of African descent; nor does everyone of African descent have a higher risk of having the abnormal hemoglobin. Large areas of northern and southern Africa are outside the malaria belt and the clinal distribution of hemoglobin S.

How people are organized into groups, or "races," depends on what traits are chosen by the organizers. For example, if people were organized into races based on their ability to digest milk and absorb the milk sugar lactose, most people of Asian, African, and Native American descent would be in one race and most people of northern European ancestry in another. However, there are important differences within these populations. For example, lactose intolerance approaches 0 percent among the Batusi people of Central Africa and affects only about 20 percent of the Fulani of West Africa (Bowman & Murray, 1990), which would put these groups in the same "race" as Swedes, Finns, and other northern European groups. To us this may seem absurd, but who is to say that skin color, eye shape, or hair texture provide more reliable bases for classification?

While there are variations between breeding populations, there is far more genetic variation within the groups we call "races" than between them. A recent study of sixteen populations around the world found that differences between members of the same population account for 84.4 percent of genetic variability (Barbujani et al., 1997). The greatest genetic variability exists amongst peoples of African ancestry (Lieberman, 1995). According to Barton (1997), this diversity would be expected if the population in Africa is the most ancient, a hypothesis supported by various genetic and fossil studies. The prevalence of genetic diversity within the African population is hypothesized as the main reason why people of African ancestry in the United States have more difficulty finding matching organ or bone marrow donors, even within the population defined as "African American" (Beatty et al., 1995). In addition, because of the "one-drop rule," the population defined as African American includes people with a variety of ancestral origins.

The probability of finding a successful organ or tissue donor/host match is dependent on the human leukocyte-system A antigens (HLA), which have the primary function of enabling the host organism to distinguish between its own tissue and that of others. When there is a close HLA match, there is less likelihood that the host will reject the donor tissue as that of an "other" (Bowman & Murray, 1990). For Asian Americans seeking donors, politically constructed panethnic (Espiritu, 1992) terms like "Asian" have limited utility if we refer back to the concept of "breeding populations," since significant genetic differences between Asian subpopulations have been reported (Geng et al., 1995; Bugawan et al., 1994).

For people of mixed ancestry, there is some overlap between the most common HLA configurations in people self-defined as "African American" and in those self-defined as "Caucasian," just as there is with the "Asian American" and "Caucasian" categories. But which HLA antigens will be inherited from which parent and whether a matching configuration can be found in a donor cannot be predicted. It thus should be clear that, while there are genetic variations based on ancestry from a particular breeding population, they don't fit neatly into our racial categories. More research on these questions is needed, particularly as the population of mixed ancestry grows.

For the vast majority of health problems, there is no clear-cut genetic basis for "racial" differences in morbidity and mortality. If there does seem to be a genetic component, as in the case of osteoporosis, its effects are further mediated by environmental and behavioral factors like physical activity, smoking, childbearing, and calcium intake. So how do we interpret "racial" differences in health status, and how should these differences be studied? As Molnar (1983: 124) states:

> The way in which we choose to group human populations depends, of course, on our purpose. We must keep this purpose in mind when working with these groups. For example, one should not establish races or ethnic units on the basis of sociopolitical criteria and then explain or interpret their existence in biological terms.

In fact, much of what has been done in the way of epidemiological research on racial differences in health status has done just that. Too many researchers have unproblematically accepted socially constructed races as biological entities and have looked for biological reasons for social causes of disease. Causal direction is at the heart of the debates about the effect of race on health status; in other words, do a person's race(s) *cause* his or her health status, or does the fact that he or she is part of a socially constructed "racial" group put the person at risk for social, economic, and environmental influences on health?

There is a need for more examination of racism, rather than race, as a factor influencing health (D. R. Williams, 1996). Some of the most thoughtful research on the health problems of people of color has looked beyond race as a cause of poor health to the long-term effects of racism. An example is Nancy Krieger and Stephen Sidney's (1996) study of the effects of racial discrimination on hypertension. There is also increasing attention to community influences on health, such as the effect of housing segregation on Black/White differences in infant mortality (Polednak, 1991).

Where Do We Go from Here?

Given the problematic origins of the conceptual bases for the treatment of race in health care research, what should be our stance regarding the use of racial categories in such studies? One of the fascinating and frustrating aspects of work on race at this moment is its contradictory nature. On the one hand, the idea of doing away with racial categories altogether is appealing as a means of attempting to demolish the myth of race. However, to do so risks masking evidence of the inequalities that have been engendered along the lines of existing racial definitions. There is a need to negotiate a space from which to consistently challenge the basis of racial classifications as reflecting a fundamentally racist epistemology, while simultaneously giving every attention to the very real effects of racism on specific populations. We are left with the challenge of how to situate race in a way that does not reinforce the assumption of a biological basis for difference, yet at the same time seeks to remedy the inequalities that the very concept of race has engendered along "racial" lines. We need to study "race," but to do it better (LaVeist, 1996), to treat it as a social variable, not a biological one, and to argue for research approaches that acknowledge its complex meanings. Acknowledging the existence of multiracial people is a key part of that agenda. When it is clear that there are many of us who are not just one "race," then people of mixed ancestry like Grace and myself will be one step closer to getting information about our health that considers the totality of who we are.

Notes

1. Osteoporosis is a condition in which the bones become more porous and thus at higher risk for fractures (Johnston & Melton, 1993).

2. Davis describes the emergence of the unique system of racial classification of people of mixed African descent in the United States in *Who Is Black? One Nation's Definition* (1991). That system eventually solidified into the "one-drop rule" whereby anyone with a "drop" of African "blood" is considered "Black."

3. The "racial worldview" of the United States as described by A. Smedley (1993) includes the universal classification of human groups as mutually exclusive entities; a hierarchical ranking of those groups; the linking of physical characteristics with innate qualities; the inheritability of these qualities; and the belief that the differences between the races are untranscendable.

Section IV

Asian-Descent Multiraciality in Global Perspective

Students of the topic of mixed race might be surprised to learn that the first academic anthology on the subject to be published in the United States was not Maria P. P. Root's *Racially Mixed People in America* (1992a); but rather a collection of international scholarly articles entitled *The Blending of Races: Marginality and Identity in World Perspective,* edited by sociologists Noel P. Gist and Anthony Gary Dworkin, and published in 1972. Unlike more recent U.S. scholars of multiraciality, Gist and Dworkin (1972: 2) approach the topic of multiracial people and populations on a global scale, as an outgrowth of European expansionism and colonialism:

> Large-scale colonialism and military conquest were for centuries a feature of Western imperialist expansion in which European powers sent troops and civil personnel to the "backwards" countries whose people usually differed racially and culturally from the Western conquerors. . . . It was almost inevitable that contacts with local people would lead to sexual unions, either in conventional marriage or in unconventional relations. . . . Their progeny thus exhibited visible genetic traits, including color, inherited from both ancestral lines. . . . It is these people of dual or multiple racial heritage who are the subject of the essays in this volume.

Reading through the chapters in *The Blending of Races* on the "Anglo-Indians of India" and the "Part-Aborigines of Australia" reminds us of three important points: (1) multiraciality is neither an entirely contemporary nor a peculiarly American phenomenon; (2) the development of a group consciousness around multiraciality and even the political mobilization around this consciousness are also neither new nor particular to the United States; and (3) the experience and condition of being racially mixed are very much matters of context. More explicitly, what it means to be "mixed race" is largely dependent on the temporal, geographical, spatial, social, and cultural context of the individual or population.

In this fourth and final section of the book, we look beyond the confines of the United States to consider multiracial Asians in a very broad sense—across time, space, culture, and society. By examining aspects of multiraciality as it has been and is currently experienced in England, Holland, Japan, Suriname, and Thailand, we hope to gain insight into the past, present, and future of multiracial Asians in America.

Writing from England, David Parker (Chapter 15) takes a look at an older generation of mixed-race Asians who are sometimes called the "Anglo-Chinese." He describes the small seaport communities where Chinese men met and married British women as historically and geographically "exemplary spaces." As Parker says, "the testimonies of 'mixed-race' Chinese people who grew up in those exemplary spaces offer rich resources for understanding how complex combinations of class, cultural, and local differences were negotiated."

In Chapter 16 Mark Taylor Brinsfield studies a population of mixed-race Asians that is several generations old and continuously evolving. His discussion of the Dutch/Indonesian Eurasians in Holland depicts a multiracial, multiethnic, transnational community that is currently experiencing what some are calling a cultural renaissance. Whether the "Indos" will continue to exist as a population and a culture, disappear into the Dutch mainstream, or become something else again is a question that parallels those asked not only about the mixed-race community in the United States but about certain Asian American communities as well.

In Chapter 17, Stephen Murphy-Shigematsu, a professor at Tokyo University, traces the representations of the American Japanese population in Japan as reflected by the terminology used to describe them. From the post–World War II era to today, the shifting terms and ideology about this multiracial/multiethnic population have reflected changing social, political, and economic conditions within and outside of Japan.

Loraine Y. Van Tuyl explores in Chapter 18 the condition of being multiracial Asian in Suriname, a country with an astonishingly diverse population and the highest percentage of Asians in South America. While the dominant culture of Suriname recognizes a very long history of mixing and is thus extremely tolerant of interracial marriage and multiracial people, the people she interviewed reveal that much of their experience with being mixed race is related to the specific ethnic groups to which they belong.

And finally, in Chapter 19 Jan R. Weisman looks at the packaging and consumption of American golf superstar Tiger Woods by the mainstream culture of Thailand. Questions of authenticity and essential "Thai-ness" have been projected onto the multiracial Woods in a way that is both familiar and unfamiliar to Americans. Using ethnographic data gathered in Thailand, Weisman examines how "the conflicts and contradictions in the Thai reception of Woods reflect the articulation between identity politics and issues of modernization and globalization evident in contemporary Thai society."

CHAPTER 15

"We Paved the Way": Exemplary Spaces and Mixed Race in Britain

David Parker

I've been wanting to write a chapter like this for many years, having been stimulated by the collections edited by Maria P. P. Root (1992c; 1996a) and having met a handful of other "mixed-race"[1] British Chinese through the course of my research (Parker, 1995). However, the final inspiration was rediscovering a group of evocative black-and-white photographs (see Photo 15-1) taken in the 1930s in London's former Chinatown in Limehouse. When I first came across these images, I was taken aback. Here was evidence that mixed-race Chinese people in Britain were nothing new. By writing this chapter I have been able to trace some of those who appear in the photographs and who can remember others who do as well.

Despite all the recent work connecting the concept of hybridity with older, uncomfortable treatments of race from the nineteenth and early twentieth centuries (see, for example, Werbner & Modood, 1997; Young, 1995), few scholars have talked to the people who were actually described as "hybrids" by sociologists such as Robert Park (1931).[2] Debates on either side of the Atlantic have instead devoted too much attention to the glamour, celebrity, and youthful vigor associated with mixed race. I hope to add an at least partially ethnographic counterpoint to the usual level of abstraction in discussions about identity. Too often, older mixed-race people are overlooked, yet their experiences might historicize voguish terms such as "hybridity" and instruct us on the long-standing intermixtures of modernity.

The particularities of racialized configurations call for small-scale archival and ethnographic work to retrace the heterographies of settlement (Hesse, 1993) and the heterochronicity of diverse historical trajectories that together have formed multicultural societies. This chapter is a report on work in progress that attempts to trace out a new genealogy of British Chinese identity. It is based on archival research and discussions with twenty-four people, primarily in two areas of established Chinese settlement in Britain: Liverpool and London.

PHOTO 15-1. "Three Little Girls in Chinatown," S&G, 4 November 1932. (Courtesy of Tower Hamlets Borough, Bancroft Library, London.)

Although the focus is on the older mixed-race generations, now in their sixties or above, I also talked to a number of people in their late twenties to examine intergenerational differences. This exploratory study is a preliminary attempt to assess what we share, and indeed whether "we" is an appropriate designation at all.

The Importance of Specificity

As I have argued elsewhere (Parker, 1995), it is important to highlight the different location of Chinese people in Britain's racialized hierarchy compared to that occupied by Asians in the United States. The term "Asian," when used in Britain, refers virtually exclusively to South Asians rather than East Asians. There are under two hundred thousand residents of Britain who were classified as "Chinese" by the 1991 census; there are no cities with concentrated Chinese populations.

However, there are historic sites of Chinese entry into Britain, which had been connected with the imperial trade with East Asia since at least the eighteenth century. This brought a small population of seafaring Chinese men to a handful of port cities, most notably London and Liverpool (Parker, 1995). By the late nineteenth century, a small settlement of Chinese seafarers had gathered in East London around the River Thames in two streets, Pennyfields and Limehouse Causeway. In Liverpool Chinese seamen and businesses clustered in a small area near the docks around Cleveland Square, Pitt Street, and Frederick Street.

There were hardly any Chinese women in Britain prior to the Second World War, so mixed marriages and relationships prevailed. In addition, as one researcher observed at the time, these were not ethnically homogeneous areas: "It seems useless to argue the pros and cons of the 'advisability' of an interracial cross, since our Imperial Commercial system is linking all possible races in our seaport towns, and has been doing so for some generations" (Fleming, 1927: 300–301).

Exemplary Spaces

In this chapter I intend to conceptualize these seaports as "exemplary spaces." Recent work in cultural studies has accentuated the spatial dimensions of social life (for example, Keith & Pile, 1993). Spatial metaphors have proliferated in discussions of cultural identity. Homi Bhabha's (1990: 211) statement that "hybridity . . . is the 'third Space' which enables other positions to emerge" marks an important intervention. Unfortunately some appropriations of this spatial turn run the risk of dehistoricizing the very processes they seek to validate (for a prime example see Soja, 1996). The term "exemplary spaces" is intended to balance the historical and geographical dimensions; a complete understanding of identity formation must give both equal weighting. In this case, seaports such as London and Liverpool are not best regarded as "third Spaces," since the term "third" could imply coming *after* first and second spaces, whose nature is not specified. Defining these cities as exemplary gives them a temporal priority in keeping with their importance as forerunners. The testimonies of mixed-race Chinese people who grew up in those exemplary spaces offer rich resources for understanding how complex combinations of class, cultural, and local differences were negotiated.

British Chinese Histories

Chinese people started arriving in Britain in significant numbers at a historical moment, the late nineteenth century, when British national self-esteem was in crisis. The growth of Germany, Japan, and the United States threatened Britain's global dominance, and the defeats suffered in the Boer War in the early 1900s led to a period of soul-searching and introspection marked by a concern with the fitness of the nation-race. It is no coincidence that in the following two decades the scientific discourse of eugenics secured cross-party support, even attracting intellectuals of the left such as Sidney and Beatrice Webb and Maynard Keynes (Searle, 1971; Hawkins, 1997; Kevles, 1986).

Mixed-race people became an object of inquiry in a very particular set of British urban spaces that could be described as "contact zones" (Pratt, 1992) or "interzones" (Mumford, 1997). These areas had a distinct social geography, wherein relations of proximity and intimacy between groups designated as radically different were simultaneously sexualized and racialized. The seaports of London and Liverpool have a very particular role in the iconography of a maritime empire professing to "rule the waves." They were critical nodal points in the circuits of imperial domination, sites where material traffic in goods and people generated new images of cosmopolitanism and decadence.

Conceptualizing port cities as exemplary spaces highlights the conjoining of spatial and temporal dimensions in the formation of social identities. Terms such as "contact zone" and "interzone" capture the spatial metaphors used to figure racial mixing, as do the "colour line," "boundaries," and "borderlines." The focal points of concern in the early twentieth century were cafés, dance halls, restaurants, laundries, and opium dens—settings where interracial contact took place. The idea of exemplarity is intended to encompass the temporality of white anxiety evident in responses to the appearance of mixed race children in British seaports. These spaces came to exemplify all the sources of difference to be held at bay if national boundaries were to be secured and national identity safely transmitted untainted to future generations. Consequently, these ports were racialized as exemplary spaces where the specters of modernity haunted the social imaginary and were to be banished by various forms of social hygiene and moral disapprobation. The culturally diverse population of these port cities and their mixed-race children became the focus for recurrent press campaigns, social investigation, and philanthropic intervention (Barkan, 1992; Rich, 1986; Fletcher, 1930). One indicator of the anxiety at impurification is the press campaign against Chinese settlement in the early twentieth century (Waller, 1970).

Stimulated by the landing of thirty-two Chinese sailors in London in November 1906, "special correspondent" Claude Blake painted a lurid picture of Liverpool's Chinatown in a series of articles in a Manchester newspaper, the *Sunday Chronicle,* that display the spatiotemporal structure of exemplarity. Firstly, the global scale of Chinese transnational migration is counterposed to the integrity of the white race:

> The whole question is in a nutshell: Is Great Britain going to profit by the bitter experience of America and Australia, by the experience of all white communities caused by the influx of the yellow man? Or is she going to wait and deal with the scourge after half a million or so of Chinamen have settled in these islands to contaminate the white race? (Blake, 1906b)

Secondly, the concern to preserve the purity of white space has a temporal dimension. Aghast at the potential introduction of permanent marks of difference, the animus toward interracial sexual relations and above all mixed-race children is clearly articulated: "when you walk along a dark, dirty, evil-smelling street and see in each ill-lighted doorway a group of half-caste youngsters—half-yellow and half-white—you must know that something is wrong" (Blake, 1906a).

In response to Blake's articles and the comment they engendered, Liverpool City Council established a commission of inquiry into Chinese settlement in the city. However, the commission reported in June 1907 that it found little to justify its appointment. No anti-Chinese immigration legislation was enacted.

However, for the next two decades local and national newspapers, together with the British state, continued to subject Chinese populations of Britain's seaports to scrutiny.[3] For example, in 1911 the monthly *London Magazine* published another series "The Chinese in England: A Growing National Problem," by Herman Scheffauer, a journalist from San Francisco who investigated Chinese settlement in Liverpool, London, and Cardiff. The structure of exemplarity is evident again as he warns Britain of the incipient Americanization of its race relations and urged it to act before it is too late. What has happened in the United States, most notably San Francisco, could happen in Britain: "Though the Chinese colonies in England are still comparatively small, they present even now many of the phases, as they may soon present many of the problems, that once confronted California before the passage of the Oriental Exclusion Act" (Scheffauer, 1911: 468).

Even more so than today, the skewed gender balance—white women and men from overseas—lent a particular charge to the documentation by white male commentators. There is a fraught, injunctive temporality of purification underlying Scheffauer's distaste (1911: 476) for what he described as "the growing evil of mixed marriages, resulting in a hybrid offspring, partly yellow and partly white."

The discussion of "half-caste pathology" (Rich, 1986) had its apogee in the application of eugenic science to the mixed-race children of Britain's seaports in the 1920s and 1930s. In 1924, for example, the London-based Eugenics Society sponsored what it termed a "Race-Crossing Investigation" in these towns. The society's secretary described the Liverpool section of the study, in which Professor Fleure, a geographer at University College, Aberystwyth, Wales, and his assistant, Rachel Fleming, were "to take anthropological measurements on slum children who are hybrid British-Chinese."[4]

The researchers' epistemological frameworks predisposed them to seek the corporeal disharmonies assumed by the indices being applied, such as the cephalic index, which was the ratio of the length to the width of the head. This objective haunts both the correspondence leading up to the research and the reports of its findings published over the next few years. The researchers were surprised at the well-being of their respondents, yet the children were still evaluated against the phenotypic norm: "A marked feature of the children of Anglo-Chinese ancestry was the complete absence of any case with the flaxen curls so common in English children up to 5 or 6 years of age" (Fleming, 1939: 60).

This context, of both popular suspicion and scientific curiosity, defined the times into which some of the people I was fortunate to interview were born (see also Kohn, 1992). I want to turn the tables on the discursive structure that demonized exemplary spaces and revisit them as positive examples that may have resonances for the present and the future.

Recollections

I managed to contact some of those who either remembered being included in the Eugenics Society's "Race-Crossing Investigation" in the interwar years, or recognized the names and addresses of households that had been contacted by the study. I gave them copies of the research to read. Mrs. Connie Hoe, age seventy-five, who grew up in the heart of Limehouse, recalled being measured and indeed photographed as a very small child for Rachel Fleming's eugenics study.

CONNIE: I can remember going into this restaurant and being taken into one of these rooms and they measured my head and took my photograph, in profile and full face. And I don't know whether they took a sample of my hair—they may have done—and asked some questions, but I can't remember what the questions were.
DP (DAVID PARKER): How did you feel, reading the study now?
CONNIE: I thought *then* that we were just objects for research!

That the vocabulary of eugenics permeated popular discourse can be gleaned from a 1935 article about Saint Michael's Church in Pitt Street, the heart of Liverpool's Chinatown, by the local priest, Reverend Bates, who concluded that, "the mating of the yellow races with the white is eugenically good, and produces a fine physical type." However, he argued, even if physicality was intact, problematization shifted to the level of cultural abnormality:

The children present a special problem. . . . They speak English, but their mode of thought is Eastern. Their real ego is wrapped in an impenetrable silence, and whilst the lips speak the face is a mask, so different from the spontaneous frankness so delightful in English children. (Bates, 1935: 589–590)

The area around Pitt Street was not "slums," as the Eugenics Society called it, but poverty undoubtedly acted as a solvent for racialized differences. Saint Michael's Church still exists (in a new building), and still merits the 1935 article's subtitle "The Church of Many Nations." Each Sunday morning some of those who grew up in Pitt Street and its surroundings return for a social gathering attended by mixed-race people with English, Irish, Spanish, African, Jewish and Filipino ancestry, as well as Chinese. Their recollections conveyed the harsh climate in the Liverpool of their youth, but also a justifiable pride in having come through those years with support from networks of family and friends that cut across racial lines. However, when I first heard their statements such as, "What we had was a wonderful life," I was skeptical, particularly considering the historical accounts of racial harassment in Britain's seaports on either side of the First World War (see May, 1973). Something of a validity check came from being able to compare the responses of those who grew up in London and Liverpool during the same years. Also, at several points in the discussions, the difficulties endured by the first generation were recalled vividly. For example, when a younger member of the Anglo-Chinese Association in Liverpool questioned the degree to which Chinese people had suffered from racism, she was quickly challenged:

BARBARA: I don't think the Chinese have experienced anything like the prejudice the blacks have, nothing on the same scale.
SEVERAL PEOPLE: Oh, they did.
DOREEN: You had to live with it.
SEVERAL PEOPLE: No, you don't remember . . .
DACK: If your father was Chinese, they couldn't get anywhere in this country.
LIN: And they had to make their own work, they couldn't have got a job. They made their own living.

To a degree, this self-sufficiency insulated the early settlers and their children from the wider world, but poverty also dictated an intensely local childhood:

DOREEN: We had to stay together in our own little circle.
DACK: As Doreen said, we had nothing. When I tell my children that, to have a holiday, that was for other people, it wasn't for the likes of us.
DP: So, Pitt Street was basically your world?
DACK: Yes, it was.

Respondents were keen to stress the inaccuracy of the stereotypical depictions of Chinatowns. In the discussions, I actually showed copies of newspaper articles that perpetuated these images, which in one case drew the following comments:

LESLIE: Really and truly, and Connie [his wife] tells me this, but I never did it, she used to read these sordid accounts in these two-penny magazines. . . . And this is the thing—she used to look for all this and couldn't find it! [Laughs] We used to think there must be something going on here, why don't they let us in on it?
CONNIE: Do you know . . . this is the sort of thing I used to look for when I was a child [reading from an article in the *Star* newspaper on April 26, 1922, describing the visit of the film director D. W. Griffith to London's Chinatown]. Never heard such rubbish in all my life! That's the sort of thing I used to look for!

In both Liverpool and London, life as children in multicultural streets and schools was recalled warmly:

EDIE: Everybody was friendly, whether you were black, white, or yellow, you were all friendly together, there was no ill-feeling amongst anybody. . . . Nobody argued, no racism, nothing at all. . . . Just one big happy family, wouldn't matter whether you were black, yellow, or whatever colour. . . . You see we're all intermingled with foreigners!

Lin Wong's (1989) respondents in an earlier study of Liverpool concurred with this view. Further support for what, to us, seem almost utopian testimonies of peaceful coexistence can be found in secondary sources, for even otherwise stereotypical press accounts acknowledged the special character of the areas around the early Chinatowns. For example, the following description of Pitt Street appeared in a Liverpool paper in 1906, just before Claude Blake's attacks:

> In this short and narrow, but by no means dismal thoroughfare dwells in concert a motley population of British, Chinese, Negroes, Manillamen [Filipinos] and Malays; the little ones are attractive in all cases, and in many are decidedly pretty. Here, at least, racial prejudice is unknown, and these children of varied parentage play, and work, in the neighbouring schools, in perfect equality with their white friends. (*Liverpool Weekly Courier,* 1906: 3)

It is important not to overestimate the presence of what today we might call "hybridity," or a precursor to multiraciality. The precise cultural habitus is hard to re-create at such a historical distance. However, from the interviews and secondary sources, several features of these settlements can be discerned. The Chinese fathers were often absent; either at sea, or, when at port, in a largely self-contained cultural world of Chinese freemason societies and gambling houses. The children were brought up mainly by white mothers or "aunties," described by Lin Wong (1989: 72) as "strong women" who, on occasion, took in children who couldn't be cared for by their parents. As a result, few of the interviewees spoke Chinese fluently, and most regretted a lack of facility in the spoken and written form of the language, despite the efforts in both cities in the 1920s and 1930s to institute Chinese-language classes. Yet, in spite of this there were Chinese elements to their everyday lives, most notably food.

Although it would unfairly recast the past into the mold of the present to assume that the interviewees had formed blended mixed-race identities, they did convey a clear sense of both being pioneers and continually negotiating differences through the years. Their words confound any straightforward narrative of assimilation.

DOREEN: If I lived my life over again, and they said you could be white, I wouldn't have it.

LIN: We had the best of both worlds, you had your Chinese and now you've got your English part of you. You can mix equally with the both.

DOREEN: The thing is you always defend your Chinese side, don't you?

LIN: It's getting easier to live in England now, as it's becoming more multicultural, but I think as children we paved the way, we had to pave the way.

Neither Limehouse nor Pitt Street survived the Second World War air raids. However, the people who grew up there embody a continuing legacy, a distinctive set of experiences that mark out the mixed-race Chinese in London and Liverpool.

Postwar Generations

In both cities, there was a postwar generation of mixed-race Chinese—the children of the first generation (some of whom had married each other) as well as the children of new wartime and early postwar Chinese settlers who had married white women. Their experiences differed from those of both their parents and their children. Rather than a residential focus, they shared socioeconomic locations. The young men in Liverpool had invariably followed their Chinese fathers onto work on the Blue Funnel Line, whose ships sailed to Asia out of the Merseyside docks. They shared a camaraderie hardened in the face of continuing employment discrimination:

HAROLD: The Blue Funnel Line was an exploiter of Chinese, it was cheap labor, we did the same work as the Europeans, but for lower wages. . . . It was ideal for the Blue Funnel to exploit the Chinese population of Liverpool, which they did, and the reason I suppose why we mingled together. . . . It was split up into gangs of men and they used to stay with the same men more or less all the way through, that's why we all knew each other.

Some needed to change their surnames to avert discrimination:

HAROLD: I was just thinking then, some people said we weren't discriminated against, but a lot of them in their minds must have thought they were, 'cause there was an awful lot of half-caste Chinese who, when they applied for jobs, changed their names to an English name.
TONY: I know half-caste Chinese lads like us, who have met, courted, and wanted to get married, and their parents wouldn't let 'em unless they changed the name.
KEN: The girl's parents don't want their families with a Chinese name.
TONY: This was *our* generation, that's how recent.
KEN: Even the Chinese looked down on us, the full Chinese, 'cause we were half-breeds, half-breeds—"half breeds, go away."

This slightly younger generation of Liverpool residents were clearly linked:

TONY: We had our own roots, we made our own bond, us half-caste lads and girls in Liverpool.

These connections persist; for example, there is a group of mixed-race Chinese door staff working in clubs in Liverpool. Whilst talking inside one of these venues, Ken remarked, "We are a race of our own," and I was prompted to reflect on whether there was a purely racialized solidarity in these exemplary spaces.

In both cities, the first generation have formed associations that periodically reforge old bonds. In Liverpool, the Anglo-Chinese Association was established in 1984 as a result of former Pitt Street residents informally coming together and seeking to rediscover a closeness they once shared. The association's first dance attracted three-hundred people.

In London there has been the same pattern of the renewal of ties in later life amongst those who grew up in Chinatown. The Chinese Children's Club, established by English

Methodists in 1927, offered educational and recreational activities to the children of Limehouse. Mrs. Hoe describes its members as sharing "this marvelous feeling of fellowship and belonging and feeling of being something special." Today, the original members organize an annual reunion at which they and their children and grandchildren gather for a meal. Old photographs are displayed, and people are asked to identify older relatives and those whose names are not known.

DP: Why do you think you've kept together?

LESLIE: I think it is an affinity for the people of the same kind as yourself, you feel more secure with the people that are of the same race as you . . . We all know one another intimately . . . one big family existing with a common bond, as you would with your brothers and sisters, where nothing is hidden. You know of their troubles, tribulations, and achievements. If you know all of this, you know you have to be as one. With meeting strangers and neighbors, it's not the same because there's no love involved.

Read starkly, the above quotations imply a strong and separate identity as Anglo-Chinese, or mixed race. However, these collectives are informal and occasional social gatherings, not distinct political entities. Memories and affiliations are shared, but not to the exclusion of all other sources of identity. The localities themselves are at least as important as being of Chinese descent. As Mrs. Hoe states, "I think of myself as being a Cockney."[5]

That the crucial factors underpinning the identities of the first multiracial Chinese are shared locality and historical memory, rather than an automatic affinity as being multiracial or mixed race, is demonstrated by comparison with respondents from my generation. Whether they had grown up in England, Hong Kong, or Singapore, those in their twenties and thirties did not have the same closeness or collective identification as the older generations, who were more definite about naming at least part of their identity as Anglo-Chinese or Eurasian:

HAROLD: When I was a kid, when someone got up and called you a "Chink" you'd get up and start fighting, but nowadays the Eurasian kids now are not really into that. I think the Eurasian kids now regard themselves more English. Years ago with them having fathers that were full Chinese, it was part of them, now I don't think they have that in them.

FRANKIE: The thing is there's not the encouragement like in Pitt Street or Nelson Street, today, there's no real community of the Chinese community like there was many years ago.

Those who didn't grow up in a multiracial collective expressed more doubt about possessing a racialized social identity. Indeed, for two creative artists being mixed race became the point of departure for a broader social vision of multiple affiliations and alignments:

ERIKA: When I say "my mixed-race heritage," it becomes no longer just about biological things, but it becomes a conceptual thing. . . . When I say, "I was interested in film"—I became more interested in nonlinear film, not this sort of straight progression to one end, but several branches at one time. And I can kind of trace that back to being mixed-race, but I'm not meaning racially . . . but the sense that I've had to be a lot more open because I was mixed race in the society that I grew up in [Singapore].

LIAM: You grow up knowing in your bones, in your heart, that no one's sense of values and ideas are universal and are final. The British/West sense of values is not universal, the Chinese is not universal, because you embody them both, all the contradictions, all the compatibilities, you have it all . . . and . . . people say it's unusual, but I've known nothing else, don't tell me that's unusual, to me this is normality. People from one culture they are linked to, that's unusual for me . . . It sets you up to be a bona fide postmodernist! What better grounding could you have?

It would be foolish to offer more than a tentative summary of remarks from such a small set of respondents. However, the older generations who either grew up together in prewar Chinatowns or worked together at sea had a much sharper sense of collective identity as at least partly Chinese, as well as a deep attachment to the neighborhoods they knew as children. Contemporary mixed-race Chinese are far more dispersed and for that reason are less likely to feel connected to each other.

Conclusion

I wrote this chapter partly to explore what links might exist between three generations of mixed race Chinese people in Britain. As in previous work, I encountered a complex dynamic of commonality and difference (Song & Parker, 1995). When I met respondents, I encountered an immediacy of visual recognition and the experience of being claimed as "one of us":

LESLIE: Every time an Anglo-Chinese person achieves something we feel it is an achievement for us.

But this recognition could also be coupled with a heightened awareness of significant dissimilarities of class, locality, and education:

TONY: Both our Mum and Dad took a detour before they got to us, and as we're going along on this parallel conversation, we're finding places where we go "bink" . . . "bink" [gestures intermittently coming together] but not very often—and we find that with a lot of half-caste Chinese.

Tony's remarks indicate the limit of a racially based identity; there are some commonalities, but less so than I had first thought. As Michael Thornton (1996) has implied, the richness of multiracial experience will only be appreciated by recognizing the multiple dimensions shaping our existence.

The task of theorizing mixed race is at an early stage. As Werner Sollors (1986: 15) argues, "we have to develop a terminology that goes beyond the organicist imagery of roots and can come to terms with the pervasiveness and inventiveness of syncretism." Paradoxically, this will be done only through recognizing the lack of correlation in experiences between different generations of multiracials. The positing of a "mixed-race

race" ignores powerful influences of class and locality on the formation of identities. The sources of particularity are not simply differential racializations, but multiple, power-laden vectors that produce distinctive experiences of place. In this instance, the structuring of local labor markets and the racialized sexualization of exemplary spaces in the early twentieth century require more detailed historical enquiry.

The deeply felt memories of unique localities count against an immediately all-inclusive racial designation. John Yau's (1989) poem captures this, albeit with a tinge of melancholy, by showing how little can be left to us by our parents, how much has to be invented and produced anew. Those who grew up in the exemplary spaces of Liverpool and London undoubtedly paved the way, but we in the present day are on different journeys:

Their Shadows

According to my mother,
unlike most English farmer's daughters,
my grandmother had social pretensions.
Yet this opinion does not explain why
she decided to marry grandfather.
In 1916, he taught, while the rest of England
fought in the muddy trenches of World War I.
"I do not think many Chinese fought in that war"
was my father's only remark.

If anything, this is their achievement
and their fame. He died in Hong Kong
shortly before she died in Liverpool.
My father was informed by two letters:
one from an aunt, one from a solicitor.
Nothing left to him in either case,
but their shadows mingling on his face. (Yau, 1989: 16)

Notes

Acknowledgments: I wish to thank all the people in Liverpool and London who shared their thoughts with me, especially Graham Chan, Tony Chinn, the members of the Anglo-Chinese Association in Liverpool, and Mr. and Mrs. Hoe.

1. The terminology used to describe persons of "mixed race" is a vexed issue, further from a resolution in Britain than in North America. I have chosen to stick to "mixed race" for the moment, as this is the most recognized term in Britain.

2. Maria Lin Wong's (1989) study of the early Chinese settlers in Liverpool and their mixed-race children is a notable exception.

3. Home Office file PRO HO 45/11843/139147, Public Record Office, London.

4. Letter from Mrs. Hodson to Lady Barr, November 27, 1924, SA/EUG/D179.

5. The term "Cockney," which is the local vernacular for East Londoner, implies an attachment to the district and is often associated with a distinctive accent.

CHAPTER 16

A Dutch Eurasian Revival?

Mark Taylor Brinsfield

Introduction

On December 27, 1949, the Dutch government formally transferred sovereignty of the Netherlands East Indies to the United States of Indonesia. From that date until the 1960s, some 300,000 "Europeans" migrated from their formal colony to the Netherlands; about 180,000 were Dutch Eurasians (Cottaar & Willems, 1985; Willems et al., 1990).[1] For many years, sociological texts generally assumed that Dutch Eurasians had quickly and smoothly assimilated into Dutch society (Ellemers, 1994). This assumption has often been used, both at home and abroad, as a primary example to support the reputation of the Netherlands as a racially and culturally tolerant country (Cottaar & Willems, 1984).

Since the early 1980s, however, a younger generation of scholars[2] have questioned the factual basis of this theory of a "geruisloze assimilatie" (quiet assimilation).[3] First of all, they point out, a systematic study of this assimilation process has never been done. Moreover, new research indicates that the Dutch government and population had not so easily tolerated, let alone accepted, Dutch Eurasians upon their arrival. Rather than warmly welcoming them as fellow Netherlanders, many Dutch people harbored against them an array of negative stereotypes which had developed in the three and a half centuries of Dutch control over Indonesia.[4] Indeed, the Dutch government had done everything possible to prevent most of the Eurasians from coming to the Netherlands in the first place (Cottaar & Willems, 1984: Rijsdijk, 1985; Gielen & Hommerson, 1987; Pollmann & Harms, 1987; Godeschalk, 1988).[5] Because of the prejudices against their physical appearance and culture, many Eurasians had a long and hard struggle to find a place for themselves in Dutch society (Lucassen & Pennix, 1994).

Nevertheless, today scholars of Dutch Eurasian history generally agree that the Netherlands has largely succeeded in assimilating Dutch Eurasians, especially the young, into the mainstream of Dutch society (Ellemers & Vaillant, 1985; Willems et al., 1990; Ellemers, 1994). At the same time, however, one can observe the development of a revival of Dutch Eurasian ethnic consciousness that has been growing since the 1980s, despite the fact that many Hollanders and even Dutch Eurasians attempt to deny, ignore, or trivialize its existence (Van der Geugten & Van der Linden, 1996). The aim of this chapter is to identify some examples of this revival, to examine some of the factors behind its emergence, and finally to assess very briefly its depth, breadth, and possible longevity. Comparisons with the American and British multiracial scenes are left to the reader.

Examples of the Revival

There are many examples of the development of a "revival" of Dutch Eurasian ethnic consciousness in Holland over the past two decades. From events that celebrate traditional clothing and food to rock bands and Websites, Dutch Indonesian Eurasians are exploring their complex identities and cultures in a context that has been both supportive and dismissive.

Among the first signs of a renaissance in ethnic consciousness was the formation, in 1980, of the youth association NINES (Nazaten Indische Nederlanders En Sympathisanten, or Descendants of Dutch Eurasians and Sympathizers), a cultural organization that holds a variety of events highlighting aspects of Eurasian culture and its Indonesian roots, including literature, theater, music, dance, the visual arts, and food (Van der Linden & Simons, 1990; *Moesson,* 1998, vol. 42, no. 11).

Shortly after the formation of NINES, the Eurasian art world in Holland began to explode. Novels and short stories by Eurasians started to appear on the literary scene in the early 1980s, such as Marion Bloem's novel *Geen gewoon Indisch meisje* (An Unusual Eurasian Girl) and Jill Stolk's novel *Scherven van smaragd* (Fragments of Emerald), both published in 1983. Documentaries by Eurasian filmmakers, exploring family and collective histories, also began to proliferate.[6] Photo exhibits portraying subjects such as colonial schools in Indonesia from 1875 to 1960 (*Moesson,* 1998, vol. 42, no. 11), and Japanese concentration camps for Europeans and Eurasians during World War II (*Moesson,* 1997, vol. 41, no. 7), have presented historical representations of the Eurasian experience. And paintings by pre–World War II Eurasian artists such as Adolfs and Dezentjé a.o. are enjoying a renewed interest and increase in value (*Moesson,* 1997, vol. 41, no. 9). In 1987, a group of Eurasian artists formed the National Association of Indische Artists to serve as a source of professional and personal support (Willems et al., 1990).

The Dutch mass media has also offered a venue for the assertion of Dutch Eurasian identity and culture in the television program "Tante Lien" (The Late, Late Show), a specifically Eurasian talk show that enjoyed immense popularity in the 1980s (Kortendick, 1990). Taking its place today are radio programs such as Meity Janssen's *Tjampoer Adoek* (*From Everything, Something*) and Lucette Schotel's *Radio Tokèh* (Janssen, 1996).

Eurasian consciousness has also expressed itself politically since the early 1980s. Several political organizations, such as the Vrije Indische Partij (Free Indies Party), INDO (Dutch Eurasian Democratic Organization), and the Committee for the Historical Restitution of Honor in the Dutch East Indies have been founded with the purpose of representing Eurasian interests. One major success on this front has been the establishment, by the Dutch government in 1991, of the Indisch Platform, a consultative body covering a wide spectrum of Eurasian issues. Through the Indisch Platform, funds have been made available to finance several Dutch Eurasian projects, such as scholarly work on Dutch Eurasian history, the film *De Indische Diaspora,* and a memorial center recognizing Dutch and Eurasian victims of World War II.

Another important area in the growing discussion on Dutch Eurasian history, culture, and identity is the academy. As mentioned, since the early 1980s a number of scholars have begun to rethink Dutch Eurasian history. At first these historians and sociologists worked mostly in isolation from each other, until a small group of Dutch and Eurasian scholars at the University of Leiden organized a conference meant to bring together academics from diverse fields and representatives from Dutch Eurasian organizations (Willems, 1998). From 1989 to 1995, five such conferences took place, yielding five anthologies.[7] As a result, many new areas of research have opened up; for example, three major Dutch research organizations are currently doing a joint oral history project, interviewing some one thousand Dutch Eurasians who lived in Indonesia from 1940 to 1965 (Willems, 1998).[8]

Because of these academic developments and the Indisch Platform, the Dutch government subsidized the publication of *Uit Indie Geboren (Born from the Indies)* (Willems et al., 1997b) in 1995, a richly illustrated book aimed at a nonacademic audience, summarizing all of the research done on Dutch Eurasians since the 1980s (Willems, 1998). The Dutch government is also currently funding educational projects that present newly revised versions of Dutch Eurasian history for Hollanders in grade school all the way up to the universities (Seriese, 1997; Van der Geugten, 11, 1998).

The Revival Abroad

Outside the Netherlands, there have also been signs of a Dutch Eurasian revival since the 1980s. In the United States, which is home to the second largest Dutch Eurasian population in the world,[9] older Eurasians are maintaining contact with each other through a variety of Indiesi organizations, barbeques, *koempoelans* (parties), and reunions.[10]

The magazine *De Indo,* the monthly publication of De Soos, the Indo community center in Walnut, California, is now thirty-five years old and has a growing circulation. Originally intended for Dutch Eurasian immigrants to the United States, *De Indo* now has subscribers in at least nineteen countries (Creutzburg, 1995). Each issue is filled with information on Dutch Eurasian history, culture, and identity, as well as personal narratives, poems, notifications of events, photos, recipes, and much more. For many years, the Indies Archive in America in Upland, California, has been collecting documents reflecting the experiences of American Eurasians (Creutzburg, 1998). Toward this end, a project is now underway to record as many of their life histories as possible (Willems, 1998). And finally, over the past decade, Dutch Eurasians in the United States have set up several charitable organizations such as HABINI, HECALI, and Het KNIL-FONDS to assist poor and sick Eurasian soldiers and civilians still in Indonesia (Broers, 1998).

Australia has also been home to a renaissance of Dutch Eurasian ethnic consciousness (Willems, 1998). It was largely through the initiative of the Eurasian community there that an international reunion was held in Bali in 1997 (Creutzburg, 1997). Beyond all national borders, the revival has recently become visible in cyberspace. In early 1997, a Website called *The Dutch East Indies Informationpoint* was launched as an experiment to see how much interest it would attract. Within nine months, the site received some 12,000 hits from around the globe (R. Van den Broeke, personal communication, 17 October 1997).

Why the Revival Emerged in the 1980s

The renaissance in Dutch Eurasian ethnic consciousness became increasingly visible in the 1980s and 1990s for several reasons. To understand these factors, we must look historically at the past fifty years of Eurasian resettlement and acculturation in Holland.

Upon settling down in the Netherlands in the 1950s and 1960s, the vast majority of Dutch Eurasians wanted to forget their colonial past and quickly and quietly become "Dutch" (L. Rijkschroeff, 1997), just as the Dutch government and people so uncompromisingly demanded of them (Surie, 1971; Mullard, 1988; Schuster, 1991). This, however, was often difficult to do. Although a prosperous economy found many Eurasians satisfied with the material aspects of Dutch life, a denigrating attitude toward their skin color and customs, an indifferent ignorance of the cruelty that they had endured during the Japanese occupation in World War II, and a lack of understanding of their motivations for immigrating created an often uncomfortable and unwelcoming environment. In addition, many of the Eurasians in the Netherlands were very unhappy with the government's handling of the decolonization process in Indonesia (Kwik, 1989; Boon & van Geleuken, 1993; Van der Geugten, 1990; Beerhorst, 1996; Stoltenborgh-Indorf, 1997; Willems, 1998). For these and other reasons, some Eurasians compared Dutch society to a stifling prison, and withdrew into themselves (Beets, 1981; Anthonio, 1990; Ducelle, 1994).

Conditions began to change somewhat for Holland's Eurasian community in the 1970s, beginning with the Dutch Queen Juliana's visit to Indonesia. Until this time, mainstream Hollanders remembered World War II only in the European context, and recognition and reparations were not offered to those Dutch citizens (including Eurasians) who had suffered the war in Asia. But during the queen's visit in 1970, the Dutch and Eurasian victims of World War II in Asia were officially commemorated for the first time. This event, followed by a series of articles about World War II in Asia by Dutch journalist Rudy Kousbroek (1992; see also Seriese, 1997), precipitated an intense discussion within the "Indies" community. Although there were bitter disagreements and angry charges, these discussions began the process of remembering for the Eurasian community, and functioned to reawaken the ethnic consciousness of many Dutch Eurasians.

Also in the 1970s, the government's policy toward immigrants began to shift away from assimilation and toward the motto "integration with the maintenance of one's own culture" (Van der Geugten & Van der Linden, 1996). This new policy, reflecting a general liberalization of Dutch society that had been occurring since the late 1960s (Ellemers, 1981; Shetter, 1987), was not intended for the Eurasian community, who were assumed to be already completely "Dutchified."[11] But many in the Eurasian community took note of this change, and felt a certain amount of envy toward newer immigrant populations (Lucassen & Pennix, 1994; Van der Geugten & Van der Linden, 1996). In the schools, the movement toward multiculturalism encouraged many of the second generation to become interested in their ethnic history, culture, and identity (Van der Linden & Simmons, 1990). These younger Eurasians, having fluency in the Dutch language and culture, have been more vocal and aggressive than their parents' generation, contributing to the emergence and the visibility of the revival.[12] For example, the young people who founded NINES were very critical of the first generation's silent acceptance of assimilation policies (Seriese, 1997).[13]

Still another force leading up to the Dutch Eurasian revival merits mention: namely, the initiatives of the Dutch Eurasian journalist, writer, and activist Jan Boon, alias Tjalie Robinson and Vincent Mahieu. After World War II, he, along with a handful of others in his Tong Tong movement,[14] kept the Indisch flame burning in a cold social climate (Willems et al., 1990).

Tjalie Robinson: The Voice of Indisch Nederland

Jan Johannes Theodorus Boon was born in 1911 in the Netherlands, but was raised in the city of Batavia (now Jakarta) in Java. He strongly identified with the Eurasian culture and identity of his mother, Fela Robinson, the daughter of an Indonesian woman and a British man (Anthonio, 1990: Seriese, 1997). As a prisoner of war of the Japanese in Malaysia during World War II, Boon took on the pseudonym Tjalie Robinson— "Tjalie" is the Indo word for "Charlie" and Robinson is his mother's maiden name—in order to assert his Eurasian identity (see Photo 16-1). Boon/Robinson later used the nom de plume Vincent Mahieu for his fictional stories featuring Eurasian protagonists.[15]

As a journalist and an activist, Tjalie Robinson sought to unite the diverse Indo community and to preserve Dutch Eurasian culture. He also fought to change the often well intended yet paternalistic and humiliating Dutch attitudes toward Indos. Toward these ends, Tjalie founded the magazine Tong Tong (now Moesson),[16] the Pasar Malam Besar (Large Evening Market) Tong Tong,[17] the Indische Kunstkring (Indies Art Circle) Tong Tong,[18] the Indisch Wetenschappelijk Instituut (Indies' Research Institute), a publishing house, a book shop, and an Indonesian general store in The Hague. At one point,

PHOTO 16-1. Tjalie
Robinson in his later years.
(Courtesy of Vivan Boon.)

he led a movement to have Petjo, the Dutch Eurasian patois language, recognized as a legitimate Dutch dialect.[19]

Tjalie's dream was someday to found a self-sufficient Indo village, to be called El Atabal, in Spain. But in the social climate of the Netherlands in the 1950s, with its push toward assimilation, he found very little support (Anthonio, 1990; Seriese, 1997; Willems, 1994). He became frustrated with the Dutch Eurasian community for its acquiescence to assimilation, and many denounced him as nostalgic for colonial times. But Tjalie felt that Eurasians needed to remember their past as a means to reorient themselves to their new environment, and that Dutch culture would be enriched in the process (L. Rijkschroeff, 1997). Moreover, he rejected the goal of Europeanization, because he felt it was based on the myth of the superiority of White Western culture.[20]

Tjalie thus began to look outside of Europe for places where Indo culture might have a better chance of surviving. After visits to Indo migrant communities in the Dutch Antilles, Suriname, and the United States in 1961, he and his family moved to southern California. He was attracted to the United States not only because it was quickly becoming home to the world's second largest Indo population, but also because of the social changes being brought about by racial and ethnic minorities.[21] Tjalie continued his work in the United States, starting the magazine *American Tong Tong* and founding the Indo community center De Soos. But again his radical attempts to create a strong Dutch Eurasian community faltered. Heated disagreements over subjects such as what it means to be Indisch and assimilation versus isolation were followed by periods of bitter silence. In addition, many disagreed with Tjalie's demand that only Eurasians be allowed to join De Soos.

After only two and one-half years, *American Tong Tong* collapsed, and Tjalie returned to the Netherlands to try to rescue his Tong Tong movement there (Anthonio, 1990; Seriese, 1997; Willems, 1998). But his ideas found even less of an echo in Holland's Eurasian community than before. Subscriptions to his magazine continued to fall dramatically, and divisions formed within the movement. Tjalie continued to search for a new biotope for Indos in the mestizo cultures of Latin America, albeit in vain (Seriese, 1997).

In 1974, Tjalie died, thinking that the Dutch Eurasian culture and community would perish with the passing of the first generation. Nevertheless, he felt some comfort in the knowledge that he had left behind his "visiting card"—his Tong Tong—as evidence for future generations that Indos had once existed. He could not have foreseen that he had actually laid much of the foundations for the Dutch Eurasian revival of the 1980s and 1990s (Van der Geugten & Van der Linden, 1996).

The Depth, Breadth, and Longevity of the Revival

Based on the foregoing, it is clear that a Dutch Eurasian identity is still alive. Indeed, one finds a revival in the areas of culture, politics, and academics. Yet there are skeptical voices that attempt to minimize its importance. For example, some critics claim that there is something artificial about the revival, as the younger generations of Dutch Eurasians have been born and educated in the Netherlands and do not have direct experiences with colonial life, decolonization, or migration. Therefore, the argument goes, although interest in Indo history and culture has increased, a "real Indische" culture no longer exists in the Netherlands, and the revival is confined mostly to recreational activities (Vaillant, 1991).

Some research seems to confirm this. One study found that less than 25 percent of the second generation of Dutch Eurasians have Indische friends, and that only 30 percent have a Eurasian partner (Coldenhoff, 1988).[22] In a series of interviews with third-generation Dutch Eurasians in 1996, many said that being Indisch meant nothing other than becoming Netherlanders (Van de Broek, 1996; Regensburg, 1996).

Perhaps another way to look at Dutch Eurasian identity and culture is that it is a dynamic process that changes with time and circumstances. Either way, because of the Dutch Eurasian revival, Indische culture and identity did not die out with the first generation of Dutch Eurasians, as Tjalie Robinson had feared, but has continued to evolve, in the Netherlands and beyond, into the twenty-first century.

Notes

1. In this chapter, "Dutch Eurasians" are defined as a multiracial/multicultural population that, partly because of paternal pride and Christian responsibility, but perhaps mostly for practical reasons (i.e., fear of an Eurasian/Indonesian alliance against the Dutch), gained Dutch citizenship in colonial Indonesia on July 1, 1893. This definition distinguishes them from the vast majority of Eurasians, who were classified as "Natives" and disappeared into Indonesian society. I use the term Dutch Eurasians for lack of a better translation of *Indische Nederlanders* a Dutch phrase that gained currency in the mid-twentieth century (Mansvelt, 1932; Blumberger, 1939; Wertheim, 1947, 1949; Van Marle, 1951–52; Van der Veur, 1955; Surie, 1971; Taylor, 1983; Willems et al., 1997a).

2. The line between young and old is, of course, never absolute.

3. This newer research has been slow to filter into the English-speaking world. In the absence of competitors, the book *The Dutch Plural Society* (1973), by the British Canadian scholar Dr. Christopher Bagley, remains the dominant English-language representation of Dutch Eurasian colonial and postcolonial experiences. However, in my opinion, much of his thesis is unfair and incorrect, even in light of the research available when he wrote the book twenty-five years ago. For example, he places a positive value on the Dutch government's assimilation policy, while many scholars recognize that it ignored and trampled on Dutch Eurasian culture and identity.

4. Dutch rule in Indonesia was characterized by the political and economic domination, by a small group of Europeans, over a mass of "Natives" and "Foreign Orientals," with Eurasians functioning as a buffer zone. To rationalize this arrangement, a myth of biologically determined Dutch supremacy, backed by God's will, developed. With full-blooded Netherlander as the racial and cultural ideal, Eurasians who were lighter skinned, who had more European ancestry, and who behaved in a more culturally Dutch manner were rewarded. Except for the stereotype of the sensuous Eurasian beauty, all of the supposedly inferior characteristics of Eurasians (such as laziness, disloyalty, etc.) were attributed to their Asian heritage (Surie, 1971; Alatas, 1977; Cottaar & Willems, 1984; Wertheim, 1990; Van der Geugten & Van der Linden, 1996).

5. Although Dutch Eurasians in Indonesia had been brought up to esteem their Dutch citizenship as a birthright, during decolonization the Dutch government encouraged them to give it up (since they were no longer of any practical value to the Netherlands). Because the government worried that Eurasians would become an "undigested lump" in Dutch society (Van der Veur 1954: 133), they attempted to develop a distinction between "Western" Netherlanders (i.e., the pure Dutch and a very small top layer of Dutch Eurasians), who could immigrate, and the poorer "Oriental" Netherlanders, who were to be excluded because of their "natural, inherently Indonesian characteristics" (Van der Veur, 1955: 51). However, many "Oriental" Netherlanders could not be prevented from migrating on the technical grounds that they kept their Dutch citizenship during the two-year option period after 1949 (Van der Veur, 1955, 1960; Cottaar & Willems, 1984).

6. For example, the films *Het land van mijn ouders* (1983), *Stille Intocht* (1992), *Oorlog, Bersiap, Dekolonisatie* (1995), *De Geschiedenis van een Keuze* (1995), and *Indisch in Nederland: Beeld and zelfbeeld van Indische Nederlanders* (1996).

7. These five anthologies are: *Indische Nederlanders in de ogen van de wetenschap* (Willems, 1990); *Bronnen vankennis over Indische Nederlanders* (Willems, 1991); *Sporen van een Indisch verleden* (Willems, 1992); *Het onbekende vaderland: De repatrilring van Indische Nederlanders 1946–1964* (Willems & Lucassen, 1994); and *Het einde van Indil: Indische Nederlanders tijdens de Japanse bezetting, de bersiap en de dekolonisatie* (Willems & de Moor 1995).

8. These research institutes are the Royal Institute of Language and Anthropological Studies

(Leiden); the Department of Asian Studies at the University of Amsterdam, and the State Institute for Research on the Second World War (W. Willems, personal communication, 19 May 1998).

9. American Dutch Eurasians live in all parts of the United States, but the largest population lives in southern California (Kwik, 1989: Rijkschroeff, 1989).

10. This desire to participate in Dutch Eurasian community activities does not seem to extend beyond the first generation of American Eurasians (M. Loeffen, personal communication, 19 February 1996; S. Krancher, personal communication, 3 December 1997; W. Willems, personal communication, 19 May 1998). For this reason, some older American Indos have jokingly referred to themselves as the "Last of the Mohicans" (Annink, 1994).

11. For example, when the Eurasian author Marion Bloem requested a subsidy for her film from the government Arts Council, they replied, "Why do you want to drag all that up again? After all, the assimilation process went so smoothly" (Bloem, 1996: 15).

12. Even in 1960 the Dutch scholar De Boer-Lasschuyt (1960: 42) wrote: "This next Indo-European generation may be tougher and to a great extent 'Dutchified'; it will most probably not completely forget nor forgive the sacrifice required from its parent-generation, by the government which believed that they 'simply must disappear.'"

13. The first generation of Dutch Eurasians often practiced their traditional customs at home, but because they were not allowed to be proud of their culture, they often told their children to act "Dutch" in the outside world (Willems, 1997). Also, parents generally sheltered their children from disturbing stories of colonial life, of World War II, of the Indonesian Revolution, and of the migration process, so when they learned of these events as young adults, it caused many to begin their journeys of self-discovery (Seriese, 1997).

14. The name "Tong Tong" refers to a hollow log that was struck with a stick to bring Indonesian villagers together, often in times of danger (Anthonio, 1990).

15. Unlike depictions of Eurasians in most fictional works, the Indos in Vincent Mahieu's stories were not stereotypical "marginal men," but multidimensional and believable characters. Although many of his protagonists meet a tragic end, they do so in defiance of externally imposed barriers (Willems, 1994; Seriese, 1997).

16. Moesson is the Dutch word for "monsoon." Today, Moesson has subscribers in thirty-seven countries. About 750 subscribers are in the United States (Vivian Boon, letter to the author, 7 June 1998).

17. The Pasar Malam Besar is perhaps his most famous legacy left. Founded in 1958, it has become the largest Eurasian festival in the world (Boon, 1997). In 1995, this bazaar, which features food, music, art, theater, lectures, and much more, attracted 115,000 visitors in eleven days (Derksen, 1996).

18. Interestingly, most of the young people who formed NINES in 1980 are the children of members of this organization.

19. Although Tjalie usually wrote in Dutch, he also wrote in Petjo, which had evolved in colonial times. In the seventeenth century, Indos spoke mainly pidgin Portuguese. In the eighteenth century, the influence of Malay grew, and in the nineteenth century, Petjo emerged as a combination of Dutch words and Malay grammar. Only by 1930 did most Dutch Eurasians gain fluency in Dutch, and Petjo was relegated to mostly the lower classes of Indos. While Tjalie was not a member of the lower class, he valued Petjo as a powerful expression of Indo culture (Van der Veur, 1968; Anthonio, 1990).

20. His concerns have been substantiated by research done by the Stichting Informie-en Coordinate Dienstverlening Oologsgetroffenen (Foundation for Information and Coordination to Aid War Victims), which found that many Indos suffered from depression, low self-esteem, lack of

confidence, and difficulty establishing intimate relationships due to their inability to talk about the trauma that they had experienced (Anthonio, 1990; Seriese, 1997).

21. Due to such factors as Holland's cold and rainly climate, housing and employment crises, and attitudes, more than 24,000 Dutch Eurasians eventually made a secondary migration to the United States. If not for American immigration quotas on Dutch citizens, more Eurasians would have possibly come (B. Rijkschroeff, 1989). But, according to Wim Willems (1997, 1998), the U.S government was, at first, reluctant to accept the "colored" Indos as Dutch refugees.

22. Although Dutch Eurasian women had frequently married Dutch men since the early seventeenth century, by World War II the Dutch Eurasian population in Indonesia had become largely endogamous (Kraak, 1957). However, in Holland, marriage with Dutch people has steadily increased with each generation. The fact that Eurasians constitute less than 3 percent of the Dutch population, and remain dispersed throughout the country makes this trend all the more inevitable (Boudre Rijkschroeff, personal communication, November 1997). Interestingly, in the third generation of Eurasians, it is more common for a person to have an Indo father and Dutch mother than the reverse (Boon, 1996).

CHAPTER 17

Multiethnic Lives and Monoethnic Myths: American-Japanese Amerasians in Japan

Stephen Murphy-Shigematsu

Representations of Amerasians in Japan have evolved considerably in the decades since World War II, as have the terms attributed to them. From the derogatory associations of "Ainoko" in the postwar period, to the definition of "Konketsuji" as a social problem in the 1960s and 1970s, from the stylish image associated with "Haafu" in the 1980s, to the international character of "Kokusaiji" and "Daburu" today, the changing terms and images of multiethnic American Japanese people do, to a certain extent, reflect changing social conditions, but are also based on stereotypes and misrepresentations. In general, more positive social attitudes and legal conditions have improved the quality of life for American-Japanese. However, continued belief in the myth of Japanese ethnic purity remains a barrier to their acceptance.

Introduction

The diverse society of Japan is composed of people of various ethnic groups, including a majority population of heterogeneous origins. Among these persons are those whose ancestry has been mixed in recent generations and who are referred to in this chapter as "multiethnic." These individuals are usually the products of relationships between majority Japanese and members of various ethnic minority groups. The largest number of multiethnic people are those of mixed Korean and Japanese ancestry. There are also

This article was originally published as "Representations of Amerasians in Japan" in *Japanese Society*, vol. 1, 1996, pp. 61–76, issued by the Japanese Society Research Institute, Tsukuba, Tokyo, Calgary (Main address: 2-36-14 Sakuradai, Nerimaku, Tokyo, 176-0002 Japan), and with the permission of that Institute is reprinted, with revisions, in this volume.

the offspring of marriages between Japanese of Okinawan ancestry and majority Japanese, as well as persons of partial Chinese, Taiwanese, Ainu, and other heritages.

This chapter explores the social representations of the most conspicuous multiethnic group in Japan, those of American and Japanese ancestry. As the first of many such groups of so-called Amerasians who are products of American hegemonic military operations in Asia, their seemingly marginal story bears significant meaning for the prominent issues of race and nationality in Japan. Description and analysis of their representations in postwar Japanese society are done through the context of the evolution of popular terms used to label them. How social perceptions, attitudes, and treatment of American-Japanese and other people of mixed ancestry have been influenced by the state-endorsed mythology of ethnic purity will also be examined.

The term "multiethnic" is used here, but it begs the question of what makes a person "ethnic." In reality, there is likely to be a great deal of variation from family to family, and from individual to individual. Grouping all persons who are racially and ethnically mixed denies individual difference as well as choice. The construction of such an artificial category also ignores the heterogeneous origins of majority Japanese, and therefore indirectly reinforces the myth of their racial/ethnic purity. Despite these limitations, "multiethnic" is used as a term of convenience, to limit and define the scope of the discussion. It is a term that is more appropriate for some of the persons included in this essay, and less so for others.

Multiethnicity and International Marriage in Japan

It is extremely difficult to count the multiethnic individuals in Japan, because the government does not identify its citizens by ethnic background. The residents of Japan are distinguished only by nationality. So, mixed marriage in Japan usually refers to the number of marriages between Japanese and persons of foreign nationality. From these statistics we can see an increasing rate of so-called international marriages, which, since 1990, have exceeded 25,000 each year. The 1990 figure of 25,626 represents a more than 350 percent increase of the 1980 number. By 1994, international marriages comprised approximately 3.5 percent of all marriages in Japan (Japan, Ministry of Health and Welfare, 1995). These international marriages, which occur most often between Japanese and highly acculturated Koreans who are born and raised in Japan yet maintain South Korean nationality, are what would be called "interethnic" marriages in the United States.

After a long period of denial, Japanese society is gradually recognizing itself as a nation composed of people of various backgrounds. References are now made to Japan as a "*takokuseki shakai*" (multinational society) due to the increased presence of people of foreign nationalities. Even descriptions of Japan as a "*tan'itsu minzoku kokka*" (monoethnic state) are now qualified by using such words as "*hobo*" (nearly) or by explaining that although it is thought of in this way, the reality might be different.

However, at the end of the twentieth century, awareness in Japan of the existence of multiethnic persons is still very low. But as their numbers grow, and as individual assertions of identity become more possible and common, acknowledgment of their presence is increasingly likely. And, with spouses and children of Japanese citizens receiving preferential treatment in immigration, permanent residence, and naturalization, their tendency to settle in Japan has grown, guaranteeing an increase in the number of multiethnic individuals born from international marriages. Finally, as social barriers between certain ethnic groups are lowered, interethnic marriages will continue to increase.

Ainoko

Significant numbers of American-Japanese Amerasians first appeared following Japan's devastating military defeat in World War II. During the American Occupation period, American men and Japanese women met in a wide variety of circumstances, and sometimes formed relationships. However, the legitimization of these relationships was marred by social and legal barriers, including the refusal of the U.S. military and government to encourage their men to hold any responsibility in birth control or in fathering. In fact, U.S. policies were enacted that actually blocked the legalization of American-Japanese relationships, which contributed directly to massive child abandonment (Shade, 1981). It was not until 1952 that American legal barriers to American-Japanese marriages were finally lifted, and the relationships were allowed to flourish. Since then, more than eighty thousand such couples have come to the United States (Thornton, 1992b), with thousands of multiethnic children accompanying them.

For those American-Japanese children who remained in Japan, nationality law based on patriarchal family systems, and racial attitudes based on the myth of the ethnic purity of the Japanese people contributed to the perception of them as non-Japanese. Multiethnic children could only receive Japanese citizenship if their American father did not acknowledge his paternity. However, the legal status of those who did obtain Japanese citizenship was in direct contrast to prevalent social attitudes that regarded them as foreign and made them targets of prejudice and discrimination.

The most conspicuous group of American-Japanese in postwar Japan were the abandoned orphans who became a target for hostility, as well as political activism, during the Occupation. Mitsubishi heiress Sawada Miki was their staunchest advocate during the dark days when they first came to public attention. In 1948, she established the Elizabeth Saunders Home for them (Hemphill, 1980). (Two decades later, in 1967, Nobel laureate Pearl S. Buck formed a similar foundation in her own name to assist the population she called "Amerasians" [Shade, 1981].) Concerned persons debated whether these orphaned children should be isolated in a protective environment and gradually integrated into Japanese society, or were better off sent abroad, either as individuals, to the United States for adoption, or as a group, to a "friendly" environment like Brazil (Hemphill, 1980). Those who favored their integration into Japanese society believed that the best solution was to eliminate their foreignness through intermarriage with majority Japanese.

During this period, multiethnic American-Japanese were commonly referred to as "Ainoko." The word literally means a "child of mixture" and is considered derogatory, evoking images of poverty, illegitimacy, racial impurity, prejudice, and discrimination. It is used for animals as well as for any kind of ethnically mixed person. As in many societies, in postwar Japan the multiethnic person was viewed as a problem, as an impure being of questionable belonging (Gist & Dworkin, 1972). Cultural confusion was also associated with the marginal qualities of the Ainoko. The extremely negative social attitudes toward them in Japan are reflected in the American film *Sayonara*, when the Japanese woman asks her American lover, "But our children . . . what would they be?" His confident answer—that they would simply be "half-yellow, half-white; half-Japanese, half-American"—was based on the assumption that they would be raised in the (supposedly) more hospitable environment of American society.

Some Japanese authorities became concerned with protecting "good" Japanese women from the sexual aggression of American males. They saw the abandoned children of this era as a social problem that was caused by the callous behavior of Americans. However, their attempts to count these children and investigate their situation were squashed by Occupation authorities, as the United States refuted claims of massive irresponsibility as "cruel Communist lies" (Hemphill, 1980). The multiethnic children were occasionally presented to the American public as unfortunate and delinquent street children, but mostly they were ignored as a by-product of the war and an inevitable but small price to pay for fighting for world peace.

Konketsuji

As the Occupation era came to an end and memories of the war began to fade, the pejorative label "Ainoko" was gradually replaced in public usage with the more neutral term "Konketsuji"—meaning literally the "mixed-blood child." Konketsuji had been used previously to refer to various kinds of ethnic mixtures, including Korean-Japanese people. But despite the shift in terms, multiethnic American-Japanese continued to be associated with the social problems caused by the U.S. military presence. The end of the Occupation did not mean a complete withdrawal of American military forces, as the U.S.–Japan Security Agreement continued to allow the maintenance of large facilities in Japan. The bases were especially active during the Korean and Vietnam wars, and the stationing of troops in Japan continued the maintenance of a service industry and thus the continued births of children fathered by Americans, both in and out of marriage.

Throughout Japan, the Konketsuji era was marked by their discrimination in education, employment, and marriage. Multiethnic American-Japanese became concentrated in large cities and in employment in the fashion, entertainment, and service industries, often on or near the military bases (Strong, 1978). The Japanese media promoted images of Amerasians as living fast and loose lives, due to the confusion created by the mixture of their genes (DeVos et al., 1983). The harsh reality was that Konketsuji were over-represented in single-parent families, were oftentimes school dropouts, and frequently had identity issues that were complicated by racial and class prejudice and abandonment (Wagatsuma, 1976).

In the 1960s some of the more fortunate Amerasians emerged as popular entertainers, creating a *"Konketsuji boomu."* Talent scouts descended on schools that had large populations of American-Japanese to sign up attractive females and males for modeling and acting. A sexual fascination was attached to the erotic and exotic images of the Konketsuji. However, feelings of fascination and admiration for these models and singers were mixed with repulsion, and Konketsuji were still objectified and set apart from the majority population (Lebra, 1976).

The less fortunate of the Amerasians became associated with the phrase *"Konketsuji mondai,"* meaning the "problem of the Konketsuji." *"Konketsuji mondai"* was publicized as evidence of the social problems caused by the U.S. military's presence, with its large concentration of relatively uneducated, aggressive young males, passing through on their way to uncertain futures in battle (Murphy-Shigematsu, 1994b).

Once Okinawa reverted to Japanese governance in 1972, the phrase *"Konketsuji mondai"* became symbolic of the protests of its residents that, as unequal members of the Japanese state, they were forced to bear the brunt of the responsibility for housing the American military. During this period, U.S. military operations had become increasingly concentrated in Okinawa, as did the population of Konketsuji, who were depicted as a burden that Okinawans were forced to deal with as part of Japan's support of the American war in Vietnam (Fukuchi, 1980; Oshiro, 1984). Although Okinawans often claim that the social environment in Okinawa has been kinder to American-Japanese than that on the Japanese mainland, in reality the Konketsuji there have been the targets of severe prejudice, aggravated by the U.S. military defeat in Vietnam and the prolonged presence of American bases (Namihira, 1980). Stereotyping and scapegoating of Amerasians have been common as Okinawan Japanese continue to struggle with the American and Japanese governments for their right of self-determination.

The conditions of this period were symbolized by the particularly poignant problem of statelessness that afflicted some American-Japanese multiethnics. The issue was highly publicized through the 1970s, and many Amerasians who had become stateless as a result of loopholes in U.S. and Japanese nationality laws were taken up as celebrated causes by various groups with different agendas (Honda, 1982). As will be explained, the resolution of this problem signified the dawning of a new era for the American-Japanese in Japan.

Haafu

The popularity of Konketsuji entertainers eventually led to the coining of a new term to describe persons of mixed ancestry—"Haafu," which comes from the English word *"half."* Turning English words into Japanese is one way of avoiding the use of emotionally laden Japanese terms that have a history of associations. "Haafu" is used to refer to a person who is "half foreigner"—thus implying that the person is also "half-

Japanese"—and was created in an attempt to attach a trendy label, particularly to those who are considered phenotypically White. From sometime during the 1970s until this day, "Haafu" has become the most popular term to describe not only American-Japanese multiethnics but certain other mixtures, mostly those considered to be phenotypically White.

The shift to "Haafu" occurred in an era in which Japan experienced an enormous economic ascent. It was no longer true that the Americans were so rich and powerful and the Japanese so poor and weak; the two nations came to relate more as equals. Also, "Haafu" lacks associations with the military, single mothers, and poverty, as the number of Amerasians born into these kinds of situations decreased considerably in the late 1970s and 1980s. As the U.S. military presence declined and the Japanese economy flourished, relatively fewer Japanese-American marriages were of the military sort. More and more they were between Japanese nationals and foreign civilians, of various types, residing in Japan.

For young people today, the terms "Ainoko" and "Konketsuji" are either unknown or pejorative terms from the past, while "Haafu" signifies a bright image of a fashionable, foreign-looking Japanese who speaks fluent English. Much of this concept is based on physical appearance, as the "White" Haafu is perhaps the ideal physical type in the minds of the Japanese majority: long legs and "hakujin" (White) features, but sufficiently Japanese to be familiar and comfortable. The idealization of a Westernized Haafu relates to the long-standing admiration of the Western powers in Japan, dating back to the Meiji era (1868–1923). This idealization also distinguishes American-Japanese multiethnics from those related to Japan's colonial empire, mostly Korean-Japanese and Taiwanese-Japanese.

The acceptance of White American standards of beauty by majority Japanese has contributed to more positive yet equally narrow images of Amerasians and to their popularity as fictionalized heroes in the entertainment world. But while there were certain positive aspects to the Konketsuji stereotype, they were limited to admiration for their attractive bodies and superior physical skills (for example, the belief that Amerasians are superior in sports, based on the fact that some of Japan's most famous professional athletes are multiethnic). The Haafu image, on the other hand, also includes the stereotype of intelligence. For example, these days, sexy Haafu idols not only model and act, but also appear as English instructors or television and radio announcers. The popular sound of these people who speak a smooth blend of native Japanese and English also represents the new image of Haafu as bilingual, bicultural, and intelligent. That this image often falls short of reality is illustrated by the singing group that helped to popularize the term "Haafu"—the Golden Haafu. Although they were promoted as bilingual, only one of the members actually spoke native English, while the others spoke it at the level of an ordinary Japanese (Williams, 1992).

Thus, the increased appearance in the Japanese media of Amerasians who have been raised bilingually and biculturally has added a much more positive, even fashionable, image to the popular stereotypes of Haafu. But whether denigrated or exoticized, the American-Japanese are always depicted as "the Other," making it difficult for them to be treated as individuals or as ordinary Japanese. Unlike many other multiethnic people in Japan, most Amerasians are physically identifiable and therefore are easy targets of daily social discrimination. The phenomenon of "passing" that is widely practiced by most Japanese minorities—including many multiethnic persons—is generally not possible for most American-Japanese. They are automatically labeled as foreigners, although many speak no language other than Japanese and have spent their whole lives in Japan. In a society in which being different can be a sin punishable by ostracism, this obvious racial difference can lead to bullying and rejection.

The positive aspects of the shift to the term "Haafu" are also marred by the fact that it generally leaves out Amerasians who have African American heritage. Those regarded as phenotypically Black are often considered to have undesirable physical features and to be culturally inferior outside of the areas of music, dance, and sports. While phenotypically White Amerasians still encounter ambivalent and hostile attitudes, those regarded as Black face considerably more negative stereotypes and discrimination by majority Japanese. The positive aspects of the Haafu image also do not include those American-Japanese who are physically indistinguishable from majority Japanese, such as those who are the children of native Japanese and Asian Americans.

Kokusaiji and Daburu

In 1979, the International Year of the Child, the term "Kokusaiji" (meaning "international child") was advanced as an alternative label for American-Japanese (Oshiro, 1984). Its usage has been limited, but it was especially promoted in the years preceding the passage of a revised Japanese nationality law in 1985. This period was marked by several highly publicized legal cases that challenged the Japanese state's right to deny citizenship to children born to Japanese women and foreign men. The new law was a major social and legal reform because it eliminated the gender discrimination inherent in the old one: all children with Japanese mothers were now allowed to acquire Japanese citizenship, making them eligible for such benefits as welfare, single-parent allowances, and national health insurance (Kokusai Kekkon o Kangaeru Kai, 1991). (Ironically, the revised nationality law has led to a new problem of statelessness for individuals born to foreign mothers and Japanese fathers who fail to acknowledge their paternity.)

The term "Kokusaiji" represents an attempt to redefine multiethnic people in a positive way by emphasizing the international quality of their parentage and cultural backgrounds. It also reflects changing social conditions. In this age of so-called internationalization and globalism, there is a wide range of international marriages involving Japanese and people from many different countries. These marriages usually do not involve military personnel and include all social classes. Also, international marriages today involve Japanese men three times as often as Japanese women. However, Japanese-American marriages remain the exception, which mostly still involve Japanese women and American men (Japan, Ministry of Health and Welfare, 1995).

There has been some opposition to the terms "Ainoko," "Konketsuji," and "Haafu" in Japan that is similar to the American movement away from terms that emphasize blood or percentage of ancestry, such as "mixed-blood" or "half-breed." "Haafu" and the newer term "Kuohta" (from the English word "quarter") label the multiethnic person according to the amount of non-Japanese "blood," much like the old racial terminology "quadroon" and "octoroon" in the United States. In the same way that the American "one-drop rule" supposedly makes a person with any amount of Black ancestry "Black" and "not White," any amount of non-Japanese ancestry has been thought to make a person foreign and not Japanese. Of course this is only in a social sense, as legally there are no racial barriers to being either American or Japanese as defined by nationality.

This irrational racial classification is offensive and alienating to many multiethnic people in Japan. Some English-speaking parents of American-Japanese, and some bilingual American-Japanese themselves, resent the English origin of the word "Haafu" and feel that it is derogatory. Therefore, they have advocated for the use of the word "Daburu," from the English word "double," to correct the deficiencies of "Haafu." "Daburu" emphasizes that American-Japanese are not "half" anything, but have the ethnicity of both sides of their parentage. With its emergence in the media it has been embraced by some American-Japanese, as well as other multiethnics, as a term of empowerment.

But even "Daburu" does not avoid criticism. While there are people who use it as an explanatory concept, it is rarely used as a self-identifying label by Amerasians. Some feel that it is unnecessary or unnatural, reflecting an overcompensation on behalf of a positive self-assertion. Others reject it because it continues to identify them as different when they would prefer a term that indicates their actual ancestry, such as "Amerikakei Nihonjin" (American-Japanese). And many feel that the term "Haafu" is fine, because it is used without a sense of its original English meaning. These people claim that, despite objections by English-speaking parents and concerned others, self-definition has paradoxically taken place as they embrace and redefine the inherently racist and negative term "Haafu." While claiming to be both Japanese and American, many youths still use "Haafu" as a term of self-identification.

As compared to "Ainoko" and "Konketsuji," the words "Haafu," "Kokusaiji," and "Daburu" reflect the fact that Amerasians in Japan are increasingly associated with children of intact and well-to-do families who have lived abroad. They tend to reside in areas that are relatively sheltered from prejudice and discrimination by the status of their families and the friendly environment of international schools or schools on the military bases (Murphy-Shigematsu, 1994a). These American-Japanese have had much greater access than many of their predecessors to gaining the skills of bilingualism and multiculturalism that have earned them respect in Japanese society and increased their opportunities in the United States.

Although old associations and stereotypes of the military, poverty, and illegitimacy are fading, they continue to pressure many of those American-Japanese who do have military fathers to deny their background and instead to claim that their fathers are businessmen (Williams, 1992). Also, in Okinawa the lives of Amerasians are still strongly influenced by the presence of U.S. military forces. Despite its reversion to Japanese rule in 1972 (twenty years after the end of the Occupation), the United States still maintains enormous military bases in Okinawa, where they continue to exercise control over large land areas and create tensions that are always potentially dangerous to the scapegoating of multiethnic Japanese (Murphy-Shigematsu, 1993).

Interestingly, the multiethnic American-Japanese in Okinawa have assumed a very symbolic role in the popular media and the arts. They have come to represent not only the American military and the troubles it has caused in Okinawa but, more complexly, the reality of American cultural and political influence on the island and its people (Oshiro, 1992). As victims themselves, Amerasians symbolize how Okinawa has been negatively affected by the aggression of others, yet also how Okinawa's resilient spirit thrives in spite of this oppression.

In 1998, multiethnic American-Japanese once again emerged in the Japanese media with the founding of the AmerAsian School. The stated aim of the school is "Daburu education," meaning it offers the languages and cultures of both ancestries of the students. Its founders have, for the first time, used the Japanese version of the term "Amerasian" ("*Amerajian*") to symbolize multiethnic American-Japanese unity with others whose lives have been directly influenced by American hegemony in Asia. Although it was commonly thought that the issues around being Amerasian were largely a thing of the past, this new school has attracted considerable attention and a growing enrollment. Some of the students are "refugees" from the violence of public schools, but most simply want an education that fits their personal needs better than that offered by public or private schools.

Discussion

Tachihara Masaaki (1980: 27), a writer of Korean and Japanese ancestries, once posed this question: "I wonder if the day will ever come when the fact of being of mixed blood would be understood in Japan." This day may still be far off. The existence of people of multiethnic backgrounds remains clouded by ignorance, stereotypes, prejudices, and disinterest.

But after a long period of denial, Japan is gradually recognizing itself as a society composed of people of various backgrounds, including those who are mixed. Representations of American-Japanese and others of mixed ancestry have evolved along with the sociopolitical situation in Japan. The generally more positive images of people of mixed ancestry have enhanced their quality of life, by making them less the objects of scorn and more the objects of admiration. The objectified nature of their experience, however, remains for many individuals, as they are treated as "Others"—outside the boundaries of ordinary Japanese.

Beneath this consciousness is the myth of "Japaneseness" fed by a state ideology of ethnic purity. Japan is still commonly depicted as a homogeneous nation-state, and the Japanese are said to be a pure race, endowed with special qualities that distinguish them from others (Dale, 1986). "Japanese blood" is therefore thought to be intimately connected with the possession of Japanese cultural knowledge (Yoshino, 1992). This popular and officialized belief that being Japanese is a matter of "race" ignores the nonracialistic nationality law, which designates persons as Japanese regardless of their ethnic or racial background. Such consciousness hinders the acceptance of Japanese, such as those of mixed ancestry, who do not conform to the narrow standards of "Japaneseness."

During my research, I was told an interesting story by an Okinawan couple. The husband is of American and Japanese ancestry and is a Japanese citizen. The wife, who is an American citizen, is also of American and Japanese ancestry, but her American father was from the Philippines. Going through the immigration check at the airport in Japan, they commonly encounter the following situation: together, they each hand their own passports to the official, who glances at their faces, and, without opening the passports, switches them and warns the couple not to mix up their passports.

American-Japanese regularly encounter this type of situation because of the common belief that the Japanese are a pure race rather than a multiethnic nationality. In my teaching, it is always interesting to provide Japanese groups with examples of people who do not fit this myth, such as George Johnson, a Japanese citizen, who speaks native Japanese, and has green eyes and brown hair. Or Taro Suzuki, who is a black-eyed, black-haired American who speaks only English. Such an exercise creates considerable confusion, and, while many Japanese have become able to acknowledge that Taro is an American, they still cannot imagine that George is Japanese.

This is the very challenge that multiethnics, and others, pose to Japanese society. Besides those of mixed ancestry, and the non-Japanese who are born and raised in Japan and do not "look Japanese" but "act Japanese," there is also the growing presence of large numbers of people who "look Japanese" but do not "act Japanese." Among these individuals are returnee students who are Japanese citizens born and/or raised in another country, as well as foreigners of Japanese ancestry, such as Brazilians. These persons challenge the assumptions of the relationship between "Japanese blood" and Japanese cultural knowledge. Such people remind all of us that a person's identity cannot be determined by his or her phenotype, and that nationalistic either/or identities are increasingly unsuitable for a world in which many individuals transcend these artificial boundaries and have multiple affiliations.

It may take several generations before majority Japanese can fully grasp the concept of Japan as a multiethnic society and conceive of "Japanese" as a nonracialistic label. This development will be enhanced by the presence and participation in Japanese society of those who challenge the limits of common conceptions, stereotypes, and prejudices. Persons of multiethnic ancestry may pose this challenge of expanding the mental and spiritual boundaries of Japan, simply by being both Japanese and not Japanese.

CHAPTER 18

The Racial Politics of Being *Dogla* and of "Asian" Descent in Suriname

Loraine Y. Van Tuyl

The Surinamese Racial Context

During the last decade, academicians have become more sophisticated in illustrating that the variability in experiences reported by multiracial people tends to relate to the differences in race relations found within their surrounding environments (Kerwin et al., 1993; King, 1997; Root, 1990, 1995, 1996; Spickard, 1995; Yoshimi, 1997). Yet despite our understanding of the important role that context plays, we have only focused on a limited number of racial climates within the United States—mostly West and East Coast (sub)urban middle-class settings (e.g., San Francisco, New York, Los Angeles) and, to a lesser degree, Hawai'i—as possible influential subcontexts within the national context (Kerwin et al., 1993; King, 1997; Spickard, 1995; Yoshimi, 1997). Within these subcontexts, we have primarily studied the experiences of multiracials who have either Black-White ancestry or, more recently, Asian-White ancestry (Gibbs & Moskowitz-Sweet, 1991; King, 1997; Yoshimi, 1997). Consequently, we know relatively little about multiracials who have Latino, Native American, or Middle Eastern heritages, and almost nothing on mixtures not involving "Whites" (Hall, 1980).

Similarly, only a few social scientists have explored the experiences of multiracials embedded within a racial ecology that is nationally and culturally different than that of the United States (Ropp, 1997; Weisman, 1998a). Two important contributors to cross-national research on race are Howard Winant (1994), who applied his "racial formation" theory to Brazilian constructions of race, and George Fredrickson (1981), who did a comparative analysis of historical and colonial race relations between South Africa and the United States. Both of these authors argue that certain differences between national contexts (i.e., geography, resources, indigenous people, national and cultural background of the colonizers, and racial/ethnic composition of a region) help us to recognize and expel American culture-bound myths of race. This comparative analysis also enables us to broaden our understanding of historical and national race relations, and how they influence attitudes toward racial mixing and the experiences of multiracials. In an attempt to address some of the limitations in the scientific research on multiracial issues, I interviewed fifteen multiracial people in Paramaribo, the capital of my home country, Suriname, which is on the north shore of South America. Suriname is unusual amongst its Caribbean and South American neighbors in that a little over 50 percent of its four hundred thousand citizens are, by American standards, "Asian"—having ancestors from India, Java (an island in Indonesia), and China who largely immigrated to Suriname as contract laborers (Dew, 1996). The descendants of these three primary "Asian" groups are locally referred to as the Hindustanis (Indians), the Javanese, and the Chinese, respectively, and are perceived as three separate racial/ethnic groups rather than as one racial group (Mitrasingh, 1980; Takaki, 1989; Williams, 1991). The rest of Suriname's population consists mostly of a group of people who call themselves "Creole" or "Negro." They are predominantly descendants of African slaves and European colonists (Buddingh, 1995; Dew, 1996; McLeod, 1996; Mitrasingh, 1980). The "Maroons" (locally known as the "Bushland Creoles" or by a tribe name) and the "Amerindians" (locally known as the "Indians" or by a tribe name) largely reside in the savannas and the rain forests, which cover about 75 percent of Suriname (Dew, 1996). Those considered "White" or "European" account for just 1.1 percent of the population (Dew, 1996).

The purpose of this chapter is to explore the experiences of a small group of multiracial people in a geographical, social, and cultural context that is, in terms of its racial composition, economic and political instability, colonial history, and non-Western, non-industrialized climate, very different from the mainland United States. Because Suriname, which had been colonized by the Dutch from 1667 to 1975, was primarily used as a plantation colony rather than as a settlement, race relations between the small percentage of predominantly White male colonists and the indigenous Amerindian and African slaves and their descendants were quite different than race relations in the United States (Fredrickson, 1981; McLeod, 1996; Root, 1992; Winant, 1994). For instance, segregation laws were never strictly enforced, not even when the institution of slavery was legal (McLeod, 1996). Although White supremacist ideologies were similarly practiced and institutionalized in both Suriname and the United States beginning in the seventeenth century, free Blacks nevertheless had more civil rights (i.e., the right to own land, hold paid jobs, and share schools, churches, and neighborhoods with Whites) compared to their counterparts in the United States, starting in the eighteenth century (Fredrickson, 1981; McLeod, 1996; Winant, 1994). For example, the first marriage between an (unmixed) Black woman and a White Dutchman occurred in 1767, precisely two hundred years before the last antimiscegenation laws were overturned by the Supreme Court in the United States (McLeod, 1996; Root, 1996). Apparently, a long tradition of interracial mixing and mutual acculturation between people of African, European, and Amerindian descent became more complex as contract workers from China, Java, and India entered the mixed society of Suriname between 1853 and 1939 and as African slaves were emancipated in 1863 (Buddingh, 1995; Dew, 1996; Mitrasingh, 1980).

As in Hawai'i, the contract laborers from Asia were initially separated by national origin on the plantations surrounding the politically, linguistically, and culturally dominant Creole capital (Mitrasingh, 1980; Takaki, 1989). After their five- to ten-year contracts ended, many of these laborers migrated to the capital (Mitrasingh, 1980). Because of the small number of White colonists and the growing presence of other groups in Suriname, no one local group has historically and consistently been dominant in terms of cultural practices, language, religion, numerical majority, or economic and political rule (McLeod, 1996; Mitrasingh, 1980). Similar to the racial climate in Hawai'i, the lack of a clear majority group seems to have facilitated the preservation of traditional cultural practices and enabled the integration of the various groups' cultural traditions, spiritual beliefs, language, and food practices (Takaki, 1989).

Although Dutch is the official language, and is the one that is most often spoken in academic, legal, and political settings, the Creole language, locally known as Sranan Tongo (Surinamese Tongue), Sranan, or Negro English, is currently the one that is most frequently spoken in social settings and on the streets. Its social prevalence promotes the transmission of many Creole expressions, values, and communication patterns. The use of Sranan enables interaction and communication, particularly between less acculturated members of each of the main groups in Suriname. However, it is also used by politicians and people in prominent positions to draw support from the "masses" (Dew, 1996).

Racial Integration and Multiculturalism

The current American racial climate has been born out of an era of legalized racial exploitation, segregation, and social oppression of non-White groups. After the major civil rights movements of the 1960s, there was a push for color-blind, cultural assimilation of racial minority groups into dominant White society, which was followed by a reactive movement promoting cultural pluralism and racial separation, but this time with equal access to resources and opportunities (Root, 1996; Williams, 1997). In contrast, the predominantly collectivistic and non-White people of Suriname share a common history of slavery and exploitation, but also have a long colonial history of racial mixing and mutual cultural assimilation (Dew, 1996; Mitrasingh, 1980).

In my discussion, I will draw from interview data from nine participants between the ages of eighteen and thirty, each with partial Asian ancestry, to explore their perceptions of race relations in the capital of Suriname and of the way in which the regional racial climate has affected their experiences as multiracial people. The participants in this study appeared to perceive their primary support group and other Surinamese people in general, whether multiracial or not, as multicultural and racially integrated. Although there is no demographic data to confirm this, most participants also believed that more than half of the people in Suriname were multiracial, which seems to explain the sense of majority status and privilege that many associate with being multiracial. Arianne, who is Javanese and Creole, states:

> I also interact a lot with people who are mixed. Or actually, most people in Suriname are mixed, so it does not make a difference for me . . . In my class, there were very few mixed people, but in general at my school there are many mixed people . . . Surinamese people are totally mixed, because the entire population is mixed.

Ann, whose ancestors are Creole, Javanese, and Chinese, describes how Surinamese people celebrate official national holidays that actually have specific ethnic origins:

> Phagwa is a Hindustani holiday. . . . All of Suriname celebrates it, you know. . . . You just participate in everything. Yeah, like that, most of the time with holidays everyone participates. . . . Hindu, Muslim, whatever, they all celebrate Christmas, you know, and almost everyone also celebrates Shubdewali [a Muslim festival], and you have other festivals where everyone participates just like that. They don't understand the reason for the celebration, but everyone participates.

Nelson, who has Hindustani, Chinese, Creole, Amerindian, and Jewish roots, confirms that Surinamese people are multicultural in terms of their participation in ethnic holidays and their food choices:

> If you look at certain holidays, Phagwa, the entire population participates. Everyone celebrates Phagwa, or Christmas, everyone celebrates Christmas nowadays, and yes, the food also, people eat more or less everything there is.

Cindy, who identifies herself as Chinese, Jewish, and Creole, describes the type of music that she listens to on the radio:

> All kinds. But especially European music. Once in a while Javanese. Chinese, eh, we did not really listen to that because you only have one radio station that now really knows how to play a few Chinese songs. . . . So you had more Hindustani, Javanese, eh, Maroon, like Kawina music, Amerindian music, and for the rest, European music.

The extended families and neighborhoods of the participants tended to be equally diverse. Don, who is Amerindian, Chinese, and Creole, explains:

> My uncle, on my mother's side . . . is married to a Javanese woman. The other uncle is married to a Hindustani woman. Another uncle is married to a Creole woman. She is also half-Hindustani. And another uncle is married to a Dutch woman.

Mandy, of Hindustani, Chinese, Jewish, Creole, Portuguese, and Dutch background, describes how people in Trinidad reacted to Suriname's diverse population and to a musical performance she had participated in:

> When we went to Trinidad, there was something like an "Ala Kondre" [Sranan for All Countries] [music] festival, where you have all cultures of Suriname in one, so you see a Hindus-

tani with a *sari,* and a Javanese person with a *slendang* [traditional clothing], and a Chinese person, and then they make [one piece of music] together, so parts of their culture, of their music, they use in one, so it actually becomes one big thing. One piece [of music], that is why they call it "Ala Kondre," and the musical part, there you have all the instruments that are typical of the Surinamese cultures. . . . You have the Hindustani drum, you have the *tabla,* you also have the guitar, you have the harmonium, but then you also have the *apinti drum* of the Maroons, you have the *gamalan* of the Javanese, so you have all the instruments together, and it was really very beautiful, it was just incredible, and that's why people were also amazed by it, like how is that possible, you know?

Racial Hierarchy

In contrast to the United States, Whites in Suriname were never numerically dominant and are no longer politically dominant, although they are still in a dominant position from a historical and international perspective (Dew, 1996). Starting at the beginning of the twentieth century, the Creoles were culturally and politically the most dominant group, but in recent years have been struggling with competition from the increasingly economically successful Hindustanis and Chinese for local control (Mitrasingh, 1980). Whether their beliefs are stereotypes, truths, or a combination of both, most study participants seemed to share a collective reality about their interactions with other groups that affected their experiences as multiracials in a similar way, despite their diverse backgrounds. Most of the participants believed that the Hindustanis are currently the most powerful group.

Ann explains how culture rather than race is responsible for the higher socioeconomic status of Hindustanis:

Look, there are many Hindustanis with power. Why? Because Hindustanis help each other to get higher up. . . . They have more power, but this does not mean that they are better. They are perhaps raised differently. Look, Hindustanis are most of the time more upwardly mobile than Creoles. And, Hindustanis will help each other. I see it with my boyfriend's family—if there is something, the family will help you. Let's say, you need something, they will help you; you need a job, they will help you. You know, while not all ethnic groups are like that, which makes it seem that they are better, but that is totally not true, it is just the way in which they were raised, and the way they approach things and they are the reason that they help each other so that they can improve, but it has nothing to do with culture. It has something to do with culture because they were raised that way, but it is not tied down to their race.

Mark, who is Javanese, Creole, and Amerindian, struggles every day to make ends meet. He discusses the power that Whites still have in Suriname and also comments on how local groups vie for resources:

First of all, the Netherlands still has a lot of impact here, because everyone, if they get the opportunity, well not everyone, many who are not well off here, want to go to Holland. Why, I don't know, because you work rock hard over there, you will have to exhaust yourself, you will have to scramble first to get ahead. But among the different ethnic groups here, the Hindustanis tend to be at the top in terms of money, businesses, the Hindustanis are at the top. [That has] a whole lot of impact, because if they are the type of Hindustanis that I just described, that only help other Hindustanis, then a Creole or other ethnic group does not easily get ahead, because the Hindustani person with a business will more easily help another Hindustani instead of a Creole. Yes, preferential treatment plays a big role.

Mandy elaborates on the interconnections of class and race that inform social relations in Suriname:

The people with money naturally are most powerful, and the people with money are the Chinese and the Hindustanis, Whites also, yes, actually, Whites, people still tend to look up to Whites, and then I am speaking about foreigners, and also Surinamese, but White Surinamese, yes, but in general it is how much money you have.

Hindustani-Creole Relations

There was full agreement among the participants that the greatest amount of racial conflict appeared to exist between the largest groups, the Creoles and Hindustanis. This racial tension and the corresponding mixed-race experience appear to parallel the Black-White racial dichotomy and biracial experience in the United States.

By comparing the racial tension in Suriname with that of Trinidad, Mandy illustrates the different gradations of conflict that exist in the Caribbean:

I am proud that we have so many ethnic groups, and that we still don't live in some kind of civil war, because I have seen that you have more Creoles and Hindustanis in Trinidad . . . yet they are still more distanced toward each other, and when they see that Suriname has so many different ethnic groups, then they are baffled, how can they live with each other, and stuff, while they have only two, and then they already live like that. So I am proud about that. What I do think is a pity, is that . . . you have a few that really put each other down, so that they maybe say, look at that Hindustani person, he is greedy, while you can actually learn something from all of them, and that you can work on your own shortcomings when you learn from each other, so I think we should adopt more from each other, we live together, so we should not take things out on each other.

Arianne suspects that the Hindustani-Creole tension is related to the unequal distribution of resources between them, and describes the negative attributions that each group makes about the other on the basis of this inequality:

Hindustanis are stingy people and because of that are often well-to-do, and Creoles often are not well-off, . . . and they see a Hindustani with a large house, and he gets jealous and then they say a lot of negative things.

Nelson is certain that most of the conflict exists

among Hindustanis and Creoles. At parties, just at school, you also see it. I have seen it a few times that they just provoke each other to fight. I think it is stupid, I mean, why would you just pick a fight because one looks different than the other?

Ann has also experienced Hindustani-Creole tension in various areas:

I know an incidence of a Hindustani woman who was with a Creole man, and that is just the combination from hell, really, it just can't be worse.. . . . The [Hindustani] father was so against the relationship, so he wanted to cut the man into pieces, but eventually . . . they [the couple] came over [to the parents house], and eventually [the couple] had to sleep in the pig barn, even though the woman came from well-to-do parents. . . . At school you really have it, Hindustanis against Creoles. . . . For example, if you have a Hindustani professor, then Creoles always think that he is boycotting them, or if it is a Creole man, then the Hindustanis think he is boycotting them, you know, they are always looking for something, they just look for things, you know. . . . There are many Hindustanis in politics and there are many Creoles in politics. The Hindustanis hate the Creoles and the Creoles hate the Hindustanis, but they work together because there is money to be made. But, if it is up to them, the Creoles can drop dead as far as the Hindustanis are concerned, and vice versa.

Horizontal and Vertical Individualism and Collectivism

In the United States, conceptualizations of "racism," White supremacy, and the Black-White dualism model are culturally bounded and based on the manifestation of White supremacy ideologies in practically all institutional domains (e.g., culture, language, education, economics, religion, politics, etc.) of this society (Fredrickson, 1981; Winant, 1994). Consequently, lay people as well as academics have often ironically attributed the problem of racism to Whiteness, which has limited our understanding of the psychological, social, and cultural components that magnify the oppressive potential of all humans, White or non-White. It also makes it difficult to understand racial tension between two groups who seem more similar than different in terms of skin color, such as the Hindustanis and Creoles. In recent meta-analyses of studies that have paid particular attention to the main cultural differences between racialized groups, J. S. Phinney (1996) found that people from mainstream American and Western European cultures generally emphasized the individual over the group and viewed people as independent, autonomous, and self-contained. On the other hand, people from Asia, Latin America, Africa, and indigenous cultures tended to emphasize the group over the individual and viewed people as interdependent and connected.

The broad cultural differences of individualism and collectivism that are readily apparent between Western and non-Western people can be further divided into the horizontal and vertical dimensions, with horizontally oriented people promoting equal rankings within and between groups, and vertically oriented people promoting hierarchical rankings. The interaction between individualism and collectivism and between the vertical and horizontal dimensions may help us gain a better understanding of how the social structures within certain racial and ethnic groups may or may not lead to racial supremacy over other groups (Singelis et al., 1995).

For instance, vertical collectivism is a cultural pattern found in India, Japan, and China, in which the individual sees the self as an interdependent aspect of an in-group, even though some members of the group have more status than others (Singelis et al., 1995). There is an acceptance of unequal distributions of privileges and resources based on characteristics endowed at birth (such as race, skin color, gender, caste, etc.) within and between groups. Vertical individualism, on the other hand, is a cultural pattern found in the United States and France, in which the self is viewed as being independent, and individuals see themselves as being different from others. Competition is an important aspect of this pattern. A high degree of freedom and a low level of equality in privileges are accepted and justified based on premises of equal opportunity and individual differences, such as effort, ability, intelligence, and talent. In contrast, horizontal collectivism is a cultural pattern found in the Israeli kibbutz, and based on its defining characteristics, also appears to be the social structure most characteristic of many Surinamese Creole, Javanese, and Amerindian groups. The individual in this community sees the self as being interdependent and the same as others. Each person is believed to deserve equal access to resources because of birthright and equal human value, regardless of contribution to the group. Lastly, horizontal individualism is a cultural pattern found in Sweden, Australia, and the Netherlands, in which the self is considered independent and unique, but perceived to have the same right to privileges and resources as others.

These vertical and horizontal dimensions prevent us from paradoxically attributing ideological sources of racial supremacy to a racial feature (i.e., Whiteness), and may provide a theoretical explanation of how cultural factors, such as a vertical orientation, may propel oppressive behavior and hierarchical ranking of cultural and racial features among individualists as well as collectivists. It is also important to acknowledge that a delicate balance of superior and subordinate roles within the self, a household, and a society in certain collectivistic and hierarchical cultures can promote spiritual development when principles of reincarnation and eternal equilibrium are also taken into account (Roland, 1988). However, collectivistic as well as individualistic ethnic groups with a more horizontal orientation are bound to clash with and end up in an inferior position toward people who continuously strive to elevate their social status and operate from a superior or hierarchical worldview (Root, 1997b; Williams, 1991).

Racial Purity

The participants in my research agreed that the Hindustani and Chinese, who are theoretically also the most hierarchically oriented, were the most committed to maintaining ethnic and racial "purity," and perceived themselves to be superior to other groups. They reported that the Javanese, Amerindians, and Creoles were less dogmatic in preserving their cultural traditions and racial purity, and Whites were completely left out of this discussion.

Mercedes, who had been primarily raised by her Creole/Amerindian mother and grandfather, and had never met her Hindustani father, lived until age seventeen in an agricultural community half an hour outside of the city. This area is more segregated and is predominantly populated by Javanese and Hindustani people, who also tend to be more traditional than people in the city. As Mercedes explains:

> Actually, living outside [of the city] in Saramacca, you have a big group of Hindustanis, a big group of Javanese, and a handful of Creole people. You know, so you just come in contact with those people. You have two Amerindian towns there, so, you just come into contact with these people. They have their own style of living, you know, that is indeed a bit different, that what I told you about Hindustanis, they really have tight family bonds: What is uncle going to say? What is aunt going to say? What is the community going to say? You know, you don't find that as much among Creoles. With the Javanese, you have the same thing. . . . What is the priest going to say? What is the community going to say about certain things? So they also comply a little bit to tight rules. With the Amerindian, I have to say, you don't have that as much, they live . . . as they like. I don't know. There is quite a bit of difference.

Mercedes also reports that interracial relationships are strictly prohibited in traditional Hindustani families, and are sometimes controlled through the use of violence and by limits on women's sexual expression. She also illustrates how women who are in a more horizontal family system (i.e., Creole matriarchal culture) tend to experience more freedom regarding their choice of partners and their expression of sexuality than those who are in a vertical family system (i.e., Hindustani patriarchal culture):

> Look, with the Hindustani it is like this. The boy is a little freer. Hey, even if he starts a relationship with a Creole woman, yes, he is then yelled at, but if he later breaks off this relationship and marries a Hindustani girl, then people say, no problem. But with the Hindustani woman, you really have the tight . . . like, you can't interact with others and actually, I don't know if it is still like that, but in the past a Hindustani girl had to enter into a marriage as a virgin, and the moment the family would notice, eh, she is no longer a virgin, and worse, with another ethnic group, then I think that such a girl would be disowned, and I have personally witnessed this. Such a child is rejected by the family, sorry, everyone turns their back on her. If she has a relationship with a Creole boy, well, she gets beaten up, she gets kicked out of the house, and if, worse, if they discover it after the wedding, then she gets a beating from both her family-in-law and her own family, because it brings shame to the family. . . . With the Creoles, you don't have that as much. Look, you accept what the child does. People say you can't buy love for the child. If the child says, "I have a relationship with a Javanese person," or someone from another race, you just accept that. Especially with the woman, you say, "Oh, it is my daughter's child," so you just accept the child, you know, or [you say,] "It is the child of my son," so the child is accepted in the family, you are not going to pay attention [and say], "She is Javanese, I am Creole," or something like that, you really don't see that very much, really, really not often. The Creole is in this respect raised with more freedom.

Ann, who lives in the city and has had a Hindustani boyfriend for five years, endured a period of coldness and disapproval from his family, but is now fully accepted (as an exception) and practices many aspects of the Hindustani culture (religion, language, food, etc.). She reports:

> I like it very much that there are diverse racial groups, but you do have certain groups who want their race to stick together and not mix. I, of course, think it is stupid, but yes, I do like it that there are different racial groups. OK, of course it also leads to problems, because you

really have people, for example, at work, they give preference to someone of a certain race because it is their race . . . [Which racial groups don't want to mix with others?] Hindustanis, you have it with Hindustanis, Javanese less, and Chinese people usually. Yes, but with Hindustanis it is worse. For example, a Hindustani has to marry a Hindustani. . . . If they, for example, go out, you will very rarely see other races in their company, they really box [stick] together. And you know, that is why, for instance, a few people can speak Javanese, very few people can speak Hindi, while everyone, for example, can speak Surinamese [Creole language], and Chinese people also act that way, because they really see it as their culture, and mind your own business, you know? They see it as theirs, it can't mix.

Interestingly, multiracials without any Hindustani nor Chinese heritage appeared to share the experiences that were reported by multiracials with partial Hindustani or Chinese ancestry, demonstrating the high degree of contact people tend to have with all the different racial groups. Mark explains his interactions with and views of Hindustani and Chinese people:

An ex-girlfriend was Hindustani, full Hindustani, [so] her family opposed that she went with me. After I met the mother, the mother thought it was ok, but the brother-in-law and the rest of the family were against it. . . . Her family is very traditional, that I noticed. With the Hindustanis I do see that, well, Hindustanis are the most, they feel the strongest about passing traditions along. I think it is dumb, stupid; I think it is idiotic. I mean, even if you pass along traditions, you can't control love. I mean, what difference should it make if a Hindustani girl wants to marry a Creole guy? They have to determine which culture they will adopt to further pass it along to the children. [Same-race arranged marriages occur] more with Hindustanis, Javanese, to a lesser degree. . . . others don't, Hindustanis and Javanese. . . . Creoles very rarely prevent their children to mix with another.

Mark also had interactions with Chinese people who seemed to have objections to interracial relations, particularly with Creoles:

With Chinese [the belief against mixing] is very strong, with Hindustani it happens once in a while; it is strong, but you have a few. . . . But I think 99 out of 100 Chinese people who I see, I don't see that they welcome Creole people in the house. They get them inside to clean the house. . . . An average Chinese person, at least, what I think they think, they see every Creole person as bad, someone who steals, someone who robs, they are very suspicious, Chinese people, very suspicious. I have personally had to have contact for a long time before I could enter the house to play mah-jongg. . . . It lasted a long time to build that friendship, I even had to prove myself. . . . [How?] I was helpful, if there was something laying around, I would not poke around or touch it. If money was just laying around, you don't go, you don't ask questions, and then people notice, and start [to accept you]. It is like that everywhere, they start to talk, "What do you think of Mark?" etc., etc., and then you are accepted.

The Multiracial Experience

The participants share similar experiences of rejection by Hindustani and Chinese people who value "purity." However, those with Chinese and Hindustani ancestry appeared to report the most distress from being denied full access to their heritage. Nevertheless, all of the participants thought that there were more advantages than disadvantages to being multiracial. They seemed to feel fully accepted and representative of the larger multiracial and multicultural community, and also thought that they were still more easily accepted than monoracials by all the different groups.

Ronald, who is Hindustani, Creole, and Amerindian, explains that he has felt excluded by "pure" Hindustani people through the use of language:

> Look, if you are with Hindustanis, for example, and I do not speak Hindi, and you join them, suddenly only Hindi is spoken. So I find that annoying. One time I made a comment, so I had just joined the company of a few girls and they started to speak in Hindi, then I said, "I am also here," then she said, "But you came yourself," so in other words, "Go away," because she knew that I could not speak Hindi.

Don, who has Amerindian, Chinese, and Creole heritages, had a similar experience with people of Chinese background:

> Look, if I go to a place where you only have Amerindians, then I also feel like an Amerindian. If there are sometimes only Creoles, I feel like a Creole. Only with Chinese people it is difficult. Because I don't understand Chinese. And if a Chinese man speaks, the man, you know, they often point toward you. That is their habit. . . . With them, the difficult part is, because Chinese people are, I don't know, I believe that they are racist. As soon as you don't look Chinese, then you are not Chinese in their eyes.

Nelson had considerable contact with his Chinese, Hindustani, and Creole heritages. He comments on the priority given to racial features over racial blood or kinship ties in gaining acceptance in the Chinese community:

> I have seen that a few Hindustanis and a few Chinese people, the parents do not like to accept another race in the family. Why, I don't know. . . . When my sister [who "looks" Chinese] goes to visit Chinese people, and I am with her, it is really great. [What is it like without her?] They just see me as an acquaintance [because I "look" more Hindustani and am darker skinned]. Only when she says, "Hey, this is my brother," [do I feel accepted]. . . . It is a bit annoying. It can be annoying, because you have the feeling that you are perhaps not accepted because of your physical appearance, you know?

Identity conflicts arising from arbitrary authenticity tests of racial "purity" or rigid adherence to traditional and "pure" cultural beliefs were also experienced by the participants, as Ronald reports:

> So in fact, sometimes you don't know where you belong, you know. . . . Hindustanis don't accept me as Hindustani, then I have to explain that I am Hindustani and Black, and from the other side too, with Creoles, some of them, I mean I have been in the same class with some guys, and they thought I was full-blood [Hindustani], and if I talked with them about rap music, that is, according to them, authentic Black man's music, then they really looked up, eh, wow, you know, only then you are accepted. And I have since high school a friend, I think he is mixed himself, Amerindian and Black, but he just says Black, and he also told me, he does not like Hindustanis. I am the only one who he befriended. It is discrimination. And when I asked him, why, he then said because they discriminate themselves.

Mercedes, who bases her Creole identity on her monocultural upbringing, explains that being raised by more traditional parents who have not reconciled their cultural differences can be particularly problematic for Hindustani-Creole biracials:

I have only known one style of being raised, that of my mother, so I never had to sit in between both, the Creole and the Hindustani. . . . With a colleague I did notice that she was in a tug-of-war. . . . Your mother's family is Creole, the father's family is Hindustani, and they sometimes stand directly opposite to one another, you know. So, I don't know, she just was not able to figure things out. If she was seen on the street with a boy, now, then her father's family always came home, and said, "Yes, I saw her; you should not allow that," and more of those things. While her mother thought, the child is an adult, so the child is allowed to. But the pressure of the father's family, that comes down on the father, and he says no, just so that he does not drop his [extended] family, I assume, so then you got a battle between the mother and father. . . . And at a certain point, she got from both sides messages about what she could and could not do, and then at a certain point, you don't know anymore where you stand. That caused her to get out of the house.

In contrast, Arianne, who is of Javanese and Creole background, appears to easily switch cultural and national identities based on the context, and does not seem to experience an either/or cultural identity conflict or to dichotomize her cultural experiences:

With Javanese people, I have a Javanese mentality. Javanese people do not like problems, they will often keep quiet, also in certain, difficult situations. Javanese people believe in *rukut.* That is the belief that they must live in harmony with everything that lives, and also with what does not live, so with the spirits. . . . I feel more Creole than Javanese because I was raised between Creoles. I am not tied to traditional values and norms, so I am not obligated to do things that Javanese people do. . . . I am totally Surinamese, my way of thinking. Well, I don't know how to explain it. Surinamese people are easygoing people, they are hospitable, they like to party. [How are you otherwise?] Oh, yeah, I also have a little bit of a Javanese mentality.

Rather than focusing on the rejection by some members of the "pure" groups, the multiracial participants tended to look at their advantaged position in terms of having easier entry into many ethnic groups, as Ann describes.

The mixed people start a conversation more easily with other races who are full [pure], because they realize that they themselves have different backgrounds and they probably have better insight in the different races, and they probably also know that all races have their good things, and I mean, you can't say that one is good, that one is bad, and mixed people actually have all those cultures in them. Even if you have not learned it from your parents, you will, because you know that you are it, you will research it, with the result, I assume, that they will accept nonmixed races more easily.

In more racially segregated societies, such as the United States, this multiracial privilege may not be the same or may be overshadowed by the difficulty in being accepted into groups of one's own racial background. However, in Suriname multiracials are saved from the grip of racial determinism because they are not expected to follow cultural traditions. Ann explains that some people have a certain idea how a certain race is. And if you are of that race, then people distance themselves. Maybe they don't know you, and maybe you are not even like that but people distance themselves. Look, in my class, everyone said, "Why are you hanging around the Hindustanis?" Because the Hindustanis distanced themselves from them, but not me . . . .People say very easily, for example, Javanese people are so sweet, they are like this, and they are like this, but what is a mixed person? You know? It depends on how you were raised, your circumstances, etc., and that is why people are more likely to talk to a mixed person.

Mandy also shared this sense of fluidity and boundary-crossing. However, she also wonders if she may be missing out by not being able to identify fully with one ethnic group:

You are a little bit of everything, you feel like, at least, I feel, you feel more at home with everything. But a disadvantage might be that you are actually also nothing; you are a little bit of everything but you are actually not really something. So you can't identify perhaps with the Hindustanis or the Javanese, and stuff, not that it is a problem, but still, sometimes you think for a minute, you know, like that.

Ronald appears to have experienced a greater sense of rejection by "pure" groups compared to Mandy, but feels nevertheless more privileged being multiracial:

Advantages? I just feel better like this. . . . I think to myself, if I were a typical, if I were just Creole, or just Hindustani, that I would also think differently, you know, that my religion, or that I had to move within my own social circles, so I think that because I am mixed, that I look at things a little different. . . . And disadvantages, that you are not accepted in certain circles, but for the rest, that is the only thing.

Conclusion

The experiences that were reported by these Surinamese research participants suggest that our current understanding of race relations, racism, and the multiracial experience is tightly bounded by unique cultural and national circumstances. In contrast to the United States, the strong precedence of racial and cultural mixing within the Creole group; the predominance of non-Western, interdependent ethnic groups; and the lack of legalized segregation and antimiscegenation laws in Suriname continued a legacy of racial mixing and mutual acculturation when new immigrant groups arrived. Unlike multiracials in the United States, who are outnumbered and often marginalized by the dominant White and subdominant ethnic minority groups, Surinamese multiracials perceive themselves as a numerically dominant group that experiences easier entry into a wider range of "pure" groups compared to monoracials.

Moreover, in the United States, there appears to be a greater investment in maintaining White racial purity and racial separation, which seems to derive more from a desire to protect White privilege rather than a wish to avoid cultural conflicts between racial groups. There also appears to be a historical trend to create or amplify differences in racial socialization, power, and privilege when cultural differences begin to fade due to acculturation and more equal access to resources. In contrast, Surinamese people who object to racial mixing seem to be more invested in preserving cultural traditions than racial purity. "Purists" in Suriname still commonly believe in the racial determinism myth that cultural norms are biologically determined by racial genes and are "given away" by racial appearance. Hence, racial mixing and racial ambiguity are viewed as problematic because they automatically translate into cultural impurity and, more importantly, religious impurity. The objective is not so much to guarantee material well-being (although this is used as a means to an end), but to assure spiritual well-being and salvation.

As speculated, "traditional" Hindustanis and Chinese most strongly adhere to ideologies promoting racial and cultural "purity," although participants had many recollections of "modern" people, including their parents, who had broken away from these cultural beliefs and practices. Nevertheless, within traditional Chinese and Hindustani communities, in-groups and out-group members are ranked according to social status as well as skin color, so that dark-skinned Creoles are most often perceived to be the most inferior racial group. In contrast, the Creole, Javanese, and Amerindian people appear to be more horizontally oriented and less racially deterministic, so that the "purity" of their cultural traditions is not threatened by developing multiple cultural identities or by mixing racially. Unfortunately, the internalization of White supremacist ideas, rejection by other groups (including the multiracial majority group), acculturation levels, class and religious differences, and ethnocentrism at times also create friction within each of these horizontal groups and their interactions with other ethnic groups.

Acknowledgments

I want to thank the Universe for making Suriname the place where my Chinese, African, and Dutch ancestors' paths crossed and I first discovered the world. I am grateful to my parents, Josta and Jules Tjen A Looi, for offering models for how to step out of the boundaries of race, culture, gender, class, religion, and nationality. I am particularly indebted to Dr. Philip Akutsu, Dr. Maria Root, Dr. Janet Negley, Wim Biervliet, Bernise Stevens, Dr. Maureen Silos, Gloria Wekker, Edwin Marshall, Steve Masami Ropp, and Cindy Nakashima for enabling me to explore, process, understand, and integrate my Surinamese and American multiracial experiences. I thank my research participants in Suriname for their honesty, their graciousness, and their ability to make me feel so deeply connected to my roots. A very special thank you is reserved for Robert Van Tuyl, for sharing and engaging himself so fully in our journey and discovery of life and love.

CHAPTER 19

The Tiger and His Stripes: Thai and American Reactions to Tiger Woods's (Multi-) "Racial Self"

Jan R. Weisman

Introduction

Tiger Woods landed at Bangkok's Don Muang International Airport on the evening of February 4, 1997. The part–African American, part-Thai twenty-one-year-old was making his third visit to his mother's homeland, and his first visit as a competitor in a professional golf tournament.[1] His arrival was greeted by pandemonium. The president of Thai Airways welcomed him with garlands on board his plane, while television and newspaper reporters, military and government officials, and a troupe of Thai classical dancers awaited him in the airport's VIP arrival lounge. The entire proceedings were broadcast live on all of Thailand's television networks. Woods was entertained at a formal dinner, engaged in a recreational round of golf with the prime minister, and was awarded honorary Thai citizenship and a royal decoration by the Minister of Foreign Affairs.

Throughout his five-day stay in Thailand, the Thai media emphasized Woods's supposed *Thai*-ness and exalted him as a model of *Thai* achievement.[2] This positioning, however, was complicated by the fact that Woods does not fit the traditional image of a public embodiment of *Thai*-ness. Hybridity is "in" in contemporary Thailand, and many racially mixed stars have captured the public imagination. However, Woods is the offspring of an American military man and a nonelite Thai woman (who, by virtue of her association with Woods's father, is of suspect morality), while the Thai glamorization of hybridity favors mixed-race stars from the more elite classes who carry no hint of GI connections. In addition, Woods is part-Black, and Thai nationalists have historically denigrated Black people as models of behavior that is to be avoided by Thais, while presenting Whites (whose phenotype is also greatly preferred) as models to be emulated. Further confounding the Thai attempt to claim him was the fact that, throughout his visit, Woods self-identified as a multiracial American. In the face of an undercurrent of public criticism regarding his *Thai* authenticity, Thai image managers' attempts to appropriate Woods's image toward *Thai* ends ultimately failed.

T. K. Williams (1995: 84–85) states that "the presentation of their outward racial selves [is not] something biracial people necessarily manipulate, but rather something that is viewed by and responded to contextually by their audiences." In this paper, I will examine Thai views of and responses to Tiger Woods's "racial self." Utilizing ethnographic data gathered in Thailand during the period surrounding and including Woods's visit, I will illustrate how the conflicts and contradictions in the Thai reception of Woods reflect the articulation between identity politics and issues of modernization and globalization evident in contemporary Thai society, drawing comparisons between the Thai and American cases in order to illuminate and expand the discourse of identity politics as it relates to multiracial Asian Americans in the United States.

Multiraciality in Thai Perspective

Studies of identity politics as they relate to multiracial Americans have typically been informed by the American racial taxonomy and the American dynamics of race relations. It has been noted, however, that the American system—with its roots in a history of African slavery and European slave mastery; its continuing emphasis on hypodescent, particularly with respect to individuals of African ancestry; and its ubiquitous directives to "check one box only"—is actually unique in world perspective (Davis, 1991: 13–16). Thailand—with a history of freedom from European colonial domination, a social structure that has traditionally defined the polity in terms of its center (i.e., the ruling monarch) rather than its margins (i.e., racial or ethnic group boundaries), and an officially mandated absence of "boxes"[3]—presents quite a different picture.

The scope of this paper does not allow for an extensive description and analysis of Thai views of what in the United States is called "race." However, three important points should be kept in mind in considering the Thai case. First, although genotype is sometimes noted, both ascription of group membership and differential treatment in Thai society tend to be phenotypically rather than genotypically based.[4] Second, where differential treatment does occur, issues of socioeconomic class may be found to figure prominently, often serving to obscure both phenotype and genotype. Third, any discussion of, or research into, Thai attitudes surrounding what in the United States is called "race" is complicated by the fact that the Thai language uses the same word— *chat*—to refer to race, ethnicity, and citizenship. Likewise, the word *Thai*, when applied to an individual or group, can refer to aspects of biological and/or cultural and/or national heritage.

Earlier scholarship on Thailand has held that total acceptance as *Thai* is possible for any individual or group who subscribes to certain principles, namely, proficiency in the Thai language, long-term residence in Thailand, allegiance to the Thai monarchy and nation-state, and (although there is some flexibility on this point) adherence to Theravada Buddhism (Basham, 1987: 2). However, I have questioned this position in other works (Weisman, 1997), taking as one point of argument the distinction that is often made in the Thai discourse between the categories *Thai* or *Thai tae* ("true Thai") and *luk kreung* (half-child).

In Thai terms, the salient feature of Tiger Woods's identity is the fact that he is *luk kreung,* a term that has, since the 1960s, carried strong connotations of racial hybridity. However, it is not limited to such usage. The term may also be applied to individuals whose parents are of different citizenships or, in some cases, ethnicities. In other words, *luk kreung* refers to an individual whose parents are of different *chat.* With respect to Tiger Woods, then, Thais are responding to and constructing his hybrid *chat,* and ascribing to him an identity as part-*Thai,* with all the polysemy inherent in those terms. These points will be elucidated below, first in an analysis of the phenomenon of the fetishization of *luk kreung* and *luk kreung*-ness that is taking place in contemporary Thai society, and then in a return to the particular case of Tiger Woods.

Luk Kreung and the Racialization of Modernity

Thai popular perceptions of *luk kreung*—in particular, those *luk kreung* who are racially mixed—have undergone significant changes in recent decades. Eurasians occupied a neutral social category for much of Thai history. Their numbers were small, their parents were of high socioeconomic status, and their Thai lineage was usually a paternal connection.[5] This situation changed dramatically in the 1960s and 1970s, during the period of Vietnam War–related American military presence in Thailand. As thousands of Amerasian children were born to nonelite Thai women and American military men, *luk kreung* came to be seen as a marker of unbridled, illegitimate, female sexuality and lower-class origins.[6] The situation has changed again in the 1990s, as Thailand has become a significant regional economic power and increasingly seeks a role on the world socioeconomic stage. *Luk kreung*-ness has now become a positive—even desirable—status, viewed as linking not only the individual but the nation with the (positive, desired, Western) world beyond Thailand's borders.

Earlier scholarship has elucidated a "top-down" approach to the construction of Thai national identity, including the definition of *Thai*-ness, and the development and promotion of public embodiments thereof.[7] In contemporary Thailand, images of *luk kreung* are being constructed and commodified by those "at the top" in order to support evolving idea(l)s of Thai modernity, to convey those idea(l)s to the Thai mass public, and, in turn, to project a "modern," "developed," and "cosmopolitan" picture of the country to an international audience. Various agents, from beauty contest organizers to the National Olympic Committee, look to *luk kreung* to bring assets such as fluency in English, physical attractiveness, and well-developed talent to international competitions.[8] *Luk kreung* have been positioned as public embodiments—whether of consumer products, new musical genres, or (the professional image managers would have the Thai public believe) Thailand's ascendant position in the international socioeconomic community.[9]

It should be noted, however, that almost without exception, the *luk kreung* who have been so positioned have been part-White. The exceptions, of which there is but a very small handful, are locally popular comedians and pop musicians, and members of national sports teams. The public embodiment of *luk kreung* of other than part-White ancestry—especially of those who are part-Black—is incomplete and problematic. The problematics are rooted in popular Thai Buddhist thought regarding the correlation between physical appearance and presumed moral character, and in modern reinterpretations of this belief, as described below.

In popular Thai Buddhist thought, physical attributes have traditionally been considered a marker of one's accumulated merit. As Penny Van Esterik (1989: 12) states, "Clarity of complexion, grace, and serenity were reflections of moral goodness, one guide to knowing merit store. Ugliness, unfortunately, conveyed the opposite." Of these attributes, perhaps none is more salient than that of complexion. In conversations with me, Thais have often commented upon the *wen kam* (extreme misfortune in this life due to a paucity of accumulated merit from previous lives) of part-Black *luk kreung* whose Black ancestry is evident in their appearance. They have spoken approvingly of the fact that my own part-Black ancestry has given me *phiu khlam* (dusky skin) rather than *phiu dam* (black or very dark skin), and *phiu muean khon Thai* (skin like a Thai) rather than *phiu muean khon nigro* (skin like a Negro [*sic*]). Such comments have often been preceded or followed by the comment that I must *mii bun* (have [a lot of] merit) because I have *phiu suai* (pretty skin).

In modern-day Thailand, fair skin is a marker not only of moral achievement but also of the achievement or possession of secular modernity. Indeed, on many occasions, Thai compliments on my complexion such as those mentioned above have been linked with comments regarding my educational achievement or the fact that I am able to travel regularly to Thailand (both considered, following a multilinked logic, to be further evidence of my accumulated merit).[10] Mary Beth Mills (1995: 259) notes that the process of rural labor migration to the city is sometimes colloquially referred to as *pai aw phiu*, or "going to get [fair] skin." Thus, in contemporary Thailand, those Thai *luk kreung* who have inherited fair skin from a White parent are often seen as possessing more accumulated merit, being more meritorious in this life, and having reached a higher level of secular achievement than those who have inherited dark skin from Black progenitors.[11]

Traditional conceptions of complexion as a marker of morality and modernity became racialized during the 1920s and 1930s, as members of the Thai elite returning from study in Europe began promoting a Thai nationalism that was derivative in part of the European discourses of nationalism, nationality, and race of that era.[12] In other works (Weisman, 2000), I have discussed how the extolment of Westernness that is so much a part of contemporary Thai life is based on a view of the West—particularly the United States—as White. Thus, the achievement of modernity, with the West as its model, has been seen by Thais as a process of striving toward goals represented by images of White people. At the same time, images of Blacks have been taken to represent the conditions away from which Thais should move.

The racialization of modernity was given official currency during the 1940s, when a government-sponsored radio program elucidated the purported characteristics of Black and White foreigners. The program—which was presented as a series of simulated conversations between two patriotic men, Man Chuchat and Khong Rakthai[13]—was designed to popularize *Ratthaniyom,* a series of state pre- and proscriptions aimed at educating the Thai populace as to the proper behavior of the citizenry of a modern nation-state. Some excerpts from a June 4, 1942, broadcast of this program will be illustrative here:

> KHONG RAKTHAI: What I have noticed is that White people are neat when they are eating. They do not use their hands to pick up food. They use knives and forks no matter where they are. . . . [B]ut whoever would like to be as the Africans—to use hands instead of forks, to use mouths instead of spoons and to use teeth instead of knives—he could continue to do so if he likes. . . .

> MAN CHUCHAT: [Sleeping on raised beds as Whites do] is the correct way because it would be good for health. But for the Africans, they would lie down wherever like monkeys. The difference in living style between the White people and the Africans is very noticeable. Civilized and uncivilized people are different in every respect of their daily lives.

(quoted in Chaloemtiarana, 1978: 309–310)

In summary, in contemporary Thailand, part-White hybridity has come to be valued inasmuch as it provides its subject with the phenotypical markers of both moral and secular accomplishment. Part-Black hybridity has not been so favored. Enter, however, Tiger Woods.

Tiger Woods and the Construction of *Thai*-ness, Part I

Tiger Woods is an international sensation, and no country is more enamored of celebrities than Thailand. If a celebrity has some connection with Thailand, all the better. Woods's decision to play golf professionally has made him a wealthy man, and in Thailand, wealth can overshadow any number of otherwise negative factors. When Woods arrived in Bangkok in 1997, a bevy of Thai image managers leapt to the task of appropriating him toward various Thai ends. Television talk show hosts eagerly competed to secure his appearance. Advertisers rushed to contract his image to grace their various promotionals. Even the National Olympic Committee—which, through its *Chang Phuak,* or "Albino Elephant," program, seeks to recruit amateur athletes of Thai or part-Thai ancestry from overseas to compete on the Thai National Olympic Team—attempted to recruit the now-professional athlete Woods to make publicity appearances on its behalf.[14]

The commodification of Tiger Woods, however, required a process of *Thai*-ification.

As noted, while in Thailand Tiger Woods self-identified as a multiracial American. While he acknowledged his part-Thai-ness—for example, speaking of how happy he was to be able to compete in a tournament in his mother's homeland (*The Nation*, 1997b)—this was not sufficient to legitimate his *Thai*-ness in the eyes of a Thai audience. The Thai hybridity that Woods claimed encompassed only two of the three possible connotations of *Thai*-ness, and these only imperfectly. That Woods's genetic heritage was part Thai could not be denied. However, his non-Thai genetic heritage—including, as it does, a Black element—was problematic. Attempts to portray him as culturally *Thai* were also problematic. He did not speak the Thai language—one of the criteria of *Thai tae*–ness, as described. He also appeared, to the Thai audience, to be lacking in the Thai social graces. Many Thais to whom I spoke during Woods's visit to Thailand commented disparagingly on the fact that he had come off the plane in Bangkok chewing gum and had not made the proper gestures of respect to the high-ranking officials who had turned out to meet him. Furthermore, Woods had never lived in Thailand and, as a single- rather than a dual-national, did not pledge allegiance to the Thai monarchy and nation-state. He therefore did not possess the requisites for any sort of claim to national *Thai*-ness.

Thus, while the media was compelled to note Woods's part-American heritage—his *luk kreung*–ness being a major factor in his marketability—it also consciously sought to *Thai*-ify him. Particular attention was paid to his profession of the Buddhist religion. Throughout Woods's visit to Thailand, much was made of the fact that he wears a Buddhist amulet and credits his Buddhist beliefs for his golfing success (*Bangkok Post*, 1997; *Thai Rath*, 1997; *The Nation*, 1997b). Notice was also made of his (presumably Thai, not American) filial piety, as demonstrated by his purchase of a new, well-appointed home for his mother[15] and by his mother's desire that he marry a Thai woman (*The Nation*, 1997c). In my conversations with Thais during Woods's visit, I also noted that they made much of his supposed non-Black, very Thai appearance—thus if not positioning him nearer the part-White public embodiment ideal, at least distancing him from its negatively valued antithesis.

Other "corrective" measures were also taken. In constructing Woods's image for a Thai audience, Thai image managers were faced with the problem of an unerasable public perception of his mother as decidedly nonelite. Many Thais with whom I spoke questioned the media's reports that his mother had been employed as a secretary at a U.S. military installation, insinuating that she had instead met Woods's father in the course of a less legitimate line of work. When the popular talk show *Sii Tum Sa-khwae* (Ten P.M. Square) broadcast a video tour of his mother's new home on February 25, 1997, public reaction was that she had—as befitting her nonelite status—been vulgar in her display of her new-found wealth. Many of those with whom I spoke expressed the opinion that she was crassly using her son's celebrity to raise her own status in the eyes of the Thai public.

Realizing the difficulty (or, perhaps, the futility) of changing public opinion of a Thai woman who had entered into a liaison (albeit a legal marriage) with an American GI during the Vietnam War era, the Thai image managers turned their attention to Woods's father. Many reports of Woods's stay in Thailand made a point of noting that the elder Woods was a former member of the elite Green Berets,[16] thereby raising him to a status above that of the ordinary GIs who fathered the majority of Thailand's Vietnam War–era Amerasians. This distinction served to counter the otherwise negative connotations of Tiger's nonelite maternity, GI paternity, and part-black ancestry—thus illuminating the persistence of Thai prejudices surrounding these issues at the same time that his celebrity in his mother's homeland seemingly overshadowed them.

Tiger Woods and the Construction of *Thai*-ness, Part II

The positioning of Tiger Woods as one of the latest public embodiments of *Thai*-ness was not without its disclaimers and detractors. Criticism began on the night of his arrival in Bangkok, when television viewers called the networks and newspapers to complain about their favorite shows being preempted by coverage of Woods at the airport. Protests that too much attention was being paid to someone who wasn't even *Thai* prompted a response from Chingchai Mongkoltham, an official of the Office of the Prime Minister and overseer of the National Sports Commission, in the following morning's edition of a Bangkok newspaper: "The government doesn't consider Tiger Woods as simply a famous person; rather, we see him as an American-Thai [*Thai*?—author's note] mixed person who has been raised by his mother in the style of Thai Buddhist young people" (*Matichon,* 1997: 1). Some objected to the fact that Woods was awarded Thai citizenship (albeit honorary) after only days in Thailand, while many Thai-born residents of the country—particularly members of some of the country's upland minority groups—have yet to be granted citizenship (*Bangkok Post,* 1997). Several sports fans to whom I spoke objected to reports that the royal decoration presented to the *luk kreung* Woods was of a higher order than the one given to the *Thai tae* boxer Somrak Khamsingh after he won a gold medal at the 1996 Olympics in Atlanta. And during the Asian Honda Classic tournament, Prayad Maksaeng, Thailand's top-rated professional golfer, complained that the crowd paid attention only to Woods: noise and moving to the next hole as soon as Woods had played, and seemingly not supporting the other players. "I am proud of myself," Maksaeng said. "I represent my country in this championship. If I do not represent the country, then who else will?" (Sriseub, 1997; see also Pongudom, 1997).

Criticisms that part-Thai *luk kreung* from outside of Thailand do not "represent the country" have been heard in Thailand for many years. Such complaints have probably been directed most often toward the field of beauty pageants, an arena replete with *luk kreung,* including many who come from overseas to enter contests in Thailand, recruited by Thai image managers who hope to cash in on the value of their *luk kreung*-ness as a commodity in international competitions.[17] Khanitsa Wirasiri (1994) and Anusorn Jornvong (1995) note that the television and film industries, in particular, are experiencing a backlash against the fetishization of *luk kreung.* These fields are being hurt by the promotion of individuals whose primary asset is a foreign (or ambiguous) phenotype or English-language ability. Often, according to Wirasiri and Jornvong, these *luk kreung* actors cannot act; some cannot even speak Thai well. While the appeal of their *luk kreung*-ness may lull their audiences into overlooking these faults and discrepancies, some Thai image managers are calling for increased attention to talent and decreased attention to *luk kreung*-ness in the selection and promotion of stars.

A common criticism of the fetishization of *luk kreung* focuses on the perception that, through the commodification that characterizes the phenomenon, Thailand is trying to take the easy way to international recognition. This criticism was also heard in the particular case of Tiger Woods. One editorial that appeared during his visit summarized the situation as follows: "In Thailand, a nation which feels less secure as a supplier of national heroes . . . Tiger is another *luk kreung* to bless national pride" (*The Nation,* 1997a). A newspaper article appearing on the same date stated that Thais "want achievers but they seem to have no idea [how] to produce them" (Pongudom, 1997). Another article asked, "Are we obstinately claiming people for our own?," going on to assert that "currently, Thai society only has instant successes, like instant noodles" (Mayawii, 1997).

Many *luk kreung* beauty pageant contestants, actors, models, and other hopefuls who have come to Thailand from other countries have been only too willing to be *Thai*-ified by their Thai image managers, realizing that this process could be a key to their success in the Thai arena. Through their participation in this process, they have endeared themselves to their Thai audiences. Tiger Woods, however, had little if anything to gain from acquiescing to the attempts to construct a passable *Thai*-ness for him. When he arrived in Bangkok in 1997, he was already a millionaire and an internationally recognized star. Herein lay the final step in the breakdown of the efforts to *Thai*-ify him: Woods himself simply did not play along.

Comparative Commodification: The U.S. Case

If the profitable appropriation of Tiger Woods and his image required a concerted process of *Thai*-ification in Thailand, it has required no less effort to package him for U.S. consumption. In both cases, professional image managers have attempted to take a portion of his "racial self" and fashion it into a whole for commercial gain. In both cases, the problematics presented by his part-Black ancestry have been surmounted through reference to the elite nature of the same.[18] However, only in the U.S. case have efforts to appropriate his "racial self" arisen not only from the image-managing elite but also from nonelite, racialized consumers of the images so created.

One of the primary applications of Woods's image by American image managers has been in the wooing of domestic consumers from previously underrepresented demographic groups—in particular, the young and the non-White. Speaking of Woods's appeal as a commodity, James Raia (1997) quotes an advertising executive specializing in sports endorsements as saying that Woods's "mixed ethnicity . . . brings a whole new market into the world of golf. Urban basketball fans are getting into it." This positioning of Woods has not been unproblematic, however. While seemingly legitimizing Woods's multi-"racial self," such portrayals in fact depend upon the assumption (or hope) that consumers of the image will infuse it, and Woods, with the (mono-)"racial self" that most closely reflects their own. Nike was chastised in 1996 when it ran a television ad in which Woods was quoted as saying that there were still some golf courses in the United States on which he would not be allowed to play. Explicit objections to the campaign focused on issues of class and status—that is, that, as a star of his sport, Woods would likely not be denied tee time on any course on which he might wish to play (Glassman, 1996; Dorman, 1996) However, for African American viewers, implicit in the criticism of Nike was a criticism of Woods himself. The interpretation that African Americans applied to the ad was that Woods was portraying himself as a victim of anti–African American racism, while being unwilling to position himself squarely within the African American "box." Thus, not only was his agency in claiming a nonapportionable, multi-"racial self" denied (albeit in a less overt fashion than in the Thai case), but (as in the Thai case) the image managers' objectives were subverted by a public that denied the legitimacy of his membership in the group into which the professionals had hoped to position him.

Danzy Senna (1998) plays upon African American criticism of Woods's refusal to be "boxed" in a satirical work set in the year 2000, when "mulattos" have taken over the United States. Without specifically mentioning Woods (certain that the reader would immediately recognize the reference), Senna (1998: 26) includes the following paragraph in a list of "types of mulattos":

> Cablinasian: A rare exotic breed found mostly in California. This is the mother of all mixtures, and when caught may be displayed for large sums of money. The Cablinasian is a mixture of Asian, American Indian, Black, and Caucasian (thus the strange name). A show mulatto, with great performance skills, the Cablinasian will be whoever the crowd wants him to be, and can switch at the drop of a dime. Does not, however, answer to the name "Black."

Miki Turner (1997: 40) observes that class differences are evident in the African American reaction to Woods's multi-"racial self," stating that his refusal to identify solely as African American "offended a large part of his fan base and caused yet another rift in the Black class wars. Lower income Blacks were quick to label him as a sellout. . . . More affluent Blacks, however, supported his multiculturalism." In other words, nonelite African Americans are seemingly more invested in the racial appropriation of Woods than are members of the elite.

The African American reaction to Tiger Woods is in contrast to the Thai case, in which the attempt to appropriate his "racial self" originated with, and circulates within, the elite sector of the population.[19] I posit that members of the African American elite gain both socioeconomic benefit and a sense of security in their elite position not through the modeling of African American images, but through the appropriation of the forms and images of success of the dominant group. In the U.S. situation, socioeconomic dominance is racialized as White. Furthermore, under the American discourse of race, Whiteness is defined as "pure," and any admixture thereto is considered to be necessarily non-White. Therefore, Tiger Woods is neither perceived to be a member of the dominant group, nor held to be a model of the means to dominance.

For nonelite African Americans, on the other hand, dominant group models are perceived as more distant or less relevant to group and individual socioeconomic development, while the appropriation of as many phenotypically and/or genotypically qualified African Americans as possible (again, applying the "one-drop" clause of the American racial discourse) is an important strategy in political mobilization. It is nonelite African Americans, then, who stand to gain the most from the appropriation of Tiger Woods's image—and for whom his refusal to be so appropriated is a particular affront, reminding many of nothing so much as ungratefulness, as he is perceived as having benefited from the struggles of an earlier African American generation while remaining unwilling to lend his support to the struggles still under way.

This section has focused on African American responses to Woods's "racial self" because, among all the American racial and ethnic communities in which he claims ancestry, the African American community has expressed the strongest desire to appropriate him racially and the strongest reaction to his refusal to be appropriated. The Asian American community (with the possible exception of a few members of the Thai American media, which, following the lead of image managers in Thailand, have made some attempts at *Thai*-ification) has demonstrated little if any such effort. Turner (1997: 40) suggests that Asian Americans, including those of Thai ancestry, have no interest in Woods's "racial self" because they have no interest in golf (an assumption I would question). She also suggests that Asian Americans are only supportive of sports figures who are "all [Asian] American, all the time," thus raising the question of whether Woods is perceived as not authentically "Asian" because of his refusal to be "boxed" as "Asian American." I would posit, however, that the reasons that the politics of Tiger Woods's identity has not been as salient an issue for Asian Americans as it has been for African Americans might lie in the Asian American community's models of socioeconomic advancement. That is, perhaps it is not so much that Woods's Asian-ness is unrecognized or unlegitimated by other Asian Americans, as it is that upwardly mobile Asian Americans simply do not look within the group for images and models. The topic of Asian American reactions to Tiger Woods's multi-"racial self" requires additional research and analysis.

Epilogue

Tiger Woods returned to Thailand in January 1998. He won the Johnnie Walker Classic tournament, played on the southern island of Phuket. A large photograph of him appeared in an English-language Bangkok newspaper. In bold type, one-and-a-half-inches high, the caption proclaimed, "Yes, I'm Thai." Beneath this line, in letters one-quarter-inch high, it continued, "Yes, I'm American. Yes, I'm Black. . . . I'm Tiger Woods" (*Bangkok Post,* 1998). Meanwhile, Nike announced that it was ending its distribution contract with a Thai-based corporation and would be managing its own wholesaling in Thailand, effective January 1998. Noting that Thailand was already Nike's largest Asian market, the managing director of Nike (Thailand) reported that the company planned to spend 100 million baht (more than US$2,500,000 at the exchange rate at the time) on advertising in Thailand in 1998, and, despite Thailand's economic troubles, expected revenue of 400 million baht (more than US$10,500,000). He stated that he foresaw "plenty of potential in Thailand because the brand [is] well-accepted [and] its main promoter, champion golfer Tiger Woods, [is] half-Thai" (Jitpleecheep & Intarakomalyasut, 1997).

Notes

1. Woods went on to win the Asian Honda Classic, played on a course just outside Bangkok on February 5–8, 1997.

2. Where italicized, the word *Thai* refers to the Thai-language term of that pronunciation; its denotations and connotations should be interpreted according to the Thai worldview as explicated herein.

3. On August 2, 1939, the Office of the Prime Minister issued the following proclamation (the third proclamation in the *Ratthaniyom* series, discussed below):

"As the Government is of the opinion that the names by which the Thais in some parts of the country have been called do not correspond to the name of the race and the preference of the people so called, and also that the appellation of the Thai people by dividing them into many groups such as the Northern Thais, the Northeastern Thais, the Southern Thais, [and] Islamic Thais, is not appropriate, for Thailand is one and indivisible, it thereby notifies that the State Preference is as follows: 1) Do not call the Thais in contradiction to the name of the race or the preference of those referred to. 2) *Use the word "Thai" for all of the Thais without any of the above-mentioned divisions.* (quoted in Chaloemtiarana, 1978:246 [emphasis added]

4. Ascription of group identity also relies heavily on cultural and linguistic criteria, as described below.

5. In the nineteenth and early twentieth centuries, most Thai Eurasians were the offspring of Thai men from the nobility or other elite groups, who married European (and later, American) women during their studies abroad and returned to Thailand to raise their families. Also during this period (and extending back as far as the 1500s), Eurasian children were born to Thai women and Western men of various nationalities who were resident in Thailand in the service of the king, or who served in other high-ranking and respected positions. Although racially mixed children were also born to other, nonsanctioned liaisons, the preponderance of the first type of union, the small total number of mixed unions, and sociopolitical factors such as the granting of rights of extraterritoriality (with the concomitant legal ascription of Eurasian children to the foreign expatriate community) worked to help ensure the acceptance of these *luk kreung* in Thai society (see Bunchua, 1984; Hunter & Chakrabongse, 1994; Kambhu, 1963; Minney, 1962; and Smith, 1971).

6. Although the Thai government does not keep statistics on such births, private organizations, notably the U.S.–based Pearl S. Buck Foundation, estimate that 5,000–7,000 Amerasian children were born in Thailand between 1962 and 1975, the period of official, Vietnam War–related U.S. presence in Thailand (Pearl S. Buck Foundation, n.d.). For demographic and socioeconomic data on the mothers of Vietnam War–era Amerasians, see Anan Wiriyaphinit (1972) and Wiraprawat Wongphuaphan (1972).

7. See, for example, T. Winichakul (1995).

8. The vast majority of Vietnam War-era Amerasians, because of their nonelite backgrounds and concomitant lack of access to life opportunities, do not possess these assets and are therefore excluded from the fetishization of *luk kreung* that has been evident in Thailand for the past several years. For a discussion of the effects of the fetishization of other *luk kreung* on this excluded group, see Weisman (2000).

9. The desire of those "at the top" to present the Thai nation in such a way as to pass international muster may be traced to the reign of King Mongkut (Rama IV, ruled 1851–68). I have described the history of this desire—as well as the processes through which the prescribed appearance of the public embodiment of the Thai nation has changed over the course of the country's history so that it increasingly approximates a Western ideal—in Weisman (1997).

10. On other occasions—or sometimes at the same time—the fact that my skin is not as fair as that of other (i.e., White) foreigners, or that I do not have straight blond hair and sky-blue eyes, has occasioned commiseration or confusion on the part of my Thai interlocutors. For a more detailed discussion of Thai reactions to my "racial self," see Weisman (2000).

11. Wiriyaphinit (1972), in a survey of Vietnam War–era Amerasians, estimates the ratio of part-Black to part-White children as 1:3.5. The number of children of other racial paternities (e.g., Native or Asian American) is so small as to be statistically insignificant. While figures for non-GI-fathered Amerasians and Eurasians are not available, given the racial demographics of the community of resident expatriates in Thailand, the vast majority of these individuals may be assumed to be mixed Thai-White.

12. The bases for the racialization process were laid even earlier, when the Thai appropriated French racial discourse, turning it against the French in a largely successful effort to retain Thai sovereignty over territory sought by French colonial expansionists (see Streckfuss, 1993).

13. The names mean "Secure/Uplifting the Nation" and "Enduring/Love Thai," respectively.

14. The name of the program is not intended to indicate a preference for fair-complected or part-White athletes. Rather, it refers to the special place held by albino elephants in Thai mythology. Rare in nature, when found in the Thai jungle, albino elephants have traditionally been presented to the Thai monarch. Thus, the name of the program is intended to conjure images of something rare and valuable.

15. Woods's father remained in the family home. He said of the new house: "[When Tiger turned pro,] his first order of business was to buy his mother her dream home. . . . Tida had always wanted a large showy home. . . . She has her home, I have mine. Some people would call that separated. I call it affluence" (Woods, 1998: 63).

16. Health problems prevented Woods's father from accompanying him to Thailand on this trip.

17. For a discussion of *luk kreung* in Thai beauty pageants, see Weisman (2000).

18. Henry Yu (1998) states that "Tiger Woods combine[s] a number of standard ways in which African American men are perceived as safe and non-threatening. His Green Beret father, like Colin Powell, was a war hero, embodying the safe Black man who sacrifices himself for the nation. Tiger's father correctly channeled the violent imagery ascribed to African American males." In the United States, it is Woods's father's sexuality, rather than his mother's, that threatens his own position as a public embodiment. (Indeed, as a male of African American descent, Woods himself may be perceived as sexually threatening.) However, Yu argues that "Tiger's father directed the dangerous sexual desirability of his Black masculinity not towards White women, but the safe option of a foreign, Asian war bride." Isabel Wilkerson (1997: 99–100) also notes the "safety" factor, stating that "as a Black man . . . [Woods] is wholesome and colorless. . . . He is the very opposite of the gangsta boyz 'n the hood. . . . [H]e's prep school and Pepsodent. He puts a pretty face on Blackness."

19. In other works (e.g., Weisman, 1997, 1998a, 1998b, 2000), I have argued that the linking of *Thai*-ness to the global capitalist enterprise through the commodification of *luk kreung* imagery is rooted in a desire to establish a sense of control over the course of the country's socio-economic development that is felt to have been lost to the Thai elite during the Vietnam War era. In the Thai case, then, it is the elite who stand to benefit from the successful appropriation of Woods as *Thai*—both in monetary terms, as his image is utilized in the marketing of high-end consumer goods to other members of the elite class, and in terms of the sense of security (i.e., in Thailand's position as an up-and-coming member of the international elite), which is gained as *Thai* control is exerted over something that is, at the same time, part-Western (and thus a model of that to which the Thai elite aspire). Interestingly, criticisms of the attempt are also limited to the Thai elite. The issue of the seeming uninvestment in the politics of Woods's identity on the part of nonelite Thais requires further research and analysis.

Bibliography

Adams, Romanzo. (1937). *Interracial Marriage in Hawaii: A Study of the Mutually Conditioned Processes of Acculturation and Amalgamation*. New York: MacMillan Co.

Alatas, S. H. (1977). *The Myth of the Lazy Native: A Study of the Image of the Malays, Filipinos, and the Javanese from the 16th to the 20th Century and Its Function in the Ideology of Colonial Capitalism*. London: F. Cass.

Alba, Richard A. (1985). "The Twilight of Ethnicity Among Americans of European Ancestry: The Case of Italians." *Ethnic and Racial Studies*, 8: 134–158.

Alba, Richard A. (1991). *Ethnic Identity: The Transformation of White America*. New Haven: Yale University Press.

Alexander, A. (1991). *Ambiguous Lives: Free Women of Color in Rural Georgia, 1789-1879*. Fayetteville: University of Arkansas Press.

Allman, K. M. (1996). "(Un)Natural Boundaries: Mixed Race, Gender, and Sexuality." In M.P.P. Root (ed.), *The Multiracial Experience: Racial Borders as the New Frontier* (pp. 277–290). Thousand Oaks, CA: Sage Publications.

Allport, G. (1979). *The Nature of Prejudice*. Reading, MA: Addison-Wesley Publishing Co.

Alvarado, Diana. (1999, Winter). "Multiracial Student Experience: What Faculty and Campus Leaders Need to Know." *Diversity Digest*, pp. 1–2.

Anderson, B. (1983). *Imagined Communities*. London: Verso.

Anderson, K. S. (1993). *Ethnic Identity in Biracial Asian Americans*. Unpublished doctoral dissertation, California School of Professional Psychology, Berkeley.

Anderson, M. (1988). *The American Census: A Social History*. New Haven: Yale University Press.

Anderson, W. (1999, August 12). "Voices/Who Are We? Rules of Identity Change as Borders Fade." *AsianWeek*, p. 5.

Annink, C. (1994). "Orang Indo en Indonesian-Dutch: Indische Nederlanders in Indonesië en de Verenigde Staten van Amerika." In W. Willems & L. Lucassen (Eds.), *Het onbekende vaderland: De repatriëring van Indische Nederlanders (1946–1964)* (pp. 145–159). The Hague: Sdu Uitgeverij Koninginnegracht.

Anthias, S., & Yuval-Davis, N. (1992). *Racialized Boundaries: Race, Nation, Gender, Colour, and Class and the Anti-Racist Struggle*. New York: Routledge.

Anthonio, W. (1990). *Tjalie Robinson: "Reflections in a Brown Eye."* Unpublished doctoral dissertation, University of Michigan, Ann Arbor.

Anzaldua, Gloria. (1987). *Borderlands/La Frontera: The New Mestiza*. San Francisco: Aunt Lute Books.

Arboleda, Teja. (1998). *In the Shadow of Race: Growing Up as a Multiethnic, Multicultural, and "Multiracial" American*. Mahwah, NJ: Lawrence Erlbaum Associates Publishers.

Arkoff, Abe, & Weaver, H. B., (1966). "Body Image and Body Dissatisfaction in Japanese Americans." *Journal of Social Psychology,* 68: 323–330.

AsianWeek (January, 1997), pp. 14–16. "Few Back Multiracial Label, Survey by Census Reaffirmed" (May 16, 1997), p. A12.

AsianWeek (1997, October 11). "Earning His Stripes," p. 9.

Association of Bay Area Governments Regional Data Center. Oakland (1992), August, p. 2.

Atkinson, D., Morten, G., & Sue, D. (Eds.). (1979). *Counseling American Minorities: A Cross-Cultural Perspective* (3rd ed.). Dubuque, IA: William C. Brown.

Awkward, M. (1995). *Negotiating Difference: Race, Gender, and the Politics of Positionality,* Chicago: The University of Chicago Press.

Bagley, C. (1973). *The Dutch Plural Society: A Comparative Study in Race Relations*. London: Oxford University Press.

Bailey, B., & Farber, D. (1992). *The First Strange Place: Race and Sex in World War II Hawaii*. Baltimore: The Johns Hopkins University Press.

Bangkok Post. (1997, February 7). "Tiger Speaks About Secrets of His Success," p. 12.

Bangkok Post. (1998, January 20). "Yes, I'm Thai" [Photo caption].

Barbujani, G., Magagini, A., Minch, E., & Cavalli-Sforza, L. L. (1997). "An Apportionment of Human DNA Diversity." *Proceedings of the National Academy of Sciences of the United States of America,* 94(9): 4516–4519.

Barkan, E. (1992). *The Retreat of Scientific Racism*. Cambridge: Cambridge University Press.

Barr, S., & Fletcher, M. A. (1997, July 9). "U.S. Proposes Multiple Racial Identification for 2000 Census." *Washington Post,* p. A1.

Barton, N.H. (1997). "Population Genetics: A New Apportionment of Human Diversity." *Current Biology,* 7: R757–R758.

Basham, R. (1987). "Ethnicity and Worldview in Chiang Mai, Thailand." *Journal of the National Research Council of Thailand,* 19 (2): 1–11.

Bates, R. (1935). "Behind the Scenes in Church Life: St. Michael's Pitt Street. The Church of Many Nations." *Liverpool Diocesan Review,* 10(8): 589–590.

Beatty, P. G., Mori, M., & Milford, E. (1995). "Impact of Racial Genetic Polymorphism on the Probability of Finding an HLA-Matched Donor." *Transplantation,* 60(8): 778–783.

Beerhorst, H. (1996). "De Indische stem als mijn geschiedenis verhaal." In T. van der Geugten & L. van der Linden (Eds.), *Indisch in Nederland: Leerlingenboek, Versie D*. 's-Hertogenbosch: KPC.

Beets, N. (1981). *De verre oorlog. Lot en levensloop van krijgsgevangenen onder de Japanners*. Meppel.

Begley, S. (1995, February 13). "Three Is Not Enough." *Newsweek,* pp. 67–69.

Berger, P. L., & Berger, B. (1979). "Becoming a Member of Society." In P. Rose (Ed.), *Socialization and the Life Cycle* (pp. 4–20). New York: St. Martin's Press.

Berlant, Lauren. (1997). *The Queen of America Goes to Washington City: Essays on Sex and Citizenship*. Durham: Duke University Press.

Berzon, J. R. (1978). *Neither White nor Black: The Mulatto Character in American Fiction*. New York: New York University Press.

Bhabha, H. (1990). "The Third Space." In J. Rutherford (Ed.), *Identity* (pp. 207–221). London: Lawrence and Wishart.

Billson, J. M. (1995). *Keepers of the Culture: The Power of Tradition in Women's Lives*. New York: Lexington Books.

Blake, C. (1906a, December 2). "Chinese Vice in England: A View of Terrible Conditions at Close Range." *Sunday Chronicle*, p. 1.

Blake, C. (1906b, December 9). "Should England Welcome the Yellow Man?" *Sunday Chronicle*, p. 2.

Blake, F. (1996). "Interethnic Humor in Hawaii." In J. Cohn (Ed.), *The Comic in the Culture* (pp. 7–8). Honolulu: University of Hawaii Press.

Bloem, M. (1983). *Geen gewoon Indisch meisje*. Haarlem: In de Knipscheer.

Bloem, M. (1996). "De Indische stem als mijn Geschiedenisverhaal." In T van der Geugten & L. van der Linden (Eds.), *Indisch in Nederland: Leerlingenboek, Versie D*. 's-Hertogenbosch: KPC.

Blumberger, J. Th. Petrus. (1939). *De Indo-Europeesche Beweging in Nederlansch - Indië*. Haarlem: H. D. Tjeenk Willink & Zaon.

Bogle, D. (1989). *Toms, Coons, Mulattoes, Mammies, and Bucks: An Interpretive History of Blacks in American Films* (Rev. ed.). New York: Continuum.

Boon, S. (1997). *Pasarkrant*. The Hague: Stichting Tong Tong.

Boon, S., & van Geleuken, E. (1993). *Ik wilde eigenlijk niet gaan: de repatriëring van Indische Nederlandes, 1946–1964*. The Hague: Stichting Tong Tong.

Bordo, Susan. (1993). *Unbearable Weight: Feminism, Western Culture, and the Body*. Berkeley: University of California Press.

Bourdieu, P. (1977). *Outline of a Theory of Practice*. Cambridge: Cambridge University Press.

Bourdieu, P. (1990). *In Other Words: Essays Towards a Reflexive Sociology*. Stanford: Stanford University Press.

Bowman, J. E., & Murray R. F. (1990). *Genetic Variation and Disorders in Peoples of African Origin*. Baltimore: The Johns Hopkins University Press.

Bowman, K. (n.d.). *No Talk Stink!* [Audio recording]. Honolulu: Hula Records.

Bradshaw, Carla K. (1992). "Beauty and the Beast: On Racial Ambiguity." In M.P.P. Root (Ed.), *Racially Mixed People in America* (pp. 77–88). Newbury Park, CA: Sage Publications.

The Bridge. "Southeast Asian Refugee Activity 1994–95 (Cumulative Since April 1975)." 11: (4).

Brinkerhoff, M. B. & Jacob, J. C. (1994). "Racial, Ethnic, and Religious Social Distance in Surinam: An Exploration on the 'Strategic Alliance Hypothesis' in a Caribbean Community." *Ethnic and Racial Studies*, 17 (4), 636–661.

Browne, M. (1986, March 30). "What Accounts for Asian Students' Success?" *New York Times*, p. C-9.

Buddingh, H. (1995). *Geschiedenis van Suriname* [History of Suriname]. Utrecht: Uitgevery Het Spectrum.

Bugawan, T. L., Chang, J. D., Klitz, W., & Erlich, H. A. (1994). "PCR/Oligonucleotide Probe Typing of HLA Class II Alleles in a Filipino Population Reveals an Unusual Distribution of HLA Haplotypes." *American Journal of Human Genetics*, 54(2): 331–340.

Bumatai, A. (1980). *All in the Ohana* [Audio recording]. Honolulu: Bluewater Records.

Bumatai, A. (1994). *Andy Bumatai: Stand Up Comic 198421994* [Audio recording]. Honolulu: Tropical Jam Recording Studios.

Bunchua, K. (c.1984). "The Portuguese Descendants in Thailand." In *Thai Politics and Government: Minority Groups*. Bangkok: Thai Studies Program, Chulalongkorn University.

Burkhardt, W. R. (1983). "Institutional Barriers, Marginality, and Adaptation Among the American-Japanese Mixed Bloods in Japan." *Journal of Asian Studies,* 42: 519–544.

Butler, J. (1993). *Bodies That Matter: On the Discursive Limits of Sex.* New York: London: Routledge.

Butterfield, Fox. (1986, August 3). "Why Asians Are Going to the Head of the Class." *New York Times.* pp. 18–23.

Buttery, T. (1987). "Helping Biracial Children Adjust." *Education Digest,* 52: 38–41.

Callahan, J. F. (1995). *The Collected Essays of Ralph Ellison.* New York: Random House.

Camper, C. (Ed.): (1994). *Miscegenation Blues: Voices of Mixed-Race Women.* Toronto: Sister Vision.

Casas, J. M., & Pytluk, S. D. (1995). "Hispanic Identity Development: Implications for Resarch and Practice." In J. Ponterotto, M. Casas, L. Suzuki, & C. Alexander (Eds.), *Handbook of Multicultural Counseling* (pp. 155–180). Thousand Oaks, CA: Sage Publications.

Cauce A., Hiraga Y., Mason, C., Aguilar, T., Ordonez, N., & Gonzalez, N. (1992). "Between a Rock and a Hard Place: Social Adjustment of Biracial Youth." In M.P.P. Root (Ed.), *Racially Mixed People in America* (pp. 207–222). Thousand Oaks, CA: Sage Publications.

Census Advisory Committee on the Asian and Pacific American Population. (1979). *Summary Report by the Census Advisory Committee on the Asian and Pacific American Population for the 1980 Census.* Mimeograph. Los Angeles: UCLA Asian American Studies Center.

Chaloemtiarana, T. (Ed.) (1978). *Thai Politics: 1932–1957* Vol. 1. Bangkok: The Social Science Association of Thailand.

Chan, S. (1991). *Asian Americans: An Interpretive History.* Boston: Twayne.

Chapkis, Wendy. (1986). *Beauty Secrets: Women and the Politics of Appearance.* Boston: Sage Publications.

Char, Tin-Yuke. (1975). *The Sandalwood Mountains: Readings and Stories of the Early Chinese in Hawai'i.* Honolulu: University Press of Hawai'i.

Cheng, C. K., and Yamamura, D. (1957). "Interracial Marriage and Divorce in Hawaii." *Social Forces,* 36: 77–84.

Chiong, Jane Ayers. (1998). *Racial Categorization of Multiracial Children in Schools.* Westport, CT: Bergin and Garvey.

Chodorow, Nancy J. (1999). *The Power of Feelings.* New Haven: Yale University Press.

Cisneros, Sandra. (1984). *The House on Mango Street.* New York: Vintage Books.

Cohen, C. B., Wilk, Richard, & Stoeltje, B. (1996). *Beauty Queens on the Global Stage: Gender, Contests, and Power.* New York: Routledge.

Cohen, L. M. (1984). *Chinese in the Post–Civil War South: A People Without a History.* Baton Rouge: Louisiana State University Press.

Coldenhoff, B. J. (1988). *Schoolloopbanen van Indische jongeren.* Doctoraal scriptie, Vakgroep Onderwijssociologie en Ondewijsbeleid, Erasmus Universiteit, Rotterdam.

Collins, S. (1996, August 18). "Playing the Name Game: Newscasters with Anglo-Sounding Last Names Are Switching to Ethnic Handles. It Gets Them Work—But Some Ask if It's Ethical." *Los Angeles Times,* calendar sec, p. 6.

Comas-Diaz, L. (1994). "LatiNegra: Mental Health Issues of African Latinas." In R. V. Almeida (Ed.), *Expansions of Feminist Family Theory Through Diversity* (pp. 35–74). New York: Haworth.

Connery, Christopher L. (1995). "Pacific Rim Discourse: The U.S. Global Imaginary in the Late Cold War Years." In Rob Wilson & Arif Dirlik (Eds.), *Asia/Pacific as Space of Cultural Production* (pp. 30–56). Durham: Duke University Press.

Connor, J. W. (1977). *Tradition and Change in Three Generations of Japanese Americans*. Chicago: Nelson-Hall.

Consumer Guide. (1995). *The Ultimate Baby Name Book*. Lincolnwood, IL: Publications International Ltd.

Cooke, T. (1997). *Biracial Identity Development: Psychosocial Contributions to Self-Esteem and Racial Identity*. Unpublished dissertation, Arizona State University, Tempe.

Cooley, C. H. (1902). *Human Nature and the Social Order*. New York: Scribner.

Cose, E. (1997). *Color-Blind: Seeing Beyond Race in a Race-Obsessed World*. New York: HarperCollins Publishers.

Cose, E. (2000, January 1). "The 21st Century: Our New Look: The Colors of Race." New York: *Newsweek*, pp. 28–30.

Cottaar, A., & Willems, W. (1984). *Indische Nederlanders: Een onderzoek naar beeldvorming*. The Hague: Moesson.

Cottaar, A., & Willems, W. (1985). "De geassimileerde Indische Nederlander: mythe of werkelijkeid?" *Gids*, 148 (3–4).

Cottaar, A., & Willems, W. (1987). "Indische Nederlanders, een ondergeschoven bevolkingsgroep" In J. E. Dubbelman (Ed.)., *Vreemd Gespuis*. Amsterdam: Anne Frank Stichting, Ambo/Novib.

Creutzburg, R. (1995). "Onze kabar koening 'De Indo' Still Going Strong in 1995." *Moesson*, 40 (5).

Creutzburg, R. (1997). "Voorlopig programma van de Indo Reunie in Maart '97 te Bali." *Internationaal Tijdschrift "De Indo," Officieel Orgaan van het Indo Community Center "De Soos," Inc.*, 34 (6).

Creutzburg, R. (1998). "Indies Archive in America." *Internationaal Tijdschrift "De Indo," Officieel Orgaan van het Indo Community Center "De Soos," Inc.*, 35 (10).

Crevecoeur, J. Hector St. John de. (1782 [1981]). *Letters from an American Farmer and Sketches of Eighteenth-Century America*. New York: Penguin Books.

Crohn, J. (1995). *Mixed Matches: How to Create Successful Interracial, Interethnic, and Interfaith Relationships*. New York: Fawcett Columbine Books.

Cross, W. E. (1971). "The Negro to Black Conversion Experience: Toward a Psychology of Black Liberation." *Black World*, 20 (9): 13–19.

Cross, W. E. (1991). *Shades of Black: Diversity in African American Identity*. Philadelphia: Temple University Press.

Crouch, Stanley. (1996, September 29). "Race Is Over." *New York Times Magazine*, p. 170.

Dale, P. (1986). *The Myth of Japanese Uniqueness*. London: Croom Helm.

Daniel, G. R. (1992a). "Beyond Black and White: The New Multiracial Consciousness." In M. P.P. Root (Ed.), *Racially Mixed People in America* (pp. 333–341). Thousand Oaks, CA: Sage Publications.

Daniel, G. R. (1992b). "Passers and Pluralists: Subverting the Racial Divide." In M. P. P. Root (Ed.), *Racially Mixed People in America* (pp. 91–107). Thousand Oaks, CA: Sage Publications.

Davies, C. (1990). *Ethnic Humor Around the World: A Comparative Analysis*. Bloomington: Indiana University Press.

Davis, F. J. (1991). *Who Is Black? One Nation's Definition*. University Park: Pennsylvania State University Press.

Davis, F. J. (1995). "The Hawaiian Alternative to the One-Drop Rule." In N. Zack (Ed.), *American Mixed Race: The Culture of Microdiversity* (pp. 115–132). Lanham, MD: Rowman and Littlefield.

Davis, K. (1989). *Too Deep for Tears*. New York: Pocket Books.

DeAngelis, T. (1997, December). "Study Shows Black Children More Intimidated by Peers." *Monitor*, p. 28.

De Boer-Lasschuyt, T. (1960). "Eurasian Repatriates in Holland." *R.E.M.P. Bulletin*, 8 (April–June).

Debonis, S. (1995). *Children of the Enemy: Oral Histories of Vietnamese Amerasians and Their Mothers*. Jefferson, NC: McFarland.

Degler, C. N. (1991). *In Search of Human Nature: The Decline and Revival of Darwinism in American Social Thought*. New York: Oxford University Press.

De la Cruz, Enrique. (1998). "Essays into American Empire in the Philippines, Part II: Culture, Community, and Capital." *Amerasia Journal* (Centennial Commemorative Issue), 24 (3).

De Lima, F. (1978). *Frank De Lima Presents a Taste of Malasades* [Audio recording]. Honolulu: Hula Records.

De Lima, F. (1988). *The Best of De Lima* [Videotape]. Honolulu: Pocholinga Productions.

De Lima, F. (1991a). *The Best of De Lima Too!* [Videotape]. Honolulu: Pocholinga Productions.

De Lima, F. (1991b). *De Lima's Joke Book*. Honolulu: Bess Press.

De Lima, F., & Kolohe, N. (1980). *Don't Sneeze When You Eat Saimin: Live at the Noodle Shop* [Audio recording]. Honolulu: Pocholinga Productions.

Der, Henry. (1994). "Statement of Henry Der, National Coalition for an Accurate Count of Asians and Pacific Islanders." In *Review of Federal Measurements of Race and Ethnicity; Hearings Before the Subcommittee on Census, Statistics, and Postal Personnel* (House of Representatives, Serial No. 103–07). Washington, DC: U.S. Government Printing Office.

Derksen, E. (1996). "De Indisch stem als mijn geschiedenis verhaal." In T. van der Geugten & L. van der Linden (Eds.), *Indisch in Nederland: Leerlingenboek, Versie D*. 's-Hertogenbosch: KPC.

DeVos, G. (1973). *Personality Patterns and Problems of Adjustment in American-Japanese Intercultural Marriages*. Taipei: The Orient Cultural Service.

DeVos, G., Wetherall, W., & Stearman, K. (1983). *Japan's Minorities*. London: Minority Rights Group.

Dew, E. (1996). *The Difficult Flowering of Surinam: Ethnicity and Politics in a Plural Society*. The Hague: Martinus Nijhoff.

De Waal Malefijit, A. M. (1960). *The Javanese Population of Suriname*. Published doctoral dissertation. Ann Arbor: University Microfilms, Inc.

Dickason, C. (1987). *Indochine*. New York: Bantam Books.

Dominguez, V. (1986). *White by Definition: Social Classification in Creole Louisiana*. New Brunswick: Rutgers University Press.

Dorinson, J., & Boskin, K. (1998). *Humor in America: A Research Guide to Genres and Topics*. Westport, CT: Greenwood Publishing Group.

Dorman, L. (1996, September 1). "We'll Be Right Back After This Hip and Distorted Commercial Break." *New York Times*, p. S13(L).

Doss, R. C., & Gross, A. M. (1994). "The Effects of Black English and Code-Switching on Intraracial Perceptions." *Journal of Black Psychology*, 20 (3): 282–293.

D'Souza, D. (1991). *Illiberal Education*. New York: Free Press.

Dubinin, N. P. (1956). "Race and Contemporary Genetics." In *Race, Science, and Society*. Paris: The UNESCO Press.

DuBois, W.E.B. (1994). *The Souls of Black Folks*. Mineola, NY: Dover Publications, Inc.

Ducelle, L. (1994). "Repatriëring: de winst en het grote verlies." In W. Willems & L. Lucassen (Eds.), *Het onbekende vaderland: De repatriëring van Indische Nederlanders (1946–1964)*. The Hague: Sdu Uitgeverij Koninginnegracht.

Dunn, L. C. (1956). "Race and Biology." In *Race, Science and Society* (pp. 31–67). Paris: The UNESCO Press.

DuPlessis, M. (1996). "Blatantly Bisexual: Or, Unthinking Queer Theory." In D. Hall & M. Pramaggiore (Eds.), *Representing Bisexualities: Subjects and Cultures of Fluid Desire*. New York: New York University Press.

Du Puy, W. A. (1932). *Hawaii and Its Race Problem*. Washington, DC: U.S. Government Printing Office.

Ebony. (1997, July). "Black America and Tiger's Dilemma."

Eddings, J. (1997, July 14). "Counting a 'New' Type of American: The Dicey Politics of Creating a 'Multiracial' Category in the Census." *U.S. News and World Report*, pp. 22–23.

Efron, S. (1998, February 1). "Weighty Issue: Tabloids Take Sumo's Akebono to Task for Engagement to Japanese-American Woman." *Los Angeles Times*, N5.

Eggebeen, D., Chew, K., & Uhlenburg, P. (1989). "American Children in Multiracial Households." *Sociological Perspectives*, 32: 65–85.

Elfenbein, A. S. (1989). *Women on the Color Line: Evolving Stereotypes and the Writings of George Washington Cable, Grace King, Kate Chopin*. Charlottesville: University Press of Virginia.

Ellemers, J. E. (1981). "The Netherlands in the Sixties and Seventies." *Netherlands Journal of Sociology*, 17 (2).

Ellemers, J. E. (1994). "De migratie uit Indonesië als proces: meerdere beelden of toch één genuanceerd beeld?" In W. Willems & L. Lucassen (Eds.), *Het onbekende vaderland: De repatriëring van Indische Nederlanders (1946–1964)*. The Hague: Uitgeverij Koninginnegracht.

Ellemers, J. E., & Vaillant, R.E.F. (1985). *Indische Nederlanders en gerepatrieerden*. Muiderberg: Coutinho.

Ellison, Ralph. (1995). "Hidden Name and Complex Fate: A Writer's Experience in the United States." In John F. Callahan (Ed.), *The Collected Essays of Ralph Ellison* (pp. 189–209). New York: Modern Library.

Emerson, R. (1988). *Contemporary Field Research: A Collection of Readings*. Prospect Heights, IL: Waveland Press.

Erikson, E. (1968). *Identity: Youth and Crisis*. Toronto: Norton.

Espiritu, Y. L. (1992). *Asian American Panethnicity: Bridging Institution and Identities*. Philadelphia: Temple University Press.

Espiritu, Y. L. (1995). *Filipino American Lives*. Philadelphia: Temple University Press.

Espiritu, Y. L. (1997). *Asian American Women and Men*. Thousand Oaks, CA: Sage Publications.

Far, S. S. (1996). *Mrs. Spring Fragrance and Other Stories*. Urbana: University of Illinois Press.

Farley, R., & Allen, W. (1989). *The Color Line and the Quality of Life in America*. Thousand Oaks, CA: Sage Publications.

Fernandez, C. (1995). "Testimony of the Association of Multiethnic Americans." In N. Zack (Ed.), *American Mixed Race: The Culture of Microdiversity* (pp. 191-210). Lanham, MD: Rowman and Littlefield.

Fernandez, C. (1996). "Goverment Classification of Multiracial/Multiethnic People." In M.P.P. Root (Ed.), *The Multiracial Experience: Racial Borders as the New Frontier* (pp. 15–36). Newbury Park, CA: Sage Publications.

Fiore, F. (1997, October 30). "Multiple Race Choices to Be Allowed on 2000 Census." *Los Angeles Times*, p. A1+.

Fleming, R. (1927). "Anthropological Studies of Children." *Eugenics Review*, pp. 294–301.

Fleming, R. (1939). "Physical Heredity in Human Hybrids." *Annals of Eugenics*, 9: 55–81.

Fletcher, M. E. (1930). *Report of an Investigation into the Colour Problem in Liverpool and Other Ports*. Liverpool: Liverpool Association for the Welfare of Half-Caste Children.

Fong, C., & Yung, J. (1995-96). "In Search of the Right Spouse: Interracial Marriage Among Chinese and Japanese Americans." *Amerasia Journal,* (3): 77–98.

Fong, T. P. (1998) *The Contemporary Asian American Experience: Beyond the Model Minority Myth.* Upper Saddle River, NJ: Prentice Hall.

Fong, T. P., & Shinagawa, L. H. (2000). *Asian Americans: Experiences and Perspectives.* Upper Saddle River, NJ: Prentice Hall.

Foucault, M. (1980a). *The History of Sexuality. 1, An Introduction.* Trans. Robert Hurley. New York: Vintage Books.

Foucault, M. (1980b). *Power/Knowledge: Selected Interviews and Other Writings.* Trans. C. Gordon, L. Marshall, J. Mepham, & K. Sopor. New York: Pantheon Books.

Frankenberg, R. (1993). *White Women, Race Matters: The Social Construction of Whiteness.* Minneapolis: University of Minnesota Press.

Fredrickson, G. M. (1981). *White Supremacy: A Comparative Study in American and South African History.* New York: Oxford University Press.

Freeman, Harold P. (1997, April 9). *Report of the Chairman: Highlights and Recommendations from the President's Cancer Panel Meeting.* Presented at "The Meaning of Race in Science—Considerations for Cancer Research," Bethesda, MD: National Institutes of Health, National Cancer Institute.

Freeman, J. M. (1995). *Changing Identities: Vietnamese Americans, 1975–1995.* Boston: Allyn and Bacon.

Freeman, J. M. (1996, January 7). "Ribald Tales Hide Clever Truths." *San Jose Mercury News,* p. 1B.

Freire, P. (1970a). *Cultural Action for Freedom.* Cambridge: Harvard Education Review.

Freire, P. (1970b). *Pedagogy of the Oppressed.* Trans. M. Ramos. New York: Herder and Herder.

Freire, P. (1973). *Education for Critical Consciousness.* New York: Seabury Press.

Friday, N. (1996). *The Power of Beauty.* New York: Harper Collins, Inc.

Frisby, M. K. (1996, January). "Black, White, or Other." *Emerge,* pp. 48–54.

Fuchs, L. (1961). *Hawaii Pono: A Social History.* New York: Harcourt, Brace and World.

Fugita, Stephen, & O'Brien, David. (1991). *Japanese American Ethnicity: The Persistence of Community.* Seattle: University of Washington Press.

Fujino, D. (1997). "The Rates, Patterns, and Reasons for Forming Heterosexual Interracial Dating Relationships Among Asian Americans." *Journal of Social and Personal Relationships,* 14 (6): 809–828.

Fukuchi, H. (1980). *Okinawa no konketsuji to hahatachi.* Okinawa: Aoi Umi Shuppansha.

Funderburg, L. (1994). *Black, White, Other: Biracial Americans Talk About Race and Identity.* New York: William Morrow and Co.

Furutani, Warren. (1990, September). "Encore." *Tozai Times,* p. 1.

Fusco, Coco. (1995). *English Is Broken Here: Notes on Cultural Fusion in the Americas.* New York: The New York Press.

Gabaccia, D. (1996). *From the Other Side: Women, Gender, and Immigrant Life in the U.S., 1820–1990.* Bloomington: Indiana University Press.

Gans, H. (1979). "Symbolic Ethnicitiy: The Future of Ethnic Groups and Cultures in America." *Ethnic and Racial Studies* 2 (January): 1–20.

Gaskins, P. (1999). *What Are You? Voices of Mixed-Race Young People.* New York: Henry Holt.

Geng, L., Imanishi, T., Tokunaga, K., Zhu, D., Mizuki, N., Xu, S., Geng, Z., Gojobori, T., Tsuji, K., & Inoko, H. (1995). "Determination of HLA Class II Alleles by Genotyping in a Manchu

Population in the Northern Part of China and Its Relationship with Han and Japanese Populations." *Tissue Antigens,* 46 (2): 111–116.

Ghandi, Leela. (1998). *Postcolonial Theory: A Critical Introduction.* New York: Columbia University Press.

Gibbs, J. T., & Moskowitz-Sweet, G. (1991). "Clinical and Cultural Issues in the Treatment of Biracial and Bicultural Adolescents." *Families in Society: The Journal of Contemporary Human Services,* 17: 579–590.

Gielen, C., & Hommerson, M. (1987). *De boot afgehouden: Het Nederlandse beleid ten aanzien van de repatriëring van Indische Nederlanders op Rijksvoorschotbasis.* Doctoraalscriptie, Katholieke Universiteit, Nijmegen.

Gingrich, Newt. (1997, July 25). "Testimony of Speaker Newt Gingrich." In U.S. House of Representatives, 105th Congress, First Session, Committee on Government Reform and Oversight, Subcommittee on Government Management, Information, and Technology. Hearings. *Federal Measures of Race and Ethnicity and the Implications for the 2000 Census,* (pp. 661–662). Washington, D.C.: U.S. Government Printing Office.

Ginsberg, E. K. (Ed.). (1996). *Passing and the Fictions of Identity.* Durham: Duke University Press.

Gist, N. P., & Dworkin, A. G. (1972). *The Blending of Races: Marginality and Identity in World Perspective.* New York: Wiley and Sons, Inc.

Glassman, J. K. (1996, September 17). "A Dishonest Ad Campaign." *Washington Post,* p. A15.

Glassman, J. K. (1997, June 12). "Multiracial (the Colorblind Choice)." *San Jose Mercury News,* p. 10B.

Glick, Clarence E. (1980). *Sojourners and Settlers: Chinese Migrants in Hawai'i.* Honolulu: University Press of Hawaii.

Godeschalk, M. (1988). *Assimilatie en heropvoeding: Beleid van de overheid en kerkelijk en partikulier initiatief ten aanzien van gerepatrieerden uit Indonesië.* Doctoraalscriptie, Katholieke Universiteit, Nijmegen.

Goffman, E. (1959). *The Presentation of Self in Everyday Life.* New York: Doubleday Anchor.

Goldberg, D. T. (1997). *Racial Subjects:Writing on Race in America.* New York: Routledge.

Gordon, M. (1964). *Assimilation in American Life.* New York: Oxford University Press.

Gould, S. J. (1981). *The Mismeasure of Man.* New York: W. W. Norton & Company.

Graham, S. (1995). "Grassroots Advocacy." In N. Zack (Ed.), *American Mixed Race: The Culture of Microdiversity* (pp. 185–190). Lanham, MD: Rowman and Littlefield.

Grove, K. J. (1991). "Identity Development in Interracial Asian/White Late Adolescents: Must It Be So Problematic?" *Journal of Youth and Adolescence,* 20: 617–628.

Grover, K. P. (1989). *An Exploratory Study of Offspring with an Asian-Indian and Non-Asian-Indian Parent Examining Self-Concept, Identity and Psychological Adjustment.* Unpublished doctoral dissertation, University of Southern California, Los Angeles.

Guillermo, E. (1996, September 13). "Made-for-TV Asians: Anchors Exploit Limited Ethnicity." *AsianWeek,* p. 5.

Guillermo, E. (1997, April 18). "Diversity's Champ: Tiger Woods and the Bold New World." *AsianWeek,* p. 5.

Gulick, S. L. (1914). *The American Japanese Problem.* New York: Scribner.

Gulick, S. L. (1937). *Mixing the Races in Hawaii: A Study of the Coming of the Neo-Hawaiian American Race.* Honolulu: Hawaiian Board Book Rooms.

Gutwirth, M. (1993). *Laughing Matter: An Essay on the Comic*. Ithaca, NY: Cornell University Press.

Hahn, R. A. (1992, January 8). "The State of Federal Health Statistics on Racial and Ethnic Groups." *Journal of the American Medical Association*, 267: pp. 268–279.

Hahn, R. A., Mulinare, J., & Teutsch, S. M. (1992, January 8). "Inconsistencies in Coding of Race and Ethnicity Between Birth and Death in U.S. Infants." *Journal of the American Medical Association*, 267: pp. 259–263.

Hahn, R. A., & Stroup, D. F. (1994, January–February). "Race and Ethnicity in Public Health Surveillance: Criteria for the Scientific Use of Social Categories." *CDC-ATSDR Workshop, Public Health Reports*, pp. 7–15.

Haizlip, S. (1994.) *The Sweeter the Juice: A Family Memoir in Black and White*. New York: Simon and Schuster.

Hall, C.C.I. (1980). *The Ethnic Identity of Racially Mixed People: A Study of Black-Japanese*. Unpublished doctoral dissertation, University of California, Los Angeles.

Hall, C.C.I. (1992). "Please Choose One: Ethnic Identity Choices for Biracial Individuals." In M.P.P. Root (Ed.), *Racially Mixed People in America* (pp. 250–264). Thousand Oaks, CA: Sage Publications.

Hall, C.C.I. (1995a). "Asian Eyes: Body Image and Eating Disorders of Asian and Asian American Women." *Eating Disorders*, (1): 8–17.

Hall, C.C.I. (1995b). "Beauty Is in the Soul of the Beholder: Psychological Implications of Beauty and African American Women." *Cultural Diversity and Mental Health*, 1(2): 125–137.

Hall, C.C.I. (1996). "2001: A Race Odyssey." In M.P.P. Root (Ed.), *The Multiracial Experience: Racial Borders as the New Frontier* (pp. 395–410). Thousand Oaks, CA: Sage Publications.

Hall, C.C.I. (1997). "Best of Both Worlds: Body Image and Satisfaction of a Sample of Black-Japanese Biracial Individuals. *Amerasia Journal*, 23 (1): 87–97.

Hall, S. (1993). "Cultural Identity and Diaspora." In J. Rutherford (Ed.), *Identity: Community, Culture, Difference* (pp. 222–237). London: Lawrence & Wishart.

Hall, K., & Bucholtz, M. (Eds.). (1995). *Gender Articulated: Language and the Socially Constructed Self*. New York: Routledge.

Hamamoto, D. Y. (1994). *Monitored Peril: Asian Americans and the Politics of Rrepresentation*. Minneapolis: University of Minnesota Press.

Haney Lopez, I. F. (1996). *White by Law*. New York: New York University Press.

Hara, M., & Keller, N. O. (1999). *Intersecting Circles: The Voices of Hapa Women in Poetry and Prose*. Honolulu, HI: Bamboo Ridge Press.

Harada, W. (1981). *Andy Bumatai's Ohana*. New York: Lee Publishers.

Harajiri, H. (1995). "Nihon ni okeru Ibunkakan Kyoiku no Rinen Zainichi Chosenjin Kenkyu no Tachiba kara. Intercultural/Transcultural Education." *The Bulletin of Intercultural Education Society, Japan*, No. 9.

Harris, S. M. (1995). "Family, Self, and Sociocultural Contributions to Body Image Attitudes of African American Women." *Psychology of Women Quarterly*, 19: 129–145.

Hassankhan, M. S., Ligeon, M., & Scheepers, P. (1995). "De sociaal-economische verschillen tussen Creolen, Hindoestanen en Javanen: 130 jaar na afschaffing van de slavernij." In L. Gobardhan-Rambocus, M. S. Hassankhan, & J. Egger (Eds.). *De erfenis van de slavernij* (pp. 249–274). Paramaribo: Anto-de-Kom Universiteit.

Hawkins, K. (1997). *Social Darwinism in European and American Thought, 1860–1945*. Cambridge: Cambridge University Press.

Helms, J. E. (1990). *Black and White Racial Identity: Theory, Research, and Practice*. Westport, CT: Greenwood Press.

Hemphill, E. (1980). *The Least of These*. New York: Weatherhill.

Henry, W. A. III. (1993, Fall). "The Politics of Separation." *Time*, (special issue), pp. 73–75.

Hernandez, C. A. (1996). "Government Classification of Multiracial/Multiethnic People." In M.P.P. Root (Ed.), *The Multiracial Experience: Racial Borders as the New Frontier* (pp. 15–36). Thousand Oaks, CA: Sage Publications.

Herodotus. (1954). *The Persian Wars*. Trans. Aubrey de Selincourt. Baltimore: Penguin.

Herring, R. D. (1992). "Biracial Children: An Increasing Concern for Elementary and Middle School Counselors." *Elementary School Guidance and Counseling*, 27 (2): 123–130.

Herrnstein, R. J., & Murray, C. (1994). *The Bell Curve*. New York: Free Press.

Hesse, B. (1993). "Black to Front and Black Again: Racialization Through Contested Times and Spaces." In M. Keith & S. Pile (Eds.), *Place and the Politics of Identity* (pp. 162–182). London: Routledge.

Hing, Bill Ong. (1983). *Making and Re-Making of Asian American Through Immigration Policy, 1850–1990*. Stanford, CA: Stanford University Press.

Hirabayashi, L. R. (1998). *Teaching Asian America: Diversity and the Problem of Community*. Lanham, MD: Rowman and Littlefield.

Ho, S. C. (1996, February). "Body Measurements, Bone Mass, and Fractures. Does the East Differ from the West?" *Clinical Orthopaedics and Related Research*, 323: p. 75–80.

Honda, H. (1982). *Sonzai shinai kodomotachi: Okinawa no mukokusekiji mondai*. Tokyo: Shobunsha.

Hoogbergen, W. (1998). "Rituelen voor de doden: Europees-Afrikaanse wortels." *Oso, Tijdschrift voor Surinaamse Taalkunde, Letterkunde, Cultuur en Geschiedenis*, 17 (1): 5–22.

hooks, b. (1982). *Ain't I a Woman*. London: Pluto.

hooks, b. (1992). *Black Looks: Race and Representation*. Boston: South End Press.

Hooper, P. F. (1980). *Elusive Destiny: The Internationalist Movement in Modern Hawaii*. Honolulu: University of Hawaii Press.

Hoppe, A. (1997, June 18). "Confessions of a Racist." *San Francisco Chronicle*, p. A19.

Hormann, B. L. (1972). "Hawaii's Mixing People." In N. P. Gist & A. G. Dworkin (Eds.), *The Blending of the Races: Marginality and Identity in World Perspective* (pp. 213–236). New York: Wiley.

Horner, C. (1995, August 13). "Out of the Chute." *San Jose Mercury News*, pp. 1C, 5C.

Houston, V. H. (1991). "The Past Meets the Future: A Cultural Essay." *Amerasia Journal*, 17 (1): 53–56.

Houston, V. H. (1997). "To the Colonizer Goes the Spoils: American Progeny in Vietnam War Films and Owning up to the Gaze." *Amerasia Journal*, 23 (1): 69–86.

Houston, V. H., & Williams, T. K. (1997). "No Passing Zone: The Artistic and Discursive Voices of Asian-Descent Multiracials." *Amerasia Journal*, 23 (1): vii–xii.

Huang, C., et al. (1996). "Determinants of Vertebral Fracture Prevalence Among Native Japanese Women and Women of Japanese Descent Living in Hawaii." *Bone*, 18(5): 437–442.

Hubbard, R. (1995). "The Social Construction of Sexuality." In P. S. Rothenberg (Ed.), *Race, Class, and Gender in the United States: An Integrated Study*. (3rd ed., pp. 48–51). New York: St. Martin's Press.

Hu-DeHart, Evelyn. (1996a). "P. C. and the Politics of Multiculturalism in Higher Education." In S. Gregory & R. Sanjek (Eds.), *Race* (pp. 243–256). New Brunswick: Rutgers University Press.

Hu-DeHart, Evelyn. (1996b). "A to Be or Not to Be, That Is the Question: A Multiracial Statistic." *Black Issues in Higher Education, 13* (August 22): 44–45.

Hune, S. (1993). "An Overview of Asian Pacific American Futures: Shifting Paradigms." In *The State of Asian Pacific America: Policy Issues to the Year 2020* (pp. 1–9). Los Angeles, CA: LEAP Asian Pacific American Public Policy Institute and UCLA Asian American Studies Center.

Hunter, E., & Chakrabongse, N. (1994). *Katya and the Prince of Siam*. Bangkok: River Books.

Hutchins, L. & Kaahumanu, L. (1991). *Bi Any Other Name: Bisexual People Speak Out*. Boston: Alyson.

In re Young. (1912). *Federal Reporter, 198*: 715–717.

Interrace Magazine. (1991, September/October). "Passing for White: The Outing of Mixed Race People" (special issue).

"Interracial Children Pose Challenge for Classifiers." (1993, January 27). *Wall Street Journal*.

Irwin, W. (1921 [1979]). *Seed of the Sun*. Salem: Ayer.

Ishikawa, Michiji. (1938). "A Study of Intermarried Japanese Families in USA." *Cultural Nippon, 3*: 457–487

Jacobs, J. (1996, October 3). "Melting in America." *San Jose Mercury*, p. 9B.

Jacobs, J. (1997, July 14). "Over Time, the Racial Lines Will Blur." *San Jose Mercury News*, p. 7B.

Jacobs, J., & Labov, T. (1995, August 21). *Sex Difference in Intermarriage: Asian Exceptionalism Reconsidered*. Paper presented at the meeting of the American Sociological Association, Washington, DC.

Janssen, M. (1996). "Hier Radio Tjamoer Adoek, Hier Meity Janssen!" *Moesson, 40(9)*.

Japan, Ministry of Health and Welfare. (1994). *Jinko Dotai Tokei*. Tokyo.

Japan, Ministry of Health and Welfare. (1995). *Jinko Dotai Tokei*. Tokyo.

Japan Times. (1993, September 17). "American Tractor Made in Japan," p. 8.

Jitpleecheep, Sukanya, & Intarakomalyasut, Nondhanada. (1997, December 1). "Nike Drops Saha in Distribution Revamp." *Bangkok Post Online*. Available at http//:www.bkkpost.samart.co.th/news/BParchive/BP971201/0112_busi04.html.

Johnson, D. J. (1992). "Developmental Pathways: Toward an Ecological Theoretical Formulation of Race Identity in Black-White Biracial Children." In M.P.P. Root (Ed.), *Racially Mixed People in America*. (pp. 37–49). Thousand Oaks, CA: Sage Publications.

Johnson, J. C. (1992). "Offspring of Cross-Race and Cross-Ethnic Marriage in Hawaii." In M.P.P. Root (Ed.), *Racially Mixed People in America* (pp. 239–249). Thousand Oaks, CA: Sage Publications.

Johnson, R., & Nagoshi, C. (1986). "The Adjustment of Offspring of Within-Group and Interracial/Intercultural Marriages: A Comparison of Personality Factor Scores" *Journal of Marriage and the Family, 38*: 279–284.

Johnston, C. C., Jr., & Melton, L. J., III. (1993). "Bone Density Measurement and the Management of Osteoporosis." In J. Favus Murray (Ed.), *Primer on the Metabolic Bone Diseases and Disorders of Mineral Metabolism* (2nd ed, pp. 137–145). New York: Raven Press.

Jones, C. P., LaVeist, T., & Lillie-Blanton, M. (1991). "'Race' in the Epidemiologic Literature: An Examination of the American Journal of Epidemiology, 1921–1990." *American Journal of Epidemiology, 134(10)*: 1079–1084.

Jones, L. (1994). *Bulletproof Diva: Tales of Race, Sex and Hair*. New York: Doubleday.

Jordan, June. (1998). "A New Politics of Sexuality." In M. Andersen & P. H. Collins (Eds.), *Race, Class, Gender: An Anthology* (pp. 437–441). New York: Wadsworth Publishers.

Jornvong, Anusorn. (1995, January 15–31). "Mixed Blood Stars Are the Rage." *Nation Junior*, 3(59): 26–27.

Kaahumanu, Lani, & Hutchins, Loraine. (1991). *Bisexual People Speak Out*. Boston: Alyson Publications.

Kambhu, L. R. (1962). *Thailand Is Our Home: A Study of Some American Wives of Thais*. Cambridge: The Center for International Studies, Massachusetts Institute of Technology.

Kame'eleihiwa, L. (1992). *Native Land and Foreign Desires*. Honolulu: Bishop Museum.

Kaw, Eugenia. (1993). "Medicalization of Racial Features: Asian American women and Cosmetic Surgery." *Medical Anthropology Quarterly*, 7(1):74–89.

Keith, M., & Pile, S. (Eds.) (1993). *Place and the Politics of Identity* . London: Routledge.

Kerwin, C., Ponterotto, J. G., Jackson, B. L., & Harris, A. (1993). "Racial Identity in Biracial Children: A Qualitative Investigation." *Journal of Counseling Psychology*, 40 (2): 221–231.

Kevles, D. (1986). *In the Name of Eugenics*. London: Penguin.

Kevles, D. (1992). *Dope Girls: The Birth of the British Drug Underground*. London: Lawrence and Wishart.

Kibria, Nazli. (1997). "The Construction of 'Asian American': Reflections on Intermarriage and Ethnic Identity Among Second-Generation Chinese and Korean Americans." *Ethnic and Racial Studies*, 20(3): 525–544.

Kich, G. K. (1982). *Eurasians: Ethnic/Racial Identity Development of Biracial Japanese/White Adults*. Unpublished doctoral dissertation, Wright Institute of Professional Psychology, Berkeley, CA.

Kich, G. K. (1992). "The Developmental Process of Asserting a Biracial, Bicultural Identity. In M.P.P. Root (Ed.), *Racially Mixed People in America*. (pp. 304–317). Thousand Oaks, CA: Sage Publications.

Kich, G. K. (1996). "In the Margins of Sex and Race: Difference, Marginality and Flexibility." In M.P.P. Root (Ed.), *The Multiracial Experience: Racial Borders as the New Frontier* (pp. 263–276). Thousand Oaks, CA: Sage Publications.

Kim, E. H. (1982). *Asian American Litreature: An Introduction to the Writings and Their Social Context*. Philadelphia: Temple University Press.

King, R. C. (1997). "Multiraciality Reigns Supreme? Mixed-Race Japanese Americans and the Cherry Blossom Queen Pageant." *Amerasia Journal*, 23(1): 113–128.

King, R.C., & DaCosta, K. (1996). "Changing Face, Changing Race: The Remaking of Race in the Japanese American and African American Communities." In M.P.P. Root (Ed.), *The Multiracial Experience: Racial Borders as the New Frontier* (pp 227–244). Thousand Oaks, CA: Sage Publications.

Kitano, H.H.L. (1993). *Generations and Identity: The Japanese American*. Needham Heights, MA: Ginn Press.

Kitano, H.H.L., Fujino, D. C., & Sato, J. T. (1998). "Interracial Marriages: Where Are the Asian Americans and Where Are They Going?" In L. C. Lee & N. W. Zane (Eds.), *Handbook of Asian American Psychology* (pp. 233–260). Thousand Oaks, CA: Sage Publications.

Kitano, H.H.L., & Yeung, W. (1982). "Chinese Interracial Marriage." *Marriage and Family Review*, 5: 35–48.

Kitano, H.H.L., Yeung, W., Chai, L., & Hatanaka, H. (1984). "Asian-American Interracial Marriage." *Journal of Marriage and the Family*, 46 (1): 179–190.

Kohn, M. (1992). *Dope Girls: The Birth of the British Drugs Underground*. London: Lawrence and Wishart.

Kokusai Kekkon o Kangaeru Kai. (1991). *Nijukokuseki*. Tokyo.

Kondo, D. (1997). *About Face: Performing Race in Fashion and Theater*. New York: Routledge.

Kortendick, O. (1990). *Indische Nederlanders und Tante Lien: eine Strategie zur Konstruktion ethnischer Identität*. Cologne: Spiegelbild.

Kousbroek, R. (1992). *Het Oostindische kampsyndroom*. Amsterdam: Meulenhoff.

Kraak, J. H., et al. (1957). *De Repatriëring uit Indonesië: een Ondezoek naar de Integratie van de Gerepatrieerden uit Indonesië in de Nederlandse Samenleving*. The Hague: Staatsuitgeverij.

Krieger, N. (1987). "Shades of Difference: Theoretical Underpinnings of the Medical Controversy on Black/White Differences in the United States, 1830–1870." *International Journal of Health Services*, 17(2): 259–278.

Krieger, N., & Sidney, S. (1996). "Racial Discrimination and Blood Pressure: The CARDIA Study of Young Black and White Adults." *American Journal of Public Health*, 86(10):1370–1378.

Kwik, G. (1989). *The Indos in Southern California*. New York: AMS.

La'ia, B. (1995a). *Ask Bu: Bu La'ia Ansas All Kine Questions, Li'dat*. Honolulu: Keefah.

La'ia, B. (1995b). *False Crack* [Audio recording]. Honolulu: Big Poi Records.

La'ia, B. (1996). *Hawaii's Most Wanted* [Audio recording]. Honolulu: Kanaka.

Lakoff, R. T., & Scherr, R. L. (1984). *Face Value: The Politics of Beauty*. Boston: Routledge & Kegan Paul.

Landrine, H., & Klonoff, E. A. (1994). "The African American Acculturation Scale: Development, Reliability, and Validity." *Journal of Black Psychology*, 20(2): 104–127.

Larson, L. A. (1995). *Black-White Biracial Adolescents: Ethnic Identity, Self-Label and Adaptive Functioning*. Unpublished doctoral dissertation, California School of Professional Psychology, Los Angeles.

Lasker, Bruno. (1931). *Filipino Immigration*. Chicago: University of Chicago Press.

Last, J. M., Abramson, J. H., Friedman, G. D., Porta, M., Spasoff, R. A., & Thuriaux, M. (Eds.). (1995). *A Dictionary of Epidemiology*. 3rd ed. New York: Oxford University Press.

Lau, E. M., & Cooper, C. (1996). "The Epidemiology of Osteoporosis. The Oriental Perspective in a World Context." *Clinical Orthopaedics and Related Research*, 323: 65–74.

LaVeist, T. A. (1996). "Why We Should Continue to Study Race . . . but Do a Better Job: An Essay on Race, Racism, and Health." *Ethnicity & Disease*, 6 (Winter-Spring): 21–29.

Lawsin, E. P. (1998). "Empowering the *Bayanihan* Spirit: Teaching Filipina/o American Studies." In L. Hirabayashi (Ed.) *Teaching Asian America: Diversity and the Problem of Community* (pp. 187–198). Lanham, MD: Rowman and Littlefield.

Lebra, T. S. (1976). *Japanese Patterns of Behavior*. Honolulu: East-West Press.

Lee, M. B. (1997). *A Simple Start For Monoracial-Multiethnic Asians*. Student paper, Asian American Studies 137, University of California, Santa Barbara.

Leland, J., & Beals, G. (1997, May 5). "In Living Colors." *Newsweek*. pp. 58–60.

Leonard, K. I. (1992). *Making Ethnic Choices: California's Punjabi Mexican Americans*. Philadelphia: Temple University Press.

Leslie, C., Elam, R., Samuels, A., and Senna, D. (1995, February 13). "The Loving Generation." *Newsweek*, p. 72.

Lewontin, R. C., Rose, S., & Kamin, L. J. (1984). *Not in Our Genes*. New York: Pantheon Books.

Li, Chui. (1992, November). "The Asian American Market for Personal Products." *Drug and Cosmetic Industry*, pp. 32–36.

Lichtveld, J. (1993). "Indiaans denken and voelen." *Oso, Tijdschrift voor Surinaamse Taalkunde, Letterkunde, Cultuur en Geschiedenis*, 12(2): 152–160.

Lieberman, L. (1995). "Race and Three Models of Human Origin." *American Anthropologist,* 97(2): 231–242.

Lieberson, S. (1986). "Ethnic Groups in Flux: The Changing Ethnic Responses of American Whites." *Annals,* 487 (September): 79–91.

Lieberson, S., & Waters, M. (1985). "Ethnic Mixtures in the United States." *Sociology and Social Research,* 70 (October): 43–51.

Lim-Hing, S. (Ed.). (1994). *The Very Inside: An Anthology of Writings by Asian and Pacific Islander Lesbian and Bisexual Women.* Toronto: Sister Vision Press.

Lind, A. (1938). *An Island Community: Ecological Succession in Hawaii.* Chicago: University of Chicago Press.

Lind, Michael. (1998, August 18). "The Beige and the Black." *New York Times Magazine,* pp. 38–39.

Linnekin, J. (1985). *Children of the Land: Exchange and Status in a Hawaiian Community.* New Brunswick: Rutgers University Press.

Lin Wong, M. (1989). *Chinese Liverpudlians.* Wirral: Liver Press.

Little, K. (1952). *Race and Society* (UNESCO, "The Race Question in Modern Science). Paris: UNESCO.

Liverpool Weekly Courier. (1906, December 1). p.3.

Livingstone, F. B. (1964 [1993]). "On the Nonexistence of the Human Races." In S. Harding, (Ed.), *The Racial Economy of Science* (pp. 133–141). Bloomington: Indiana University Press.

Lloyd-Tarrisyna, D. (1989). *Perceived Ethnic Identity, Conflicts, and Needs of Biracial Individuals.* Unpublished master's thesis, California State University, Long Beach.

Loewen, J. W. (1971). *The Mississippi Chinese: Between Black and White.* Cambridge: Harvard University Press.

Loewen, J. W. (1988). *The Mississippi Chinese: Between Black and White.* 2nd Ed. Prospect Heights, IL: Waveland Press.

Lopez-Baez, S. (1997). "Counseling Interventions with Latinas." In C. Lees (Ed.), *Multicultural Issues in Counseling: New Approaches to Diversity* (pp. 257–267). Alexandria: American Counseling Associations.

Lott, Juanita Tamayo. (1998). *Asian Americans: From Racial Category to Multiple Identities.* Walnut Creek, CA: Altmira Press.

Lowe, J. (1986). "Theories of Ethnic Humor: How to Enter, Laughing." *American Quarterly,* 38(3): 439–460.

Lowe, L. (1991). "Heterogeneity, Hybridity, Multiplicity: Marking Asian American differences." *Diaspora,* 1: 24–44.

Lowe, L. (1996). *Immigrant Acts: On Asian American Cultural Politics.* London: Duke University Press.

Lowry, I. S. (1982). "The Science and Politics of Ethnic Enumeration." In W. A. Van Horne (Ed.), *Ethnicity and Public Policy* (pp. 42–61). Madison: University of Wisconsin.

Lucassen, J., & Penninx, R. (1994). *Nieuwkomers, Nakomelingen, Nederlanders: Immigranten in Nederland, 1550–1993.* Amsterdam: Het Spinhuis.

Luckey, M. M., Wallenstein, S., Lapinski, R., & Meier, D. E. (1996). "A Prospective Study of Bone Loss in African-American and White Women—A Clinical Research Center Study." *Journal of Clinical Endocrinology and Metabolism,* 81(8): 248–256.

Lyotard, J. F. (1984). *The Postmodern Condition: A Report on Knowledge.* Trans. G. Bennington & B. Massumi. Minneapolis: University of Minnesota Press.

Malajuwara, F. (1998). "Begrafenis- en rouwrituelen bij de Kalihna." *Oso, Tijdschrift voor Suri-naamse Taalkunde, Letterkunde, Cultuur en Geschiedenis,* 17 (1): 63–70.

Manalansan, M. F., IV. (1994). "Searching for Community: Filipino Gay Men in New York City." *Amerasia Journal,* 20 (1): 59–73.

Mansvelt, W.M.F. (1932). "De Positie der Indo-Europeanen." *Koloniale Studiën: Tijdschrift van de Vereeniging voor Studie van Koloniaal-Maatschappelijke Vraagstukken,* 16 (Eerste Deel).

Mar, J. B. (1988). *Chinese Caucasian Interracial Parenting and Ethnic Identity.* Unpublished doctoral dissertation, University of Massachusetts, Amherst.

Marc, D. (1992). *Comic Visions: Television Comedy and American Culture.* Winchester, MA: Unwin Hyman.

Marr, D. G., & White, C. P. (Eds.) (1988). *Postwar Vietnamese: Dilemmas in Socialist Development.* New York: Southeast Asia Program.

Marriott, Michel. (1996, July 20). "Multiracial Americans Ready to Claim Their Own Identity." *New York Times,* p. A1.

Mass, A. I. (1992). "Interracial Japanese Americans: The Best of Both Worlds or the End of the Japanese American Community?" In M.P.P. Root (Ed.), *Racially Mixed People in America* (pp. 265–279). Thousand Oaks, CA: Sage Publications.

Matichon. (1997, February 5). "Hae Rap Tigeur Wud Some Kiat Woi Lan Tiwi Sum Hua Thai Sod Bangkap Du," pp. 1, 23.

Matsumoto, G. M., Meredith, G.M., & Masuda, M. (1973). "Ethnic Identity: Honolulu and Seattle Japanese-Americans." In S. Sue & N. Wagners (Eds.), *Asian Americans: Psychological Perspectives.* Palo Alto: Science & Behavior Books, Inc.

May, J. P. (1973). *The British Working Class and the Chinese, 1870–1911, with Particular Reference to the Seamen's Union Strike of 1911.* Unpublished master's dissertation, University of Warwick.

Mayawii. (1997, February 7). "Up Ma Pen Khong Rao Aow Deu Deu Reu Plao?" *Nechan Sapda,* p. 9.

McCleod, R. G. (1997, April 24). "Tiger Woods: An Emblem for Census Issue." *San Francisco Chronicle,* p. A23.

McCunn, R. L. (1988). *Chinese American Portraits.* San Francisco: Chronicle Books.

McIntosh, Peggy. (1992). "White Privilege and Male Privilege: A Personal Account of Coming to See Correspondences Through Work in Women's Studies." In A. L. Anderson & P. H. Collins (Eds.), *Race, Class, and Gender: An Anthology* (pp. 70–81). Belmont, CA: Wadsworth.

McKenney, N. R., & Bennett, C. E. (1994, January –February). "Issues Regarding Data on Race and Ethnicity: the Census Bureau Experience." *CDC-ATSDR Workshop, Public Health Reports,* pp. 16–25.

McKenney, N. R., & Cresce, A. R. (1992, April). *Measurement of Ethnicity in the United States: Experiences of the U.S. Census Bureau.* Paper presented at the joint Canada-United States conference on the Measurement of Ethnicity, Ottawa.

McLaurin, E. (1993). *A Community in Conflict: Has Hate Come to Town?* [Videotape]. Honolulu: KITV.

McLeod, C. (1996). *Elisabeth Samson, een vrije, zwarte vrouw in het 18e-eeuwse Suriname* [Elisabeth Samson, a free, Black woman in the 18th-century Suriname]. Utrecht: Uitgevery Conserve.

McRoy, R. G., & Hall, C.C.I. (1996). "Transracial Adoptions: In Whose Best Interest?" In M.P.P. Root (Ed.), *The Multiracial Experience: Race Borders as a New Frontier* (pp. 63–78). Thousand Oaks, CA: Sage Publications.

Mead, G. H. (1934). *Mind, Self, and Society.* Chicago: University of Chicago Press.

Michener, J. A. (1959). *Hawaii*. New York: Random House.

Miller, R. L. (1992). "The Human Ecology of Multiracial Identity." In M.P.P. Root (Ed.), *Racially Mixed People in America* (pp. 24–36). Thousand Oaks, CA: Sage Publications.

Miller, R. L. & Miller, B. (1990). "Mothering the Biracial Child: Bridging the Gaps Between African-American and White Parenting Styles." *Women and Therapy*, 10 (1–2): 169–179.

Miller, S. (1997). *After Death: How People Around the World Map the Journey After Life*. New York, Touchstone.

Mills, M. B. (1995). "Attack of the Widow Ghosts: Gender, Death, and Modernity in Northeast Thailand." In A. Ong & M. G. Pctctz (Eds.), *Bewitching Women, Pious Men: Gender and Body Politics in Southeast Asia* (pp. 244–273). Berkeley: University of California Press.

Minney, R. J. (1962). *Fanny and the Regent of Siam*. Cleveland: The World Publishing Co.

Mitchell, A. (1990). *Cultural Identification, Racial Knowledge and General Psychological Well-Being Among Biracial Young Adults*. Unpublished doctoral dissertation. California School of Professional Psychology, Berkeley.

Mitrasingh, F.E.M. (1980). *Suriname: Land of Seven Peoples. Social Mobility in a Plural Society*. Paramaribo, Suriname. Unpublished paper.

Moesson. (1996). 40 (7–9).

Moesson. (1997). 41(7); 42(6).

Moesson. (1998). 42(11).

Molnar, S. (1983). *Human Variation—Races, Types, and Ethnic Groups* (2nd ed.). Englewood Cliffs, NJ: Prentice-Hall.

Montero, Darrel. (1980). *Japanese Americans: Changing Patterns of Ethnic Affiliation over Three Generations*. Boulder, CO: Westview Press.

Morganthau, T. (1995, February 13). "What Color Is Black?" *Newsweek*, pp. 63–65.

Morita, Pat. (1985). *Pat Morita's Mixed Plate of Comedy* [Videotape]. Honolulu: KGMB.

Mukoyama, T. H. (1998). *Effects of Heritage Combination on Ethnic Identity, Self-Esteem, and Adjustment Among American Biethnic Adults*. Unpublished doctoral dissertation, California School of Professional Psychology, Berkeley.

Mumford, K. (1997). *Interzones: Black/White Sex Districts in Chicago and New York in the Early Twentieth Century*. New York: Columbia University Press.

Murphy-Shigematsu, S. (1987). *The Voices of Amerasians: Ethnicity, Identity, and Empowerment in Interracial Japanese Americans*. Unpublished doctoral dissertation, Harvard University, Cambridge.

Murphy-Shigematsu, S. (1993). "Multiethnic Japan and the Monoethnic Myth." *MELUS*, pp. 63–80.

Murphy-Shigematsu, S. (1994a, April). "Maruchiesunikkujin to Nihon Shakai." *Gendai no Espri*, pp. 177–185.

Murphy-Shigematsu, S. (1994b). *Okinawa no Nichibei Hafu no Stereotaipu*. Kyushu: Kyushu University Press, pp. 53–57.

Nagel, J. (1994). "Constructing Ethnicity: Creating and Recreating Ethnic Identity and Culture." *Social Problems*, 41(1): 152–176.

Nakashima, C. L. (1992). "An Invisible Monster: The Creation and Denial of Mixed-Race People in America." In M.P.P. Root (Ed.), *Racially Mixed People in America* (pp. 162–178). Thousand Oaks, CA: Sage Publications.

Nakashima, C. L. (1996). "Voices from the Movement: Approaches to Multiraciality." In M.P.P. Root (Ed.), *The Multiracial Experience: Racial Borders as the New Frontier* (pp. 79–97). Thousand Oaks, CA: Sage Publications.

Nakayama, Thomas K., & Martin, Judith N. (1999). *Whiteness: The Communication of Social Identity.* Thousand Oaks, CA: Sage Publications.

Namihira, I. (1980, June). "Torinokosareta shudan: Konketsuji no identity okangaeru." *Aoi Umi, Tokushu, Okinawa no Konketsujitachi.* pp. 21–30.

Nash, P. T. (1997). "Will the Census go Multiracial?" *Amerasia Journal,* 23(1): 17–27.

The Nation. (1997a, February 7). "Looking Beyond the Young Tiger Woods," p. A4.

The Nation. (1997b, February 7). "Woods Attributes His Mental Strength to Practice of Buddhism," p. A18.

The Nation. (1997c, January 29). "Woods' Mother Wants a Thai Bride for Son," p. A16.

Navarro, V. (1990). "Race or Class Versus Race and Class: Mortality Differentials in the United States." *Lancet,* 136: 1238–1240.

Nelan, B. W. (1993, Fall). "Not Quite So Welcome Anymore." *Time.* (special issue), pp. 10–12.

Newell, J. F. (1991). *Vietnamese Americans: A Needs Assessment.* Unpublished master's thesis, California State University, Long Beach.

Newsweek. (1988, February 22). "The Pacific Century: Is America in Decline?"

Newsweek. (1995, February 13). "What Color Is Black? Science, Politics, and Racial Identity."

Nishinaga, L. (1982). "Mixed-Ancestry Beauty Queens: Letters to the Editor." *Rafu Shimpo,* p. 3.

Nobles, W. W. (1972). "African Philosophy: Foundations for Black Psychology." In R. Jones (Ed.), *Black Psychology* (pp. 18–31). New York: Harper and Row.

Noguchi, S. (1995, February 27). "Leaving Race Behind." *San Jose Mercury News,* p. 6B.

Norment, L. (1995, August). "Am I Black, White, or in Between?" *Ebony,* pp. 108–112.

Nunez, S. (1995). *A Feather on the Breath of God.* New York: HarperCollins.

Odo, F. (1993). "Is There a Future for Our Past? Cultural Preservation Policy." In *The State of Asian Pacific America: A Public Policy Report* (pp. 113–126). California: LEAP Asian Pacific American Public Policy Institute and UCLA Asian American Studies Center.

Ogbu, J. U. (1993). "Differences in Cultural Frame of Reference." *International Journal of Behavioral Development,* 16(3): 483–506.

O'Hearn, Claudine Chiawei. (1998). *Half and Half: Writers on Growing up Biracial and Bicultural.* New York: Pantheon Books.

Oka, J. M. (1994). *Self-Concept and Parental Values: Influences on the Ethnic Identity Development of Biracial Children.* Unpublished doctoral dissertation, San Jose State University.

Okamura, Jonathan. (1995). "Why There Are Not Asian Americans in Hawai'i: The Continuing Significance of Local Identity." In Peter Manicas, (Ed.), *Social Process in Hawai'i* (2nd ed.; pp. 243–260). Boston: McGraw-Hill.

Okihiro, Gary Y. (1994). *Margins and Mainstreams: Asian American History and Culture.* Seattle: University of Washington Press.

Olden, M. (1988). *Oni.* New York: Jove Books.

Omi, M., & Winant, H. (1986). *Racial Formation in the United States from the 1960s to the 1980s.* New York: Routledge.

Omi, M. & Winant, H. (1994). *Racial Formation in the United States from the 1960s to the 1990s.* New York: Routledge.

Ong, P., Bonacich, E., & Cheng, L. (1994). *The New Asian Immigration in Los Angeles and Global Restructuring.* Philadelphia: Temple University Press.

Online, H. (1995). *Marker* [on-line]. Honolulu: Hawaii Online. Accessed September 5, 1995.

Osajima, Keith. (1995). "Postmodernism and Asian American Studies: A Critical Appropriation." In G. Y. Okihiro, M. Alquizola, D. F. Rony, & K. S. Wong (Eds.), *Privileging Positions: The Sites of Asian American Studies* (pp. 21–35). Pullman: Washington State University Press.

Oshiro, T. (1992). *Gusho kara no koe.* Tokyo: Bugeishunshu.

Oshiro, Y. (1984). "Kokusaiji no kakaeru mondai." In Y. Sasaki (Ed.), *Okinawa no bunka to seishin eisei* (pp. 192–202). Tokyo: Kobundo.

Page, C. (1996, February 11). "The Rudeness of Race." *Chicago Tribune Magazine,* pp. 12–15, 24.

Palmer, A. (1924). *The Human Side of Hawaii: Race Problems in the Mid-Pacific.* Boston: The Pilgrim Press.

Parham, T. & Helms, J. (1985). Relation of Racial Identity Attitudes to Self-Actualization and Affective States of Black Students." *Journal of Counseling Psychology,* 32: 431–440.

Paris, J. (1921). *Kimono.* London.

Park, R. E. (1926). "Our Racial Frontier on the Pacific." *Survey Graphic: East by West—Our Windows on the Pacific,* 9: 196.

Park, R. E. (1928). "Human Migration and the Marginal Man." *American Journal of Sociology,* 33: 881–893.

Park, R. E. (1931). "Mentality of Racial Hybrids." *American Journal of Sociology,* 36: 535–551.

Park, R. E. (1934). "Race Relations and Certain Frontiers." In E. B. Reuter (Ed.), *Race and Culture Contacts* (pp. 57–85). New York: McGraw Hill.

Park, R. E. (1937). Introduction to Romanzo Adams, *Intermarriage in Hawaii: A Study of Mutually Conditioned Processes of Acculturation and Amalgamation* (pp. vii-xiv). New York: The Macmillan Co.

Park, R. E. (1938). Introduction to Andrew Lind, *An Island Community: Ecological Succession in Hawaii* (pp. vii–xiv). Chicago: University of Chicago Press,

Parker, D. (1995). *Through Different Eyes: The Cultural Identities of Young Chinese People in Britain.* Aldershot: Avebury.

Pearl S. Buck Foundation, Thailand (Eds.) (n.d.). *Ongkan Kan Kuson Poen Et Bak* (pamphlet). Bangkok: Pearl S. Buck Foundation.

Pescador, J. (1995). "Andy Bumatai—Star of the Series Marker." In *Filipinos in TV, Radio, and Print* [on-line]. Available at http://pubweb.acns.nwu.edu/~flip/tv.html. Accessed September 5, 1995.

Persons, S. (1987). *Ethnic Studies at Chicago, 1905–45.* Urbana: University of Illinois Press.

Peterson, P. (1995). "A Politically Correct Solution to Racial Classification." In P. L. Peterson (Ed.), *Classifying by Race* (pp. 3–17). Princeton: Princeton University Press.

Pettit, A. G. (1980). *Images of the Mexican American in Fiction and Film.* College Station: Texas A&M University Press.

Phinney, J. S. (1992). "The Multigroup Ethnic Identity Measure: A New Scale for Use with Diverse Groups." *Journal of Adolescent Research,* 7: 156–176.

Phinney, J. S. (1996). "When We Talk About American Ethnic Groups, What Do We Mean?" *American Psychologist,* 51(9): 918–927.

Pickens, D. K. (1968). *Eugenics and the Progressives.* Nashville, TN: Vanderbilt University Press.

Pido, A.J.A. (1986). *The Pilipinos in America: Macro/Microdimensions of Immigration and Integration.* Staten Island, NY: Center for Migration Studies.

Pike, Douglas (Ed.). (1990). *History of Vietnam War Reader.* Unpublished manuscript, University of California, Berkeley.

Polednak, A. (1989). *Racial and Ethnic Differences in Disease.* New York: Oxford University Press.

Polednak, A. (1991). "Black-White Differences in Infant Mortality in 38 Standard Metropolitan Areas." *American Journal of Public Health*, 81: 1480–1482.

Polk, A. (1997). *Blasian and Jewish: How Will My Kids Identify?* Available at http://www.webcom.com/%7Eintvoice/hess2.html.

Pollmann, T., & Harms, I. (1987). *In Nederland door omstandigheden*. Baarn: Ambo.

Pongudom, M. (1997, February 7). "Petter Bears Pain to Go Ahead." *The Nation*, p. A18.

Posadas, Barbara M. (1989). "Mestiza Girlhood: Interracial Families in Chicago's Filipino American Community Since 1925." In Asian Women United of California (Eds.), *Making Waves: An Anthology of Writings by and About Asian American Women* (pp. 273–282). Boston: Beacon.

Prager, E. (1995, September). "A 21st-Century Life: The Story of Alpha." *Bazaar*, pp. 390–391.

Pratt, M. L. (1992). *Imperial Eyes: Travel Writing and Transculturation*. London: Routledge.

Price, D. L. (1997). "Humorous Hapas, Performing Identities." *Amerasia Journal*, 23:(1):99–111.

Price, D. L. (1998). "Mixed Laughter and Multiethnic Humor." In P. R. Spickard & J. Burroughs (Eds.), *We Are a People: Narrative in the Construction of Multiplicity and Ethnic Identity* (pp. 179–191). Philadelphia: Temple University Press.

Provine, W. B. (1986). "Geneticists and Race." *American Zoology*, 26: 857–887.

QV Magazine. (1998a, May–June). 1(4).

QV Magazine. (1998b, July–August). 1(5).

Raia, J. (1997). "Show Him the Money." *Eye on the Tiger: The Tiger Woods Quarterly*, 1(2): 40–49.

Rambaran, H., & Ramsoedh, H. (1998). "Concepten en praktijken onder Surinaamse hindoes in relatie to de dood." *Oso, Tijdschrift voor Surinaamse Taalkunde, Letterkunde, Cultuur en Geschiedenis*, 17(1): 40–49.

Ramirez, D. A. (1996). "Multiracial Identity in a Color-Conscious World." In M.P.P. Root (Ed.), *The Multiracial Experience: Racial Borders as the New Frontier* (pp. 49–62). Thousand Oaks, CA: Sage Publications.

Regensburg, E. (1996). "Indisch? Leuk, niet meer." *Moesson*, 41(10).

Reiplinger, R. (1995). *Rap's Hawaii* [Videotape]. Honolulu: Lee Enterprises.

Rich, P. (1986). *Race and Empire in British Politics*. Cambridge: Cambridge University Press.

Rijkschroeff, B. (1989). *Een Ervaring Rijker: De Indische immigranten in de Verenigde Staten van Amerika*. Delft: Eburon.

Rijkschroeff, L. (1997). "Gezien: Indische Nederlanders in beeld." *Moesson*, 41(10).

Rijsdijk, A. (1985). "De opvang van Indische Nederlanders: Een kille thuiskomst." *Intermediair*, 21(5).

Robello, E. (1995). *Comedy in Hawaii: A Laugh a Minute. On Dialogue* [Videotape]. Honolulu: Hawaii Public Broadcasting Authority.

Rodriguez, R. (1995, July 3). "Sorry, New York, the Real Melting Pot Is California." *San Jose Mercury News*, p. 6B.

Rogin, Michael. (1996). *Blackface, Whitenoise: Jewish Immigrants in the Hollywood Melting Pot*. Berkeley: University of California Press.

Rohmer, S. (1922). "The Daughter of Huang Chow." In *Tales of Chinatown*. New York: Doubleday, Page & Company.

Roland, A. (1988). *In Search of Self in India and Japan: Toward a Cross-Cultural Psychology*. Princeton: Princeton University Press.

Rooks, C. T. (1997). *Asian Americans in Subarctic America: A Multicultural, Multivariate Comparative Study.* Unpublished doctoral dissertation, University of California, Irvine. Ann Arbor: UMI Dissertation Services.

Rooks, N. (1996). *Hair Raising: Beauty, Culture, and African American Women.* New Brunswick: Rutgers University Press.

Root, M.P.P. (1990). "Resolving 'Other' Status: Identity Development of Biracial Individuals." In L. Brown & M.P.P. Root (Eds.), *Complexity and Diversity in Feminist Theory and Therapy* (pp. 185–205). New York: Haworth.

Root, M.P.P. (1992a). *Racially Mixed People in America.* Thousand Oaks, CA: Sage Publications.

Root, M.P.P. (1992b). "Back to the Drawing Board: Methodological Issues in Research on Multiracial People." In M.P.P. Root (Ed.), *Racially Mixed People in America* (pp. 181–189). Thousand Oaks, CA: Sage Publications.

Root, M.P.P. (1992c). "Within, Between, and Beyond Race." In M.P.P. Root (Ed.), *Racially Mixed People in America* (pp. 3–11). Thousand Oaks, CA: Sage Publications.

Root, M.P.P. (1995). "The Multiracial Contribution to the Psychological Browning of America." In N. Zack (Ed.), *American Mixed Race: The Culture of Microdiversity* (pp. 231–236). Lanham, MD: Rowman and Littlefield.

Root, M.P.P. (1996a). "The Multiracial Experience: Racial Borders as a Significant Frontier in Race Relations." In M.P.P. Root (Ed.), *The Multiracial Experience: Racial Borders as the New Frontier* (pp. xiii–xxviii). Thousand Oaks, CA: Sage Publications.

Root, M.P.P. (Ed.). (1996b). *The Multiracial Experience: Racial Borders as the New Frontier.* Thousand Oaks, CA: Sage Publications.

Root, M.P.P. (1997a). "Contemporary Mixed Heritage Filipino Americans: Fighting Colonized Identities." In M.P.P. Root (Ed.), *Filipino Americans: Transformation and Identity* (pp. 80–94). Thousand Oaks, CA: Sage Publications.

Root, M.P.P. (1997b). "Multiracial Asians: Models of Ethnic Identity." *Amerasia Journal,* 23(1): 29–42.

Root, M.P.P. (1998a). "Experiences and Processes Affecting Racial Identity Development: Preliminary Results from the Biracial Sibling Project." *Cultural Diversity and Ethnic Minority Psychology,* 1: xx.

Root, M.P.P. (1998b). "Multiracial Asian Americans: Changing the Face of Asian America." In C. Lee & N. W. Zane (Eds.) *Handbook of Asian American Psychology* (pp. 261–288). Thousand Oaks, CA: Sage Publications.

Root, M.P.P. (1998c). "Rethinking Racial Identity Development: An Ecological Framework." In P. N. Spickard & J. Burroughs (Eds.), *We the People* (pp. 205–220). Philadelphia: Temple University Press.

Ropp, S. M. (1997). "Do Multiracial Subjects Really Challenge Race? Mixed-Race Asians in the United States and the Caribbean." *Amerasia Journal,* 23 (1):1–16.

Ropp, S. M., Lee, M., Williams, T. K., & Rooks, C. T. (1995). *Prism Lives/Emerging Voices of Multiracial Asians: A Selective, Partially Annotated Bibliography.* Los Angeles: University of California Press.

Rosaldo, Renato. (1989). *Culture and Truth: The Remaking of Social Analysis.* Boston: Beacon Press.

Rushton, J. Philippe (1995). *Race, Evolution, and Behavior: A Life History Perspective.* New Brunswick: Transaction Publishers.

Russell, K., Wilson, M., & Hall, R. (1992). *The Color Complex: The Politics of Skin Color Among African Americans*. New York: Anchor Books.

SA/EUG. Eugenics Society Archives, Wellcome Institute for the History of Medicine, London.

Said, Edward. (1978). *Orientalism*. New York: Pantheon.

Saldivar, Jose David. (1997). *Border Matters: Remapping American Cultural Studies*. Berkeley: University of California Press.

Salgado de Snyder, N., Lopez, C. M., & Padilla, A. M. (1982). "Ethnic Identity and Cultural Awareness Among Offspring of Mixed Interethnic Marriages." *Journal of Early Adolescence*, 2(3): 277–282.

Sampson, E. E. (1988). The Debate on Individualism: Indigenous Psychologies of the Individual and Their Role in Personal and Societal Functioning." *American Psychologist*, 43:15–22.

Sanchez, George J. (1993). *Becoming Mexican American: Ethnicity, Culture, and Identity in Chicano Los Angeles, 1900–1945*. New York: Oxford University Press.

San Francisco Chronicle. (1997, June 8). Editorial: "Multiracial Checkoff Is a Vote for Accuracy", p. 10.

Sanjek, Roger. (1996). "The Enduring Inequalities of Race." In S. Gregory & R. Sanjek (Eds.), *Race*. New Brunswick: Rutgers University Press.

Sariman, J. (1998). "Overlijdensrituelen bij Javaanse Surinamers." *Oso, Tijdschrift voor Surinaamse Taalkunde, Letterkunde, Cultuur en Geschiedenis*, 17(1):50–62.

Sarna, Jonathan. (1978). "From Immigrants to Ethnics: Toward a New Theory of 'Ethnicization.'" *Ethnicity*, 5: 370–378.

Saunders, Debra J. (1998, September 20). "What's in a Name?" *San Francisco Chronicle and Examiner*, p. A12.

Saxton, A. (1971). *The Indispensable Enemy: Labor and the Anti-Chinese Movement in Cailfornia*. Berkeley: University of California Press.

Scheffauer, H. (1911). "The Chinese in England: A Growing National Problem." *The London Magazine*, June, pp. 465–480; July, pp. 644–657.

Scheick, W.J. (1979). *The Half-Blood: A Cultural Symbol in 19th-Century American Fiction*. Louisville: The University Press of Kentucky.

Schiebinger, L. (1993). *Nature's Body: Gender in the Making of Modern Science*. Boston: Beacon Press.

Schuster, J. (1991). "The State and Post-War Immigration into the Netherlands: The Racialisation and Assimilation of Indonesian Dutch." *European Journal of Intercultural Studies*, 3.

Searle, G. (1971). *The Quest for National Efficiency*. Oxford: Basil Blackwell.

See, L. (1995). *On Gold Mountain*. New York: St. Martin's.

Senna, D. (1998). "The Mulatto Millennium." In C. C. O'Hearn (Ed.), *Half and Half: Writers on Growing up Biracial and Bicultural*. (pp. 12–27). New York: Pantheon Books.

Seriese, E. (1997). "'Wie dit lees is gek': Het Indische na Indië." In W. Willems, R. Raben, E. Seriese, L. van der Linden, & U. Bosma (Eds.), *Uit Indië geboren: Vier eeuwen familiegeschiedenis*. Zwolle: Waanders.

Shade, J. (1981). *America's Forgotten Children: The Amerasians*. Perkasie, PA: Pearl S. Buck Foundation.

Shah, S. (Ed.). (1997). *Dragon Ladies: Asian American Feminists Breathe Fire*. Boston, MA: South End Press.

Shapiro, H. L. (1953). *Race Mixture* (UNESCOs The Race Question in Modern Science). Paris: UNESCO.

Shearer, D. (1998 Fall). "What's in a Name?" *Teaching Tolerance*, pp. 11–14.

Shetter, W. (1987). *The Netherlands in Perspective: The Organizations of Society and Environment*. Leiden: Martinus Nijhoff.

Shinagawa, L. H. (1994). *Intermarriage and Inequality: A Theoretical and Empirical Analysis of the Marriage Patterns of Asian Americans*. Berkeley: University of California at Berkeley Press.

Shinagawa, L. H., & Pang, G. Y. (1988). "Intraethnic, Interethnic, and Interracial Marriages Among Asian Americans in California, 1980." *Berkeley Journal of Sociology*, 33: 950–1104.

Shinagawa, L. H., & Pang, G. Y. (1996). "Asian American Panethnicity and Intermarriage." *Amerasia Journal*, 22(2):127–152.

Simonson, D., Sasaki, P., & Sakata, K. (1985). *Fax to Da Max*. Honolulu: Bess Press.

Singelis, T. M., Triandis, H. C., Bhawuk, D.P.S., & Gelfand, M. J. (1995). "Horizontal and Vertical Dimensions of Individualism and Collectivism: A Theoretical and Measurement Refinement." *Cross-Cultural Research*, 29(3):240–275.

Smedley, A. (1993). *Race in North America: Origin and Evolution of a Worldview*. Boulder: Westview Press.

Smith, Daniel. (1998, November). "the vibe q." *Vibe Magazine* pp. 94–98.

Smith, H. E. (1971). "Thai-American Intermarriage in Thailand." *International Journal of Sociology of the Family*, 1:127–146.

Smolowe, J. (1993, Fall). "Intermarried . . . with Children." *Time* (special issue), pp. 64–65.

Soja, E. W. (1996). *Thirdspace: Journeys to Los Angeles and Other Real-and-Imagined Places*. Oxford: Blackwell.

Sollors, W. (1986). *Beyond Ethnicity*. New York: Oxford University Press.

Sollors, W. (1997). *Neither Black nor White Yet Both: Thematic Explorations of Interracial Literature*. New York: Oxford University Press.

Song, M., & Parker, D. (1995). "Commonality, Difference, and the Dynamics of Disclosure in In-Depth Interviewing." *Sociology*, 29:241–256.

Speight, S. L., Vera, E. M., & Derrickson, K. B. (1996). "Racial Self-Designation, Racial Identity and Self-Esteem Revisited." *Journal of Black Psychology*, 22(1):37–52.

Spencer, J. M. (1993). "Trends of Opposition to Multiculturalism." *The Black Scholar*, 23(2):

Spencer, J. M. (1997). *The New Colored People: Mixed-Race Movement in America*. New York: New York University Press.

Spickard, P. R. (1986). "Injustice Compounded: Amerasians and Non-Japanese in America's Concentration Camps." *Journal of American Ethnic History*, 5(Spring): 5–22.

Spickard, P. R. (1989). *Mixed Blood: Intermarriage and Ethnic Identity in Twentieth-Century America*. Madison: University of Wisconsin Press.

Spickard, P. R. (1996). *Japanese Americans: The Formation and Transformation of an Ethnic Group*. New York: Twayne.

Spickard, P. R. (1997). "What Must I Be? Asian Americans and the Question of Multiethnic Identity." *Amerasia Journal*, 23(1):43–60.

Spickard, P. R. & Fong, R. (1995). "Pacific Islander Americans and Multiethnicity: A Vision of America's Future?" *Social Forces*, 73:(4):1365–1383.

Spickard, P. R., & Mengel, L. (1997, November–December). "Deconstructing Race: The Multiethnicity of Sui Sin Far." *Books and Culture*, pp. 43–44.

Sriseub, P. (1997 February 8). "Crowd Indifference Frustrates Prayad." *The Nation*, p. A18.

Standen, B. (1996). "Without a Template: The Biracial Korean/White Experience." In M.P.P. Root (Ed.), *The Multiracial Experience: Racial Borders as the New Frontier* (pp. 245–259). Thousand Oaks, CA: Sage Publications.

Stedman, R. W. (1982). *Shadows of the Indian: Stereotypes in American Culture.* Norman: University of Oklahoma Press.

Stephan, C. (1992). "Mixed Heritage Individuals: Ethnic Identity and Trait Characteristics." In M.P.P. Root (Ed.), *Racially Mixed People in America* (pp. 50–63). Thousand Oaks, CA: Sage Publications.

Stephan, C., & Stephan, W. (1989). "After Intermarriage: Ethnic Identity Among Mixed-Heritage Japanese-Americans and Hispanics." *Journal of Marriage and the Family,* 51:507–519.

Stephan, W., & Stephan, C. (1991). "Intermarriage: Effects on Personality, Adjustment and Intergroup Relations in Two Samples of Students." *Journal of Marriage and the Family,* 53: 241–250.

Stolk, J. (1983). *Scherven van smaragd.* The Hague: Moesson.

Stoltenborgh-Indorf, I. (1997). "Het leven na Indië." *Moesson,* 41(11).

Streckfuss, David. (1993). "The Mixed Colonial Legacy in Siam: Origins of Thai Racialist Thought, 1980–1910." In Laurie Sears (Ed.), *Autonomous Histories, Particular Truths: Essays in Honor of John R. W. Smail* (pp. 123–153). Madison: The University of Wisconsin, Center for Southeast Asian Studies.

Streeter, C. A. (1996). "Ambiguous Bodies: Locating Black/White Women in Cultural Representations." In M.P.P. Root (Ed.), *The Multiracial Experience: Racial Borders as the New Frontier,* (pp. 305–320). Thousand Oaks, CA: Sage Publications,

Strong, N. (1978). *Patterns of Social Interaction and Psychological Accommodations Among Japan's Konketsuji Population.* Unpublished doctoral dissertation, University of California, Berkeley.

Sturdevant, S. P. & Stoltzfus, B. (1992). *Let the Good Times Roll: Prostitution and the U.S. Military in Asia.* New York: The New Press.

Sue, S., Sue, W., & Sue, D. (1975). "Asian Americans as a Minority Group." *American Psychologist,* 30(9): 906–910.

Suinn, R. M., Rickard-Figueroa, K., Lew, S., & Vigil, P. (1987). "The Suinn-Lew Asian Self-Identity Acculturation Scale: An Initial Report." *Educational Psychological Measurement.* 47(2): 401–407.

Sung, Betty Lee. (1990). *Chinese American Intermarriage.* New York: Center for Migration Studies.

Surie, H. G. (1971). "De gerepatrieerden." In H. Verwey-Jonker (Ed.), *Allochtonen in Nederland.* The Hague: Ministerie van Cultuur, Recreatie en Maatschapelijk Werk.

Ta, Van Tai. (1984). "Women and the Law in Traditional Vietnam." The Vietnam Forum: A Review of Vietnamese Culture. *Yale University Southeast Asian Studies,* 3 (Winter-Spring), pp. 23–55.

Tachihara Masaaki. (1980). *Cliff's Edge and Other Stories: Cliff's Edge, The Archer, and Torchlight No,* trans. Stephen W. Kohl. Ann Arbor, MI: Midwest Publishers International.

Tajima, R. (1989). "Lotus Blossoms Don't Bleed: Images of Asian Women." In Asian Women United of California (Eds.), *Making Waves: An Anthology of Writings by and About Asian American Women* (pp. 308–317). Boston: Beacon.

Takagi, D. (1993). *The Retreat from Race: Asian American Admissions and Racial Politics.* New Brunswick: Rutgers University Press.

Takagi, D. (1996a). "Maiden Voyage: Excursion into Sexuality and Identity Politics in Asian America." In R. Leong (Ed.), *Asian American Sexualities: Dimensions of the Gay and Lesbian Experience* (pp. 21–35). New York: Routledge.

Takagi, D. (1996b). "Post–Civil Rights Politics and Asian American Identity: Admissions and Higher Education." In S. Gregory & R. Sanjek (Eds.), *Race,* (pp. 229–242). New Brunswick: Rutgers University Press.

Takaki, Ronald. (1983). *Pau Hana: Plantation Life and Labor in Hawaii.* Honolulu: University of Hawai'i Press.

Takaki, Ronald. (1989). *Strangers from a Different Shore: A History of Asian Americans.* Boston: Little, Brown, and Company.

Tamagawa, Kathleen. (1932). *Holy Prayers in a Horse's Ear.* New York.

Taylor, J. G. (1983). *The Social World of Batavia: European and Eurasian in Dutch Asia.* Madison: University of Wisconsin Press.

Tchen, J.K.W. (1990). "New York Chinese: The Nineteenth-Century Pre-Chinatown Settlement." *Chinese America: History and Perspectives,* p. 157–192.

Tchen, J.K.W. (1995). "Conjuring Ghosts in a Journey East." In G. Y. Okihiro, M. Alquizola, D. F. Rony, & K. S. Wong (Eds.), *Privileging Positions: The Sites of Asian American Studies,* (pp. 101–114). Pullman: Washington State University Press.

Thai Rath. (1997, February 8). "Cho Phra Kreung" [Photo caption]. *Thai Rath,* p. 25.

Thorne, B. (1994). *Gender Play: Girls and Boys in School.* New Brunswick: Rutgers University Press.

Thornton, M. C. (1983). *A Social History of a Multiethnic Identity: The Case of Black Japanese Americans.* Unpublished doctoral dissertation, University of Michigan, Ann Arbor.

Thornton, M. C. (1992a). "Is the Multiracial Status Unique? The Personal and Social Experience." In M.P.P. Root (Ed.), *Racially Mixed People in America,* (pp. 321–325). Thousand Oaks: Sage Publications.

Thornton, M. C. (1992b). "The Quiet Immigration: Foreign Spouses of U.S. Citizens, 1945–1985." In M.P.P. Root (Ed.), *Racially Mixed People in America* (pp. 64–76). Thousand Oaks, CA: Sage Publications.

Thornton, M. C. (1996). "Hidden Agendas, Identity Theories, and Multiracial People." In M.P.P. Root, (Ed.), *The Multiracial Experience: Racial Borders as the New Frontier* (pp. 101–120). Thousand Oaks: Sage Publications.

Thornton, M. C., & Wason, S. (1996). "Intermarriage." In D. Levinson (Ed.), *Encyclopedia of Marriage and the Family* (pp. 396–402). New York: Simon and Schuster.

Time. (1987, August 31). "Those Asian American Whiz Kids," p. 325.

Time. (1993, Fall). "The New Face of America: How Immigrants Are Shaping the World's First Multicultural Society" (special issue).

Tinker, J. (1973). "Intermarriage and Ethnic Boundaries: The Japanese American Case." *Journal of Social Issues,* 29:49–66.

Tjon A Ten, V. (1998). "Rituelen en gebruiken bij overlijden bij creolen." *Oso, Tijdschrift voor Surinaamse Taalkunde, Letterkunde, Cultuur en Geschiedenis,* 17(1): 23–28.

Tobias, J. H., Cook, D. G., Chambers, T. J. & Dalzell, N. (1994). "A Comparison of Bone Mineral Density Between Caucasian, Asian, and Afro-Caribbean Women." *Clinical Science,* 87(5): 587–591.

Trask, H. K. (1990). "Politics in the Pacific Islands: Imperialism and Native Self-Determination." *Amerasia Journal,* 16(1): 1–19.

Trautfield, M. T. (1984). "America's Responsibility to the Amerasian Children: Too Little, Too Late." *Brooklyn Journal of International Law,* 10(1): 54–82.

Tsu, Lao. (1972). *Tao Te Ching.* Trans. Gia-fu Feng and Jane English. New York: Vintage Books.

Turner, Miki. (1997). "Tiger's Stripes: Does It Really Matter What Color They Are?" *Upscale,* 9(2): 38–41.

Twine, F. W. (1996). "Heterosexual Alliances: The Romantic Management of Racial Identity." In M.P.P. Root (Ed.), *The Multiracial Experience: Racial Borders as the New Frontier* (pp. 291–304). Thousand Oaks, CA: Sage Publications.

Twine, F. W., Warren, J. F. & Ferrandiz, F. F. (1991). *Just Black? Multiracial Identity.* New York: Filmmakers Library.

Tyau, K. (1996). *A Little Too Much Is Enough.* New York: Norton.

Uehara-Carter, M. (1996). *Channel A—Community: Issues Forum. On Being Blackanese.* Available at http://www.channela.com/community/issues/guests/960917/index.html?phbdt3.

Ursul, R. G. (1977). "Local Boy Eyes Big Time: Andy Line: Struggling Comic." *Windward Sun Press,* p. A–15.

U.S. Bureau of the Census. (1963). *1960 Census: Nonwhite Population by Race* (Subject Report PC (2)-1C). Washington, DC: U.S.Government Printing Office.

U.S. Bureau of the Census. (1979). *Twenty Censuses: Population and Housing Questions, 1790–1980.* Washington, DC: U.S. Government Printing Office.

U.S. Bureau of the Census. (1990). *Census of Population and Housing.* Summary Tape, File 3A.

U.S. Bureau of the Census. (1991, June 12). "Census Bureau Releases: 1990 Census Counts on Specific Racial Groups." Press Release CB91–215.

U.S. Bureau of the Census. (1992, December). *Marital Status and Living Arrangements: March 1992.* (Current Population Reports, Population Characteristics, Series P20–468). Washington, DC: U.S. Government Printing Office.

U.S. Bureau of the Census. (1993, September). *We the Americans . . . Asians* (p. 8). U.S. Department of Commerce, Economics and 1993 Statistics Administration.

U.S. Equal Employment Opportunity Commission. (1977). "Government-Wide Standard Race/ Ethnic Categories." *Federal Register,* 42(64): 17900.

U.S. House of Representatives, 105th Congress, First Session, Committee on Government Reform and Oversight, Subcommittee on Government Management, Information, and Technology. (1997). *Hearings on the Federal Measures of Race and Ethnicity and the Implications for the 2000 Census.* Serial No. 105-57 (April 23, May 22, and July 25).

U.S. Office of Management and Budget. (1994, July 14). *Comments on OMB's Statistical Policy Directive No. 15: Race and Ethnic Standards for Federal Statistics and Administrative Reporting.* Presented at OMB Hearings, San Francisco.

U.S. Office of Management and Budget. (1995, August 28). "Interim Notice of Review and Possible Revision of OMB's Statistical Policy Directive No. 15: Race and Ethnic Standards for Federal Statistics and Administrative Reporting: Summary and Analysis of Public Comments and Brief Discussion of Research Agenda." *Federal Register,* 60:166.

U.S. Office of Management and Budget. (1997, July 9). "Recommendations from the Interagency Committee for the Review of the Racial and Ethnic Standards to the Office of Management and Budget Concerning Changes to the Standards for the Classification of Federal Data on Race and Ethnicity." *Federal Register,* 62:131.

USA Today. (1992, December 11). P. 7A.

USA Today. (1999, September 7), P. 1.

U.S. News and World Report. (1997, July 21). "A Compromise in Racial Politics," p. 37.

Uyematsu, A. (1971). "The Emergence of Yellow Power in America." In A. Tachiki et al. (Eds.), *Roots: An Asian American Reader* (p. 9). Los Angeles: UCLA Asian American Studies Center.

Vaillant, R.E.F. (1991). "Aantekeningen bij onderzoek naar de sociale positie van Indische migranten." In W. Willems (Ed.), *Bronnen van kennis over Indische Nederlanders.* Leiden: C.O.M.T.

Vallangca, Roberto V. (1977). *Pinoy: The First Wave*. San Francisco: Strawberry Hill Press.

Valverde, K.L.C. (1992). "From Dust to Gold: The Vietnamese Amerasian Experience." In M.P.P. Root (Ed.), *Racially Mixed People in America* (pp. 144–161). Thousand Oaks, CA: Sage Publications.

Van de Broek, C. (1996). "'Ik ben een Indo kesasar!'" *Moesson*, 41(5).

Van der Geugten, T. (1990). *Met gemengde gevoelens: Het zelfbeeld van Indische Nederlanders*. Doctoraalscriptie, Economische en sociale geschiedenis, tweede gecorrigeerde editie, Universiteit Amsterdam.

Van der Geugten, T. (1998). "Treffers en missers: Indische geschiedschrijving en het Nederlandse geschiedenisonderwijs (II)." *Moesson,* 42(11).

Van der Geugten, T., & Van der Linden, L. (1996). *Indisch in Nederland: Beeld en zelfbeeld van Indische Nederlanders*. 's-Hertogenbosch: KPC.

Van der Linden, L., & Simons, W. (1990). *Indo-Europeanen: Van koloniale mengbloed tot zelfbewuste Indo*. 's-Hertogenbosch: KPC.

Van der Veur, P.W. (1960). "The Eurasian Dilemma in Indonesia." *Journal of Asian Studies,* 1 (November).

Van der Veur, P.W. (1968). "Cultural Aspects of the Eurasian Community in Indonesian Colonial Society." *Indonesia,* 6 (October).

Van der Veur, P.W. J.(1995). *Introduction to a Socio-Political Study of the Eurasians of Indonesia*. Unpublished doctoral dissertation, Cornell University, Ithaca.

Van Esterik, P. (1989). *Deconstructing Display: Gender and Development in Thailand* (Paper No. 2, Working Paper Series, Thai Studies Project, Women in Development Consortium in Thailand). Toronto: York University.

Van Lustbader, E. (1980). *The Ninja*. New York: Ballantine Books.

Van Lustbader, E. (1984). *The Miko*. New York: Ballantine Books.

Van Lustbader, E. (1985). *Jian*. New York: Ballantine Books.

Van Lustbader, E. (1986). *Shan*. New York: Ballantine Books.

Van Marle, A. (1951–52). "De groep der Europeanen in Nederlands-Indië, iets over onstaan en groei." *Indonesië,* 5 (2–6).

Van Niekerk, M. (1995). "A Historical Approach to Ethnic Differences in Social Mobility: Creoles and Hindustanis in Surinam." In G. Baumann & T. Sunier (Eds.), *Post-Migration Ethnicity: De-Essentializing Cohesion, Commitments, and Comparison* (pp. 118–143). Amsterdam: Het Spinhuis.

Van Tassel, E. F. (1997). "'Only the Law Would Rule Between Us': Antimiscegenation, the Moral Economy of Dependency and the Debate over Rights After the Civil War." In R. Delgado & J. Sefancic (Eds.), *Critical White Studies: Looking Behind the Mirror* (pp. 152–156). Philadelphia: Temple University Press.

Villapando, V. (1989). "The Business of Selling Mail-Order Brides." In Asian Women United of California (Eds.), *Making Waves: An Anthology of Writings by and About Asian American Women* (pp. 318–326). Boston: Beacon Press.

Wagatsuma, H. (1967). The Social Perception of Skin Color in Japan." *Daedalus,* 96: 407–441.

Waller, P. (1970). "Racial Phobia: The Chinese Scare, 1906–1914." In *Essays to C. M. Bowra* (pp. 88–100). Oxford: Alden Press.

Waters, M. C. (1990). *Ethnic Options: Changing Identities in America*. Berkeley: University of California Press.

Waters, M. C. (1994, April). *The Social Construction of Race and Ethnicity: Some Examples from Demography*. Paper presented at "American Diversity: A Demographic Challenge for the Twenty-First Century," Center for Social and Demographic Analysis Conference, SUNY, Albany.

Weedon, C. (1987). *Feminist Practice and Poststructuralist Theory* (2nd ed). Oxford: Blackwell Publishers.

Wei, William. (1993). *The Asian American Movement*. Philadelphia: Temple University Press.

Weinrich, P. (1986). "The Operationalisation of Identity Theory in Racial and Ethnic Relations." In J. Rex & D. Mason (Eds.), *Theories of Race and Ethnic Relations* (pp. 299–320). Cambridge, MA: Cambridge University Press.

Weisman, J. (1996a). *Half-Way There: Femininity, Hybridity, and Modernity in Contemporary Thailand*. Paper presented at the annual meeting of the American Anthropological Association.

Weisman, J. (1996b). *Rice Outside the Paddy: The Form and Function of Hybridity in Thai Literature*. Unpublished manuscript, prepared in fulfillment of the research competency requirement, Department of Anthropology, University of Washington, Seattle.

Weisman, J. (1997, November 19–23). *The Emperor's Lady Transformed: Gender, Race, and Shifting Embodiments of the Nation in Contemporary Thailand*. Paper presented at the annual meeting of the American Anthropological Association, Washington, D.C.

Weisman, J. (1998a). *Multiracial Amerasia Abroad: Thai Perceptions and Constructions of Tiger Woods*. Paper presented the annual meeting of the Association for Asian American Studies, Honolulu.

Weisman, J. (1998b). "Rice Outside the Paddy: The Form and Function of Hybridity in a Thai Novel." *Crossroads: An Interdisciplinary Journal of Southeast Asian Studies*, 1(1): 51–78.

Weisman, J. (2000). *Tropes and Traces: Hybridity, Race, Sex, and Responses to Modernity in Contemporary Thailand*. Ph.D. diss., University of Washington.

Wekker, G. (1994). *Ik ben een gouden munt*. Amsterdam: Feministische Uitgevery VITA.

Welsing, F. C. (1991). *The Issis (Yssis) Papers*. Chicago: Third World Press.

Werbner, P., & Modood, T. (Eds.). (1997). *Debating Cultural Hybridity*. London: Zed Books.

Wertheim, W. F. (1947). *Het sociologisch karakter van de Indo-Maatschappij*. Amsterdam: Vrij Nederland.

Wertheim, W. F. (1949). *Het Rassenprobleem: De Ondergang van een Mythe*. The Hague: Albani.

White, J. E. (1997, May 5). "I'm Just Who I Am." *Time*, pp. 32–36.

Wiegman, R. (1995). *American Anatomies: Theorizing Race and Gender*. Durham, NC: Duke University Press.

Wilkerson, Isabel. (1997). "The Many Ways of Looking at a Black Man: The All American." *Essence*, 28(7): 99–102.

Willems, W. (Ed.). (1990). *Indische Nederlanders in de ogen van de wetenschap*. Leiden: C.O.M.T.

Willems, W. (1991). *Bronnen van kennis over Indische Nederlanders*. Leiden: C.O.M.T.

Willems, W. (1994). "Tjalie Robinson: een vooruitziend migrant." In B. Paasman et al. (Eds.), *Tjalie Robinson, de stem van Indisch Nederland*. The Hague: Stichting Tong Tong.

Willems, W. (1997). "Displaced Persons: De migratie naar Amerika." In W. Willems, R. Raben, E. Seriese, L. van der Linden, & U. Bosma (Eds.), *Uit Indië geboren: Vier eeuwen familiegeschiedenis*. Zwollers: Waanders.

Willems, W. (1998, May 1–2). *No Sheltering Sky: Migrant-Identities of the Dutch from Indonesia*. Reading for the workshop "Mixed Identities in a (Post)Colonial World," Deakin University, Toorak Campus, Melbourne, Australia.

Willems, W., Cottaar, A., & Van Aken, D. (1990). "Indische Nederlanders: Van marginale groep tot succesvolle migranten?" In D. van Arkel et al. (Eds.), *Van Oost naar West: Racisme als mondiaal verschijnsel*. The Hague: Novib.

Willems, W., & de Moor, J. (Eds.). (1995). *Het Einde van Indië: Indische Nederlanders tijdens van Japanse bezetting en de dekolonisatie*. The Hague: Sdu Uitgeverij Koninginnegracht.

Willems, W., & Lucassen, L. (Eds.). (1994). *Het onbekende vaderland: De repatriëring van Indische Nederlanders (1946–1964)*. The Hague: Sdu Uitgeverij Koninginnegracht.

Willems, W., Raben, R., Seriese, E., van der Linden, L., & Bosma, U. (1997a). "Indische geschiedschrijving." In W. Willems, R. Raben, E. Seriese, L. van der Linden, & U. Bosma (Eds.). *Uit Indië geboren: Vier eeuwen familiegeschiedenis*. Zwolle: Waanders.

Willems, W., Raben, R., Seriese, E., van der Linden, L., & Bosma, U. (Eds). (1997b). *Uit Indië geboren: Vier eeuwen familiegeschiedenis*. Zwolle: Waanders.

Williams, B. (1991). *Stains on My Name, War in My Veins: Guyana and the Politics of Cultural Struggle*. Durham: Duke University Press.

Williams, D. R. (1994). "The Concept of Race in Health Services Research: 1966 to 1990." *Health Services Research, 29*(3).

Williams, D. R. (1996). "Racism and Health: A Research Agenda." *Ethnicity and Disease, 6*: 1–6.

Williams, D. R., Lavisso-Mourey, R., & Warren, R. C. (1994, January –February). "The Concept of Race and Health Status in America." *CDC-ATSDR Workshop, Public Health Reports*, pp. 26–41.

Williams, G. (1995). *Life on the Color Line: The True Story of a White Boy Who Discovered He Was Black*. New York: Dutton.

Williams, T. K. (1992). "Prism Lives: Identity of Binational Amerasians." In M.P.P. Root (Ed.), *Racially Mixed People in America* (pp. 280–303). Thousand Oaks, CA: Sage Publications.

Williams, T. K. (1995). "The Theater of Identity: (Multi-)Race and Representation of Eurasians and Afro-Asians." In N. Zack (Ed.), *American Mixed Race: The Culture of Microdiversity* (pp. 79–96). Lanham, MD: Rowman & Littlefield.

Williams, T. K. (1996). "Race as Process: Reassessing the 'What Are You?' Encounters of Biracial Individuals." In M.P.P. Root (Ed.), *The Multiracial Experience: Racial Borders as the New Frontier* (pp. 191–210). Thousand Oaks, CA: Sage Publications.

Williams, T. K. (1997). "Race-ing and Being Raced: The Critical Interrogation of 'Passing.'" *Amerasian Journal, 23*(1): 61–65.

Williams, T. K., Nakashima, C., Kich, G., & Daniel, G. R. (1996). "Being Different Together in the University Classroom: Multiracial Identity as Transgressive Education." In M.P.P. Root (Ed.), *The Multiracial Experience: Racial Borders as the New Frontier* (pp. 359–379). Thousand Oaks, CA: Sage Publications.

Williams, T. K., & Thornton, M. C. (1998). "Social Construction of Ethnicity Versus Personal Experience: The Case of Afro-Amerasians." *Journal of Comparative Family Studies, 29*(2): 255–267.

Wilson, B. L. (1986). *Racial Identification of Black-Asian Children: 4 to 8 Years Old*. Unpublished doctoral dissertation, The Wright Institute of Professional Psychology, Berkeley, CA.

Wilson, J. (1991, Summer). "Optical Illusions: Images of Miscegenation in Nineteenth- and Twentieth-Century American Art." *American Art,* pp. 89–107.

Wilson, R. A., & Hosokawa, B. (1982). *East to America: A History of the Japanese in the United States.* New York: Quill.

Wilson, T. (1992). "Blood Quantum: Native American Mixed-Bloods." In M.P.P. Root (Ed.), *Racially Mixed People in America* (pp. 108–125). Thousand Oaks, CA: Sage Publications.

Winant, H. (1994). *Racial Conditions: Politics, Theory, Comparisons.* Minneapolis: University of Minnesota Press.

Winant, H. (1997). "Behind Blue Eyes: Whiteness and Contemporary U.S. Racial Politics." In M. Fine, L. Weis, L. C. Powell, & L. M. Wong (Eds.), *Off White: Readings on Race, Power, and Society* (pp. 40–53). New York: Routledge.

Winichakul, T. (1994). *Siam Mapped: A History of the Geo-Body of a Nation.* Honolulu: The University of Hawaii Press.

Winn, N. N. & Priest, R. (1993). "Counseling Biracial Children: A Forgotten Component of Multicultural Counseling." *Family Therapy,* 20(1): 28–36.

Wirasiri, Khanitsa. (1994). "Watthanatham 'Luk Kreung' Fuang Fa Banthoeng: Chiwit Thi Plien Pai Khong Dek Sai Luad Prasom" [The Exaltation of *Luk kreung* Culture: The Changed Lives of Mixed-Blood Children]. *Athit,* pp. 26–29.

Wiriyaphinit, A. (1972). "Dek Phom Daeng: Luk Raboet Thi Amerika Thing Nai Thai." *Sangkhomsat Parithat,* 10(8): 58–65.

Wolf, N. (1991). *The Beauty Myth: How Images of Beauty Are Used Against Women.* New York: William Morrow and Co. Inc.

Wongphuaphan, W. (1972). "Takhli: Khaya Songkram." *Sangkhomsat Parithat,* 10(8): 44–55.

Woods, Earl (1998). *Playing Through: Straight Talk on Hard Work, Big Dreams, and Adventures with Tiger.* New York: Harper Collins Publishers.

Wright, L., Jr. (1994, July 25). "One Drop of Blood." *The New Yorker,* pp. 46–55.

Wright, L., Jr. (1997). "Who's Black, Who's White, and Who Cares." In R. Delgado & J. Sefancic (Eds.), *Critical White Studies: Looking Behind the Mirror.* Philadelphia: Temple University Press.

Wu, W. F. (1982). *The Yellow Peril: Chinese Americans in American Fiction, 1850–1940.* Hamden: Archon Books.

Yamamoto, Eric. (1995). "The Significance of Local." In P. Manicas (Ed.), *Social Process in Hawai'i,* (2nd ed., pp. 138–150). Boston: McGraw-Hill.

Yancey, Williams, Ericksen, Eugene, & Juliani, Richard. (1976). "Emergent Ethnicity: A Review and a Reformulation." *American Sociological Review,* 41 (June): 391–403.

Yancey, Williams, Ericksen, Eugene, & Leon, George. (1985). "The Structure of Pluralism: 'We're All Italian Around Here, Aren't We, Mrs. O'Brien?'" *Ethnic and Racial Studies,* 8 (January): 94–116.

Yau, John. (1989). *Radiant Silhouette: New and Selected Work, 1974–1988.* Santa Rosa, CA: Black Sparrow Press.

Yinger, Milton J. (1981). "Toward a Theory of Assimilation and Dissimilation." *Ethnic and Racial Studies,* 4 (July): 249–264.

Yolk Magazine. (1995, Summer). "The Lean, Mean, Dean Machine," 2(2).

Yoshimi, J. (1997). "Hapas at a Los Angeles High School: Context and Phenomenology." *Amerasia Journal,* 23 (1): 130–148.

Young, R.J.C. (1995). *Colonial Desire: Hybridity in Theory, Culture and Race.* London: Routledge.

Yu, H. (1998, June 23–28). *How Tiger Woods Lost His Stripes: Post-National American Studies as a History of Race, Migration, and the Commodification of Culture.* Paper presented at the annual meeting of the Association for Asian American Studies, Honolulu.

Zack, N. (1993). *Race and Mixed Race.* Philadelphia: Temple University Press.

Zack, N. (Ed.). (1995). *American Mixed Race: The Culture of Microdiversity.* Lanham, MD: Rowman and Littlefield.

Zack, N. (1996). "On Being and Not-Being Black and Jewish." In M.P.P. Root (Ed.), *The Multiracial Experience: Racial Borders as the New Frontier* (pp. 140–151). Thousand Oaks, CA: Sage Publications.

Zhao, Xiaojian. (n.d.) *War Brides, Family, and Gender: The Chinese American Community in Transition.* Unpublished manuscript.

About the Contributors

MARK TAYLOR BRINSFIELD studied languages and law in Europe for ten years and received his M.A. in European Studies at the University of Exeter. Brinsfield currently lives in Northampton, Massachusetts, where he studies philosophy through the University of London External Programme, as well as the viola da gamba at Smith College and the flute at the Northampton Community Music Center.

YEN LE ESPIRITU is professor of ethnic studies at the University of California, San Diego, and the author of many important works, such as *Asian American Panethnicity: Bridging Institutions and Identities* (Temple), *Filipino American Lives* (Temple), and *The Gender Lens: Asian American Women and Men.*

HAROLD GATES holds a master of science degree in social work from the University of Wisconsin–Madison and a master of arts degree in Chinese studies from Washington University in St. Louis. He has worked as a social worker and as a university counselor, primarily with students of color, and cofounded several community-based multiracial organizations in the midwest.

CHRISTINE C. IIJIMA HALL is the director of employee services at Maricopa Community College District Office. In the late 1970s, she pioneered psychological research on identity development among Black and Japanese biracials. Her dissertation, "The Ethnic Identity of Racially Mixed People" (University of California, Los Angeles), has become a classic.

REBECCA CHIYOKO KING is an assistant professor of sociology at the University of San Francisco. She received her doctorate in sociology from the University of California, Berkeley, and is one of the founding members of Hapa Issues Forum.

STEPHEN MURPHY-SHIGEMATSU received his doctorate in education at Harvard University. He is a professor at Tokyo University's International Division.

CYNTHIA L. NAKASHIMA is a Ph.D. candidate in comparative ethnic studies at the University of California, Berkeley, and is at work on a dissertation entitled, "Mixed Race Women and Their White Mothers: Race and Gender, Close to Home."

DANIEL A. NAKASHIMA is a doctoral candidate in the Graduate School of Education at the University of California, Los Angeles.

MICHAEL OMI is a professor of Asian American studies at the University of California, Berkeley. He coauthored *Racial Formation in the United States: From the 1960s to the 1990s.*

DAVID PARKER is a lecturer in the Department of Cultural Studies and Sociology at the University of Birmingham in England. He is the author of *Through Different Eyes: The Cultural Identities of Young Chinese People in Britain* (1995) and editor, with Miri Song, of *Rethinking 'Mixed Race'* (2000).

DARBY LI PO PRICE is an assistant professor of American studies at DePaul University and earned his Ph.D. in ethnic studies at the University of California, Berkeley. He is finishing his book *Mixed Laughter: Multiracial Identities and American Comedy* and has published essays and edited several works.

CURTISS TAKADA ROOKS is an assistant professor of ethnic studies at San Jose State University. He received his Ph.D. in comparative cultures at the University of California, Irvine.

MARIA P. P. ROOT has edited several landmark volumes on multiracial identity. Her most recent book is titled *Love's Revolution: Interracial Marriage* (Temple). She is a psychologist in private practice in the Seattle area.

JOHN CHOCK ROSA is an assistant professor of Asian Pacific American studies at Arizona State University.

PAUL SPICKARD is a professor of history at the University of California, Santa Barbara.

CATHY J. TASHIRO is an assistant professor of nursing at the University of Washington in Seattle.

MICHAEL C. THORNTON has pioneered sociological studies on multiethnic identity formation. He has also studied interactions among people of color, especially the attitudes of Blacks toward Asian Americans, Latinos, and West Indians. He conducts his research in the Department of Afro-American Studies and the Asian American Studies Program at the University of Wisconsin–Madison.

TRUDE I. COOKE TURNER is the assistant dean of student services at Springfield Technical Community College in Massachusetts.

KIEU LINH CAROLINE VALVERDE received her Ph.D. from the University of California, Berkeley, and has been involved with mixed race issues for more than a decade. She has taught Asian American and Southeast Asian American history at the University of California, Berkeley. As a Fulbright scholar, she conducted research in Viet Nam for her dissertation. She is currently a Rockefeller Fellow at the University of Massachusetts, Boston.

LORAINE Y. VAN TUYL received her M.A. and Ph.D. degrees in clinical psychology from the Pacific Graduate School of Psychology in Palo Alto, California. She is currently a postdoctoral fellow at the student counseling center at the University of California, Davis, where she provides therapy to multiracial college students and develops workshops on multiracial conflict.

JAN R. WEISMAN received her Ph.D. in anthropology from the University of Washington. She has taught the Thai language at the University of California, Berkeley, and at the University of Washington and directed the Thai language program of the Southeast Asian Studies Summer Institute. At the University of Washington she has taught courses on interraciality.

TERESA WILLIAMS-LEÓN is an assistant professor at California State University, Northridge. She holds her Ph.D. in sociology from the University of California, Los Angeles, and has taught some of the first courses on multiracial identity at UCLA, UC Santa Barbara, and CSUN. Currently she is conducting research on Asian–European American, Asian–African American, and Asian–Mexican American comparative multiracial identities.